THE NATIONAL EDITION
OF ROOSEVELT'S WORKS

THE WORKS OF
THEODORE ROOSEVELT

NATIONAL EDITION

VOLUME IV

African Game Trails

AN ACCOUNT OF THE AFRICAN WANDERINGS
OF AN
AMERICAN HUNTER-NATURALIST

By
Theodore Roosevelt

New York
Charles Scribner's Sons
1926

CONTENTS

ROOSEVELT IN AFRICA

By Carl Akeley

It was in the very heart of Africa that I first came to know and love Theodore Roosevelt. For three memorable hours we sat alone in the shade of an acacia, and talked of the things nearest and dearest to the hearts of men. To be sure, I had met Roosevelt, the President, and had felt deep respect and admiration for him as the great servant of a great people. Our acquaintance had progressed as my African hunting experience enabled me to make suggestions for his own expedition. But it was not until we met on the Uasin Gishu Plateau that the wall between acquaintance and friendship crumbled away and revealed to me the simplicity, the fineness, the bigness of Roosevelt, the man. That friendship, begun in the African out-of-doors, founded on a mutual love of the free wild things of nature, has been one of my most treasured possessions.

"I cannot comprehend Roosevelt. He is so complex," a friend once remarked to me. "Back down just a minute," I replied. "You're all wrong. Roosevelt's chief trait is his simplicity. To understand him you must accept him as a very simple and primitive man." Some time afterward my friend came to me and admitted that I was right. Because other men evolve for themselves circuitous routes to their own objectives, they are not prepared for straightforwardness in a man of such great accomplishment. Roosevelt always came out in the open and then went directly to the point. He never dallied in marshes and jungles off the main trail. The result was that very few things made trouble for him. The soul of a man as free from evasion and subterfuge as Roosevelt could stand to be swept bare by the winds of the Uasin Gishu.

I first met Roosevelt on my return from Africa in 1907. On my arrival in New York, I had found awaiting me at the old Grand Union Hotel an invitation to visit the White House. He had previously become interested in my work on a visit to the Field Museum in Chicago, where he had seen my deer groups. He had called for me at the time, but unfortunately I was not there. Needless to say, I prepared for my visit to the Executive Mansion with some uneasiness. I had not seen my dinner-coat since I left Chicago and my polished social manner had grown somewhat rusty during two years in the jungle; but I soon found that formality was superfluous in Roosevelt's presence. I felt at home with him almost instantly because of his evident and intelligent interest in me and in my interests. I am sure that when he met a man he wished that man "to talk shop" in order that he might have an accurate gauge of the man and of his capabilities. He knew that if a man had anything to give, it would come out when he spoke of the things with which he was most familiar. There was encouragement, too, in the absolute frankness with which he discussed every subject that came up. In an interview, his method was simplicity itself—to lead a stranger to his own back yard, so to speak, and there to play with him.

My back yard was Africa, but there was also present at that White House dinner-party a man whose back yard was Alaska. Before dinner Roosevelt had been making him talk about the natural resources and the animal life of the territory, and as we entered the dining-room the President remarked: "When I am through with this job, I am going to Alaska for a good hunt."

I have reason to believe that we were served a most excellent dinner but this belief is not based upon gustatory observation, for the President fired questions at me so rapidly that I had little time for anything but talking. Among the stories that I told was one of sixteen lions that were seen emerging from a cave on Juja Farm. At the time certain congressmen were irritating the President considerably and, when I had finished my tale, he turned to Congressman Mann, who sat at his right, and said:

"Congressman, I wish I had those sixteen lions to turn loose on Congress."

"B-but, Mr. President," queried the congressman after some hesitation, "aren't you afraid that they might make mistakes?"

With a snap of his teeth Roosevelt replied: "Not if they stayed long enough."

So he really originated the cry with which the Senate crowd retaliated when he departed for Africa: "America expects every lion to do his duty."

When the last course appeared, I had not exhausted my repertoire, but apparently I had said enough to influence the President to change his plan. As he rose from the table, he remarked emphatically: "When I am through with this job, I am going to Africa."

"But what about Alaska?" interposed the man from the North.

The President's reply was final. "Alaska will have to wait." I always think of this as the real inauguration of his African expedition, for he began at once to make plans, assembling his naturalists, selecting camp equipment, guns, and ammunition, and conferring with other big-game hunters. Arrangements were carried on with the utmost care until his departure on March 23, 1909.

Many of my old friends and colleagues became connected with the Roosevelt expedition. Newland and Tarlton, whose first safari client I had been, acted as his agents in Nairobi, and Leslie J. Tarlton, a partner in that firm, ultimately became one of the white hunters of the expedition. R. J. Cuninghame, whom I had employed to teach me to hunt elephants in 1906, was Roosevelt's official guide. Edmund Heller, who had accompanied me to Africa in 1905, was his mammalogist. Even some of my black boys, notably Ali, the tent-boy to whose faithful service Roosevelt pays tribute in the pages of this book, went with him on safari.

In 1909 I was about to return to Africa in behalf of the American Museum of Natural History to secure material for a group of elephants, and I had set my heart on including in that group an animal shot by Theodore Roosevelt. In response to my suggestion that he should secure an elephant for me, Roosevelt had arranged to meet me in Africa for an elephant-hunt. However, I was later in reaching the game fields than I had anticipated; Roosevelt had already completed his elephant-hunting for the Smithsonian Institution on and about Mount Kenia, and it looked for a time as though our plan would have to be abandoned. When later in the year I went to the Uasin Gishu Plateau, understanding that Roosevelt had gone on to Uganda, I had given up all hope of having an elephant-hunt with the colonel. But one day as we were marching toward the 'Nzoi River, intending to camp on its banks that night, we sighted in the distance a large safari. We knew that no party except our own had been allowed to go into the country where Roosevelt was operating, and I despatched a note inquiring if it were Roosevelt and stating that we planned to go into camp on the banks of the 'Nzoi. My runner was met half-way by another black messenger with a cordial note from Roosevelt himself. The story of our meeting and of our deferred elephant-hunt he relates in his chapter "To the Uasin Gishu."

Nothing that I know of Roosevelt better illustrates his habit of coming out in the open and going straight to the point than the way in which he approached his elephants on that occasion. A herd, the trail of which he had crossed the day before, was easily overtaken. As we stood hidden by a great ant-hill, I picked out a cow for my group and pointed her out to Roosevelt. Of course I assumed that he would shoot from behind the ant-hill, well out of sight and protected, but at that time I did not know Roosevelt. The rule in elephant-hunting is to get as close as you can before shooting, and, to him, sixty yards did not seem close. He went around the hill and started straight toward the eight elephants. As Kermit and I followed, one on either side and a little behind him, I had an impulse to climb on his shoulder and whisper: "Shoot her! Don't take her alive." However, the result of that hunt proved that such a caution would have been superfluous. He always met his opponent half-way, and, as in this instance, his method usually succeeded.

While Tarlton and Kermit returned to camp for tools with which to dress the skins, Colonel Roosevelt and I sat together in the shade resting. He had not seen any one except the members of his own party for a good many months, while I was fresh from the States, fresh from Oyster Bay, and he talked to me of his wife and children at home. It was then that I first caught a vision of Roosevelt, the father and husband. I got a new view of the man, a view that only his intimate friends were privileged to see, a view that I wish every one might have had. I realized then that I could follow him anywhere; even if I doubted, I could follow him, because I knew of his sincerity, his integrity, and his splendid spirit. Had our trails not crossed there on the Uasin Gishu, I might never have known the inspiration of his friendship.

Another incident of that meeting on the banks of the 'Nzoi not mentioned by Roosevelt was particularly characteristic of the man. Mr. Oscar Straus, one of our steamer companions across the Atlantic, on learning that I was likely to meet Roosevelt, had asked me to present to him in the jungles a bottle of very choice brandy. Roosevelt's interest in the brandy was as slight as his interest in the accompanying message was great. He passed the bottle on to Cuninghame and I felt certain that it would eventually meet with just appreciation.

While Roosevelt was on safari, a cartoon was published that showed a lion sitting on its haunches, wearing an expression of extreme satisfaction, and clasping its fore paws over a drawn and bulging stomach. The cartoon bore the caption "He was a *good* President." That the lions failed to do the duty that certain elements in the United States Senate expected of them was not because Roosevelt refused to give them opportunity. As a hunter, he completely disregarded his own bodily welfare. While President of the United States he had had to accept a body-guard; but on the trail in Africa his body-guard—that is, his companions—very thoroughly understood that they were not to interfere with any attacking animal until Roosevelt was down. I recall an incident of a lion-hunt, recounted to me by one of his men. This man saw a lioness at very close quarters in the high grass, crouched to spring at Roosevelt. He was about to shoot, when fortunately Roosevelt saw the beast, fired, and killed her. His companion was very grateful for the outcome, for Roosevelt told him afterward that they would have parted company had he shot the beast for Roosevelt's protection.

There is no room to interpret this story as an indication that Roosevelt was unwilling to give a fair chance and due credit to his associates. No man was ever more eager that the men who worked with him should have their opportunity. No man was ever more generous in his expression of appreciation. "African Game Trails" abounds in such tributes. Accomplishments and virtues great or small—the efforts of the scientists that contributed permanent value to the work of his expedition, the efficient management of his big safari, the hardy qualities of the Africanders, the fine work and courteous hospitality of government officials, the pluck of a gun-bearer, or the faithful service of his tent-boy—all received his recognition. His was not empty praise, for his treatment of his associates accorded with his word.

Edmund Heller, his mammalogist, an able and conscientious naturalist, had accompanied me on one of my expeditions, with the assurance that on his return he would be permitted to do the actual scientific classification and working up of the collection. There was a change in the régime of the institution for which our work was being done, during our absence, and, when he returned with a large collection of small animals in addition to my collection of big game, he was not allowed to have anything to do with his own material. One day in Washington, I complained of this to Roosevelt. Doctor C. Hart Merriam, who was present, enlarged upon the injustice of such treatment. Roosevelt's sense of fair play came to the fore at once. He was thoroughly indignant. "The naturalists who go with me," he said, "may rest assured that they will have the opportunity for scientific work." The two published volumes, "Life Histories of African Game Animals," by Theodore Roosevelt and Edmund Heller, prove how truly he kept his word. Roosevelt was insistent that every one should have credit for the things he did. In natural-history circles his influence in that direction really marks a new era.

Among naturalists Roosevelt had his place. No fellow student ever questioned any observation of his. His honesty and integrity were just as marked in his natural-history work as in all the other observations of his thorough life. "African Game Trails," as its name implies, is primarily the narrative of his experiences in hunting big animals, but he never fails to record his observations of the flowers and birds along the way with an intimacy that adds charm and animation to his recital. The day I met him on the Uasin Gishu, he was much more excited over a honey-bird he had been watching than over the elephant trail he had just crossed. Heller, who had made an intensive study of small rodents, wrote me from the boat expressing his amazement at the colonel's knowledge of that particular field. In talking with Roosevelt, he had made some reference to a very obscure species of mouse, discovered a number of years before in the northern part of British Columbia. He supposed that none but a specialist would know anything about this rodent. When he mentioned it, however, Roosevelt immediately began to tell him all about it. He was perfectly familiar with the little animal.

There is much of killing in his book and one often hears it criticized on that account. Those who are unfamiliar with hunting conditions have asked if he did not slaughter many animals unnecessarily for the pleasure of it. Their idea arises, I think, from his habit of recording the minute details of the kill —how the animal acted when struck, how the bullet performed, and so on. As he himself frequently observes, he actually killed only those specimens that his scientists considered desirable for the Smithsonian or that his safari required for food. The detailed descriptions are not an indication of blood lust or joy in killing; rather they signify a keen interest in the technique of hunting—in the effectiveness of a particular type of gun and ammunition, and in the behavior of an animal when wounded in a certain part of its anatomy.

Conservationists may well look to "African Game Trails" for sane pronouncement of their theories. Roosevelt was one of the stanchest advocates of conservation, but his interest was never of the maudlin, sentimental type. If animals were abundant or could become abundant, he believed in making use of them and he felt that wild animals could be made to serve no greater purpose than that of leading men into the fields, into the open air, to the chase. If the animals shot were of value in scientific work or for food, it was infinitely better that they should be killed than that they should live to die of old age and be wasted. People are usually extremists in conservation. Some would never allow anything to be killed. Intelligent conservation requires only such protection as is necessary to maintain the proper balance.

Africa despises a poor sportsman, but there is nothing of scorn in the memory of Theodore Roosevelt that endures in British East. The colonel made countless friends there among all classes. One of our fellow passengers when we sailed for Africa in 1909 was Sir Percy Girouard, who was going out to take over the governorship of British East Africa. Naturally he had seen much in the papers about Roosevelt's doings and about the things he had said to the colonists. Having been irritated by something he had read, he was frankly prejudiced against the colonel and remarked one day that, when he got out, he, not Roosevelt, would be governor of East Africa. However, a few months later, after the new governor and Roosevelt had met, I found that Sir Percy no longer resented his suggestions. He had become quite as ardent an admirer of Roosevelt as were the other officials of the province, no less than three of whom expressed themselves to me in terms similar to the words of one who said: "I would give up my citizenship and follow Roosevelt anywhere, if he would have me."

Few men get as much out of a trip to Africa as Roosevelt did, for few men can take so much to it. As a statesman, he found interest in problems of control and colonization. As a student of history, he understood the condition of the country, the heritage of the settlers, and the traditions of native tribes. As a sportsman, he enjoyed the chase, whether it was a stalk involving the outwitting of the animal or a gallop across the plains on horseback. He was an ardent horseman, as we all know, and among the high spots of his African journey were the mornings when he was off by dawn borne by his sorrel horse, Tranquillity. He understood every detail of the functioning of his rifles, and took an intelligent interest in modern guns and modern ammunition. Finally, as a naturalist, he enjoyed every animal he saw or collected; for his extraordinary knowledge of the researches of others gave him the keen enthusiasm of a specialist.

No one has written an appreciation of Africa, not even in an entire book, that may be compared with Roosevelt's foreword to "African Game Trails." My opinion of Roosevelt as a writer has been completely changed by reading those few paragraphs. They furnish a clew to a literary quality of which I had been but dimly aware but which I have since found running through all his works. Still, a man to whom Africa meant less, however gifted a writer he might be, could not have written those pages. The foreword expresses completely the feeling of Roosevelt, the sportsman-naturalist, for Africa—his understanding of "the hidden spirit of the wilderness," his "delight in the hardy life of the open," and in "the thrill of the fight with dangerous game," and his joy in the "awful glory of sunrise and sunset in the wide waste spaces of the earth." Wherever one wanders in Africa— whether gazing toward Kenia or out across the hot, dry plains, whether tracking "the fiercest beasts of ravin" or "the fleetest and most timid of those beings that live in undying fear of talon and fang," whether glorying in the new stars or watching the moonlight reflected on the shining skins of singing black men— some fragment from Roosevelt's word-picture drifts into one's consciousness to give form to thought and feeling. To a man with such appreciation, Africa had much to give. Africa's friends were glad to see him go there and Africa hailed his coming.   All lovers of Africa have welcomed "African Game Trails," both as a record of the character and experience of Theodore Roosevelt and as a true sportsman's sincere interpretation of the moods and mysteries of that land of "golden joys."

AFRICAN GAME TRAILS

AN ACCOUNT OF THE AFRICAN WANDERINGS OF AN
AMERICAN HUNTER-NATURALIST

BIBLIOGRAPHICAL NOTE

AFRICAN GAME TRAILS. An account of the African wanderings of an American hunter-naturalist. By Theodore Roosevelt. Illustrated. Volume I [II]. New York: Charles Scribner's Sons, 1910.

2 vols., xvi, 268; viii, 269–529 pp., ports., illus., maps,
8vo, three-quarters pigskin, uncut.

This first edition was printed on Ruysdael hand-made paper by the De Vinne Press, limited to 500 numbered sets, each signed by the author. It was followed by the better-known single-volume edition, printed by Scribners, with the longer title, and with the preliminary material differently arranged. This edition has the following description:

AFRICAN GAME TRAILS. An account of the African wanderings of an American hunter-naturalist. By Theodore Roosevelt. With illustrations from photographs by Kermit Roosevelt and other members of the expedition, and from drawings by Philip R. Goodwin. New York: Charles Scribner's Sons, 1910.

xv, 529 pp., 8vo, brown cloth, top edges gilt, other edges uncut.
Several other editions have appeared, varying
somewhat as to illustrations.

Except for part of Chapter XI and the appendixes, which are new, this work is reprinted from *Scribner's Magazine*, October, 1909, to September, 1910.

This supplements the more scientific two-volume work: LIFE HISTORIES OF AFRICAN GAME ANIMALS. New York: Scribners, 1914.

Map showing Mr. Roosevelt's route and hunting trips in Africa

FOREWORD

"I SPEAK of Africa and golden joys"; the joy of wandering through lonely lands; the joy of hunting the mighty and terrible lords of the wilderness, the cunning, the wary, and the grim.

In these greatest of the world's great hunting-grounds there are mountain peaks whose snows are dazzling under the equatorial sun; swamps where the slime oozes and bubbles and festers in the steaming heat; lakes like seas; skies that burn above deserts where the iron desolation is shrouded from view by the wavering mockery of the mirage; vast grassy plains where palms and thorn-trees fringe the dwindling streams; mighty rivers rushing out of the heart of the continent through the sadness of endless marshes; forests of gorgeous beauty, where death broods in the dark and silent depths.

There are regions as healthy as the northland; and other regions, radiant with bright-hued flowers, birds, and butterflies, odorous with sweet and heavy scents, but treacherous in their beauty, and sinister to human life. On the land and in the water there are dread brutes that feed on the flesh of man; and among the lower things that crawl and fly and sting and bite, he finds swarming foes far more evil and deadly than any beast or reptile; foes that kill his crops and his cattle, foes before which he himself perishes in his hundreds of thousands.

The dark-skinned races that live in the land vary widely. Some are warlike, cattle-owning nomads; some till the soil and live in thatched huts shaped like bee-hives; some are fisherfolk; some are ape-like, naked savages, who dwell in the woods and prey on creatures not much wilder or lower than themselves.

The land teems with beasts of the chase, infinite in number and incredible in variety. It holds the fiercest beasts of ravin,

and the fleetest and most timid of those beings that live in undying fear of talon and fang. It holds the largest and the smallest of hoofed animals. It holds the mightiest creatures that
tread the earth or swim in its rivers; it also holds distant kinsfolk of these same creatures, no bigger than woodchucks, which
dwell in crannies of the rocks and in the tree-tops. There are
antelope smaller than hares, and antelope larger than oxen.
There are creatures which are the embodiments of grace; and
others whose huge ungainliness is like that of a shape in a nightmare. The plains are alive with droves of strange and beautiful animals whose like is not known elsewhere; and with others
even stranger that show both in form and temper something of
the fantastic and the grotesque. It is a never-ending pleasure
to gaze at the great herds of buck as they move to and fro in
their myriads, as they stand for their noontide rest in the quivering heat haze, as the long files come down to drink at the water-
ing-places, as they feed and fight and rest and make love.

The hunter who wanders through these lands sees sights which
ever afterward remain fixed in his mind. He sees the monstrous
river-horse snoring and plunging beside the boat, the giraffe
looking over the tree-tops at the nearing horseman, the ostrich
fleeing at a speed that none may rival, the snarling leopard and
coiled python with their lethal beauty, the zebras barking in the
moonlight, as the laden caravan passes on its night march through
a thirsty land. In after-years there shall come to him memories
of the lion's charge, of the gray bulk of the elephant, close at
hand in the sombre woodland; of the buffalo, his sullen eyes lowering from under his helmet of horn; of the rhinoceros, truculent
and stupid, standing in the bright sunlight on the empty plain.

These things can be told. But there are no words that can
tell the hidden spirit of the wilderness, that can reveal its mystery, its melancholy, and its charm. There is delight in the
hardy life of the open, in long rides rifle in hand, in the thrill of
the fight with dangerous game. Apart from this, yet mingled
with it, is the strong attraction of the silent places, of the large
tropic moons, and the splendor of the new stars; where the wan-

FOREWORD

derer sees the awful glory of sunrise and sunset in the wide waste
spaces of the earth, unworn of man, and changed only by the
slow change of the ages through time everlasting.

THEODORE ROOSEVELT.

KHARTOUM,
March 15, 1910.

AFRICAN GAME TRAILS

AN ACCOUNT OF THE AFRICAN WANDERINGS
OF AN AMERICAN HUNTER-NATURALIST

A RAILROAD THROUGH THE PLEISTOCENE

THE great world movement which began with the voyages of Columbus and Vasco da Gama, and which has gone on with ever-increasing rapidity and complexity until our own time, has developed along myriad lines of interest. In no way has it been more interesting than in the way in which it has brought into sudden, violent, and intimate contact phases of the world's life history which would normally be separated by untold centuries of slow development. Again and again, in the continents new to peoples of European stock, we have seen the spectacle of a high civilization all at once thrust into and superimposed upon a wilderness of savage men and savage beasts. Nowhere, and at no time, has the contrast been more strange and more striking than in British East Africa during the last dozen years.

The country lies directly under the equator; and the hinterland, due west, contains the huge Nyanza lakes, vast inland seas which gather the headwaters of the White Nile. This hinterland, with its lakes and its marshes, its snow-capped mountains, its high, dry plateaus, and its forests of deadly luxuriance, was utterly unknown to white men half a century ago. The map of Ptolemy in the second century of our era gave a more accurate view of the lakes, mountains, and headwaters of the Nile than the maps published at the beginning of the second half of the nineteenth century, just before Speke, Grant, and Baker made their great trips of exploration and adventure. Behind these explorers came others; and then adventurous missionaries, traders, and elephant-hunters; and many men, whom risk did not daunt, who feared neither danger nor hardship, traversed the country hither and thither, now for one reason, now for another, now as naturalists, now as geographers, and again as government officials or as mere wanderers who loved the wild and strange life which had survived over from an elder age.

Most of the tribes were of pure savages; but here and there were intrusive races of higher type; and in Uganda, beyond the Victoria Nyanza, and on the headwaters of the Nile proper, lived a people which had advanced to the upper stages of barbarism, which might almost be said to have developed a very primitive kind of semi-civilization. Over this people—for its good fortune—Great Britain established a protectorate; and ultimately, in order to get easy access to this new outpost of civilization in the heart of the Dark Continent, the British Government built a railroad from the old Arab coast town of Mombasa westward to Victoria Nyanza.

This railroad, the embodiment of the eager, masterful, materialistic civilization of to-day, was pushed through a region in which nature, both as regards wild man and wild beast, did not and does not differ materially from what it was in Europe in the late Pleistocene. The comparison is not fanciful. The teeming multitudes of wild creatures, the stupendous size of some of them, the terrible nature of others, and the low culture of many of the savage tribes, especially of the hunting tribes, substantially reproduces the conditions of life in Europe as it was led by our ancestors ages before the dawn of anything that could be called civilization. The great beasts that now live in East Africa were in that bygone age represented by close kinsfolk in Europe; and in many places, up to the present moment. African man, absolutely naked, and armed as our early paleolithic ancestors were armed, lives among, and on, and in constant dread of, these beasts, just as was true of the men to whom the cave-lion was a nightmare of terror, and the mammoth and the woolly rhinoceros possible but most formidable prey.

This region, this great fragment out of the long-buried past of our race, is now accessible by railroad to all who care to go thither; and no field more inviting offers itself to hunter or naturalist, while even to the ordinary traveller it teems with interest. On March 23, 1909, I sailed thither from New York, in charge of a scientific expedition sent out by the Smithsonian, to collect birds, mammals, reptiles, and plants, but especially specimens of big game, for the National Museum at Washington. In addition to myself and my son Kermit (who had entered Harvard a few months previously), the party consisted of three naturalists: Surgeon Lieutenant-Colonel Edgar A. Mearns, U. S. A., retired; Mr. Edmund Heller, of California, and Mr. J. Alden Loring, of Owego, N. Y. My arrangements for the trip had been chiefly made through two valued English friends, Mr. Frederick Courteney Selous, the greatest of the world's big-game hunters, and Mr. Edward North Buxton, also a mighty hunter. On landing we were to be met by Messrs. R. J. Cuninghame and Leslie Tarlton, both famous hunters; the latter an Australian, who served through the South African war; the former by birth a Scotchman, and a Cambridge man, but long a resident of Africa, and at one time a professional elephant-hunter—in addition to having been a whaler in the Arctic Ocean, a hunter-naturalist in Lapland, a transport-rider in South Africa, and a collector for the British Museum in various odd corners of the earth.

We sailed on the *Hamburg* from New York—what headway the Germans have made among those who go down to the sea in ships!—and at Naples transshipped to the *Admiral,* of another German line, the East African. On both ships we were as comfortable as possible, and the voyage was wholly devoid of incidents. Now and then, as at the Azores, at Suez, and at Aden, the three naturalists landed, and collected some dozens of scores of birds—which next day were skinned and prepared in my room, as the largest and best fitted for the purpose. After reaching Suez the ordinary tourist type of passenger ceased to be predominant; in his place there were Italian officers going out to a desolate coast town on the edge of Somaliland; missionaries, German, English, and American; Portuguese civil officials; traders of different nationalities; and planters and military and civil officers bound to German and British East Africa. The Englishmen included planters, magistrates, forest officials, army officers on leave from India, and other army officers going out to take command of black native levies in out-of-the-way regions where the English flag stands for all that makes life worth living. They were a fine set, these young Englishmen, whether dashing army officers or capable civilians; they reminded me of our own men who have reflected such honor on the American name, whether in civil and military positions in the Philippines and Porto Rico, working on the Canal Zone in Panama, taking care of the custom-houses in San Domingo, or serving in the army of occupation in Cuba. Moreover, I felt as if I knew most of them already, for they might have walked out of the pages of Kipling. But I was not as well prepared for the corresponding and equally interesting types among the Germans, the planters, the civil officials, the officers who had commanded, or were about to command, white or native troops; men of evident power and energy, seeing whom made it easy to understand why German East Africa has thriven apace. They are first-class men, these English and Germans; both are doing in East Africa a work of worth to the whole world; there is ample room for both, and no possible cause for any but a thoroughly friendly rivalry; and it is earnestly to be wished, in the interest both of them and of outsiders, too, that their relations will grow, as they ought to grow, steadily better—and not only in East Africa but everywhere else.

On the ship, at Naples, we found Selous, also bound for East Africa on a hunting trip; but he, a veteran whose first hunting in Africa was nearly forty years ago, cared only for exceptional trophies of a very few animals, while we, on the other hand, desired specimens of both sexes of all the species of big game that Kermit and I could shoot, as well as complete series of all the smaller mammals. We believed that our best work of a purely scientific character would be done with the mammals, both large and small.

No other hunter alive has had the experience of Selous; and, so far as I now recall, no hunter of anything like his experience has ever also possessed his gift of penetrating observation joined to his power of vivid and accurate narration. He has killed scores of lion and rhinoceros and hundreds of elephant and buffalo; and these four animals are the most dangerous of the world's big game, when hunted as they are hunted in Africa. To hear him tell of what he has seen and done is no less interesting to a naturalist than to a hunter. There were on the ship many men who loved wild nature, and who were keen hunters of big game; and almost every day, as we steamed over the hot, smooth waters of the Red Sea and the Indian Ocean, we would gather on deck around Selous to listen to tales of those strange adventures that only come to the man who has lived long the lonely life of the wilderness.

On April 21 we steamed into the beautiful and picturesque harbor of Mombasa. Many centuries before the Christian era, dhows from Arabia, carrying sea-farers of Semitic races whose very names have perished, rounded the Lion's Head at Guardafui and crept slowly southward along the barren African coast. Such dhows exist to-day almost unchanged, and bold indeed were the men who first steered them across the unknown oceans. They were men of iron heart and supple conscience, who fronted inconceivable danger and hardship; they established trading stations for gold and ivory and slaves; they turned these trading stations into little cities and sultanates, half Arab, half negro. Mombasa was among them. In her time of brief splendor Portugal seized the city; the Arabs won it back; and now England holds it. It lies just south of the equator, and when we saw it the brilliant green of the tropic foliage showed the town at its best.

We were welcomed to Government House in most cordial fashion by the acting governor, Lieutenant-Governor Jackson, who is not only a trained public official of long experience, but a first-class field naturalist and a renowned big-game hunter; indeed I could not too warmly express my appreciation of the hearty and generous courtesy with which we were received and treated alike by the official and the unofficial world throughout East Africa.   We landed in the kind of torrential downpour that only comes in the tropics; it reminded me of Panama at certain moments in the rainy season.   That night we were given a dinner by the Mombasa Club; and it was interesting to meet the merchants and planters of the town and the neighborhood as well as the officials.   The former included not only Englishmen but also Germans and Italians; which is quite as it should be, for at least part of the high inland region of British East Africa can be made one kind of "white man's country"; and to achieve this, white men should work heartily together, doing scrupulous justice to the natives, but remembering that progress and development in this particular kind of new land depend exclusively upon the masterful leadership of the whites, and that therefore it is both a calamity and a crime to permit the whites to be riven in sunder by hatreds and jealousies.   The coast regions of British East Africa are not suited for extensive white settlement; but the hinterland is, and there everything should be done to encourage such settlement.   Non-white aliens should not be encouraged to settle where they come into rivalry with the whites (exception being made as regards certain particular individuals and certain particular occupations).

There are, of course, large regions on the coast and in the interior where ordinary white settlers cannot live, in which it would be wise to settle immigrants from India, and there are many positions in other regions which it is to the advantage of everybody that the Indians should hold, because there is as yet no sign that sufficient numbers of white men are willing to hold them, while the native blacks, although many of them do fairly well in unskilled labor, are not yet competent to do the higher tasks which now fall to the share of the Goanese, and Moslem and non-Moslem Indians.   The small merchants who deal with the natives, for instance, and most of the minor railroad officials, belong to these latter classes. I was amused, by the way, at one bit of native nomenclature in connection with the Goanese. Many of the Goanese are now as dark as most of the other Indians; but they are descended in the male line from the early Portuguese adventurers and conquerors, who were the first white men ever seen by the natives of this coast. Accordingly to this day some of the natives speak even of the dark-skinned descendants of the subjects of King Henry the Navigator as "the whites," designating the Europeans specifically as English, Germans, or the like; just as in out-of-the-way nooks in the far Northwest one of our own red men will occasionally be found who still speaks of Americans and Englishmen as "Boston men" and "King George's men."

One of the government farms was being run by an educated colored man from Jamaica; and we were shown much courtesy by a colored man from our own country who was practising as a doctor. No one could fail to be impressed with the immense advance these men represented as compared with the native negro; and indeed to an American, who must necessarily think much of the race problem at home, it is pleasant to be made to realize in vivid fashion the progress the American negro has made, by comparing him with the negro who dwells in Africa untouched, or but lightly touched, by white influence.

In such a community as one finds in Mombasa or Nairobi one continually runs across quiet, modest men whose lives have been fuller of wild adventure than the life of a viking leader of the ninth century. One of the public officials whom I met at the governor's table was Major Hinde. He had at one time served under the government of the Congo Free State; and, at a crisis in the fortunes of the State, when the Arab slave-traders bade fair to get the upper hand, he was one of the eight or ten white men, representing half as many distinct nationalities, who overthrew the savage soldiery of the slave-traders and shattered beyond recovery the Arab power. They organized the wild pagan tribes just as their Arab foes had done; they fought in a land where deadly sickness struck down victor and vanquished with ruthless impartiality; they found their commissariat as best they could wherever they happened to be; often they depended upon one day's victory to furnish the ammunition with which to wage the morrow's battle; and ever they had to be on guard no less against the thousands of cannibals in their own ranks than against the thousands of cannibals in the hostile ranks, for, on whichever side they fought, after every battle the warriors of the man-eating tribes watched their chance to butcher the wounded indiscriminately and to feast on the bodies of the slain.

The most thrilling book of true lion stories ever written is Colonel Patterson's "The Man-eaters of Tsavo." Colonel Patterson was one of the engineers engaged, some ten or twelve years back, in building the Uganda Railway; he was in charge of the work, at a place called Tsavo, when it was brought to a complete halt by the ravages of a couple of man-eating lions which, after many adventures, he finally killed. At the dinner at the Mombasa Club I met one of the actors in a blood-curdling tragedy which Colonel Patterson relates. He was a German, and, in company with an Italian friend, he went down in the special car of one of the English railroad officials to try to kill a man-eating lion which had carried away several people from a station on the line. They put the car on a siding; as it was hot the door was left open, and the Englishman sat by the open window to watch for the lion, while the Italian finally lay down on the floor and the German got into an upper bunk. Evidently the Englishman must have fallen asleep, and the lion, seeing him through the window, entered the carriage by the door to get at him. The Italian waked to find the lion standing on him with its hind feet, while its fore paws were on the seat as it killed the unfortunate Englishman, and the German, my informant, hearing the disturbance, leaped out of his bunk actually onto the back of the lion. The man-eater, however, was occupied only with his prey; holding the body in his mouth he forced his way out through the window-sash, and made his meal undisturbed but a couple of hundred yards from the railway-carriage.

The day after we landed we boarded the train to take what seems to me, as I think it would to most men fond of natural history, the most interesting railway journey in the world. It was Governor Jackson's special train, and in addition to his own party and ours there was only Selous; and we travelled with the utmost comfort through a naturalist's wonderland. All civilized governments are now realizing that it is their duty here and there to preserve, unharmed, tracts of wild nature, with thereon the wild things the destruction of which means the destruction of half the charm of wild nature. The English Government has made a large game reserve of much of the region on the way to Nairobi, stretching far to the south, and one mile to the north, of the track. The reserve swarms with game; it would be of little value except as a reserve; and the attraction it now offers to travellers renders it an asset of real consequence to the whole colony. The wise people of Maine, in our own country, have discovered that intelligent game preservation, carried out in good faith, and in a spirit of common sense as far removed from mushy sentimentality as from brutality, results in adding one more to the State's natural resources of value; and in consequence there are more moose and deer in Maine to-day than there were forty years ago; there is a better chance for every man in Maine, rich or poor, provided that he is not a game-butcher, to enjoy his share of good hunting; and the number of sportsmen and tourists attracted to the State adds very appreciably to the means of livelihood of the citizen. Game reserves should not be established where they are detrimental to the interests of large bodies of settlers, nor yet should they be nominally established in regions so remote that the only men really interfered with are those who respect the law, while a premium is thereby put on the activity of the unscrupulous persons who are eager to break it. Similarly, game-laws should be drawn primarily in the interest of the whole people, keeping steadily in mind certain facts that ought to be self-evident to every one above the intellectual level of those well-meaning persons who apparently think that all shooting is wrong and that man could continue to exist if all wild animals were allowed to increase unchecked. There must be recognition of the fact that almost any wild animal of the defenseless type, if its multiplication were unchecked while its natural enemies, the dangerous carnivora, were killed, would by its simple increase crowd man off the planet; and of the further fact that, far short of such increase, a time speedily comes when the existence of too much game is incompatible with the interests, or indeed the existence, of the cultivator. As in most other matters, it is only the happy mean which is healthy and rational. There should be certain sanctuaries and nurseries where game can live and breed absolutely unmolested; and elsewhere the laws should so far as possible provide for the continued existence of the game in sufficient numbers to allow a reasonable amount of hunting on fair terms to any hardy and vigorous man fond of the sport, and yet not in sufficient numbers to jeopardize the interests of the actual settler, the tiller of the soil, the man whose well-being should be the prime object to be kept in mind by every statesman. Game-butchery is as objectionable as any other form of wanton cruelty or barbarity; but to protest against all hunting of game is a sign of softness of head, not of soundness of heart.

In the creation of the great game reserve through which the Uganda Railway runs, the British Government has conferred a boon upon mankind, and no less in the enactment and enforcement of the game-laws in the African provinces generally. Of course, experience will show where, from time to time, there must be changes. In Uganda proper, buffaloes and hippos throve so under protection as to become sources of grave danger not only to the crops but to the lives of the natives, and they had to be taken off the protected list and classed as vermin, to be shot in any numbers at any time; and only the great demand for ivory prevented the necessity of following the same course with regard to the elephant; while recently in British East Africa the increase of the zebras, and the harm they did to the crops of the settlers, rendered it necessary to remove a large measure of the protection formerly accorded them, and in some cases actually to encourage their slaughter; and increase in settlement may necessitate further changes. But, speaking generally, much wisdom and foresight, highly creditable to both government and people, have been shown in dealing with and preserving East African game while at the same time safeguarding the interests of the settlers.

On our train the locomotive was fitted with a comfortable seat across the cowcatcher, and on this, except at meal-time, I spent most of the hours of daylight, usually in company with Selous, and often with Governor Jackson, to whom the territory and the game were alike familiar. The first afternoon we did not see many wild animals, but birds abounded, and the scenery was both beautiful and interesting. A black-and-white hornbill, feeding on the track, rose so late that we nearly caught it with our hands; guinea-fowl and francolin, and occasionally bustard, rose near by; brilliant rollers, sunbirds, bee-eaters, and weaver-birds flew beside us, or sat unmoved among the trees as the train passed. In the dusk we nearly ran over a hyena; a year or two previously the train actually did run over a lioness one night, and the conductor brought in her head in triumph. In fact, there have been continual mishaps such as could only happen to a railroad in the Pleistocene! The very night we went up there was an interruption in the telegraph service due to giraffes having knocked down some of the wires and a pole in crossing the track; and elephants have more than once performed the same feat. Two or three times, at night, giraffes have been run into and killed; once a rhinoceros was killed, the engine being damaged in the encounter; and on other occasions the rhino has only just left the track in time, once the beast being struck and a good deal hurt, the engine again being somewhat crippled. But the lions now offer, and have always offered, the chief source of unpleasant excitement. Throughout East Africa the lions continually take to man-eating at the expense of the native tribes, and white hunters are continually being killed or crippled by them. At the lonely stations on the railroad the two or three subordinate officials often live in terror of some fearsome brute that has taken to haunting the vicinity; and every few months, at some one of these stations, a man is killed or badly hurt by, or narrowly escapes from, a prowling lion.

The stations at which the train stopped were neat and attractive; and besides the Indian officials there were usually natives from the neighborhood. Some of these might be dressed in the fez and shirt and trousers which indicate a coming under the white man's influence, or which, rather curiously, may also indicate Mohammedanism. But most of the natives are still wild pagans, and many of them are unchanged in the slightest particular from what their forefathers were during the countless ages when they alone were the heirs of the land— a land which they were utterly powerless in any way to improve. Some of the savages we saw wore red blankets, and in deference to white prejudice draped them so as to hide their nakedness. But others appeared—men and women—with literally not one stitch of clothing, although they might have rather elaborate hairdresses, and masses of metal ornaments on their arms and legs. In the region where one tribe dwelt all the people had their front teeth filed to sharp points; it was strange to see a group of these savages, stark naked, with oddly shaved heads and filed teeth, armed with primitive bows and arrows, stand gravely gazing at the train as it rolled into some station; and none the less strange, by the way, because the locomotive was a Baldwin, brought to Africa across the great ocean from our own country. One group of women, nearly nude, had their upper arms so tightly bound with masses of bronze or copper wire that their muscles were completely malformed. So tightly was the wire wrapped round the upper third of the upper arm, that it was reduced to about one-half of its normal size; and the muscles could only play, and that in deformed fashion, below this unyielding metal bondage.

Why the arms did not mortify it was hard to say; and their freedom of use was so hampered as to make it difficult to understand how men or women whose whole lives are passed in one or another form of manual labor could inflict upon themselves such crippling and pointless punishment. Next morning we were in the game country, and as we sat on the seat over the cowcatcher it was literally like passing through a vast zoological garden. Indeed no such railway journey can be taken on any other line in any other land. At one time we passed a herd of a dozen or so of great giraffes, cows and calves, cantering along through the open woods a couple of hundred yards to the right of the train. Again, still closer, four waterbuck cows, their big ears thrown forward, stared at us without moving until we had passed. Hartbeests were everywhere; one herd was on the track, and when the engine whistled they bucked and sprang with ungainly agility and galloped clear of the danger. A long-tailed straw-colored monkey ran from one tree to another. Huge black ostriches appeared from time to time. Once a troop of impala, close by the track, took fright; and as the beautiful creatures fled we saw now one and now another bound clear over the high bushes. A herd of zebra clattered across a cutting of the line not a hundred yards ahead of the train; the whistle hurried their progress, but only for a moment, and as we passed they were already turning round to gaze. The wild creatures were in their sanctuary, and they knew it. Some of the settlers have at times grumbled at this game reserve being kept of such size; but surely it is one of the most valuable possessions the country could have. The lack of water in parts, the prevalence in other parts of diseases harmful to both civilized man and domestic cattle, render this great tract of country the home of all homes for the creatures of the waste. The protection given these wild creatures is genuine, not nominal; they are preserved, not for the pleasure of the few, but for the good of all who choose to see this strange and attractive spectacle; and from this nursery and breeding ground the overflow keeps up the stock of game in the adjacent land, to the benefit of the settler to whom the game gives fresh meat, and to the benefit of the whole country because of the attraction it furnishes to all who desire to visit a veritable happy hunting-ground.

Soon after lunch we drew up at the little station of Kapiti Plains, where our safari was awaiting us; "safari" being the term employed throughout East Africa to denote both the caravan with which one makes an expedition and the expedition itself. Our aim being to cure and send home specimens of all the common big game—in addition to as large a series as possible of the small mammals and birds—it was necessary to carry an elaborate apparatus of naturalists' supplies; we had brought with us, for instance, four tons of fine salt, as to cure the skins of the big beasts is a herculean labor under the best conditions; we had hundreds of traps for the small creatures; many boxes of shotgun cartridges in addition to the ordinary rifle cartridges which alone would be necessary on a hunting trip; and, in short, all the many impedimenta needed if scientific work is to be properly done under modern conditions. Few laymen have any idea of the expense and pains which must be undergone in order to provide groups of mounted big animals from far-off lands, such as we see in museums like the National Museum in Washington and the American Museum of Natural History in New York. The modern naturalist must realize that in some of its branches his profession, while more than ever a science, has also become an art. So our preparations were necessarily on a very large scale; and as we drew up at the station the array of porters and of tents looked as if some small military expedition was about to start. As a compliment, which I much appreciated, a large American flag was floating over my own tent; and in the front line, flanking this tent on either hand, were other big tents for the members of the party, with a dining tent and skinning tent; while behind were the tents of the two hundred porters, the gun-bearers, the tent-boys, the askaris or native soldiers, and the horse-boys or saises. In front of the tents stood the men in two lines; the first containing fifteen askaris, the second line porters with their head men. The askaris were uniformed, each in a red fez, a blue blouse, and white knickerbockers, and each carrying his rifle and belt. The porters were chosen from several different tribes or races to minimize the danger of combination in the event of mutiny.

Here and there in East Africa one can utilize ox-wagons, or pack-trains of donkeys; but for a considerable expedition it is still best to use a safari of native porters, of the type by which the commerce and exploration of the country have always been carried on. The backbone of such a safari is generally composed of Swahili, the coast men, negroes who have acquired the Moslem religion, together with a partially Arabicized tongue and a strain of Arab blood from the Arab warriors and traders who have been dominant in the coast towns for so many centuries. It was these Swahili trading caravans, under Arab leadership, which, in their quest for ivory and slaves, trod out the routes which the early white explorers followed. Without their work as a preliminary the work of the white explorers could not have been done; and it was the Swahili porters themselves who rendered this work itself possible. To this day every hunter, trader, missionary, or explorer must use either a Swahili safari or one modelled on the Swahili basis. The part played by the white-topped ox-wagon in the history of South Africa, and by the camel caravan in North Africa, has been played in Middle Africa by the files of strong, patient, childlike savages, who have borne the burdens of so many masters and employers hither and thither, through and across, the dark heart of the continent.

Equatorial Africa is in most places none too healthy a place for the white man, and he must care for himself as he would scorn to do in the lands of pine and birch and frosty weather. Camping in the Rockies or the North woods can with advantage be combined with "roughing it"; and the early pioneers of the West, the explorers, prospectors, and hunters, who always roughed it, were as hardy as bears, and lived to a hale old age, if Indians and accidents permitted.   But in tropic Africa a lamentable proportion of the early explorers paid in health or life for the hardships they endured; and throughout most of the country no man can long rough it, in the Western and Northern sense, with impunity.

At Kapiti Plains our tents, our accommodations generally, seemed almost too comfortable for men who knew camp life only on the great plains, in the Rockies, and in the North woods. My tent had a fly which was to protect it from the great heat; there was a little rear extension in which I bathed—a hot bath, never a cold bath, is almost a tropic necessity; there was a ground canvas, of vital moment in a land of ticks, jiggers, and scorpions; and a cot to sleep on, so as to be raised from the ground.   Quite a contrast to life on the round-up!   Then I had two tent-boys to see after my belongings, and to wait at table as well as in the tent.   Ali, a Mohammedan mulatto (Arab and negro), was the chief of the two, and spoke some English, while under him was "Bill," a speechless black boy; Ali being particularly faithful and efficient.   Two other Mohammedan negroes, clad like the askaris, reported to me as my gun-bearers, Muhamed and Bakari; seemingly excellent men, loyal and enduring, no trackers, but with keen eye for game, and the former speaking a little English.   My two horse-boys, or saises, were both pagans.   One, Hamisi, must have had in his veins Galla or other non-negro blood; derived from the Hamitic, or bastard Semitic, or at least non-negro, tribes which, pushing slowly and fitfully southward and southwestward among the negro peoples, have created an intricate tangle of ethnic and linguistic types from the middle Nile to far south of the equator.   Hamisi always wore a long feather in one of his sandals, the only ornament he affected.   The other sais was a silent, gentle-mannered black heathen; his name was Simba, a lion, and as I shall later show he was not unworthy of it.   The two horses for which these men cared were stout, quiet little beasts; one, a sorrel, I named Tranquillity, and the other, a brown, had so much the cob-like build of a zebra that we christened him Zebra-shape. One of Kermit's two horses, by the way, was more romantically named after Huandaw, the sharp-eared steed of the Mabinogion. Cuninghame, lean, sinewy, bearded, exactly the type of hunter and safari manager that one would wish for such an expedition as ours, had ridden up with us on the train, and at the station we met Tarlton, and also two settlers of the neighborhood, Sir Alfred Pease and Mr. Clifford Hill. Hill was an Africander. He and his cousin, Harold Hill, after serving through the South African war, had come to the new country of British East Africa to settle, and they represented the ideal type of settler for taking the lead in the spread of empire. They were descended from the English colonists who came to South Africa in 1820; they had never been in England, and neither had Tarlton. It was exceedingly interesting to meet these Australians and Africanders, who typified in their lives and deeds the greatness of the English Empire, and yet had never seen England.

As for Sir Alfred, Kermit and I were to be his guests for the next fortnight, and we owe primarily to him, to his mastery of hunting craft, and his unvarying and generous hospitality and kindness, the pleasure and success of our introduction to African hunting. His life had been one of such varied interest as has only been possible in our own generation. He had served many years in Parliament; he had for some years been a magistrate in a peculiarly responsible post in the Transvaal; he had journeyed and hunted and explored in the northern Sahara, in the Soudan, in Somaliland, in Abyssinia; and now he was ranching in East Africa. A singularly good rider and one of the best game-shots I have ever seen, it would have been impossible to have found a kinder host or a hunter better fitted to teach us how to begin our work with African big game.

At Kapiti Station there was little beyond the station buildings, a "compound" or square enclosure in which there were many natives, and an Indian store. The last was presided over by a turbaned Mussulman, the agent of other Indian traders who did business in Machakos-boma, a native village a dozen miles distant; the means of communication being two-wheeled carts, each drawn by four humped oxen, driven by a well-nigh naked savage.

For forty-eight hours we were busy arranging our outfit; and the naturalists took much longer. The provisions were those usually included in an African hunting or exploring trip, save that, in memory of my days in the West, I included in each provision box a few cans of Boston baked beans, California peaches, and tomatoes. We had plenty of warm bedding, for the nights are cold at high altitudes, even under the equator. While hunting I wore heavy shoes, with hobnails or rubber soles; khaki trousers, the knees faced with leather, and the legs buttoning tight from the knee to below the ankle, to avoid the need of leggings; a khaki-colored army shirt; and a sun-helmet, which I wore in deference to local advice, instead of my beloved and far more convenient slouch-hat. My rifles were an army Springfield, 30-caliber, stocked and sighted to suit myself; a Winchester 405; and a double-barrelled 500–450 Holland, a beautiful weapon presented to me by some English friends.*

* Mr. E. N. Buxton took the lead in the matter when he heard that I intended making a trip after big game in Africa. I received the rifle at the White House, while I was President. Inside the case was the following list of donors:

LIST OF ZOOLOGISTS AND SPORTSMEN WHO ARE DONORS OF A DOUBLE ELEPHANT RIFLE TO THE HON. THEODORE ROOSEVELT, PRESIDENT U. S. A.

IN RECOGNITION OF HIS SERVICES ON BEHALF OF THE PRESERVATION OF SPECIES BY MEANS OF NATIONAL PARKS AND FOREST RESERVES, AND BY OTHER MEANS

E. N. Buxton, Esq.
Rt. Hon. Lord Avebury, D.C.L. ("The Pleasures of Life," etc.)
Major-Gen. Sir F. Reginald Wingate, K.C.B. (Governor-General of the Soudan.)
Sir Edmund G. Loder, Bart.
Hon. N. C. Rothschild.
The Earl of Lonsdale. (Master of Hounds.)
Sir R. G. Harvey, Bart.
The Rt. Hon. Lord Curzon of Kedleston, G.C.S.I., G.C.I.E.
St. George Littledale, Esq.
Dr. P. Chalmers Mitchell, F.R.S., F.Z.S. (Secretary of the Zoological Soc.)
C. E. Green, Esq. (Master of Essex Hounds.)

Kermit's battery was of the same type, except that instead of a Springfield he had another Winchester shooting the army

F. C. SELOUS, ESQ. ("A Hunter's Wanderings," etc.)
COUNT BLÜCHER.
LIEUT.-COL. C. DELMÉ RADCLIFFE, C.M.G., M.V.O.
MAURICE EGERTON, ESQ.
LORD DESBOROUGH, C.V.O.
CAPTAIN M. McNEILL.
CLAUDE H. TRITTON, ESQ.
J. TURNER-TURNER, ESQ.
HON. L. W. ROTHSCHILD, M.P.
RT. HON. SIR E. GREY, BART., M.P. (Foreign Secretary and author of "Dry Fly Fishing.")
SIR M. DE C. FINDLAY, C.M.G. (British Minister at Dresden.)
C. PHILLIPPS-WOLLEY, ESQ., F.R.G.S. ("Sport in the Caucasus.")
RT. HON. SIR G. O. TREVELYAN, BART., D.C.L. ("The American Revolution.")
WARBURTON PIKE, ESQ.
SIR WM. E. GARSTIN, G.C.M.G.
HIS GRACE THE DUKE OF BEDFORD, K.G. ("A Great Estate.")
HER GRACE THE DUCHESS OF BEDFORD.
LORD BRASSEY, G.C.B., M.V.O. (Owner of *The Sunbeam.*)
HON. T. A. BRASSEY. (Editor of the *Naval Annual.*)
RHYS WILLIAMS, ESQ.
MAJOR-GEN. A. A. A. KINLOCH, C.B. ("Large Game in Thibet.")
SIR WM. LEE-WARNER, K.C.S.I. ("The Protected Princes of India.")
THE RT. REV. THE LORD BISHOP OF LONDON.
MAJOR-GEN. DALRYMPLE WHITE.
COLONEL CLAUDE CANE.
RT. HON. SYDNEY BUXTON, M.P. (Postmaster General, "Fishing and Shooting.")
MAJOR C. E. RADCLYFFE, D.S.O.
SIR A. E. PEASE, BART. ("Cleveland Hounds.")
SIR H. H. JOHNSTON, K.C.B., G.C.M.G. ("The Uganda Protectorate.")
ABEL CHAPMAN, ESQ. ("Wild Spain.")
J. G. MILLAIS, ESQ., F.Z.S. ("A Breath from the Veldt.")
E. LORT-PHILLIPS, ESQ. (Author of ornithological works.)
R. KEARTON, ESQ., F.Z.S. ("Wild Nature's Ways.")
J. H. GURNEY, ESQ., F.Z.S. (Works on ornithology.)
F. J. JACKSON, C.B., C.M.G., LIEUT.-GOVERNOR EAST AFRICAN PROTECTORATE. ("Big Game," Badminton Library.)
COL. SIR F. LUGARD, K.C.M.G., C.B., D.S.O.
LADY LUGARD. ("A Tropical Dependency.")
SIR CLEMENT L. HILL, K.C.B., M.P. (Late Head of the African Department: Foreign O.)
SIR H. SETON-KARR, M.P., C.M.G. ("My Sporting Holidays.")
CAPTAIN BOYD ALEXANDER. ("From the Niger to the Nile.")
SIR J. KIRK, K.C.B., G.C.M.G. (Dr. Livingstone's companion, 1858-64.)
MORETON FREWEN, ESQ.
THE EARL OF WARWICK.
P. L. SCLATER, ESQ., D.SC., PH.D. (Late Sec. Zool. Soc.)
COL. J. H. PATTERSON, D.S.O. ("The Man-Eaters of Tsavo.")

ammunition, and his double-barrel was a Rigby. In addition I had a Fox No. 12 shotgun; no better gun was ever made.

There was one other bit of impedimenta, less usual for African travel, but perhaps almost as essential for real enjoyment even on a hunting trip, if it is to be of any length. This was the "Pigskin Library," so called because most of the books were bound in pigskin. They were carried in a light aluminum and oilcloth case, which, with its contents, weighed a little less than sixty pounds, making a load for one porter. Including a few volumes carried in the various bags, so that I might be sure always to have one with me, and Gregorovius, read on the voyage outward, the list was as printed in Appendix F.

It represents in part Kermit's taste, in part mine; and, I need hardly say, it also represents in no way all the books we most care for, but merely those which, for one reason or another, we thought we should like to take on this particular trip.

I used my Whitman tree army saddle and my army field-glasses; but, in addition, for studying the habits of the game, I carried a telescope given me on the boat by a fellow traveller and big-game hunter, an Irish hussar captain from India—and incidentally I am out in my guess if this same Irish hussar captain be not worth watching should his country ever again be engaged in war. I had a very ingenious beam or scale for weighing game, designed and presented to me by my friend, Mr. Thompson Seton. I had a slicker for wet weather, an army overcoat, and a mackinaw jacket for cold, if I had to stay out overnight in the mountains. In my pockets I carried, of course, a knife, a compass, and a water-proof match-box. Finally, just before leaving home, I had been sent, for good luck, a goldmounted rabbit's foot, by Mr. John L. Sullivan, at one time ring champion of the world.

Our camp was on a bare, dry plain, covered with brown and withered grass. At most hours of the day we could see round about, perhaps a mile or so distant, or less, the game feeding. South of the track the reserve stretched for a long distance; north it went for but a mile, just enough to prevent thoughtless or cruel people from shooting as they went by in the train. There was very little water; what we drank, by the way, was carefully boiled. The drawback to the camp, and to all this plains region, lay in the ticks, which swarmed, and were a scourge to man and beast. Every evening the saises picked them by hundreds off each horse; and some of our party were at times so bitten by the noisome little creatures that they could hardly sleep at night, and in one or two cases the man was actually laid up for a couple of days; and two of our horses ultimately got tick fever, but recovered.

In mid-afternoon of our third day in this camp we at last had matters in such shape that Kermit and I could begin our hunting; and forth we rode, he with Hill, I with Sir Alfred, each accompanied by his gun-bearers and sais, and by a few porters to carry in the game. For two or three miles our little horses shuffled steadily northward across the desolate flats of short grass until the ground began to rise here and there into low hills, or koppies, with rock-strewn tops. It should have been the rainy season, the season of "the big rains"; but the rains were late, as the parched desolation of the landscape bore witness; nevertheless there were two or three showers that afternoon. We soon began to see game, but the flatness of the country and the absence of all cover made stalking a matter of difficulty; the only bushes were a few sparsely scattered mimosas; stunted things, two or three feet high, scantily leaved, but abounding in bulbous swellings on the twigs, and in long, sharp spikes of thorns. There were herds of hartbeest and wildebeest, and smaller parties of beautiful gazelles. The last were of two kinds, named severally after their discoverers, the explorers Grant and Thomson; many of the creatures of this region commemorate the men—Schilling, Jackson, Neumann, Kirke, Chanler, Abbot—who first saw and hunted them and brought them to the notice of the scientific world. The Thomson's gazelles, or "tommies" as they are always locally called, are pretty, alert little things, half the size of our prongbuck; their big brothers, the Grant's, are among the most beautiful of all antelopes, being rather larger than a whitetail deer, with singularly graceful carriage, while the old bucks carry long lyre-shaped horns.

Distances are deceptive on the bare plains under the African sunlight. I saw a fine Grant, and stalked him in a rain-squall; but the bullets from the little Springfield fell short as he raced away to safety; I had underestimated the range. Then I shot, for the table, a good buck of the smaller gazelle, at two hundred and twenty-five yards; the bullet went a little high, breaking his back above the shoulders.

But what I really wanted were two good specimens, bull and cow, of the wildebeest. These powerful, ungainly beasts, a variety of the brindled gnu or blue wildebeest of South Africa, are interesting creatures of queer, eccentric habits. With their shaggy manes, heavy fore quarters, and generally bovine look, they remind one somewhat of our bison, at a distance, but of course they are much less bulky, a big old bull in prime condition rarely reaching a weight of seven hundred pounds. They are beasts of the open plains, ever alert and wary; the cows, with their calves, and one or more herd bulls, keep in parties of several score; the old bulls, singly, or two or three together, keep by themselves, or with herds of zebra, hartbeest, or gazelle; for one of the interesting features of African wild life is the close association and companionship so often seen between totally different species of game. Wildebeest are as savage as they are suspicious; when wounded they do not hesitate to charge a man who comes close, although of course neither they nor any other antelopes can be called dangerous when in a wild state, any more than moose or other deer can be called dangerous; when tame, however, wildebeest are very dangerous indeed, more so than an ordinary domestic bull. The wild, queer-looking creatures prance and rollic and cut strange capers when a herd first makes up its mind to flee from a stranger's approach; and even a solitary bull will some-

times plunge and buck as it starts to gallop off; while a couple
of bulls, when the herd is frightened, may relieve their feelings
by a moment's furious battle, occasionally dropping to their
knees before closing. At this time, the end of April, there
were little calves with the herds of cows; but in many places
in equatorial Africa the various species of antelopes seem to
have no settled rutting-time or breeding-time; at least we saw
calves of all ages.

Our hunt after wildebeest this afternoon was successful;
but though by velt law each animal was mine, because I hit
it first, yet in reality the credit was communistic, so to speak,
and my share was properly less than that of others. I first
tried to get up to a solitary old bull, and after a good deal of
manœuvring, and by taking advantage of a second rain-squall,
I got a standing shot at him at four hundred yards, and hit
him, but too far back. Although keeping a good distance away,
he tacked and veered so, as he ran, that by much running myself I got various other shots at him, at very long range, but
missed them all, and he finally galloped over a distant ridge,
his long tail switching, seemingly not much the worse. We
followed on horseback; for I hate to let any wounded thing
escape to suffer. But meanwhile he had run into view of
Kermit; and Kermit—who is of an age and build which better
fit him for successful breakneck galloping over unknown country dotted with holes and bits of rotten ground—took up the
chase with enthusiasm. Yet it was sunset, after a run of six
or eight miles, when he finally ran into and killed the tough
old bull, which had turned to bay, snorting and tossing its
horns.

Meanwhile I managed to get within three hundred and fifty
yards of a herd, and picked out a large cow which was unac-
companied by a calf. Again my bullet went too far back; and
I could not hit the animal at that distance as it ran. But after
going half a mile it lay down, and would have been secured
without difficulty if a wretched dog had not run forward and
put it up; my horse was a long way back, but Pease, who

had been looking on at a distance, was mounted, and sped after it. By the time I had reached my horse Pease was out of sight; but riding hard for some miles I overtook him, just before the sun went down, standing by the cow which he had ridden down and slain. It was long after nightfall before we reached camp, ready for a hot bath and a good supper. As always thereafter with anything we shot, we used the meat for food and preserved the skins for the National Museum. Both the cow and the bull were fat and in fine condition; but they were covered with ticks, especially wherever the skin was bare. Around the eyes the loathsome creatures swarmed so as to make complete rims, like spectacles; and in the armpits and the groin they were massed so that they looked like barnacles on an old boat. It is astonishing that the game should mind them so little; the wildebeest evidently dreaded far more the biting flies which hung around them; and the maggots of the bot-flies in their nostrils must have been a sore torment. Nature is merciless indeed.

The next day we rode some sixteen miles to the beautiful hills of Kitanga, and for over a fortnight were either Pease's guests at his farm—ranch, as we should call it in the West— or were on safari under his guidance.

CHAPTER II

ON AN EAST AFRICAN RANCH

THE house at which we were staying stood on the beautiful Kitanga hills. They were so named after an Englishman, to whom the natives had given the name of Kitanga; some years ago, as we were told, he had been killed by a lion near where the ranch-house now stood; and we were shown his grave in the little Machakos graveyard. The house was one story high, clean and comfortable, with a veranda running round three sides; and on the veranda were lion-skins and the skull of a rhinoceros. From the house we looked over hills and wide lonely plains; the green valley below, with its flat-topped acacias, was very lovely; and in the evening we could see, scores of miles away, the snowy summit of mighty Kilimanjaro turn crimson in the setting sun. The twilights were not long; and when night fell, stars new to Northern eyes flashed glorious in the sky. Above the horizon hung the Southern Cross, and directly opposite in the heavens was our old familiar friend the Wain, the Great Bear, upside down and pointing to a North Star so low behind a hill that we could not see it. It is a dry country, and we saw it in the second year of a drought; yet I believe it to be a country of high promise for settlers of white race. In many ways it reminds one rather curiously of the great plains of the West, where they slope upward to the foot-hills of the Rockies. It is a white man's country. Although under the equator, the altitude is so high that the nights are cool, and the region as a whole is very healthy. I saw many children, of the Boer immigrants, of English settlers, even of American missionaries, and they looked sound and well. Of course there was no real identity in any feature; but again and again the landscape struck me by its general likeness to the cattle country I knew so well. As my horse shuffled forward, under the bright, hot sunlight, across the endless flats or gently rolling slopes of brown and withered grass, I might have been on the plains anywhere, from Texas to Montana; the hills were like our Western buttes; the half-dry watercourses were fringed with trees, just as if they had been the Sandy, or the Dry, or the Beaver, or the Cottonwood, or any of the multitude of creeks that repeat these and similar names, again and again, from the Panhandle to the Saskatchewan.   Moreover, a Westerner, far better than an Easterner, could see the possibilities of the country.   There should be storage reservoirs in the hills and along the rivers— in my judgment built by the government, and paid for by the water-users in the shape of water-rents—and irrigation ditches; with the water stored and used there would be an excellent opening for small farmers, for the settlers, the actual home-makers, who, above all others, should be encouraged to come into a white man's country like this of the highlands of East Africa.   Even as it is, many settlers do well; it is hard to real-ize that right under the equator the conditions are such that wheat, potatoes, strawberries, apples, all flourish.   No new country is a place for weaklings; but the right kind of man, the settler who makes a success in similar parts of our own West, can do well in East Africa; while a man with money can undoubtedly do very well indeed; and incidentally both men will be leading their lives under conditions peculiarly at-tractive to a certain kind of spirit.   It means hard work, of course; but success generally does imply hard work.

The plains were generally covered only with the thick grass on which the great herds of game fed; here and there small thorn-trees grew upon them, but usually so small and scat-tered as to give no shelter or cover.   By the occasional water-courses the trees grew more thickly, and also on the hills and in the valleys between.   Most of the trees were mimosas, or of similar kind, usually thorny; but there were giant cactus-like euphorbias, shaped like candelabra, and named accordingly; and on the higher hills fig-trees, wild olives, and many others whose names I do not know, but some of which were stately and beautiful. Many of the mimosas were in bloom, and covered with sweet-smelling yellow blossoms. There were many flowers. On the dry plains there were bushes of the color and size of our own sagebrush, covered with flowers like morning-glories. There were also wild sweet peas, on which the ostriches fed, as they did on another plant with a lilac flower of a faint heliotrope fragrance. Among the hills there were masses of singularly fragrant flowers like pink jessamines, growing on bushes sometimes fifteen feet high or over. There were white flowers that smelt like narcissus, blue flowers, red lilies, orange tiger-lilies, and many others of many kinds and colors, while here and there in the pools of the rare rivers grew the sweet-scented purple lotus-lily.

There was an infinite variety of birds, small and large, dull-colored and of the most brilliant plumage. For the most part they either had no names at all or names that meant nothing to us. There were glossy starlings of many kinds; and scores of species of weaver-finches, some brilliantly colored, others remarkable because of the elaborate nests they built by communities among the trees. There were many kinds of shrikes, some of them big, parti-colored birds, almost like magpies, and with a kestrel-like habit of hovering in the air over one spot; others very small and prettily colored. There was a little red-billed finch with its outer tail-feathers several times the length of its head and body. There was a little emerald cuckoo, and a tiny thing, a barbet, that looked exactly like a kingfisher, four inches long. Eared owls flew up from the reeds and grass. There were big, restless, wonderfully colored plantain-eaters in the woods; and hornbills, with strange swollen beaks. A true lark, colored like our meadow-lark (to which it is in no way related), sang from bushes; but the clapper-lark made its curious clapping sounds (apparently with its wings like a ruffed grouse) while it zigzagged in the air. Little pipits sang overhead like our Missouri skylarks. There were night-jars; and doves of various kinds, one of which uttered a series of notes slightly resembling the call of our whippoorwill or chuck-will's-widow. The beautiful little sunbirds were the most gorgeous of all. Then there were bustards, great and small, and snake-eating secretarybirds, on the plains; and francolins, and African spur-fowl with brilliant, naked throats and sand-grouse that flew in packs uttering guttural notes. The wealth of bird life was bewildering. There was not much bird music, judged by the standards of a temperate climate; but the bulbuls, and one or two warblers, sang very sweetly. The naturalists caught shrews and mice in their traps; mole-rats with velvety fur, which burrowed like our pocket-gophers; rats that lived in holes like those of our kangaroo-rat; and one mouse that was striped like our striped gopher. There were conies among the rocks on the hills; they looked like squat, heavy woodchucks, but their teeth were somewhat like those of a wee rhinoceros, and they had little hoof-like nails instead of claws. There were civits and wildcats and things like a small mongoose. But the most interesting mammal we saw was a brilliantly colored yellow-and-blue, or yellow-and-slate, bat, which we put up one day while beating through a ravine. It had been hanging from a mimosa twig, and it flew well in the strong sunlight, looking like some huge, parti-colored butterfly.

It was a settled country, this in which we did our first hunting, and for this reason all the more interesting. The growth and development of East and Middle Africa are phenomena of such absorbing interest, that I was delighted at the chance to see the parts where settlement has already begun before plunging into the absolute wilderness. There was much to remind one of conditions in Montana and Wyoming thirty years ago; the ranches planted down among the hills and on the plains still teeming with game, the spirit of daring adventure everywhere visible, the hope and the heart-breaking disappointment, the successes and the failures. But the problem offered by the natives bore no resemblance to that once offered by the presence of our tribes of horse Indians, few in numbers and incredibly formidable in war. The natives of East Africa are numerous; many of them are agricultural or pastoral peoples after their own fashion; and even the bravest of them, the warlike Masai, are in no way formidable as our Indians were formidable when they went on the war-path. The ranch country I first visited was in what was once the domain of the Wakamba, and in the greater part of it the tribes still dwell. They are in most ways primitive savages, with an imperfect and feeble social, and therefore military, organization; they live in small communities under their local chiefs; they file their teeth, and though they wear blankets in the neighborhood of the whites, these blankets are often cast aside; even when the blanket is worn, it is often in such fashion as merely to accentuate the otherwise absolute nakedness of both sexes. Yet these savages are cattle-keepers and cattle-raisers, and the women do a good deal of simple agricultural work; unfortunately, they are wastefully destructive of the forests. The chief of each little village is recognized as the official head man by the British official, is given support, and is required to help the authorities keep peace and stamp out cattle disease—the two most important functions of government so far as the Wakamba themselves are concerned. All the tribes have their herds of black, brown, and white goats, of mottled sheep, and especially of small humped cattle. The cattle form their pride and joy. During the day each herd is accompanied by the herdsmen, and at night it is driven within its boma, or circular fence of thorn-bushes. Except for the milk, which they keep in their foul, smoky calabashes, the natives really make no use of their cattle; they do not know how to work them, and they never eat them even in time of starvation. When there is prolonged drought and consequent failure of crops, the foolish creatures die by the hundreds when they might readily be saved if they were willing to eat the herds which they persist in treating as ornaments rather than as made for use.

Many of the natives work for the settlers, as cattle-keepers, as ostrich-keepers, or, after a fashion, as laborers. The settlers evidently much prefer to rely upon the natives for unskilled labor rather than see coolies from Hindostan brought into the country. At Sir Alfred Pease's ranch, as at most of the other farms of the neighborhood, we found little Wakamba settlements. Untold ages separated employers and employed; yet those that I saw seemed to get on well together. The Wakamba are as yet not sufficiently advanced to warrant their sharing in the smallest degree in the common government; the "just consent of the governed" in their case, if taken literally, would mean idleness, famine, and endless internecine warfare. They cannot govern themselves from within; therefore they must be governed from without; and their need is met in highest fashion by firm and just control, of the kind that on the whole they are now getting. At Kitanga the natives on the place sometimes worked about the house; and they took care of the stock. The elders looked after the mild little humped cattle—bulls, steers, and cows; and the children, often the merest toddlers, took naturally to guarding the parties of pretty little calves, during the daytime, when they were separated from their mothers. It was an ostrich-farm, too; and in the morning and evening we would meet the great birds, as they went to the grazing-grounds or returned to the ostrich boma, mincing along with their usual air of foolish stateliness, convoyed by two or three boys, each with a red blanket, a throwing-stick, copper wire round his legs and arms, and perhaps a feather stuck in his hair.

There were a number of ranches in the neighborhood—using "neighborhood" in the large Western sense, for they were many miles apart. The Hills, Clifford and Harold, were Africanders; they knew the country, and were working hard and doing well; and in the midst of their work they spared the time to do their full part in insuring a successful hunt to me, an entire stranger. All the settlers I met treated me with the same large and thoughtful courtesy—and what fine fellows they were! And their wives even finer. At Bondoni was Percival, a tall sinewy man, a fine rider and shot; like so many other men whom I met, he wore merely a helmet, a flannel shirt, short breeches or trunks, and puttees and boots, leaving the knee entirely bare. I shall not soon forget seeing him one day, as he walked beside his twelve-ox team, cracking his long whip, while in the big wagon sat pretty Mrs. Percival with a puppy, and a little cheetah cub, which we had found and presented to her and which she was taming. They all— Sir Alfred, the Hills, every one—behaved as if each was my host and felt it peculiarly incumbent on him to give me a good time; and among these hosts one who did very much for me was Captain Arthur Slatter. I was his guest at Kilimakiu, where he was running an ostrich farm; he had lost his right hand, yet he was an exceedingly good game-shot, both with his light and his heavy rifles.

At Kitanga, Sir Alfred's place, two Boers were working, Messrs. Prinsloo and Klopper. We foregathered, of course, as I too was of Dutch ancestry; they were strong, upstanding men, good mechanics, good masons, and Prinsloo spoke English well. I afterward stopped at the farm of Klopper's father, and at the farm of another Boer named Joijs; and I met other Boers while out hunting—Erasmus, Botha, Jaubert, Meyer. They were descendants of the Voortrekkers with the same names who led the hard-fighting farmers northward from the Cape seventy years ago; and were kinsfolk of the men who since then have made these names honorably known throughout the world. There must of course be many Boers who have gone backward under the stress of a hard and semisavage life; just as in our communities of the frontier, the backwoods, and the lonely mountains, there are shiftless "poor whites" and "mean whites" mingled with the sturdy men and women who have laid deep the foundations of our national greatness. But personally I happened not to come across these shiftless "mean white" Boers. Those that I met, both men and women, were of as good a type as any one could wish for in his own coun-

trymen or could admire in another nationality. They fulfilled
the three prime requisites for any race: they worked hard,
they could fight hard at need, and they had plenty of children.
These are the three essential qualities in any and every nation;
they are by no means all-sufficient in themselves, and there is
need that many others should be added to them; but the lack
of any one of them is fatal, and cannot be made good by the
presence of any other set of attributes.

It was pleasant to see the good terms on which Boer and
Briton met. Many of the English settlers whose guest I was,
or with whom I hunted—the Hills, Captain Slatter, Heatley,
Judd—had fought through the South African war; and so had
all the Boers I met. The latter had been for the most part
members of various particularly hard-fighting commandos;
when the war closed they felt very bitterly, and wished to avoid
living under the British flag. Some moved West and some
East; those I met were among the many hundreds, indeed thousands, who travelled northward—a few overland, most of
them by water—to German East Africa. But in the part in
which they happened to settle they were decimated by fever,
and their stock perished of cattle sickness; and most of them
had again moved northward, and once more found themselves under the British flag. They were being treated precisely
on an equality with the British settlers; and every well-wisher
to his kind, and above all every well-wisher to Africa, must
hope that the men who in South Africa fought so valiantly
against one another, each for the right as he saw it, will speedily
grow into a companionship of mutual respect, regard, and consideration such as that which, for our inestimable good fortune,
now knits closely together in our own land the men who wore
the blue and the men who wore the gray and their descendants.
There could be no better and manlier people than those, both
English and Dutch, who are at this moment engaged in the
great and difficult task of adding East Africa to the domain
of civilization; their work is bound to be hard enough anyhow;
and it would be a lamentable calamity to render it more diffi-

cult by keeping alive a bitterness which has lost all point and justification, or by failing to recognize the fundamental virtues, the fundamental characteristics, in which the men of the two stocks are in reality so much alike.

Messrs. Klopper and Loijs, whose farms I visited, were doing well; the latter, with three of his sons, took me out with pride to show me the dam which they had built across a dry watercourse, so as to make a storage reservoir when the rains came. The houses were of stone, and clean and comfortable; the floors were covered with the skins of buck and zebra; the chairs were home-made, as was most of the other furniture; the "rust bunks," or couches, strongly and gracefully shaped, and filled with plaited rawhide, were so attractive that I ordered one to take home. There were neatly kept little flower-gardens, suffering much from the drought; there were ovens and outbuildings; cattle sheds for the humped oxen and the herds of pretty cows and calves; the biltong was drying in smoke-houses; there were patches of ground in cultivation, for corn and vegetables; and the wild velt came up to the door-sills, and the wild game grazed quietly on all sides within sight of the houses. It was a very good kind of pioneer life; and there could be no better pioneer settlers than Boers such as I saw.

The older men wore full beards, and were spare and sinewy. The young men were generally smooth-faced or mustached, strongly built, and rather shy. The elder women were stout, cordial, motherly housewives; the younger were often really pretty. At their houses I was received with hearty hospitality, and given coffee or fresh milk, while we conversed through the medium of the sons or daughters who knew a little English. They all knew that I was of Dutch origin, and were much interested when I repeated to them the only Dutch I knew, a nursery song which, as I told them, had been handed down to me by my own forefathers, and which in return I had repeated, so many, many times, to my children when they were little. It runs as follows, by the way; but I have no idea how the words are spelled, as I have no written copy; it is supposed to be sung by the father, who holds the little boy or little girl on his knee, and tosses him or her up in the air when he comes to the last line:

> "Trippa, troppa, tronjes,
> De varken's in de boonjes,
> De koejes in de klaver,
> De paardeen in de haver,
> De eenjes in de water-plass!
> So groot myn kleine (here insert the
>   little boy's or little girl's name) wass!"

My pronunciation caused trouble at first; but I think they understood me the more readily because doubtless their own usual tongue was in some sort a dialect; and some of them already knew the song, while they were all pleased and amused at my remembering and repeating it; and we were speedily on a most friendly footing.

The essential identity of interest between the Boer and British settlers was shown by their attitude toward the district commissioner, Mr. Humphery, who was just leaving for his biennial holiday, and who dined with us in our tent on his way out. From both Boer farmer and English settler—and from the American missionaries also—I heard praise of Humphery, as a strong man, not in the least afraid of either settler or native, but bound to do justice to both, and, what was quite as important, *sympathizing with the settlers and knowing and understanding their needs*. A new country in which white pioneer settlers are struggling with the iron difficulties and hardships of frontier life is above all others that in which the officials should be men having both knowledge and sympathy with the other men over whom they are placed and for whom they should work.

My host and hostess, Sir Alfred and Lady Pease, were on the best terms with all their neighbors, and their friendly interest was returned; now it was the wife of a Boer farmer who sent over a basket of flowers, now came a box of apples from an English settler on the hills; now Prinsloo the Boer stopped to dinner; now the McMillans—American friends, of whose farm and my stay thereon I shall speak later—rode over from their house on the Mua Hills, with their guest, Selous, to take lunch. This, by the way, was after I had shot my first lions, and I was much pleased to be able to show Selous the trophies.

My gentle-voiced hostess and her daughter had seen many strange lands and strange happenings; as was natural with a husband and father of such adventure-loving nature. They took a keen interest, untinged by the slightest nervousness, in every kind of wild creature from lions and leopards down. The game was in sight from the veranda of the house almost every hour of the day. Early one morning, in the mist, three hartbeests came right up to the wire fence, twoscore yards from the house itself; and the black-and-white striped zebra, and ruddy hartbeest, grazed or rested through the long afternoons in plain view, on the hillsides opposite.

It is hard for one who has not himself seen it to realize the immense quantities of game to be found on the Kapiti Plains and Athi Plains and the hills that bound them. The common game of the plains, the animals of which I saw most while at Kitanga and in the neighborhood, were the zebra, wildebeest, hartbeest, Grant's gazelle, and "tommies" or Thomson's gazelle; the zebra and the hartbeest, usually known by the swahili name of kongoni, being by far the most plentiful. Then there were impala, mountain reedbuck, duiker, steinbuck, and diminutive dikdik. As we travelled and hunted we were hardly ever out of sight of game; and on Pease's farm itself there were many thousand head; and so there were on Slatter's. If wealthy men who desire sport of the most varied and interesting kind would purchase farms like these, they could get, for much less money, many times the interest and enjoyment a deer-forest or grouse-moor can afford.

The wildebeest or gnu were the shyest and least plentiful, but in some ways the most interesting, because of the queer streak of ferocious eccentricity evident in all their actions.

They were of all the animals those that were most exclusively dwellers in the open, where there was neither hill nor bush. Their size and their dark-bluish hides, sometimes showing white in the sunlight, but more often black, rendered them more easily seen than any of their companions. But hardly any plains animal of any size makes any effort to escape its enemies by eluding their observation. Very much of what is commonly said about "protective coloration" has no basis whatever in fact. Black and white are normally the most conspicuous colors in nature (and yet are borne by numerous creatures who have succeeded well in the struggle for life); but almost any tint, or combination of tints, among the grays, browns and duns, harmonizes fairly well with at least some surroundings, in most landscapes; and in but a few instances among the larger mammals, and in almost none among those frequenting the open plains, is there the slightest reason for supposing that the creature gains any benefit whatever from what is loosely called its "protective coloration." Giraffes, leopards, and zebras, for instance, have actually been held up as instances of creatures that are "protectingly" colored and are benefited thereby. The giraffe is one of the most conspicuous objects in nature, and never makes the slightest effort to hide; near by its mottled hide is very noticeable, but, as a matter of fact, under any ordinary circumstances any possible foe trusting to eyesight would discover the giraffe so far away that its coloring would seem uniform, that is, would because of the distance be indistinguishable from a general tint which really might have a slight protective value. In other words, while it is possible that the giraffe's beautifully waved coloring may under certain circumstances, and in an infinitesimally small number of cases, put it at a slight disadvantage in the struggle for life, in the enormous majority of cases—a majority so great as to make the remaining cases negligible—it has no effect whatever, one way or the other; and it is safe to say that under no conditions is its coloring of the slightest value to it as affording it "protection" from foes trusting to their eyesight. So it is with the leopard; it is undoubtedly much less conspicuous than if it were black—and yet the black leopards, the melanistic individuals, thrive as well as their spotted brothers; while on the whole it is probably slightly more conspicuous than if it were nearly unicolor, like the American cougar. As compared with the cougar's tawny hide the leopard's coloration represents a very slight disadvantage, and not an advantage, to the beast; but its life is led under conditions which make either the advantage or the disadvantage so slight as to be negligible; its peculiar coloration is probably in actual fact of hardly the slightest service to it from the "protective" standpoint whether as regards escaping from its enemies or approaching its prey. It has extraordinary facility in hiding, it is a master of the art of stealthy approach; but it is normally nocturnal, and by night the color of its hide is of no consequence whatever; while by day, as I have already said, its varied coloration renders it slightly more easy to detect than is the case with the cougar.

All of this applies with peculiar force to the zebra, which it has also been somewhat the fashion of recent years to hold up as an example of "protective coloration." As a matter of fact the zebra's coloration is not protective at all; on the contrary, it is exceedingly conspicuous, and under the actual conditions of the zebra's life probably never hides it from its foes; the instances to the contrary being due to conditions so exceptional that they may be disregarded. If any man seriously regards the zebra's coloration as "protective," let him try the experiment of wearing a hunting suit of the zebra pattern; he will speedily be undeceived. The zebra is peculiarly a beast of the open plains, and makes no effort ever to hide from the observation of its foes. It is occasionally found in open forest; and may there now and then escape observation simply as any animal of any color—a dun hartbeest or a nearly black bushbuck—may escape observation. At a distance of over a few hundred yards the zebra's coloration ceases to be conspicuous simply because the distance has caused it to lose all its distinctive character—that is, all the quality which could possibly make it protective. Near by it is always very conspicuous, and if the conditions are such that any animal can be seen at all, a zebra will catch the eye much more quickly than a Grant's gazelle, for instance. These gazelles, by the way, although much less conspicuously colored than the zebra, bear when young, and the females even when adult, the dark side stripe which characterizes all sexes and ages of the smaller gazelle, the "tommy"; it is a very conspicuous marking, quite inexplicable on any theory of protective coloration. The truth is that no game of the plains is helped in any way by its coloration in evading its foes, and none seeks to escape the vision of its foes. The larger game animals of the plains are always walking and standing in conspicuous places, and never seek to hide or take advantage of cover; while, on the contrary, the little grass and bush antelopes, like the duiker and steinbuck, trust very much to their power of hiding, and endeavor to escape the sight of their foes by lying absolutely still, in the hope of not being made out against their background. On the plains one sees the wildebeest farthest off and with most ease; the zebra and hartbeest next; the gazelles last.

The wildebeest are very wary. While the hunter is still a long way off the animal will stop grazing and stand with head raised, the heavy shoulders and short neck making it unmistakable. Then, when it makes up its mind to allow no closer approach, it brandishes its long tail, springs and plunges, runs once or twice in semicircles, and is off, the head held much lower than the shoulders, the tail still lashing; and now and then a bull may toss up the dust with its horns. The herds of cows and calves usually contain one or two or more bulls; and in addition, dotted here and there over the plain, are single bulls or small parties of bulls, usually past their prime or not yet full grown. These bulls are often found in the company of hartbeests or zebras; and stray zebras and hartbeests are often found with the wildebeest herds. The stomachs of those

I opened contained nothing but grass; they are grazers, not browsers. The hartbeest are much faster, and if really frightened speedily leave their clumsy-looking friends behind; but the wildebeest, as I have seen them, are by far the most wary. The wildebeest and zebra seemed to me to lie down less frequently than the hartbeest; but I frequently came on herds of both lying down during the heat of the day. Sometimes part of the herd will stand drowsily erect and the rest lie down. Near Kitanga there were three wildebeest which were usually found with a big herd of hartbeest, and which regularly every afternoon lay down for some hours, just as their friends did. The animal has a very bovine look; and though called an antelope it is quite as close kin to the oxen as it is to many of the other beasts also called antelope. The fact is that antelope is not an exact term at all, but merely means any hollow-horned ruminant which the observer happens to think is not a sheep, goat, or ox. When, with Linnæus, the first serious effort at the systematization of living nature began, men naturally groped in the effort to see correctly and to express what they saw. When they came to describe the hollow-horned ruminants, they, of course, already had names at hand for anything that looked like one of the domestic creatures with which they were familiar; and as "antelope" was already a name of general, though vague, currency for some wild creatures, they called everything an antelope that did not seem to come in one of the more familiar domestic categories. Study has shown that sheep and goats grade into one another among the wild species; and the so-called antelopes include forms differing from one another quite as sharply as any of them differ from their kinsfolk that are represented in the farmyard.

Zebra share with hartbeest the distinction of being the most abundant game animal on the plains, throughout the whole Athi region. The two creatures are fond of associating together, usually in mixed herds; but sometimes there will merely be one or two individuals of one species in a big herd of the other. They are sometimes, though less frequently than the hartbeest, found in open bush country; but they live in the open plains by choice.

I could not find out that they had fixed times for resting, feeding, and going to water. They and the hartbeests formed the favorite prey of the numerous lions of the neighborhood; and I believe that the nights, even the moonlight nights, were passed by both animals under a nervous strain of apprehension, ever dreading the attack of their arch-enemy, and stampeding from it. Their stampedes cause the utmost exasperation to the settlers, for when in terror of the real or imaginary attack of a lion, their mad, heedless rush takes them through a wire fence as if it were made of twine and pasteboard. But a few months before my arrival a mixed herd of zebra and hartbeest, stampeded either by lions or wild dogs, rushed through the streets of Nairobi, several being killed by the inhabitants, and one of the victims falling just outside the Episcopal church. The zebras are nearly powerless when seized by lions; but they are bold creatures against less formidable foes, trusting in their hoofs and their strong jaws; they will, when in a herd, drive off hyenas or wild dogs, and will turn on hounds, if the hunter is not near. If the lion is abroad in the daytime, they, as well as the other game, seem to realize that he cannot run them down; and though they follow his movements with great alertness, and keep at a respectful distance, they show no panic. Ordinarily, as I saw them, they did not seem very shy of men; but in this respect all the game displayed the widest differences, from time to time, without any real cause, that I could discern, for the difference. At one hour, or on one day, the zebra and hartbeest would flee from our approach when half a mile off; and again they would permit us to come within a couple of hundred yards, before moving slowly away. On two or three occasions at lunch herds of zebra remained for half an hour watching us with much curiosity not over a hundred yards off. Once, when we had been vainly beating for lions at the foot of the Elukania ridge, at least a thousand zebras stood, in herds, on every side of us, throughout lunch; they were from two to four hundred yards distant, and I was especially struck by the fact that those which were to leeward and had our wind were no more alarmed than the others. I have seen them water at dawn and sunset, and also in the middle of the day; and I have seen them grazing at every hour of the day, although I believe most freely in the morning and evening. At noon and until the late afternoon those I saw were quite apt to be resting, either standing or lying down. They are noisy. Hartbeests merely snort or sneeze now and then; but the shrill, querulous barking of the "bonte quaha," as the Boers call the zebra, is one of the common sounds of the African plains, both by day and night. It is usually represented in books by the syllables "qua-ha-ha"; but of course our letters and syllables were not made to represent, and can only in arbitrary and conventional fashion represent, the calls of birds and mammals; the bark of the bonte quagga or common zebra could just as well be represented by the syllables "ba-wa-wa," and as a matter of fact it can readily be mistaken for the bark of a shrill-voiced dog. After one of a herd has been killed by a lion or a hunter his companions are particularly apt to keep uttering their cry. Zebras are very beautiful creatures, and it was an unending pleasure to watch them. I never molested them save to procure specimens for the museums, or food for the porters, who like their rather rank flesh. They were covered with ticks like the other game; on the groin, and many of the tenderest spots, the odious creatures were in solid clusters; yet the zebras were all in high condition, with masses of oily yellow fat. One stallion weighed 650 pounds.

The hartbeest—Coke's hartbeest, known locally by the Swahili name of kongoni—were at least as plentiful, and almost as tame, as the zebras. As with the other game of equatorial Africa, we found the young of all ages; there seems to be no especial breeding-time, and no one period among the males corresponding to the rutting-season among Northern animals. The hartbeests were usually inseparable companions of the zebra; but though they were by preference beasts of the bare plain, they were rather more often found in open bush than were their striped friends. There are in the country numerous ant-hills, which one sees in every stage of development, from a patch of bare earth with a few funnel-like towers to a hillock a dozen feet high and as many yards in circumference. On these big ant-hills one or two kongoni will often post themselves as lookouts, and are then almost impossible to approach. The bulls sometimes fight hard among themselves, and although their horns are not very formidable weapons, yet I knew of one case in which a bull was killed in such a duel, his chest being ripped open by his adversary's horns; and now and then a bull will kneel and grind its face and horns into the dust or mud. Often a whole herd will gather around and on an ant-hill, or even a small patch of level ground, and make it a regular stamping-ground, treading it into dust with their sharp hoofs. They have another habit which I have not seen touched on in the books. Ordinarily their droppings are scattered anywhere on the plain; but again and again I found where hartbeests—and more rarely Grant's gazelles—had in large numbers deposited their droppings for some time in one spot. Hartbeests are homely creatures, with long faces, high withers, and showing when first in motion a rather ungainly gait, but they are among the swiftest and most enduring of antelope, and when at speed their action is easy and regular. When pursued by a dog they will often play before him—just as a tommy will—taking great leaps, with all four legs inclined backward, evidently in a spirit of fun and derision. In the stomachs of those I killed, as in those of the zebras, I found only grass and a few ground plants; even in the open bush or thinly wooded country they seem to graze and not browse. One fat and heavy bull weighed 340 pounds; a very old bull, with horns much worn down, 299; and a cow in high condition, 315.

The Grant's gazelle is the most beautiful of all these plains creatures; it is about the size of a big whitetail deer; one heavy buck which I shot, although with poor horns, weighed

171 pounds. The finest among the old bucks have beautiful lyre-shaped horns, over two feet long, and their proud, graceful carriage and lightness of movement render them a delight to the eye. As I have already said, the young and the females have the dark side stripe which marks all the tommies; but the old bucks lack this, and their color fades into the brown or sandy of the dry plains far more completely than is the case with zebra or kongoni. Like the other game of the plains they are sometimes found in small parties, or else in fair-sized herds, by themselves, and sometimes with other beasts; I have seen a single fine buck in a herd of several hundred zebra and kongoni. The Thomson's gazelles, hardly a third the weight of their larger kinsfolk, are found scattered everywhere; they are not as highly gregarious as the zebra and kongoni, and are not found in such big herds, but their little bands—now a buck and several does, now a couple of does with their fawns, now three or four bucks together, now a score of individuals—are scattered everywhere on the flats. Like the Grants, their flesh is delicious, and they seem to have much the same habits. But they have one very marked characteristic: their tails keep up an incessant nervous twitching, never being still for more than a few seconds at a time, while the larger gazelle in this part of its range rarely moves its tail at all. They are grazers and they feed, rest, and go to water at irregular times, or at least at different times in different localities; and although they are most apt to rest during the heat of the day, I have seen them get up soon after noon, having lain down for a couple of hours, feed for an hour or so, and then lie down again. In the same way the habits of the game as to migration vary with the different districts, in Africa as in America. There are places where all the game, perhaps notably the wildebeests, gather in herds of thousands at certain times, and travel for scores of miles, so that a district which is teeming with game at one time may be almost barren of large wild life at another. But my information was that around the Kapiti Plains there was no such complete and extensive shift. If the

rains are abundant and the grass rank, most of the game will
be found far out in the middle of the plains; if, as was the
case at the time of my visit, there has been a long drought—
the game will be found ten or fifteen miles away, near or
among the foot-hills.

Unless there was something special on, like a lion or rhinoceros hunt, I usually rode off followed only by my sais and
gun-bearers.   I cannot describe the beauty and the unceasing
interest of these rides, through the teeming herds of game.
It was like retracing the steps of time for sixty or seventy
years, and being back in the days of Cornwallis Harris and
Gordon Cumming, in the palmy times of the giant fauna of
South Africa.   On Pease's own farm one day I passed through
scores of herds of the beautiful and wonderful wild creatures
I have spoken of above; all told there were several thousands
of them.   With the exception of the wildebeest, most of them
were not shy, and I could have taken scores of shots at a distance of a couple of hundred yards or thereabout.   Of course
I did not shoot at anything unless we were out of meat or
needed the skin for the collection; and when we took the skin
we almost always took the meat too, for the porters, although
they had their rations of rice, depended for much of their
well-being on our success with the rifle.

These rides through the wild, lonely country, with only my
silent black followers, had a peculiar charm.   When the sky
was overcast it was cool and pleasant, for it is a high country;
as soon as the sun appeared the vertical tropical rays made the
air quiver above the scorched land.   As we passed down a
hillside we brushed through aromatic shrubs and the hot,
pleasant fragrance enveloped us.   When we came to a nearly
dry watercourse, there would be beds of rushes, beautiful lilies,
and lush green plants with staring flowers, and great deep-green
fig-trees, or flat-topped mimosas.   In many of these trees there
were sure to be native beehives; these were sections of hollow
logs hung from the branches; they formed striking and characteristic features of the landscape.   Wherever there was any

moisture, there were flowers, brilliant of hue and many of them sweet of smell; and birds of numerous kinds abounded. When we left the hills and the wooded watercourses we might ride hour after hour across the barren desolation of the flats, while herds of zebra and hartbeest stared at us through the heat haze. Then the zebra, with shrill, barking neighs, would file off across the horizon, or the high-withered hartbeests, snorting and bucking, would rush off in a confused mass, as unreasoning panic succeeded foolish confidence. If I shot anything, vultures of several kinds, and the tall, hideous marabout storks, gathered before the skinners were through with their work; they usually stayed at a wary distance, but the handsome ravens, glossy-hued with white napes, big-billed, long-winged, and short-tailed, came round more familiarly.

I rarely had to take the trouble to stalk anything; the shooting was necessarily at rather long range, but by manœuvring a little, and never walking straight toward a beast, I was usually able to get whatever the naturalists wished. Sometimes I shot fairly well, and sometimes badly. On one day, for instance, the entry in my diary ran: "Missed steinbuck, pig, impala, and Grant; awful." On another day it ran in part as follows: "Out with Heller. Hartbeest, two hundred and fifty yards, facing me; shot through face, broke neck. Zebra, very large, quartering, one hundred and sixty yards, between neck and shoulder. Buck Grant, two hundred and twenty yards, walking, behind shoulder. Steinbuck, one hundred and eighty yards, standing, behind shoulder." Generally each head of game bagged cost me a goodly number of bullets; but only twice did I wound animals which I failed to get; in the other cases the extra cartridges represented either misses at animals which got clean away untouched, or else a running fusillade at wounded animals which I eventually got. I am a very strong believer in making sure, and, therefore, in shooting at a wounded animal as long as there is the least chance of its getting off. The expenditure of a few cartridges is of no consequence whatever compared to the escape of a single head of game

which should have been bagged. Shooting at long range necessitates much running. Some of my successful shots at Grant's
gazelle and kongoni were made at three hundred, three hundred
and fifty, and four hundred yards; but at such distances my
proportion of misses was very large indeed—and there were
altogether too many even at shorter ranges.

The so-called grass-antelopes, the steinbuck, and duiker,
were the ones at which I shot worst; they were quite plentiful,
and they got up close, seeking to escape observation by hiding
until the last moment; but they were small, and when they
did go they rushed half-hidden through the grass and in and
out among the bushes at such a speed, and with such jumps
and twists and turns, that I found it well-nigh impossible to
hit them with the rifle. The few I got were generally shot
when they happened to stand still.

On the steep, rocky, bush-clad hills there were little klipspringers and the mountain reedbuck or Chanler's reedbuck, a
very pretty little creature. Usually we found the reedbuck does
and their fawns in small parties, and the bucks by themselves;
but we saw too few to enable us to tell whether this represented
their normal habits. They fed on the grass, the hill plants, and
the tips of certain of the shrubs, and were true mountaineers
in their love of the rocks and rough ground, to which they fled
in frantic haste when alarmed. They were shy and elusive
little things, but not wary in the sense that some of the larger
antelopes are wary. I shot two does with three bullets, all of
which hit. Then I tried hard for a buck; at last, late one evening, I got up to one feeding on a steep hillside, and actually
took ten shots to kill him, hitting him no less than seven times.

Occasionally we drove a ravine or a range of hills by means
of beaters. On such occasions all kinds of things were put up.
Most of the beaters, especially if they were wild savages impressed for the purpose from some neighboring tribe, carried
throwing-sticks, with which they were very expert, as indeed
were some of the colonials, like the Hills. Hares, looking and
behaving much like small jack-rabbits, were plentiful both on

the plains and in the ravines, and dozens of these were knocked over; while on several occasions I saw francolins and spur-fowl cut down on the wing by a throwing-stick hurled from some unusually dexterous hand.

The beats, with the noise and laughter of the good-humored, excitable savages, and the alert interest as to what would turn up next, were great fun; but the days I enjoyed most were those spent alone with my horse and gun-bearers. We might be off by dawn, and see the tropic sun flame splendid over the brink of the world; strange creatures rustled through the bush or fled dimly through the long grass, before the light grew bright; and the air was fresh and sweet as it blew in our faces. When the still heat of noon drew near I would stop under a tree, with my water canteen and my lunch. The men lay in the shade, and the hobbled pony grazed close by, while I either dozed or else watched through my telescope the herds of game lying down or standing· drowsily in the distance. As the shadows lengthened I would again mount, and finally ride homeward as the red sunset paled to amber and opal, and all the vast, mysterious African landscape grew to wonderful beauty in the dying twilight.

III

LION-HUNTING ON THE KAPITI PLAINS

THE dangerous game of Africa are the lion, buffalo, elephant, rhinoceros, and leopard. The hunter who follows any of these animals always does so at a certain risk to life or limb; a risk which it is his business to minimize by coolness, caution, good judgment, and straight shooting. The leopard is in point of pluck and ferocity more than the equal of the other four; but his small size always renders it likely that he will merely maul and not kill a man. My friend Carl Akeley, of Chicago, actually killed bare-handed a leopard which sprang on him. He had already wounded the beast twice, crippling it in one front and one hind paw; whereupon it charged, followed him as he tried to dodge the charge, and struck him full just as he turned. It bit him in one arm, biting again and again as it worked up the arm from the wrist to the elbow; but Akeley threw it, holding its throat with the other hand, and flinging its body to one side. It luckily fell on its side with its two wounded legs uppermost, so that it could not tear him. He fell forward with it and crushed in its chest with his knees until he distinctly felt one of its ribs crack; this, said Akeley, was the first moment when he felt he might conquer. Redoubling his efforts, with knees and hand, he actually choked and crushed the life out of it, although his arm was badly bitten. A leopard will charge at least as readily as one of the big beasts, and is rather more apt to get his charge home, but the risk is less to life than to limb.

There are other animals often or occasionally dangerous to human life which are, nevertheless, not dangerous to the hunter. Crocodiles are far greater pests, and far more often man-eaters, than lions or leopards; but their shooting is not accompanied by the smallest element of risk. Poisonous snakes are fruitful sources of accident, but they are actuated only by fear and the anger born of fear. The hippopotamus sometimes destroys boats and kills those in them; but again there is no risk in hunting him. Finally, the hyena, too cowardly ever to be a source of danger to the hunter, is sometimes a dreadful curse to the weak and helpless. The hyena is a beast of unusual strength and enormous power in his jaws and teeth, and thrice over would he be dreaded were fang and sinew driven by a heart of the leopard's cruel courage. But though the creature's foul and evil ferocity has no such backing as that yielded by the angry daring of the spotted cat, it is yet fraught with a terror all its own; for on occasion the hyena takes to man-eating after its own fashion. Carrion-feeder though it is, in certain places it will enter native huts and carry away children or even sleeping adults; and where famine or disease has worked havoc among a people, the hideous spotted beasts become bolder and prey on the survivors. For some years past Uganda has been scourged by the sleeping sickness, which has ravaged it as in the Middle Ages the Black Death ravaged Europe. Hundreds of thousands of natives have died. Every effort has been made by the government officials to cope with the disease; and among other things sleeping-sickness camps have been established, where those stricken by the dread malady can be isolated and cease to be possible sources of infection to their fellows. Recovery among those stricken is so rare as to be almost unknown, but the disease is often slow, and months may elapse during which the diseased man is still able to live his life much as usual. In the big camps of doomed men and women thus established there were, therefore, many persons carrying on their avocations much as in an ordinary native village. But the hyenas found that in many of the huts the inmates were a helpless prey. In 1908 and throughout the early part of 1909, they grew constantly bolder, haunting these sleeping-sickness camps, and each night entering them, bursting into the huts and carrying off and eating the dying people. To guard against them each little group of huts was enclosed by a thick hedge; but after a while the hyenas learned to break through the hedges, and continued their ravages; so that every night armed sentries had to patrol the camps, and every night they could be heard firing at the marauders.

The men thus preyed on were sick to death and for the most part helpless. But occasionally men in full vigor were attacked. One of Pease's native hunters was seized by a hyena as he slept beside the camp-fire, and part of his face torn off. Selous informed me that a friend of his, Major R. T. Coryndon, then administrator of Northwestern Rhodesia, was attacked by a hyena but two or three years ago. At the time Major Coryndon was lying, wrapped in a blanket, beside his wagon. A hyena stealthily approaching through the night, seized him by the hand, and dragged him out of bed; but as he struggled and called out, the beast left him and ran off into the darkness. In spite of his torn hand the major was determined to get his assailant, which he felt sure would soon return. Accordingly, he went back to his bed, drew his cocked rifle beside him, pointing toward his feet, and feigned sleep. When all was still once more, a dim form loomed up through the uncertain light, toward the foot of the bed; it was the ravenous beast returning for his prey; and the major shot and killed it where it stood.

A few months ago a hyena entered the outskirts of Nairobi, crept into a hut, and seized and killed a native man. At Nairobi the wild creatures are always at the threshold of the town and often cross it. At Governor Jackson's table, at Government House, I met Mr. and Mrs. Sandiford. Mr. Sandiford is managing the railroad. A few months previously, while he was sitting, with his family, in his own house in Nairobi, he happened to ask his daughter to look for something in one of the bedrooms. She returned in a minute, quietly remarking: "Father, there's a leopard under the bed." So there was; and it was then remembered that the house cat had been showing a marked and alert distrust of the room in question—very probably the leopard had gotten into the house while trying to catch her or one of the dogs. A neighbor with a rifle was summoned, and shot the leopard.

Hyenas not infrequently kill mules and donkeys, tearing open their bellies and eating them while they are still alive. Yet when themselves assailed they usually behave with abject cowardice. The Hills had a large Airedale terrier, an energetic dog of much courage. Not long before our visit this dog put up a hyena from a bushy ravine in broad daylight, ran after it, overtook it, and flew at it. The hyena made no effective fight, although the dog—not a third its weight—bit it severely and delayed its flight so that it was killed. During the first few weeks of our trip I not infrequently heard hyenas after nightfall but saw none. Kermit, however, put one out of a ravine or dry creek-bed—a donga, as it is locally called—and though the brute had a long start he galloped after it and succeeded in running it down. The chase was a long one, for twice the hyena got in such rocky country that he almost distanced his pursuer; but at last, after covering nearly ten miles, Kermit ran into it in the open, shooting it from the saddle as it shambled along at a canter, growling with rage and terror. I would not have recognized the cry of the hyenas from what I had read, and it was long before I heard them laugh. Pease said that he had only once heard them really laugh. On that occasion he was watching for lions outside a Somali zareba. Suddenly a leopard leaped clear over the zareba, close beside him, and in a few seconds came flying back again, over the high thorn fence, with a sheep in its mouth; but no sooner had it landed than the hyenas rushed at it and took away the sheep; and then their cackling and shrieking sounded exactly like the most unpleasant kind of laughter. The normal death of very old lions, as they grow starved and feeble—unless they are previously killed in an encounter with dangerous game like buffalo—is to be killed and eaten by hyenas; but of course a lion in full vigor pays no heed to hyenas, unless it is to kill one if it gets in the way.

During the last few decades, in Africa, hundreds of white hunters, and thousands of native hunters, have been killed or wounded by lions, buffaloes, elephants, and rhinos. All are dangerous game; each species has to its gruesome credit a long list of mighty hunters slain or disabled. Among those competent to express judgment there is the widest difference of opinion as to the comparative danger in hunting the several kind of animals. Probably no other hunter who has ever lived has combined Selous's experience with his skill as a hunter and his power of accurate observation and narration. He has killed between three and four hundred lions, elephants, buffaloes, and rhinos, and he ranks the lion as much the most dangerous, and the rhino as much the least, while he puts the buffalo and elephant in between, and practically on a par. Governor Jackson has killed between eighty and ninety of the four animals; and he puts the buffalo unquestionably first in point of formidable capacity as a foe, the elephant equally unquestionably second, the lion third, and the rhino last. Stigand puts them in the following order: lion, elephant, rhino, leopard, and buffalo. Drummond, who wrote a capital book on South African game, who was for years a professional hunter like Selous, and who had fine opportunities for observation, but who was a much less accurate observer than Selous, put the rhino as unquestionably the most dangerous, with the lion as second, and the buffalo and elephant nearly on a level. Samuel Baker, a mighty hunter and good observer, but with less experience of African game than any one of the above, put the elephant first, the rhino second, the buffalo seemingly third, and the lion last. The experts of greatest experience thus absolutely disagree among themselves; and there is the same wide divergence of view among good hunters and trained observers whose opportunities have been less. Mr. Abel Chapman, for instance, regards both the elephant and the rhino as more dangerous than the lion; and many of the hunters I met in East Africa seemed inclined to rank the buffalo as more dangerous than any other animal. A man who has shot but a dozen or a score of these various animals, all put together, is not entitled to express any but the most tentative opinion as to their relative prowess and ferocity; yet on the whole it seems to me that the weight of opinion among those best fitted to judge is that the lion is the most formidable opponent of the hunter, under ordinary conditions. This is my own view. But we must ever keep in mind the fact that the surrounding conditions, the geographical locality, and the wide individual variation of temper within the ranks of each species, must all be taken into account. Under certain circumstances a lion may be easily killed, whereas a rhino would be a dangorous foe. Under other conditions the rhino could be attacked with impunity, and the lion only with the utmost hazard; and one bull buffalo might flee and one bull elephant charge, and yet the next couple met with might show an exact reversal of behavior.

At any rate, during the last three or four years, in German and British East Africa and Uganda, over fifty white men have been killed or mauled by lions, buffaloes, elephants, and rhinos; and the lions have much the largest list of victims to their credit. In Nairobi churchyard I was shown the graves of seven men who had been killed by lions, and of one who had been killed by a rhino. The first man to meet us on the African shore was Mr. Campbell, Governor Jackson's A. D. C., and only a year previously he had been badly mauled by a lion. We met one gentleman who had been crippled for life by a lioness. He had marked her into some patches of brush, and coming up, tried to put her out of one thick clump. Failing, he thought she might have gone into another thicket, and walked toward it; instantly that his back was turned, the lioness, who had really been in the first clump of brush, raced out after him, threw him down, and bit him again and again before she was driven off. One night we camped at the very spot where, a score of years before, a strange tragedy had happened. It was in the early days of the opening of the country, and an expedition was going toward Uganda; one of the officials in charge was sleeping in a tent with the flap open. There was an askari on duty; yet a lion crept up, entered the tent, and seized and dragged forth the man. He struggled and made outcry; there was a rush of people, and the lion dropped his prey and bounded off. The man's wounds were dressed, and he was put back to bed in his own tent; but an hour or two after the camp again grew still, the lion returned, bent on the victim of whom he had been robbed; he re-entered the tent, seized the unfortunate wounded man with his great fangs, and this time made off with him into the surrounding darkness, killed and ate him. Not far from the scene of this tragedy, another had occurred. An English officer named Stewart, while endeavoring to kill his first lion, was himself set on and slain. At yet another place we were shown where two settlers, Messrs. Lucas and Goldfinch, had been one killed and one crippled by a lion they had been hunting. They had been following the chase on horseback, and being men of bold nature, and having killed several lions, had become too daring. They hunted the lion into a small piece of brush and rode too near it. It came out at a run and was on them before their horses could get under way. Goldfinch was knocked over and badly bitten and clawed; Lucas went to his assistance, and was in his turn knocked over, and the lion then lay on him and bit him to death. Goldfinch, in spite of his own severe wounds, crawled over and shot the great beast as it lay on his friend.

Most of the settlers with whom I was hunting had met with various adventures in connection with lions. Sir Alfred had shot many in different parts of Africa; some had charged fiercely, but he always stopped them. Captain Slatter had killed a big male with a mane a few months previously. He was hunting it in company with Mr. Humphery, the district commissioner of whom I have already spoken, and it gave them some exciting moments, for when hit it charged savagely. Humphery had a shotgun loaded with buckshot, Slatter his rifle. When wounded, the lion charged straight home, hit

Slatter, knocking him flat and rolling him over and over in the sand, and then went after the native gun-bearer, who was running away—the worst possible course to follow with a charging lion. The mechanism of Slatter's rifle was choked by the sand, and as he rose to his feet he saw the lion overtake the fleeing man, rise on his hind legs like a rearing horse—not springing—and strike down the fugitive. Humphery fired into him with buckshot, which merely went through the skin; and some minutes elapsed before Slatter was able to get his rifle in shape to kill the lion, which, fortunately, had begun to feel the effect of his wounds, and was too sick to resume hostilities of its own accord. The gun-bearer was badly but not fatally injured. Before this, Slatter, while on a lion-hunt, had been set afoot by one of the animals he was after, which had killed his horse. It was at night and the horse was tethered within six yards of his sleeping master. The latter was aroused by the horse galloping off, and he heard it staggering on for some sixty yards before it fell. He and his friend followed it with lanterns and drove off the lion, but the horse was dead. The tracks and the marks on the horse showed what had happened. The lion had sprung clean on the horse's back, his fore claws dug into the horse's shoulders, his hind claws cutting into its haunches, while the great fangs bit at the neck. The horse struggled off at a heavy run, carrying its fearsome burden. After going some sixty yards the lion's teeth went through the spinal cord, and the ride was over. Neither animal had made a sound, and the lion's feet did not touch the earth until the horse fell.

While a magistrate in the Transvaal, Pease had under him as game officer a white hunter, a fine fellow, who underwent an extraordinary experience. He had been off some distance with his Kaffir boys to hunt a lion. On his way home the hunter was hunted. It was after nightfall. He had reached a region where lions had not been seen for a long time, and where an attack by them was unknown. He was riding along a trail in the darkness, his big boarhound trotting ahead, his native "boys" some distance behind. He heard a rustle in the bushes alongside the path, but paid no heed, thinking it was a reedbuck.   Immediately afterward two lions came out in the path behind and raced after him.   One sprang on him, tore him out of the saddle, and trotted off holding him in its mouth, while the other continued after the frightened horse.   The lion had him by the right shoulder, and yet with his left hand he wrenched his knife out of his belt and twice stabbed it.   The second stab went to the heart and the beast let go of him, stood a moment, and fell dead.   Meanwhile, the dog had followed the other lion, which now, having abandoned the chase of the horse, and with the dog still at his heels, came trotting back to look for the man.   Crippled though he was, the hunter managed to climb a small tree; and though the lion might have gotten him out of it, the dog interfered.   Whenever the lion came toward the tree the dog worried him, and kept him off until, at the shouts and torches of the approaching Kaffir boys, he sullenly retired, and the hunter was rescued.

Percival had a narrow escape from a lion, which nearly got him, though probably under a misunderstanding. He was riding through a wet spot of ground, where the grass was four feet high, when his horse suddenly burst into a run and the next moment a lion had galloped almost alongside of him. Probably the lion thought it was a zebra, for when Percival, leaning over, yelled in his face, the lion stopped short. But he at once came on again, and nearly caught the horse. However, they were now out of the tall grass, and the lion gradually drew up when they reached the open country.

The two Hills, Clifford and Harold, were running an ostrich-farm.   The lions sometimes killed their ostriches and stock; and the Hills in return had killed several lions. The Hills were fine fellows; Africanders, as their forefathers for three generations had been, and frontiersmen of the best kind. From the first moment they and I became fast friends, for we instinctively understood one another, and found that we felt alike on all the big questions, and looked at life, and especially the life of effort led by the pioneer settler, from the same standpoint. They reminded me, at every moment, of those Western ranchmen and home-makers with whom I have always felt a special sense of companionship and with whose ideals and aspirations I have always felt a special sympathy. A couple of months before my visit, Harold Hill had met with a rather unpleasant adventure. He was walking home across the lonely plains, in the broad daylight, never dreaming that lions might be abroad, and was unarmed. When still some miles from his house, while plodding along, he glanced up and saw three lions in the trail only fifty yards off, staring fixedly at him. It happened to be a place where the grass was rather tall, and lions are always bold where there is the slightest cover; whereas, unless angered, they are cautious on bare ground. He halted, and then walked slowly to one side; and then slowly forward toward his house. The lions followed him with their eyes, and when he had passed they rose and slouched after him. They were not pleasant followers, but to hurry would have been fatal; and he walked slowly on along the road, while for a mile he kept catching glimpses of the tawny bodies of the beasts as they trod stealthily forward through the sunburned grass, alongside or a little behind him. Then the grass grew short, and the lions halted and continued to gaze after him until he disappeared over a rise.

Everywhere throughout the country we were crossing were signs that the lion was lord and that his reign was cruel. There were many lions, for the game on which they feed was extraordinarily abundant. They occasionally took the ostriches or stock of the settlers, ravaged the herds and flocks of the natives, but not often; for their favorite food was yielded by the swarming herds of kongoni and zebras, on which they could prey at will. Later we found that in this region they rarely molested the buffalo, even where they lived in the same reed beds; and this though elsewhere they habitually prey on the buffalo. But where zebras and hartbeests could be obtained without effort, it was evidently not worth their while to chal-

lenge such formidable quarry. Every "kill" I saw was a kongoni or a zebra; probably I came across fifty of each. One
zebra kill, which was not more than eighteen hours old (after
the lapse of that time the vultures and marabous, not to speak
of the hyenas and jackals, leave only the bare bones), showed
just what had occurred. The bones were all in place, and the
skin still on the lower legs and head. The animal was lying
on its belly, the legs spread out, the neck vertebræ crushed;
evidently the lion had sprung clean on it, bearing it down by
his weight while he bit through the back of the neck, and the
zebra's legs had spread out as the body yielded under the lion.
One fresh kongoni kill showed no marks on the haunches, but
a broken neck and claw marks on the face and withers; in this
case the lion's hind legs had remained on the ground, while
with his fore paws he grasped the kongoni's head and shoulders, holding it until the teeth splintered the neck-bone.

One or two of our efforts to get lions failed, of course, the
ravines we beat did not contain them, or we failed to make
them leave some particularly difficult hill or swamp—for lions
lie close. But Sir Alfred knew just the right place to go to,
and was bound to get us lions—and he did.

One day we started from the ranch-house in good season for
an all-day lion-hunt. Besides Kermit and myself, there was a
fellow guest, Medlicott, and not only our host, but our hostess
and her daughter; and we were joined by Percival at lunch,
which we took under a great fig-tree, at the foot of a high,
rocky hill. Percival had with him a little mongrel bulldog, and
a Masai "boy," a fine, bold-looking savage, with a handsome
head-dress and the usual formidable spear; master, man, and
dog evidently all looked upon any form of encounter with lions
simply in the light of a spree.

After lunch we began to beat down a long donga, or dry
watercourse—a creek, as we should call it in the Western plains
country. The watercourse with low, steep banks wound in
curves, and here and there were patches of brush, which might
contain anything in the shape of lion, cheetah, hyena, or wild

dog. Soon we came upon lion spoor in the sandy bed; first the footprints of a big male, then those of a lioness. We walked cautiously along each side of the donga, the horses following close behind so that if the lion were missed we could gallop after him and round him up on the plain. The dogs—for besides the little bull, we had a large brindled mongrel named Ben, whose courage belied his looks—began to show signs of scenting the lion; and we beat out each patch of brush, the natives shouting and throwing in stones, while we stood with the rifles where we could best command any probable exit. After a couple of false alarms the dogs drew toward one patch, their hair bristling, and showing such eager excitement that it was evident something big was inside; and in a moment one of the boys called, "simba" (lion), and pointed with his finger. It was just across the little ravine, there about four yards wide and as many feet deep; and I shifted my position, peering eagerly into the bushes for some moments before I caught a glimpse of tawny hide; as it moved, there was a call to me to "shoot," for at that distance, if the lion charged, there would be scant time to stop it; and I fired into what I saw. There was a commotion in the bushes, and Kermit fired; and immediately afterward there broke out on the other side, not the hoped-for big lion, but two cubs the size of mastiffs. Each was badly wounded and we finished them off; even if unwounded they were too big to take alive.

This was a great disappointment, and as it was well on in the afternoon, and we had beaten the country most apt to harbor our game, it seemed unlikely that we would have another chance. Percival was on foot and a long way from his house, so he started for it; and the rest of us also began to jog homeward. But Sir Alfred, although he said nothing, intended to have another try. After going a mile or two he started off to the left at a brisk canter; and we, the other riders, followed, leaving behind our gun-bearers, saises, and porters. A couple of miles away was another donga, another shallow watercourse with occasional big brush patches along the winding bed; and toward this we cantered. Almost as soon as we reached it our leader found the spoor of two big lions; and with every sense acock, we dismounted and approached the first patch of tall bushes. We shouted and threw in stones, but nothing came out; and another small patch showed the same result. Then we mounted our horses again, and rode toward another patch a quarter of a mile off. I was mounted on Tranquillity, the stout and quiet sorrel.

This patch of tall, thick brush stood on the hither bank— that is, on our side of the watercourse. We rode up to it and shouted loudly. The response was immediate, in the shape of loud gruntings, and crashings through the thick brush. We were off our horses in an instant, I throwing the reins over the head of mine; and without delay the good old fellow began placidly grazing, quite unmoved by the ominous sounds immediately in front.

I sprang to one side; and for a second or two we waited, uncertain whether we should see the lions charging out ten yards distant or running away. Fortunately, they adopted the latter course. Right in front of me, thirty yards off, there appeared, from behind the bushes which had first screened him from my eyes, the tawny, galloping form of a big maneless lion. Crack! the Winchester spoke; and as the soft-nosed bullet ploughed forward through his flank the lion swerved so that I missed him with the second shot; but my third bullet went through the spine and forward into his chest. Down he came, sixty yards off, his hind quarters dragging, his head up, his ears back, his jaws open and lips drawn up in a prodigious snarl, as he endeavored to turn to face us. His back was broken; but of this we could not at the moment be sure, and if it had merely been grazed, he might have recovered, and then, even though dying, his charge might have done mischief. So Kermit, Sir Alfred, and I fired, almost together, into his chest. His head sank, and he died.

This lion had come out on the left of the bushes; the other, to the right of them, had not been hit, and we saw him galloping off across the plain, six or eight hundred yards away. A couple more shots missed, and we mounted our horses to try to ride him down. The plain sloped gently upward for three-quarters of a mile to a low crest or divide, and long before we got near him he disappeared over this. Sir Alfred and Kermit were tearing along in front and to the right, with Miss Pease close behind; while Tranquillity carried me, as fast as he could, on the left, with Medlicott near me. On topping the divide Sir Alfred and Kermit missed the lion, which had swung to the left, and they raced ahead too far to the right. Medlicott and I, however, saw the lion, loping along close behind some kongoni; and this enabled me to get up to him as quickly as the lighter men on the faster horses. The going was now slightly downhill, and the sorrel took me along very well, while Medlicott, whose horse was slow, bore to the right and joined the other two men. We gained rapidly, and, finding out this, the lion suddenly halted and came to bay in a slight hollow, where the grass was rather long. The plain seemed flat, and we could see the lion well from horseback; but, especially when he lay down, it was most difficult to make him out on foot, and impossible to do so when kneeling.

We were about a hundred and fifty yards from the lion, Sir Alfred, Kermit, Medlicott, and Miss Pease off to one side, and slightly above him on the slope, while I was on the level, about equidistant from him and them. Kermit and I tried shooting from the horses; but at such a distance this was not effective. Then Kermit got off, but his horse would not let him shoot; and when I got off I could not make out the animal through the grass with sufficient distinctness to enable me to take aim. Old Ben the dog had arrived, and, barking loudly, was strolling about near the lion, which paid him not the slightest attention. At this moment my black sais, Simba, came running up to me and took hold of the bridle; he had seen the chase from the line of march and had cut across to join me. There was no other sais or gun-bearer anywhere near, and his action was plucky, for he was the only man afoot, with the lion at bay.

Lady Pease had also ridden up and was an interested spectator only some fifty yards behind me.

Now, an elderly man with a varied past which includes rheumatism does not vault lightly into the saddle; as his sons, for instance, can; and I had already made up my mind that in the event of the lion's charging it would be wise for me to trust to straight powder rather than to try to scramble into the saddle and get under way in time. The arrival of my two companions settled matters. I was not sure of the speed of Lady Pease's horse; and Simba was on foot and it was of course out of the question for me to leave him. So I said, "Good, Simba, now we'll see this thing through," and gentle-mannered Simba smiled a shy appreciation of my tone, though he could not understand the words. I was still unable to see the lion when I knelt, but he was now standing up, looking first at one group of horses and then at the other, his tail lashing to and fro, his head held low, and his lips dropped over his mouth in peculiar fashion, while his harsh and savage growling rolled thunderously over the plain. Seeing Simba and me on foot, he turned toward us, his tail lashing quicker and quicker. Resting my elbow on Simba's bent shoulder, I took steady aim and pressed the trigger; the bullet went in between the neck and shoulder, and the lion fell over on his side, one fore leg in the air. He recovered in a moment and stood up, evidently very sick, and once more faced me, growling hoarsely. I think he was on the eve of charging. I fired again at once, and this bullet broke his back just behind the shoulders; and with the next I killed him outright, after we had gathered round him.

These were two good-sized maneless lions, and very proud of them I was. I think Sir Alfred was at least as proud, especially because we had performed the feat alone, without any professional hunters being present. "We were all amateurs, only gentlemen riders up," said Sir Alfred. It was late before we got the lions skinned. Then we set off toward the ranch, two porters carrying each lion-skin, strapped to a pole; and two others carrying the cub-skins. Night fell long before we were near the ranch; but the brilliant tropic moon lighted the trail. The stalwart savages who carried the bloody lion-skins swung along at a faster walk as the sun went down and the moon rose higher; and they began to chant in unison, one uttering a single word or sentence, and the others joining in a deep-toned, musical chorus. The men on a safari, and indeed African natives generally, are always excited over the death of a lion, and the hunting tribes then chant their rough hunting-songs, or victory songs, until the monotonous, rhythmical repetitions make them grow almost frenzied. The ride home through the moonlight, the vast barren landscape shining like silver on either hand, was one to be remembered; and above all, the sight of our trophies and of their wild bearers.

Three days later we had another successful lion-hunt. Our camp was pitched at a water-hole in a little stream called Potha, by a hill of the same name. Pease, Medlicott, and both the Hills were with us, and Heller came too; for he liked, when possible, to be with the hunters so that he could at once care for any beast that was shot. As the safari was stationary, we took fifty or sixty porters as beaters. It was thirteen hours before we got into camp that evening. The Hills had with them as beaters and water-carriers half a dozen of the Wakamba who were working on their farm. It was interesting to watch these naked savages, with their filed teeth, their heads shaved in curious patterns, and carrying for arms little bows and arrows.

Before lunch we beat a long, low hill. Harold Hill was with me; Medlicott and Kermit were together. We placed ourselves, one couple on each side of a narrow neck two-thirds of the way along the crest of the hill; and soon after we were in position we heard the distant shouts of the beaters as they came toward us, covering the crest and the tops of the slopes on both sides. It was rather disconcerting to find how much better Hill's eyes were than mine. He saw everything first, and it usually took some time before he could make me see it.

In this first drive nothing came my way except some mountain reedbuck does, at which I did not shoot. But a fine male cheetah came to Kermit, and he bowled it over in good style as it ran.

Then the beaters halted, and waited before resuming their march until the guns had gone clear round and established themselves at the base of the farther end of the hill. This time Kermit, who was a couple of hundred yards from me, killed a reedbuck and a steinbuck. Suddenly Hill said "Lion," and endeavored to point it out to me, as it crept cautiously among the rocks on the steep hillside, a hundred and fifty yards away. At first I could not see it; finally I thought I did and fired, but, as it proved, at a place just above him. However, it made him start up, and I immediately put the next bullet behind his shoulders; it was a fatal shot; but, growling, he struggled down the hill, and I fired again and killed him. It was not much of a trophy, however, turning out to be a half-grown male.

We lunched under a tree, and then arranged for another beat. There was a long, wide valley, or rather a slight depression in the ground—for it was only three or four feet below the general level—in which the grass grew tall, as the soil was quite wet. It was the scene of Percival's adventure with the lion that chased him. Hill and I stationed ourselves on one side of this valley or depression, toward the upper end; Pease took Kermit to the opposite side; and we waited, our horses some distance behind us. The beaters were put in at the lower end, formed a line across the valley, and beat slowly toward us, making a great noise.

They were still some distance away when Hill saw three lions, which had slunk stealthily off ahead of them through the grass. I have called the grass tall, but this was only by comparison with the short grass of the dry plains. In the depression or valley it was some three feet high. In such grass a lion, which is marvellously adept at hiding, can easily conceal itself, not merely when lying down, but when advancing at a crouching gait. If it stands erect, however, it can be seen.

There were two lions near us, one directly in our front, a hundred and ten yards off. Some seconds passed before Hill could make me realize that the dim yellow smear in the yellow-brown grass was a lion; and then I found such difficulty in getting a bead on him that I overshot. However, the bullet must have passed very close—indeed, I think it just grazed him—for he jumped up and faced us, growling savagely. Then, his head lowered, he threw his tail straight into the air and began to charge. The first few steps he took at a trot, and before he could start into a gallop I put the soft-nosed Winchester bullet in between the neck and shoulder. Down he went with a roar; the wound was fatal, but I was taking no chances, and I put two more bullets in him. Then we walked toward where Hill had already seen another lion—the lioness, as it proved. Again he had some difficulty in making me see her; but he succeeded and I walked toward her through the long grass, repressing the zeal of my two gun-bearers, who were stanch, but who showed a tendency to walk a little ahead of me on each side, instead of a little behind. I walked toward her because I could not kneel to shoot in grass so tall; and when shooting offhand I like to be fairly close, so as to be sure that my bullets go in the right place. At sixty yards I could make her out clearly, snarling at me as she faced me; and I shot her full in the chest. She at once performed a series of extraor-dinary antics, tumbling about on her head, just as if she were throwing somersaults, first to one side and then to the other. I fired again, but managed to shoot between the somersaults, so to speak, and missed her. The shot seemed to bring her to herself, and away she tore; but instead of charging us she charged the line of beaters. She was dying fast, however, and in her weakness failed to catch any one; and she sank down into the long grass. Hill and I advanced to look her up, our rifles at full cock, and the gun-bearers close behind. It is tick-lish work to follow a wounded lion in tall grass, and we walked carefully, every sense on the alert. We passed Heller, who had been with the beaters. He spoke to us with an amused smile. His only weapon was a pair of field-glasses, but he always took things as they came, with entire coolness, and to be close to a wounded lioness when she charged merely interested him. A beater came running up and pointed toward where he had seen her, and we walked toward the place. At thirty yards' distance Hill pointed, and eagerly peering, I made out the form of the lioness showing indistinctly through the grass. She was half crouching, half sitting, her head bent down; but she still had strength to do mischief. She saw us, but before she could turn I sent a bullet through her shoulders; down she went, and was dead when we walked up. A cub had been seen, and another full-grown lion, but they had slunk off and we got neither.

This was a full-grown but young lioness of average size; her cubs must have been several months old. We took her entire to camp to weigh; she weighed 283 pounds. The first lion, which we had difficulty in finding, as there were no identifying marks in the plain of tall grass, was a good-sized male, weighing about 400 pounds, but not yet full grown; although he was probably the father of the cubs.

We were a long way from camp, and, after beating in vain for the other lion, we started back; it was after nightfall before we saw the camp-fires. It was two hours later before the porters appeared, bearing on poles the skin of the dead lion, and the lioness entire. The moon was nearly full, and it was interesting to see them come swinging down the trail in the bright silver light, chanting in deep tones, over and over again, a line or phrase that sounded like:

"Zou-zou-boulé ma ja guntai; zou-zou-boulé ma ja guntai."

Occasionally they would interrupt it by the repetition in unison, at short intervals, of a guttural ejaculation, sounding like "huzlem." They marched into camp, then up and down the lines, before the rows of small fires; then, accompanied by all the rest of the porters, they paraded up to the big fire where I was standing. Here they stopped and ended the ceremony by a minute or two's vigorous dancing amid singing and wild shouting. The firelight gleamed and flickered across the grim dead beasts, and the shining eyes and black features of the excited savages, while all around the moon flooded the landscape with her white light.

IV

ON SAFARI; RHINO AND GIRAFFE

WHEN we killed the last lions we were already on safari, and the camp was pitched by a water-hole on the Potha, a half-dried stream, little more than a string of pools and reed beds, winding down through the sun-scorched plain. Next morning we started for another water-hole at the rocky hill of Bondoni, about eight miles distant.

Safari life is very pleasant, and also very picturesque. The porters are strong, patient, good-humored savages, with something childlike about them that makes one really fond of them. Of course, like all savages and most children, they have their limitations, and in dealing with them firmness is even more necessary than kindness; but the man is a poor creature who does not treat them with kindness also, and I am rather sorry for him if he does not grow to feel for them, and to make them in return feel for him, a real and friendly liking. They are subject to gusts of passion, and they are now and then guilty of grave misdeeds and shortcomings; sometimes for no conceivable reason, at least from the white man's standpoint. But they are generally cheerful, and when cheerful are always amusing; and they work hard, if the white man is able to combine tact and consideration with that insistence on the performance of duty and lack of which they despise as weakness. Any little change or excitement is a source of pleasure to them. When the march is over they sing; and after two or three days in camp they will not only sing, but dance when another march is to begin. Of course at times they suffer greatly from thirst and hunger and fatigue, and at times they will suddenly grow sullen or rebel without what seems to us any adequate cause; and they have an inconsequent type of mind which now and then leads them to commit follies all the more exasperating because they are against their own interest no less than against the interest of their employer. But they do well on the whole, and safari life is attractive to them. They are fed well; the government requires that they be fitted with suitable clothes and given small tents, so that they are better clad and sheltered than they would be otherwise; and their wages represent money which they could get in no other way. The safari represents a great advantage to the porter; who in his turn alone makes the safari possible.

When we were to march, camp was broken as early in the day as possible. Each man had his allotted task, and the tents, bedding, provisions, and all else were expeditiously made into suitable packages. Each porter is supposed to carry from fifty-five to sixty pounds, which may all be in one bundle or in two or three. The American flag, which flew over my tent, was a matter of much pride to the porters, and was always carried at the head or near the head of the line of march; and after it in single file came the long line of burden-bearers. As they started, some of them would blow on horns or whistles and others beat little tom-toms; and at intervals this would be renewed again and again throughout the march; or the men might suddenly begin to chant, or merely to keep repeating in unison some one word or one phrase which, when we asked to have it translated, might or might not prove to be entirely meaningless. The head men carried no burdens, and the tent-boys hardly anything, while the saises walked with the spare horses. In addition to the canonical and required costume of blouse or jersey and drawers, each porter wore a blanket, and usually something else to which his soul inclined. It might be an exceedingly shabby coat; it might be, of all things in the world, an umbrella, an article for which they had a special attachment. Often I would see a porter, who thought nothing whatever of walking for hours at midday under the equatorial sun with his head bare, trudging along with solemn pride either under an open umbrella, or carrying the umbrella (tied much like Mrs. Gamp's) in one hand, as a wand of dignity. Then their head-gear varied according to the fancy of the individual. Normally it was a red fez, a kind of cap only used in hot climates, and exquisitely designed to be useless therein because it gives absolutely no protection from the sun. But one would wear a skin cap; another would suddenly put one or more long feathers in his fez; and another discarding the fez, would revert to some purely savage head-dress which he would wear with equal gravity whether it were, in our eyes, really decorative or merely comic. One such head-dress, for instance, consisted of the skin of the top of a zebra's head, with the two ears. Another was made of the skins of squirrels, with the tails both sticking up and hanging down. Another consisted of a bunch of feathers woven into the hair, which itself was pulled out into strings that were stiffened with clay. Another was really too intricate for description because it included the man's natural hair, some strips of skin, and an empty tin can.

If it were a long journey and we broke it by a noon-day halt, or if it were a short journey and we reached camp ahead of the safari, it was interesting to see the long file of men approach. Here and there, leading the porters, scattered through the line, or walking alongside, were the askaris, the rifle-bearing soldiers. They were not marksmen, to put it mildly, and I should not have regarded them as particularly efficient allies in a serious fight; but they were excellent for police duty in camp, and were also of use in preventing collisions with the natives. After the leading askaris might come one of the head men; one of whom, by the way, looked exactly like a Semitic negro, and always travelled with a large dirty-white umbrella in one hand; while another, a tall, powerful fellow, was a mission boy who spoke good English; I mention his being a mission boy because it is so frequently asserted that mission boys never turn out well. Then would come the man with the flag, followed by another blowing on an antelope horn, or perhaps beating an empty can as a drum; and then the long line of men, some carrying their loads on their heads, others on their shoulders, others, in a very few cases, on their backs. As they approached the halting place their spirits rose, the whistles and horns were blown, and the improvised drums beaten, and perhaps the whole line would burst into a chant.

On reaching the camping-ground each man at once set about his allotted task, and the tents were quickly pitched and the camp put in order, while water and firewood were fetched. The tents were pitched in long lines, in the first of which stood my tent, flanked by those of the other white men and by the dining tent. In the next line were the cook tent, the provision tent, the store tent, the skinning tent, and the like; and then came the lines of small white tents for the porters. Between each row of tents was a broad street. In front of our own tents in the first line an askari was always pacing to and fro; and when night fell we would kindle a camp-fire and sit around it under the stars. Before each of the porters' tents was a little fire, and beside it stood the pots and pans in which the porters did their cooking. Here and there were larger fires, around which the gun-bearers or a group of askaris or of saises might gather. After nightfall the multitude of fires lit up the darkness and showed the tents in shadowy outline; and around them squatted the porters, their faces flickering from dusk to ruddy light, as they chatted together or suddenly started some snatch of wild African melody in which all their neighbors might join. After a while the talk and laughter and singing would gradually die away, and as we white men sat around our fire, the silence would be unbroken except by the queer cry of a hyena, or much more rarely by a sound that always demanded attention—the yawning grunt of a questing lion.

If we wished to make an early start we would breakfast by dawn and then we often returned to camp for lunch. Otherwise we would usually be absent all day, carrying our lunch with us. We might get in before sunset or we might be out till long after nightfall; and then the gleam of the lit fires was a welcome sight as we stumbled toward them through the darkness. Once in, each went to his tent to take a hot bath; and then, clean and refreshed, we sat down to a comfortable dinner, with game of some sort as the principal dish.

On the first march after leaving our lion-camp at Potha I shot a wart-hog. It was a good-sized sow, which, in company with several of her half-grown offspring, was grazing near our line of march; there were some thorn-trees which gave a little cover, and I killed her at a hundred and eighty yards, using the Springfield, the lightest and handiest of all my rifles. Her flesh was good to eat, and the skin, as with all our specimens, was saved for the National Museum. I did not again have to shoot a sow, although I killed half-grown pigs for the table, and boars for specimens. This sow and her porkers were not rooting, but were grazing as if they had been antelope; her stomach contained nothing but chopped green grass. Wart-hogs are common throughout the country over which we hunted. They are hideous beasts, with strange protuberances on their cheeks; and when alarmed they trot or gallop away, holding the tail perfectly erect with the tassel bent forward. Usually they are seen in family parties, but a big boar will often be alone. They often root up the ground, but the stomachs of those we shot were commonly filled with nothing but grass. If the weather is cloudy or wet they may be out all day long, but in hot, dry weather we generally found them abroad only in the morning and evening. A pig is always a comical animal; even more so than is the case with a bear, which also impresses one with a sense of grotesque humor—and this notwithstanding the fact that both boar and bear may be very formidable creatures. A wart-hog standing alertly at gaze, head and tail up, legs straddled out, and ears cocked forward, is rather a figure of fun; and not the less so when with characteristic suddenness he bounces round with a grunt and scuttles madly off to safety. Wart-hogs are beasts of the bare plain or open forest, and though they will often lie up in patches of brush they do not care for thick timber.

After shooting the wart-hog we marched on to our camp

at Bondoni. The gun-bearers were Mohammedans, and the dead pig was of no service to them; and at their request I walked out while camp was being pitched and shot them a buck; this I had to do now and then, but I always shot males, so as not to damage the species.

Next day we marched to the foot of Kilimakiu Mountain, near Captain Slatter's ostrich-farm. Our route lay across bare plains thickly covered with withered short grass. All around us as we marched were the game-herds, zebras and hartbeests, gazelles of the two kinds, and now and then wilde-beests. Hither and thither over the plain, crossing and recross-ing, ran the dusty game trails, each with its myriad hoof-marks; the round hoof-prints of the zebra, the heart-shaped marks that showed where the hartbeest-herd had trod, and the delicate etching that betrayed where the smaller antelope had passed. Occasionally we crossed the trails of the natives, worn deep in the hard soil by the countless thousands of bare or sandalled feet that had trodden them. Africa is a country of trails. Across the high velt, in every direction, run the tangled trails of the multitudes of game that have lived thereon from time immemorial. The great beasts of the marsh and the forest made therein broad and muddy trails which often offer the only pathway by which a man can enter the sombre depths. In wet ground and dry alike are also found the trails of savage man. They lead from village to village, and in places they stretch for hundreds of miles, where trading parties have worn them in the search for ivory, or in the old days when raiding or purchasing slaves. The trails made by the men are made much as the beasts make theirs. They are generally longer and better defined, although I have seen hippo tracks more deeply marked than any made by savage man. But they are made simply by men following in one another's footsteps, and they are never quite straight. They bend now a little to one side, now a little to the other, and sudden loops mark the spot where some vanished obstacle once stood; around it the first trail-makers went, and their successors have ever trodden in their footsteps, even though the need for so doing has long passed away.

Our camp at Kilimakiu was by a grove of shady trees, and from it at sunset we looked across the vast plain and saw the far-off mountains grow umber and purple as the light waned. Back of the camp, and of the farmhouse near which we were, rose Kilimakiu Mountain, beautifully studded with groves of trees of many kinds. On its farther side lived a tribe of the Wakamba. Their chief with all the leading men of his village came in state to call upon me, and presented me with a fat hairy sheep, of the ordinary kind found in this part of Africa, where the sheep very wisely do not grow wool. The head man was dressed in khaki, and showed me with pride an official document which confirmed him in the position by direction of the government, and required him to perform various acts, chiefly in the way of preventing his tribespeople from committing robbery or murder, and of helping to stamp out cattle disease. Like all the Wakamba they had flocks of goats and sheep, and herds of humped cattle; but they were much in need of meat and hailed my advent. They were wild savages with filed teeth, many of them stark naked, though some of them carried a blanket. Their heads were curiously shaved so that the hair tufts stood out in odd patterns, and they carried small bows, and arrows with poisoned heads.

The following morning I rode out with Captain Slatter. We kept among the hills. The long drought was still unbroken. The little pools were dry and their bottoms baked like iron, and there was not a drop in the watercourses. Part of the land was open and part covered with a thin forest or bush of scattered mimosa-trees. In the open country were many zebras and hartbeests, and the latter were found even in the thin bush. In the morning we found a small herd of eland at which, after some stalking, I got a long shot and missed. The eland is the largest of all the horned creatures that are called antelope, being quite as heavy as a fattened ox. The herd I approached consisted of a dozen individuals, two of them huge bulls, their coats having turned a slaty blue, their great dewlaps hanging down, and the legs looking almost too small for the massive bodies. The reddish-colored cows were of far lighter build. Eland are beautiful creatures and ought to be domesticated. As I crept toward them I was struck by their likeness to great, clean, handsome cattle. They were grazing or resting, switching their long tails at the flies that hung in attendance upon them and lit on their flanks, just as if they were Jerseys in a field at home. My bullet fell short, their size causing me to underestimate the distance, and away they went at a run, one or two of the cows in the first hurry and confusion skipping clean over the backs of others that got in their way—a most unexpected example of agility in such large and ponderous animals. After a few hundred yards they settled down to the slashing trot which is their natural gait, and disappeared over the brow of a hill.

The morning was a blank, but early in the afternoon we saw the eland-herd again. They were around a tree in an open space, and we could not get near them. But instead of going straight away they struck off to the right and described almost a semicircle, and though they were over four hundred yards distant, they were such big creatures and their gait was so steady that I felt warranted in shooting. On the dry plain I could mark where my bullets fell, and though I could not get a good chance at the bull I finally downed a fine cow; and by pacing I found it to be a little over a quarter of a mile from where I stood when shooting.

It was about nine miles from camp, and I dared not leave the eland alone, so I stationed one of the gun-bearers by the great carcass and sent a messenger in to Heller, on whom we depended for preserving the skins of the big game. Hardly had this been done when a Wakamba man came running up to tell us that there was a rhinoceros on the hillside three-quarters of a mile away, and that he had left a companion to watch it while he carried us the news. Slatter and I immediately rode in the direction given, following our wild-looking guide; the other gun-bearer trotting after us. In five minutes we had reached the opposite hill crest, where the watcher stood, and he at once pointed out the rhino. The huge beast was standing in entirely open country, although there were a few scattered trees of no great size at some little distance from him. We left our horses in a dip of the ground and began the approach; I cannot say that we stalked him, for the approach was too easy. The wind blew from him to us, and a rhino's eyesight is dull. Thirty yards from where he stood was a bush four or five feet high, and though it was so thin that we could distinctly see him through the leaves, it shielded us from the vision of his small, pig-like eyes as we advanced toward it, stooping and in single file, I leading. The big beast stood like an uncouth statue, his hide black in the sunlight; he seemed what he was, a monster surviving over from the world's past, from the days when the beasts of the prime ran riot in their strength, before man grew so cunning of brain and hand as to master them. So little did he dream of our presence that when we were a hundred yards off he actually lay down.

Walking lightly, and with every sense keyed up, we at last reached the bush, and I pushed forward the safety of the double-barrelled Holland rifle which I was now to use for the first time on big game. As I stepped to one side of the bush so as to get a clear aim, with Slatter following, the rhino saw me and jumped to his feet with the agility of a polo-pony. As he rose I put in the right barrel, the bullet going through both lungs. At the same moment he wheeled, the blood spouting from his nostrils, and galloped full on us. Before he could get quite all the way round in his headlong rush to reach us, I struck him with my left-hand barrel, the bullet entering between the neck and shoulder and piercing his heart. At the same instant Captain Slatter fired, his bullet entering the neck vertebræ. Ploughing up the ground with horn and feet, the great bull rhino, still head toward us, dropped just thirteen paces from where we stood.

This was a wicked charge, for the rhino meant mischief

and came on with the utmost determination. It is not safe to generalize from a few instances. Judging from what I have since seen, I am inclined to believe that both lion and buffalo are more dangerous game than rhino; yet the first two rhinos I met both charged, whereas we killed our first four lions and first four buffaloes without any of them charging, though two of each were stopped as they were on the point of charging. Moreover, our experience with this bull rhino illustrates what I have already said as to one animal being more dangerous under certain conditions, and another more dangerous under different conditions. If it had been a lion instead of a rhino, my first bullet would, I believe, have knocked all the charge out of it; but the vitality of the huge pachyderm was so great, its mere bulk counted for so much, that even such a hard-hitting rifle as my double Holland— than which I do not believe there exists a better weapon for heavy game—could not stop it outright, although either of the wounds inflicted would have been fatal in a few seconds.

Leaving a couple of men with the dead rhino, to protect it from the Wakamba by day and the lions by night, we rode straight to camp, which we reached at sunset. It was necessary to get to work on the two dead beasts as soon as possible in order to be sure of preserving their skins. Heller was the man to be counted on for this task. He it was who handled all the skins, who, in other words, was making the expedition of permanent value so far as big game was concerned; and no work at any hour of the day or night ever came amiss to him. He had already trained eight Wakamba porters to act as skinners under his supervision. On hearing of our success, he at once said that we ought to march out to the game that night so as to get to work by daylight. Moreover, we were not comfortable at leaving only two men with each carcass, for lions were both bold and plentiful.

The moon rose at eight and we started as soon as she was above the horizon. We did not take the horses, because there was no water where we were going, and furthermore we did

not like to expose them to a possible attack by lions. The
march out by moonlight was good fun, for though I had been
out all day, I had been riding, not walking, and so was not
tired. A hundred porters went with us so as to enable us
to do the work quickly and bring back to camp the skins
and all the meat needed, and these porters carried water, food
for breakfast, and what little was necessary for a one-night
camp. We tramped along in single file under the moonlight,
up and down the hills, and through the scattered thorn forest.
Kermit and Medlicott went first, and struck such a pace that
after an hour we had to halt them so as to let the tail end
of the file of porters catch up. Then Captain Slatter and I
set a more decorous pace, keeping the porters close up in line
behind us. In another hour we began to go down a long
slope toward a pin-point of light in the distance which we
knew was the fire by the rhinoceros. The porters, like the
big children they were, felt in high feather, and began to chant
to an accompaniment of whistling and horn-blowing as we
tramped through the dry grass which was flooded with silver
by the moon, now high in the heavens.

As soon as we reached the rhino, Heller with his Wakamba
skinners pushed forward the three-quarters of a mile to the
eland, returning after midnight with the skin and all the best
parts of the meat.

Around the dead rhino the scene was lit up both by the
moon and by the flicker of the fires. The porters made their
camp under a small tree a dozen rods to one side of the
carcass, building a low circular fence of branches on which
they hung their bright-colored blankets, two or three big fires
blazing to keep off possible lions. Half as far on the other
side of the rhino a party of naked savages had established
their camp, if camp it could be called, for really all they
did was to squat down round a couple of fires with a few
small bushes disposed round about. The rhino had been
opened, and they had already taken out of the carcass what
they regarded as tidbits and what we certainly did not grudge

them.   Between the two camps lay the huge dead beast, his hide glistening in the moonlight.   In each camp the men squatted around the fires chatting and laughing as they roasted strips of meat on long sticks, the fitful blaze playing over them, now leaving them in darkness, now bringing them out into a red relief.   Our own tent was pitched under another tree a hundred yards off, and when I went to sleep, I could still hear the drumming and chanting of our feasting porters; the savages were less at ease, and their revel was quiet.

Early next morning I went back to camp, and soon after reaching there again started out for a hunt.   In the afternoon I came on giraffes and got up near enough to shoot at them. But they are such enormous beasts that I thought them far nearer than they were.   My bullet fell short, and they disappeared among the mimosas, at their strange leisurely looking gallop.   Of all the beasts in an African landscape none is more striking than the giraffe.   Usually it is found in small parties or in herds of fifteen or twenty or more individuals. Although it will drink regularly if occasion offers, it is able to get along without water for months at a time, and frequents by choice the dry plains or else the stretches of open forest where the trees are scattered and ordinarily somewhat stunted. Like the rhinoceros—the ordinary or prehensile-lipped rhinoceros—the giraffe is a browsing and not a grazing animal.   The leaves, buds, and twigs of the mimosas or thorn-trees form its customary food.   Its extraordinary height enables it to bring into play to the best possible advantage its noteworthy powers of vision, and no animal is harder to approach unseen.   Again and again I have made it out a mile off or rather have seen it a mile off when it was pointed out to me, and looking at it through my glasses, would see that it was gazing steadily at us.   It is a striking-looking animal and handsome in its way, but its length of leg and neck and sloping back make it appear awkward even at rest.   When alarmed it may go off at a long swinging pace or walk, but if really frightened it strikes into a peculiar gallop or canter.   The tail is cocked and twisted,

and the huge hind legs are thrown forward well to the outside
of the fore legs. The movements seem deliberate and the
giraffe does not appear to be going at a fast pace, but if it
has any start a horse must gallop hard to overtake it. When
it starts on this gait, the neck may be dropped forward at
a sharp angle with the straight line of the deep chest, and
the big head is thrust in advance. They are defenseless things
and, though they may kick at a man who incautiously comes
within reach, they are in no way dangerous.

The following day I again rode out with Captain Slatter.
During the morning we saw nothing except the ordinary game,
and we lunched on a hilltop, ten miles distant from camp,
under a huge fig-tree with spreading branches and thick, deep-
green foliage. Throughout the time we were taking lunch
a herd of zebras watched us from near by, standing motionless
with their ears pricked forward, their beautifully striped bodies
showing finely in the sunlight. We scanned the country round
about with our glasses, and made out first a herd of elands, a
mile in our rear, and then three giraffes a mile and a half
in our front. I wanted a bull eland, but I wanted a giraffe
still more, and we mounted our horses and rode toward where
the three tall beasts stood, on an open hillside with trees
thinly scattered over it. Half a mile from them we left the
horses in a thick belt of timber beside a dry watercourse, and
went forward on foot.

There was no use in trying a stalk, for that would merely
have aroused the giraffe's suspicion. But we knew they were
accustomed to the passing and repassing of Wakamba men
and women, whom they did not fear if they kept at a reasonable
distance, so we walked in single file diagonally in their direction; that is, toward a tree which I judged to be about three
hundred yards from them. I was carrying the Winchester
loaded with full metal-patched bullets. I wished to get for
the museum both a bull and a cow. One of the three giraffes
was much larger than the other two, and as he was evidently
a bull I thought the two others were cows.

As we reached the tree the giraffes showed symptoms of uneasiness. One of the smaller ones began to make off, and both the others shifted their positions slightly, curling their tails. I instantly dropped on my knee, and getting the bead just behind the big bull's shoulder, I fired with the three-hundred-yard sight. I heard the "pack" of the bullet as it struck just where I aimed; and away went all three giraffes at their queer rocking-horse canter. Running forward, I emptied my magazine, firing at the big bull and also at one of his smaller companions, and then, slipping into the barrel what proved to be a soft-nosed bullet, I fired at the latter again. The giraffe was going straightaway and it was a long shot, at four or five hundred yards; but by good luck the bullet broke its back and down it came. The others were now getting over the crest of the hill, but the big one was evidently sick, and we called and beckoned to the two saises to hurry up with the horses. The moment they arrived we jumped on, and Captain Slatter cantered up a neighboring hill so as to mark the direction in which the giraffes went if I lost sight of them. Meanwhile I rode full speed after the giant quarry. I was on the tranquil sorrel, the horse I much preferred in riding down game of any kind, because he had a fair turn of speed, and yet was good about letting me get on and off. As soon as I reached the hill crest I saw the giraffes ahead of me, not as far off as I had feared, and I raced toward them without regard to rotten ground and wart-hog holes. The wounded one lagged behind, but when I got near he put on a spurt, and as I thought I was close enough I leaped off, throwing the reins over the sorrel's head, and opened fire. Down went the big bull, and I thought my task was done. But as I went back to mount the sorrel he struggled to his feet again and disappeared after his companion among the trees, which were thicker here, as we had reached the bottom of the valley. So I tore after him again, and in a minute came to a dry watercourse. Scrambling into and out of this I saw the giraffes ahead of me just beginning the

ascent of the opposite slope; and touching the horse with the
spur we flew after the wounded bull. This time I made up
my mind I would get up close enough; but Tranquillity did
not quite like the look of the thing ahead of him. He did
not refuse to come up to the giraffe, but he evidently felt
that, with such an object close by and evident in the landscape, it behooved him to be careful as to what might be
hidden therein, and he shied so at each bush we passed that
we progressed in a series of loops. So off I jumped, throwing
the reins over his head, and opened fire once more; and this
time the great bull went down for good.

Tranquillity recovered his nerve at once and grazed contentedly while I admired the huge proportions and beautiful
coloring of my prize. In a few minutes Captain Slatter
loped up, and the gun-bearers and saises followed. As if by
magic, three or four Wakamba turned up immediately afterward, their eyes glistening at the thought of the feast ahead
for the whole tribe. It was mid-afternoon, and there was
no time to waste. My sais, Simba, an excellent long-distance
runner, was sent straight to camp to get Heller and pilot him
back to the dead giraffes. Beside each of the latter, for they
had fallen a mile apart, we left a couple of men to build
fires. Then we rode toward camp. To my regret, the smaller
giraffe turned out to be a young bull and not a cow.

At this very time, and utterly without our knowledge, there
was another giraffe-hunt going on. Sir Alfred had taken out
Kermit and Medlicott, and they came across a herd of a
dozen giraffes right out in the open plains. Medlicott's horse
was worn out and he could not keep up, but both the others
were fairly well mounted. Both were light men and hard
riders, and although the giraffes had three-quarters of a
mile the start, it was not long before both were at the heels
of the herd. They singled out the big bull, which by the way
turned out to be an even bigger bull than mine, and fired
at him as they galloped. In such a headlong, helter-skelter
chase, however, it is no easy matter to score a hit from horse-

back unless one is very close up; and Sir Alfred made up his mind to try to drive out the bull from the rest of the herd. He succeeded; but at this moment his horse put a forefoot into a hole and turned a complete somersault, almost wrenching out his shoulder. Sir Alfred was hurled off head over heels, but even as he rolled over, clutching his rifle, he twisted himself round to his knees, and took one last shot at the flying giraffe. This left Kermit alone and he galloped hard on the giraffe's heels, firing again and again with his Winchester. Finally his horse became completely done out and fell behind; whereupon Kermit jumped off, and being an excellent long-distance runner, ran after the giraffe on foot for more than a mile. But he did not need to shoot again. The great beast had been mortally wounded and it suddenly slowed down, halted, and fell over dead. As a matter of curiosity we kept the Winchester bullets both from Kermit's giraffe and from mine. I made a point of keeping as many as possible of the bullets with which the different animals were slain so as to see just what was done by the different types of rifles we had with us.

When I reached camp I found that Heller had already started. Next morning I rode down to see him and found him hard at work with the skins; but as it would take him two or three days to finish them and put them in condition for transport, we decided that the safari should march back to the Potha camp, and that from thence we would send Percival's ox-wagon to bring back to the camp all the skins, Heller and his men accompanying him. The plan was carried out, and the following morning we shifted the big camp as proposed.

Heller, thus left behind, came near having an unpleasant adventure. He slept in his own tent, and his Wakamba skinners slept under the fly not far off. One night they let the fires die down and were roused at midnight by hearing the grunting of a hungry lion apparently not a dozen yards off in the darkness. Heller quickly lit his lantern and sat up with his shotgun loaded with bird-shot, the only weapon he had with him. The lion walked round and round the tent, grunting at intervals. Then, after some minutes of suspense, he drew off. While the grunting had been audible, not a sound came from the tent of the Wakambas, who all cowered under their blankets in perfect silence. But once he had gone there was a great chattering, and in a few minutes the fires were roaring, nor were they again suffered to die down.

Heller's skinners had grown to work very well when under his eye. He had encountered much difficulty in getting men who would do the work, and had tried the representatives of various tribes, but without success until he struck the Wakamba. These were real savages who filed their teeth and delighted in raw flesh, and Heller's explanation of their doing well was that their taste for the raw flesh kept them thoroughly interested in their job, so that they learned without difficulty. The porters speedily christened each of the white men by some title of their own, using the ordinary Swahili title of Bwana (master) as a prefix. Heller was the Bwana Who Skinned; Loring, who collected the small mammals, was named, merely descriptively, the Mouse Master, Bwana Pania. I was always called Bwana Makuba, the chief or Great Master; Kermit was first called Bwana Medogo, the young master, and afterward was christened "the Dandy," Bwana Merodadi.

From Potha the safari went in two days to McMillan's place, Juja Farm, on the other side of the Athi. I stayed behind, as I desired to visit the American Mission Station at Machakos. Accordingly, Sir Alfred and I rode thither. Machakos has long been a native town, for it was on the route formerly taken by the Arab caravans that went from the coast to the interior after slaves and ivory. Riding toward it we passed herd after herd of cattle, sheep, and goats, each guarded by two or three savage herdsmen. The little town itself was both interesting and attractive. Besides the natives there were a number of Indian traders and the English commissioner and assistant commissioner, with a small body of native soldiers. The latter not a long time before had been just such savages as those round about them, and the change for the better wrought in their physique and morale by the ordered discipline to which they had submitted themselves could hardly be exaggerated. When we arrived the commissioner and his assistant were engaged in cross-examining some neighboring chiefs as to the cattle sickness. The English rule in Africa has been of incalculable benefit to Africans themselves, and indeed this is true of the rule of most European nations. Mistakes have been made, of course, but they have proceeded at least as often from an unwise effort to accomplish too much in the way of beneficence, as from a desire to exploit the natives. Each of the civilized nations that has taken possession of any part of Africa has had its own peculiar good qualities and its own peculiar defects. Some of them have done too much in supervising and ordering the lives of the natives, and in interfering with their practices and customs. The English error, like our own under similar conditions, has, if anything, been in the other direction. The effort has been to avoid wherever possible all interference with tribal customs, even when of an immoral and repulsive character, and to do no more than what is obviously necessary, such as insistence upon keeping the peace and preventing the spread of cattle disease. Excellent reasons can be advanced in favor of this policy, and it must always be remembered that a fussy and ill-considered benevolence is more sure to awaken resentment than cruelty itself; while the natives are apt to resent deeply even things that are obviously for their ultimate welfare. Yet I cannot help thinking that with caution and wisdom it would be possible to proceed somewhat farther than has yet been the case in the direction of pushing upward some at least of the East African tribes; and this though I recognize fully that many of these tribes are of a low and brutalized type. Having said this much in the way of criticism, I wish to add my tribute of unstinted admiration for the disinterested and efficient work being done, alike in the interest of the

white man and the black, by the government officials whom
I met in East Africa. They are men in whom their country
has every reason to feel a just pride.

We lunched with the American missionaries. Mission work
among savages offers many difficulties, and often the wisest
and most earnest effort meets with dishearteningly little reward; while lack of common sense, and of course, above all,
lack of a firm and resolute disinterestedness, insures the worst
kind of failure. There are missionaries who do not do well,
just as there are men in every conceivable walk of life who do
not do well; and excellent men who are not missionaries, including both government officials and settlers, are only too apt to
jump at the chance of criticising a missionary for every al-
leged sin of either omission or commission. Finally, zealous
missionaries, fervent in the faith, do not always find it easy
to remember that savages can only be raised by slow steps,
that an empty adherence to forms and ceremonies amounts to
nothing, that industrial training is an essential in any permanent upward movement, and that the gradual elevation of mind
and character is a prerequisite to the achievement of any kind
of Christianity which is worth calling such. Nevertheless,
after all this has been said, it remains true that the good done
by missionary effort in Africa has been incalculable. There are
parts of the great continent, and among them I include many
sections of East Africa, which can be made a white man's
country; and in these parts every effort should be made to
favor the growth of a large and prosperous white population.
But over most of Africa the problem for the white man is to
govern, with wisdom and firmness, and when necessary with
severity, but always with an eye single to their own interests
and development, the black and brown races. To do this
needs sympathy and devotion no less than strength and wisdom, and in the task the part to be played by the missionary
and the part to be played by the official are alike great, and
the two should work hand in hand.

After returning from Machakos, I spent the night at Sir

Alfred's, and next morning said good-by with most genuine regret to my host and his family. Then, followed by my gun-bearers and sais, I rode off across the Athi Plains. Through the bright white air the sun beat down mercilessly, and the heat haze wavered above the endless flats of scorched grass. Hour after hour we went slowly forward, through the morning, and through the burning heat of the equatorial noon, until in mid-afternoon we came to the tangled tree growth which fringed the half-dried bed of the Athi. Here I off-saddled for an hour; then, mounting, I crossed the river-bed where it was waterless, and before evening fell I rode up to Juja Farm.

V

JUJA FARM; HIPPO AND LEOPARD

A T Juja Farm we were welcomed with the most generous hospitality by my fellow countryman and his wife, Mr. and Mrs. W. N. McMillan. Selous had been staying with them, and one afternoon I had already ridden over from Sir Alfred's ranch to take tea with them at their other house on the beautiful Mua hills.

Juja Farm lies on the edge of the Athi Plains, and the house stands near the junction of the Nairobi and Rewero Rivers. The house, like almost all East African houses, was of one story, a broad, vine-shaded veranda running around it. There were numerous outbuildings of every kind; there were flocks and herds, corn-fields, a vegetable-garden, and, immediately in front of the house, a very pretty flower-garden, carefully tended by unsmiling Kikuyu savages. All day long these odd creatures worked at the grass and among the flower-beds; according to the custom of their tribe their ears were slit so as to enable them to stretch the lobes to an almost unbelievable extent, and in these apertures they wore fantastically carved native ornaments. One of them had been attracted by the shining surface of an empty tobacco can, and he wore this in one ear to match the curiously carved wooden drum he carried in the other. Another, whose arms and legs were massive with copper and iron bracelets, had been given a blanket because he had no other garment; he got along quite well with the blanket excepting when he had to use the lawn-mower, and then he would usually wrap the blanket around his neck and handle the lawn-mower with the evident feeling that he had done all that the most exacting conventionalism could require.

The house-boys and gun-bearers, and most of the boys who took care of the horses, were Somalis, whereas the cattle-keepers who tended the herds of cattle were Masai, and the men and women who worked in the fields were Kikuyus. The three races had nothing to do with one another, and the few Indians had nothing to do with any of them. The Kikuyus lived in their beehive huts scattered in small groups; the Somalis all dwelt in their own little village on one side of the farm; and half a mile off the Masai dwelt in their village. Both the Somalis and Masai were fine, daring fellows; the Somalis were Mohammedans and horsemen; the Masai were cattle-herders, who did their work as they did their fighting, on foot, and were wild heathen of the most martial type. They looked carefully after the cattle, and were delighted to join in the chase of dangerous game, but regular work they thoroughly despised. Sometimes when we had gathered a mass of Kikuyus or of our own porters together to do some job, two or three Masai would stroll up to look on with curiosity, sword in belt and great spear in hand; their features were well cut, their hair curiously plaited, and they had the erect carriage and fearless bearing that naturally go with a soldierly race.

Within the house, with its bedrooms and dining-room, its library and drawing-room, and the cool, shaded veranda, everything was so comfortable that it was hard to realize that we were far in the interior of Africa and almost under the equator. Our hostess was herself a good rider and good shot, and had killed her lion; and both our host and a friend who was staying with him, Mr. Bulpett, were not merely mighty hunters who had bagged every important variety of large and dangerous game, but were also explorers of note, whose travels had materially helped in widening the area of our knowledge of what was once the dark continent.

Many birds sang in the garden, bulbuls, thrushes, and warblers; and from the narrow fringe of dense woodland along the edges of the rivers other birds called loudly, some with harsh, some with musical, voices. Here for the first time we saw the honey-guide, the bird that insists upon leading any man it sees to honey, so that he may rob the hive and give it a share.

Game came right around the house. Hartbeests, wildebeests, and zebras grazed in sight on the open plain. The hippopotami that lived close by in the river came out at night into the garden. A couple of years before a rhino had come down into the same garden in broad daylight, and quite wantonly attacked one of the Kikuyu laborers, tossing him and breaking his thigh. It had then passed by the house out to the plain, where it saw an ox-cart, which it immediately attacked and upset, cannoning off after its charge and passing up through the span of oxen, breaking all the yokes but fortunately not killing an animal. Then it met one of the men of the house on horseback, immediately assailed him, and was killed for its pains.

My host was about to go on safari for a couple of months with Selous, and to manage their safari they had one of the noted professional hunters of East Africa, Mr. W. Judd, and Judd was kind enough to take me out hunting almost every day that we were at Juja. We would breakfast at dawn and leave the farm about the time that it grew light enough to see; ordinarily our course was eastward, toward the Athi, a few miles distant. These morning rides were very beautiful. In our front was the mountain mass of Donyo Sabuk, and the sun rose behind it, flooding the heavens with gold and crimson. The morning air blew fresh in our faces, and the unshod feet of our horses made no sound as they trod the dew-drenched grass. On every side game stood to watch us, herds of hartbeests and zebras, and now and then a herd of wildebeests or a few straggling old wildebeest bulls. Sometimes the zebras and kongoni were very shy, and took fright when we were yet a long way off; at other times they would stand motionless and permit us to come within fair gunshot, and after we had passed we could still see them regarding us without their having moved. The wildebeests were warier; usually when we were yet a quarter of a mile or so distant, the herd, which had been standing with heads up, their short, shaggy necks and heavy withers giving the animals an unmistakable look, would take fright, and, with heavy curvets, and occasionally running in semicircles, would make off, heads held down and long tails lashing the air.

In the open woods which marked the border between the barren plains and the forested valley of the Athi, Kermit and I shot water-buck and impala. The water-buck is a stately antelope with long, coarse gray hair and fine carriage of the head and neck; the male alone carries horns. We found them usually in parties of ten or a dozen, both of bulls and cows; but sometimes a party of cows would go alone, or three or four bulls might be found together. In spite of its name, we did not find it much given to going in the water, although it would cross the river fearlessly whenever it desired; it was, however, always found not very far from water. It liked the woods and did not go many miles from the streams, yet we frequently saw it on the open plains a mile or two from trees, feeding in the vicinity of the zebra and the hartbeest. This was, however, usually quite early in the morning or quite late in the afternoon. In the heat of the day it clearly preferred to be in the forest, along the stream's edge, or in the bush-clad ravines.

The impala are found in exactly the same kind of country as the water-buck, and often associate with them. To my mind they are among the most beautiful of all antelope. They are about the size of a white-tailed deer, their beautiful annulated horns making a single spiral, and their coat is like satin with its contrasting shades of red and white. They have the most graceful movements of any animal I know, and it is extraordinary to see a herd start off when frightened, both bucks and does bounding clear over the tops of the tall bushes, with a peculiar bird-like motion and lightness. Usually a single old buck will be found with a large company of does and fawns; the other bucks go singly or in small parties. It was in the middle of May, and we saw fawns of all ages. When in the open, where, like the water-buck, it often went in the morning and evening, the impala was very shy, but I did not find it particularly so among the woods. In connection with shooting two of the impala, there occurred little incidents which are worthy of mention.

In one case I had just killed a water-buck cow, hitting it at a considerable distance and by a lucky fluke, after a good deal of bad shooting. We started the porters in with the water-buck, and then rode west through an open country, dotted here and there with trees and with occasional ant-hills. In a few minutes we saw an impala buck, and I crept up behind an ant-hill and obtained a shot at about two hundred and fifty yards. The buck dropped, and as I was putting in another cartridge I said to Judd that I didn't like to see an animal drop like that, so instantaneously, as there was always the possibility that it might only be creased, and that if an animal so hurt got up, it always went off exactly as if unhurt. When we raised our eyes again to look for the impala it had vanished. I was sure that we would never see it again, and Judd felt much the same way, but we walked in the direction toward which its head had been pointed, and Judd ascended an ant-hill to scan the surrounding country with his glasses. He did so, and after a minute remarked that he could not see the wounded impala; when a sudden movement caused us to look down, and there it was, lying at our very feet, on the side of the ant-hill, unable to rise. I had been using a sharp-pointed bullet in the Springfield, and this makes a big hole. The bullet had gone too far back, in front of the hips. I should not have wondered at all if the animal had failed to get up after falling, but I did not understand why, as it recovered enough from the shock to be able to get up, it had not continued to travel, instead of falling after going one hundred yards. Indeed, I am inclined to think that a deer or prong-buck, hit in the same fashion, would have gone off and would have given a long chase before being overtaken. Judging from what others have said, I have no doubt that African game is very tough and succumbs less easily to wounds than is the case with animals of the northern temperate zone; but in my own experience, I several times saw African antelopes succumb to wounds quicker than the average northern animal would have succumbed to a similar wound. One was this impala. Another was the cow eland I first shot; her hind leg was broken high up, and the wound, though crippling, was not such as would have prevented a moose or wapiti from hobbling away on three legs; yet in spite of hard struggles the eland was wholly unable to regain her feet.

The impala thus shot by the way, although in fine condition and the coat of glossy beauty, was infested by ticks; around the horns the horrid little insects were clustered in thick masses for a space of a diameter of some inches. It was to me marvellous that they had not set up inflammation or caused great sores, for they were so thick that at a distance of a few feet they gave the appearance of there being some big gland or bare place at the root of each horn.

The other impala buck also showed an unexpected softness, succumbing to a wound which I do not believe would have given me either a white-tailed or a black-tailed deer. I had been vainly endeavoring to get a water-buck bull, and as the day was growing hot I was riding homeward, scanning the edge of the plain where it merged into the trees that extended out from the steep bank that hemmed in one side of the river-bottom. From time to time we would see an impala or a water-buck making its way from the plain back to the river-bottom, to spend the day in the shade. One of these I stalked, and after a good deal of long-range shooting broke a hind leg high up. It got out of sight and we rode along the edge of the steep descent which led down into the river-bottom proper. In the bottom there were large, open, grassy places, while the trees made a thick fringe along the river course. We had given up the impala and turned out toward the plain, when one of my gun-bearers whistled to us and said he had seen the wounded animal cross the bottom and go into the fringe of trees bounding a deep pool in which we knew there were both hippos and crocodiles. We were off our horses at once, and, leaving them at the top, scrambled down the descent and crossed the bottom to the spot indicated. The impala had lain down as soon as it reached cover, and as we entered the fringe of wood I caught a glimpse of it getting up and making off. Yet fifty yards farther it stopped again, standing right on the brink of the pool, so close that when I shot it, it fell over into the water.

When, after arranging for this impala to be carried back to the farm, we returned to where our horses had been left, the boys told us with much excitement that there was a large snake near by; and sure enough a few yards off, coiled up in the long grass under a small tree, was a python. I could not see it distinctly, and using a solid bullet I just missed the back-bone, the bullet going through the body about its middle. Immediately the snake lashed at me with open jaws, and then, uncoiling, came gliding rapidly in our direction. I do not think it was charging; I think it was merely trying to escape. But Judd, who was utterly unmoved by lion, leopard, or rhino, evidently held this snake in respect, and yelled to me to get out of the way. Accordingly, I jumped back a few feet, and the snake came over the ground where I had stood; its evil genius then made it halt for a moment and raise its head to a height of perhaps three feet, and I killed it by a shot through the neck. The porters were much wrought up about the snake, and did not at all like my touching it and taking it up, first by the tail and then by the head. It was only twelve feet long. We tied it to a long stick and sent it in by two porters.

Another day we beat for lions, but without success. We rode to a spot a few miles off, where we were joined by three Boer farmers. They were big, upstanding men, looking just

as Boer farmers ought to look who had been through a war
and had ever since led the adventurous life of frontier farmers
in wild regions. They were accompanied by a pack of big,
rough-looking dogs, but were on foot, walking with long and
easy strides. The dogs looked a rough-and-ready lot, but on
this particular morning showed themselves of little use; at
any rate they put up nothing.

But Kermit had a bit of deserved good luck. While the
main body of us went down the river-bed, he and McMillan,
with a few natives, beat up a side ravine, down the middle
of which ran the usual dry watercourse fringed with patches
of brush. In one of these they put up a leopard, and saw it
slinking forward ahead of them through the bushes. Then
they lost sight of it, and came to the conclusion that it was in
a large thicket. So Kermit went on one side of it and McMillan
on the other, and the beaters approached to try and get the
leopard out. Of course none of the beaters had guns; their
function was merely to make a disturbance and rouse the
game, and they were cautioned on no account to get into
danger. But the leopard did not wait to be driven. Without
any warning, out he came and charged straight at Kermit,
who stopped him when he was but six yards off with a bullet
in the fore part of the body; the leopard turned, and as
he galloped back Kermit hit him again, crippling him in the
hips. The wounds were fatal, and they would have knocked
the fight out of any animal less plucky and savage than the
leopard; but not even in Africa is there a beast of more un-
flinching courage than this spotted cat. The beaters were
much excited by the sight of the charge and the way in which
it was stopped, and they pressed jubilantly forward too heed-
lessly; one of them, who was on McMillan's side of the thicket,
went too near it, and out came the wounded leopard at him.
It was badly crippled or it would have got the beater at once;
as it was, it was slowly overtaking him as he ran through
the tall grass, when McMillan, standing on an ant-heap, shot
it again. Yet, in spite of having this third bullet in it, it ran

down the beater and seized him, worrying him with teeth and claws; but it was weak because of its wounds, and the powerful savage wrenched himself free, while McMillan fired into the beast again; and back it went through the long grass into the thicket. There was a pause, and the wounded beater was removed to a place of safety, while a messenger was sent on to us to bring up the Boer dogs. But while they were waiting, the leopard, on its own initiative, brought matters to a crisis, for out it came again straight at Kermit, and this time it dropped dead to Kermit's bullet. No animal could have shown a more fearless and resolute temper. It was an old female, but small, its weight being a little short of seventy pounds. The smallest female cougar I ever killed was heavier than this, and one very big male cougar which I killed in Colorado was three times the weight. Yet I have never heard of any cougar which displayed anything like the spirit and ferocity of this little leopard, or which in any way approached it as a dangerous foe. It was sent back to camp in company with the wounded beater, after the wounds of the latter had been dressed; they were not serious, and he was speedily as well as ever.

The rivers that bounded Juja Farm, not only the Athi, but the Nairobi and Rewero, contained hippopotami and crocodiles in the deep pools. I was particularly anxious to get one of the former, and early one morning Judd and I rode off across the plains, through the herds of grazing game seen dimly in the dawn, to the Athi. We reached the river, and, leaving our horses, went down into the wooded bottom, soon after sunrise. Judd had with him a Masai, a keen-eyed hunter, and I my two gun-bearers. We advanced with the utmost caution toward the brink of a great pool; on our way we saw a bush-buck, but of course did not dare to shoot at it, for hippopotami are wary, except in very unfrequented regions, and any noise will disturb them. As we crept noiselessly up to the steep bank which edged the pool, the sight was typically African. On the still water floated a crocodile, nothing but his eyes and nostrils visible. The bank was covered with a dense growth of trees, festooned with vines; among the branches sat herons; a little cormorant dived into the water; and a very small and brilliantly colored kingfisher with a red beak and large turquoise crest, perched unheedingly within a few feet of us. Here and there a dense growth of the tall and singularly graceful papyrus rose out of the water, the feathery heads, which crowned the long smooth green stems, waving gently to and fro.

We scanned the waters carefully, and could see no sign of hippos, and, still proceeding with the utmost caution, we moved a hundred yards farther down to another lookout. Here the Masai detected a hippo head a long way off on the other side of the pool; and we again drew back and started cautiously forward to reach the point opposite which he had seen the head.

But we were not destined to get that hippo. Just as we had about reached the point at which we had intended to turn in toward the pool, there was a succession of snorts in our front and the sound of the trampling of heavy feet and of a big body being shoved through a dense mass of tropical bush. My companions called to me in loud whispers that it was a rhinoceros coming at us, and to "Shoot, shoot." In another moment the rhinoceros appeared, twitching its tail and tossing and twisting its head from side to side as it came toward us. It did not seem to have very good horns, and I would much rather not have killed it; but there hardly seemed any alternative, for it certainly showed every symptom of being bent on mischief. My first shot, at under forty yards, produced no effect whatever, except to hasten its approach. I was using the Winchester, with full-jacketed bullets; my second bullet went in between the neck and shoulder, bringing it to a halt. I fired into the shoulder again, and as it turned toward the bush I fired into its flank both the bullets still remaining in my magazine.

For a moment or two after it disappeared we heard the

branches crash, and then there was silence. In such cover a wounded rhino requires cautious handling, and as quietly as possible we walked through the open forest along the edge of the dense thicket into which the animal had returned. The thicket was a tangle of thorn-bushes, reeds, and small, low-branching trees; it was impossible to see ten feet through it, and a man could only penetrate it with the utmost slowness and difficulty, whereas the movements of the rhino were very little impeded. At the far end of the thicket we examined the grass to see if the rhino had passed out, and sure enough there was the spoor, with so much blood along both sides that it was evident the animal was badly hit. It led across this space and into another thicket of the same character as the first; and again we stole cautiously along the edge some ten yards out. I had taken the heavy Holland double-barrel, and with the safety-catch pressed forward under my thumb, I trod gingerly through the grass, peering into the thicket and expectant of developments. In a minute there was a furious snorting and crashing directly opposite us in the thicket, and I brought up my rifle; but the rhino did not quite place us, and broke out of the cover in front, some thirty yards away; and I put both barrels into and behind the shoulder. The terrific striking force of the heavy gun told at once, and the rhino wheeled, and struggled back into the thicket, and we heard it fall. With the utmost caution, bending and creeping under the branches, we made our way in, and saw the beast lying with its head toward us. We thought it was dead, but would take no chances; and I put in another, but as it proved needless, heavy bullet.

It was an old female, considerably smaller than the bull I had already shot, with the front horn measuring fourteen inches as against his nineteen inches; as always with rhinos, it was covered with ticks, which clustered thickly in the folds and creases of the skin, around and in the ears, and in all the tender places. McMillan sent out an ox-wagon and brought it in to the house, where we weighed it. It was a little over two thousand two hundred pounds. It had evidently been in the neighborhood in which we found it for a considerable time, for a few hundred yards away we found its stamping-ground, a circular spot where the earth had been all trampled up and kicked about, according to the custom of rhinoceroses; they return day after day to such places to deposit their dung, which is then kicked about with the hind feet. As with all our other specimens, the skin was taken off and sent back to the National Museum. The stomach was filled with leaves and twigs, this kind of rhinoceros browsing on the tips of the branches by means of its hooked, prehensile upper lip.

Now I did not want to kill this rhinoceros, and I am not certain that it really intended to charge us. It may very well be that if we had stood firm it would, after much threatening and snorting, have turned and made off; veteran hunters like Selous could, I doubt not, have afforded to wait and see what happened. But I let it get within forty yards, and it still showed every symptom of meaning mischief, and at a shorter range I could not have been sure of stopping it in time. Often under such circumstances the rhino does not mean to charge at all, and is acting in a spirit of truculent and dull curiosity; but often, when its motions and actions are indistinguishable from those of an animal which does not mean mischief, it turns out that a given rhino does mean mischief. A year before I arrived in East Africa a surveyor was charged by a rhinoceros entirely without provocation; he was caught and killed. Chanler's companion on his long expedition, the Austrian Von Höhnel, was very severely wounded by a rhino and nearly died; the animal charged through the line of march of the safari, and then deliberately turned, hunted down Von Höhnel, and tossed him. Again and again there have been such experiences, and again and again hunters who did not wish to kill rhinos have been forced to do so in order to prevent mischief. Under such circumstances it is not to be expected that men will take too many chances when face to face with a creature whose actions are threatening and whose intentions it is absolutely impossible to divine. In fact, I do not see how the rhinoceros can be permanently preserved, save in very out-of-the-way places or in regular game reserves. There is enough interest and excitement in the pursuit to attract every eager young hunter, and, indeed, very many eager old hunters; and the beast's stupidity, curiosity, and truculence make up a combination of qualities which inevitably tend to insure its destruction.

As we brought home the whole body of this rhinoceros, and as I had put into it eight bullets, five from the Winchester and three from the Holland, I was able to make a tolerably fair comparison between the two. With the full-jacketed bullets of the Winchester I had mortally wounded the animal; it would have died in a short time, and it was groggy when it came out of the brush in its final charge; but they inflicted no such smashing blow as the heavy bullets of the Holland. Moreover, when they struck the heavy bones they tended to break into fragments, while the big Holland bullets ploughed through. The Winchester and the Springfield were the weapons, one of which I always carried in my own hand, and for any ordinary game I much prefer them to any other rifles. The Winchester did admirably with lions, giraffes, elands, and smaller game, and, as will be seen, with hippos. For heavy game like rhinoceroses and buffaloes, I found that for me personally the heavy Holland was unquestionably the proper weapon. But in writing this I wish most distinctly to assert my full knowledge of the fact that the choice of a rifle is almost as much a matter of personal idiosyncrasy as the choice of a friend. The above must be taken as merely the expression of my personal preferences. It will doubtless arouse as much objection among the ultrachampions of one type of gun as among the ultrachampions of another. The truth is that any good modern rifle is good enough. The determining factor is the man behind the gun.

In the afternoon of the day on which we killed the rhino Judd took me out again to try for hippos, this time in the

Rewero, which ran close by the house.   We rode upstream a couple of miles.   Then we sent back our horses and walked down the river-bank as quietly as possible, Judd scanning the pools, and the eddies in the running stream, from every point of vantage.   Once we aroused a crocodile, which plunged into the water.   The stream was full of fish, some of considerable size; and in the meadow-land on our side we saw a gang of big, black wild geese feeding.   But we got within half a mile of McMillan's house without seeing a hippo, and the light was rapidly fading.   Judd announced that we would go home, but took one last look around the next bend, and instantly sank to his knees, beckoning to me.   I crept forward on all fours, and he pointed out to me an object in the stream, fifty yards off, under the overhanging branch of a tree, which jutted out from the steep bank opposite.   In that light I should not myself have recognized it as a hippo head; but it was one, looking toward us, with the ears up and the nostrils, eyes, and forehead above water.   I aimed for the centre; the sound told that the bullet had struck somewhere on the head, and the animal disappeared without a splash.   Judd was sure I had killed, but I was by no means so confident myself, and there was no way of telling until next morning, for the hippo always sinks when shot and does not rise to the surface for several hours.   Accordingly, back we walked to the house.

At sunrise next morning Cuninghame, Judd, and I, with a crowd of porters, were down at the spot.   There was a very leaky boat in which Cuninghame, Judd, and I embarked, intending to drift and paddle downstream while the porters walked along the bank.   We did not have far to go, for as we rounded the first point we heard the porters break into guttural exclamations of delight, and there ahead of us, by a little island of papyrus, was the dead hippo.   With the help of the boat it was towed to a convenient landing-place, and then the porters dragged it ashore.   It was a cow, of good size for one dwelling in a small river, where they never approach the dimensions of those making their homes in a great

lake like the Victoria Nyanza. This one weighed nearly two
thousand eight hundred pounds, and I could well believe that
a big lake bull would weigh between three and four tons.

In wild regions hippos rest on sandy bars, and even come
ashore to feed, by day; but wherever there are inhabitants
they land to feed only at night. Those in the Rewero continually entered McMillan's garden. Where they are numerous they sometimes attack small boats and kill the people in
them; and where they are so plentiful they do great damage
to the plantations of the natives, so much so that they then
have to be taken off the list of preserved game and their
destruction encouraged. Their enormous jaws sweep in quantities of plants or lush grass or corn or vegetables, at a mouth-
ful, while their appetites are as gigantic as their bodies. In
spite of their short legs, they go at a good gait on shore,
but the water is their real home, and they always seek it when
alarmed. They dive and float wonderfully, rising to the
surface or sinking to the bottom at will, and they gallop at
speed along the bottoms of lakes or rivers, with their bodies
wholly submerged; but as is natural enough, in view of their
big bodies and short legs, they are not fast swimmers for any
length of time. They make curious and unmistakable trails
along the banks of any stream in which they dwell; their short
legs are wide apart, and so when they tread out a path they
leave a ridge of high soil down the centre. Where they have
lived a long time, the rutted paths are worn deep into the soil,
but always carry this distinguishing middle ridge.

The full-jacketed Winchester bullet had gone straight into
the brain; the jacket had lodged in the cranium, but the lead
went on, entering the neck and breaking the atlas vertebra.

At Juja Farm many animals were kept in cages. They
included a fairly friendly leopard, and five lions, two of which
were anything but friendly. There were three cheetahs, nearly
full grown; these were continually taken out on leashes, Mrs.
McMillan strolling about with them and leading them to the
summer-house. They were good-tempered, but they did not

lead well.   Cheetahs are interesting beasts; they are aberrant cats, standing very high on their legs, and with non-retractile claws like a dog.   They are nearly the size of a leopard, but are not ordinarily anything like as ferocious, and prey on the smaller antelope, occasionally taking something as big as a half-grown kongoni.   For a short run, up to say a quarter of a mile or even perhaps half a mile, they are the swiftest animals on earth, and with a good start easily overtake the fastest antelope; but their bolt is soon shot, and on the open plain they can readily be galloped down with a horse.   When they sit on their haunches their attitude is that neither of a dog nor of a cat so much as of a big monkey.   On the whole, they are much more easily domesticated than most other cats, but, as with all highly developed wild creatures, they show great individual variability of character and disposition.   They have a very curious note, a bird-like chirp, in uttering which they twist the upper lip as if whistling.   When I first heard it I was sure that it was uttered by some bird, and looked about quite a time before finding that it was the call of a cheetah.

Then there was a tame wart-hog, very friendly, indeed, which usually wandered loose, and was as comical as pigs generally are, with its sudden starts and grunts.   Finally, there was a young tommy buck and a Grant's gazelle doe, both of which were on good terms with every one and needed astonishingly little looking after to prevent their straying.   When I was returning to the house on the morning I killed the rhinoceros, I met the string of porters and the ox-wagon just after they had left the gate on their way to the carcass.   The Grant doe had been attracted by the departure, and was following immediately behind the last porter; a wild-looking Masai warrior, to whom, as I learned, the special care of the gazelle had been intrusted for that day, was running as hard as he could after her from the gate; when he overtook her he ran in between her and the rearmost porter, and headed her for the farm gate, uttering what sounded like wild war-cries and brandishing his spear. They formed a really absurd couple, the little doe slowly and decorously walking back to the farm, quite unmoved by the clamor and threats, while her guardian, the very image of what a savage warrior should look when on the war-path, walked close behind, waving his spear and uttering deep-toned shouts, with what seemed a ludicrous disproportion of effort to the result needed.

Antelopes speedily become very tame and recognize clearly their friends. Leslie Tarlton's brother was keeping a couple of young kongoni and a partly grown Grant on his farm just outside Nairobi. (The game comes right to the outskirts of Nairobi; one morning Kermit walked out from the McMillans' town house, where we were staying in company with Percival, the game-ranger, and got photographs of zebras, kongoni, and Kavirondo cranes; and a leopard sometimes came up through the garden on to the veranda of the house itself.) Tarlton's young antelopes went freely into the country round about, but never fled with the wild herds; and they were not only great friends with Tarlton's dogs, but recognized them as protectors. Hyenas and other beasts frequently came round the farm after nightfall, and at their approach the antelopes fled at speed to where the dogs were, and then could not be persuaded to leave them.

We spent a delightful week at Juja Farm, and then moved to Kamiti Ranch, the neighboring farm, owned by Mr. Hugh H. Heatley, who had asked me to visit him for a buffalo-hunt. While in the highlands of British East Africa it is utterly impossible for a stranger to realize that he is under the equator; the climate is delightful and healthy. It is a white man's country, a country which should be filled with white settlers; and no place could be more attractive for visitors. There is no more danger to health incident to an ordinary trip to East Africa than there is to an ordinary trip to the Riviera. Of course, if one goes on a hunting trip there is always a certain amount of risk, including the risk of fever,

just as there would be if a man camped out in some of the
Italian marshes. But the ordinary visitor need have no more
fear of his health than if he were travelling in Italy, and it
is hard to imagine a trip better worth making than the trip
from Mombasa to Nairobi and on to the Victoria Nyanza.

VI

A BUFFALO-HUNT BY THE KAMITI

HEATLEY'S RANCH comprises twenty thousand acres lying between the Rewero and Kamiti Rivers. It is seventeen miles long, and four across at the widest place. It includes some as beautiful bits of natural scenery as can well be imagined, and though Heatley—a thorough farmer, and the son and grandson of farmers—was making it a success-ful farm, with large herds of cattle, much improved stock, hundreds of acres under cultivation, a fine dairy, and the like, yet it was also a game reserve such as could not be matched either in Europe or America. From Juja Farm we marched a dozen miles and pitched our tent close beside the Kamiti.

The Kamiti is a queer little stream, running for most of its course through a broad swamp of tall papyrus. Such a swamp is almost impenetrable. The papyrus grows to a height of over twenty feet, and the stems are so close together that in most places it is impossible to see anything at a distance of six feet. Ten yards from the edge, when within the swamp, I was wholly unable to tell in which direction the open ground lay, and could get out only by either following my back track or listening for voices. Underfoot, the mud and water are hip-deep. This swamp was the home of a herd of buffalo numbering perhaps a hundred individuals. They are semi-aquatic beasts, and their enormous strength enables them to plough through the mud and water and burst their way among the papyrus stems without the slightest difficulty, whereas a man is nearly helpless when once he has entered the reed beds. They had made paths hither and thither across the swamp, these paths being three feet deep in ooze and black water. There were little islands in the swamp on which they could rest. Toward its lower end, where it ran into the Nairobi, the Kamiti emerged from the papyrus swamp and became a rapid brown stream of water with only here and there a papyrus cluster along its bank.

The Nairobi, which cut across the lower end of the farm, and the Rewero, which bounded it on the other side from the Kamiti, were as different as possible from the latter. Both were rapid streams broken by riffle and waterfall, and running at the bottom of tree-clad valleys. The Nairobi Falls, which were on Heatley's Ranch, were singularly beautiful. Heatley and I visited them one evening after sunset, coming home from a day's hunt. It was a ride I shall long remember. We left our men, and let the horses gallop. As the sun set behind us, the long lights changed the look of the country and gave it a beauty that had in it an element of the mysterious and the unreal. The mountains loomed both larger and more vague than they had been in the bright sunlight, and the plains lost their look of parched desolation as the afterglow came and went. We were galloping through a world of dim shade and dying color; and, in this world, our horses suddenly halted on the brink of a deep ravine from out of which came the thunder of a cataract. We reined up on a jutting point. The snowy masses of the fall foamed over a ledge on our right, and below at our feet was a great pool of swirling water. Thick-foliaged trees, of strange shape and festooned with creepers, climbed the sheer sides of the ravine. A black-and-white eagle perched in a blasted tree-top in front; and the bleached skull of a long-dead rhinoceros glimmered white near the brink to one side.

On another occasion we took our lunch at the foot of Rewero Falls. These are not as high as the falls of the Nairobi, but they are almost as beautiful. We clambered down into the ravine a little distance below and made our way toward them, beside the brawling, rock-choked torrent. Great trees towered overhead, and among their tops the monkeys chattered and screeched. The fall itself was broken in two parts like a miniature Niagara, and the spray curtain shifted to and fro as the wind blew.

The lower part of the farm, between the Kamiti and Rewero and on both sides of the Nairobi, consisted of immense rolling plains, and on these the game swarmed in almost incredible numbers. There were Grant's and Thomson's gazelles, of which we shot one or two for the table. There was a small herd of blue wildebeest, and among them one unusually large bull with an unusually fine head; Kermit finally killed him. There were plenty of wart-hogs, which were to be found feeding right out in the open, both in the morning and the evening. One day Kermit got a really noteworthy sow with tusks much longer than those of the average boar. He ran into her on horseback after a sharp chase of a mile or two, and shot her from the saddle as he galloped nearly alongside, holding his rifle as the old buffalo-runners used to hold theirs, that is, not bringing it to his shoulder. I killed two or three half-grown pigs for the table, but I am sorry to say that I missed several chances at good boars. Finally one day I got up to just two hundred and fifty yards from a good boar as he stood broadside to me; firing with the little Springfield I put the bullet through both shoulders, and he was dead when we came up.

But of course the swarms of game consisted of zebra and hartbeest. At no time, when riding in any direction across these plains, were we ever out of sight of them. Sometimes they would act warily and take the alarm when we were a long distance off. At other times herds would stand and gaze at us while we passed within a couple of hundred yards. One afternoon we needed meat for the safari, and Cuninghame and I rode out to get it. Within half a mile we came upon big herds both of hartbeest and zebra. They stood to give me long-range shots at about three hundred yards. I wounded a zebra, after which Cuninghame rode. While he was off, I killed first a zebra and then a hartbeest, and shortly afterward a cloud of dust announced that Cuninghame was bringing a herd of game toward me. I knelt motionless, and the long files of red-coated hartbeest and brilliantly striped zebra came galloping past. They were quite a distance off, but I had time for several shots at each animal I selected, and I dropped one more zebra and one more hartbeest, in addition, I regret to add, to wounding another hartbeest. The four hartbeest and zebra lay within a space of a quarter of a mile; and half a mile farther I bagged a tommy at two hundred yards—his meat was for our own table, the kongoni and the zebra being for the safari.

On another day, when Heatley and I were out together, he stationed me among some thin thorn-bushes on a little knoll, and drove the game by me, hoping to get me a shot at some wildebeest. The scattered thorn-bushes were only four or five feet high, and so thin that there was no difficulty in looking through them and marking every movement of the game as it approached. The wildebeest took the wrong direction and never came near me—though they certainly fared as badly as if they had done so, for they passed by Kermit, and it was on this occasion that he killed the big bull. A fine cock ostrich passed me and I much wished to shoot him, but did not like to do so, because ostrich-farming is one of the staple industries of the region, and it is not well to have even the wild birds shot. The kongoni and the zebra streamed by me, herd after herd, hundreds and hundreds of them, many passing within fifty yards of my shelter, now on one side, now on the other; they went at an easy lope, and I was interested to see that many of the kongoni ran with their mouths open. This is an attitude which we usually associate with exhaustion, but such cannot have been the case with the kongoni—they had merely cantered for a mile or so. The zebra were, as usual, noisy, a number of them uttering their barking neigh as they passed. I do not know how it is ordinarily, but these particular zebra, all stallions by the way, kept their mouths open throughout the time they were neighing, and their ears pricked forward; they did not keep their mouths open while merely galloping, as did the kongoni. We had plenty of meat, and the naturalists had enough specimens; and I was glad that there was no need to harm the beautiful creatures. They passed so close that I could mark every slight movement, and the ripple of the muscles under the skin. The very young fawns of the kongoni seemed to have little fear of a horseman, if he approached while they were lying motionless on the ground; but they would run from a man on foot.

There were interesting birds, too. Close by the woods at the river's edge, we saw a big black ground-hornbill walking about, on the lookout for its usual dinner of small snakes and lizards. Large flocks of the beautiful Kavirondo cranes stalked over the plains and cultivated fields, or flew by with mournful, musical clangor. But the most interesting birds we saw were the black whydah-finches. The female is a dull-colored, ordinary-looking bird, somewhat like a female bobolink. The male in his courtship dress is clad in a uniform dark glossy suit, and his tail-feathers are almost like some of those of a barnyard rooster, being over twice as long as the rest of the bird, with a downward curve at the tips. The females were generally found in flocks, in which there would often be a goodly number of males also, and when the flocks put on speed the males tended to drop behind. The flocks were feeding in Heatley's grain-fields, and he was threatening vengeance upon them. I was sorry, for the male birds certainly have habits of peculiar interest. They were not shy, although if we approached too near them in their favorite haunts, the grass-land adjoining the papyrus beds, they would fly off and perch on the tops of the papyrus stems. The long tail hampers the bird in its flight, and it is often held at rather an angle downward, giving the bird a peculiar and almost insect-like appearance. But the marked and extraordinary peculiarity was the custom the cocks had of dancing in artificially made dancing-rings. For a mile and a half beyond our camp, down the course of the Kamiti, the grass-land at the edge of the papyrus was thickly strewn with these dancing-rings. Each was about two feet in diameter, sometimes more, sometimes less. A tuft of growing grass perhaps a foot high was left in the centre. Over the rest of the ring the grass was cut off close by the roots, and the blades strewn evenly over the surface of the ring. The cock bird would alight in the ring and hop to a height of a couple of feet, wings spread and motionless, tail drooping, and the head usually thrown back. As he came down he might or might not give an extra couple of little hops. After a few seconds he would repeat the motion, sometimes remaining almost in the same place, at other times going forward during and between the hops so as finally to go completely round the ring. As there were many scores of these dancing-places within a comparatively limited territory, the effect was rather striking when a large number of birds were dancing at the same time. As one walked along, the impression conveyed by the birds continually popping above the grass and then immediately sinking back, was somewhat as if a man was making peas jump in a tin tray by tapping on it. The favorite dancing times were in the early morning, and, to a less extent, in the evening. We saw dancing-places of every age, some with the cut grass which strewed the floor green and fresh, others with the grass dried into hay and the bare earth showing through.

But the game we were after was the buffalo-herd that haunted the papyrus swamp. As I have said before, the buffalo is by many hunters esteemed the most dangerous of African game. It is an enormously powerful beast with, in this country, a coat of black hair which becomes thin in the old bulls, and massive horns which rise into great bosses at the base, these bosses sometimes meeting in old age so as to cover the forehead with a frontlet of horn. Their habits vary much in different places. Where they are much persecuted, they lie in the densest cover, and only venture out into the open to feed at night. But Heatley, though he himself had killed a couple of bulls, and the Boer farmer who was working for him another, had preserved the herd from outside molestation, and their habits were doubtless much what they would have been in regions where man is a rare visitor.

The first day we were on Heatley's farm, we saw the buffalo, to the number of seventy or eighty, grazing in the open, some hundreds of yards from the papyrus swamp, and this shortly after noon. For a mile from the papyrus swamp the country was an absolutely flat plain, gradually rising into a gentle slope, and it was an impossibility to approach the buffalo across this plain save in one way to be mentioned hereafter. Probably when the moon was full the buffalo came out to graze by night. But while we were on our hunt the moon was young, and the buffalo evidently spent most of the night in the papyrus, and came out to graze by day. Sometimes they came out in the early morning, sometimes in the late evening, but quite as often in the bright daylight. We saw herds come out to graze at ten o'clock in the morning, and again at three in the afternoon. They usually remained out several hours, first grazing and then lying down. Flocks of the small white cow-heron usually accompanied them, the birds stalking about among them or perching on their backs; and occasionally the whereabouts of the herd in the papyrus swamp could be determined by seeing the flock of herons perched on the papyrus tops. We did not see any of the red-billed tick-birds on the buffalo; indeed, the only ones that we saw in this neighborhood happened to be on domestic cattle—in other places we found them very common on rhinoceros. At night the buffalo sometimes came right into the cultivated fields, and even into the garden close by the Boer farmer's house; and once at night he had shot a bull. The bullet went through the heart but the animal ran to the papyrus swamp, and was found next day dead just within the edge. Usually the main herd, of bulls, cows, and calves, kept together; but there were outlying bulls found singly or in small parties. Not only the natives but the whites were inclined to avoid the immediate neighborhood of the papyrus swamp, for there had been one or two narrow escapes from unprovoked attacks by the buffalo. The farmer told us that a man who was coming to see him had been regularly followed by three bulls, who pursued him for quite a distance. There is no doubt that under certain circumstances buffalo, in addition to showing themselves exceedingly dangerous opponents when wounded by hunters, become truculent and inclined to take the offensive themselves. There are places in East Africa where as regards at least certain herds this seems to be the case; and in Uganda the buffalo have caused such loss of life, and such damage to the native plantations, that they are now ranked as vermin and not as game, and their killing is encouraged in every possible way. The list of white hunters that have been killed by buffalo is very long, and includes a number of men of note, while accidents to natives are of constant occurrence.

The morning after making our camp, we started at dawn for the buffalo-ground, Kermit and I, Cuninghame and Heatley, and the Boer farmer with three big, powerful dogs. We walked near the edge of the swamp. The whydah-birds were continually bobbing up and down in front of us as they rose and fell on their dancing-places, while the Kavirondo cranes called mournfully all around. Before we had gone two miles, buffalo were spied, well ahead, feeding close to the papyrus. The line of the papyrus which marked the edge of the swamp was not straight, but broken by projections and indentations; and by following it closely and cutting cautiously across the points, the opportunity for stalking was good. As there was not a tree of any kind anywhere near, we had to rely purely on our shooting to prevent damage from the buffalo. Kermit and I had our double-barrels, with the Winchesters as spare guns, while Cuninghame carried a 577, and Heatley a magazine rifle.

Cautiously threading our way along the edge of the swamp, we got within a hundred and fifty yards of the buffalo before we were perceived. There were four bulls, grazing close by the edge of the swamp, their black bodies glistening in the early sun-rays, their massive horns showing white, and the cow-herons perched on their backs. They stared sullenly at us with outstretched heads from under their great frontlets of horn. The biggest of the four stood a little out from the other three, and at him I fired, the bullet telling with a smack on the tough hide and going through the lungs. We had been afraid they would at once turn into the papyrus, but instead of this they started straight across our front directly for the open country. This was a piece of huge good luck. Kermit put his first barrel into the second bull, and I my second barrel into one of the others, after which it became impossible to say which bullet struck which animal, as the firing became general. They ran a quarter of a mile into the open, and then the big bull I had first shot, and which had no other bullet in him, dropped dead, while the other three, all of which were wounded, halted beside him. We walked toward them, rather expecting a charge; but when we were still over two hundred yards away they started back for the swamp, and we began firing. The distance being long, I used my Winchester. Aiming well before one bull, he dropped to the shot as if poleaxed, falling straight on his back with his legs kicking; but in a moment he was up again and after the others. Later I found that the bullet, a full-metal patch, had struck him in the head but did not penetrate to the brain, and merely stunned him for the moment. All the time we kept running diagonally to their line of flight. They were all three badly wounded, and when they reached the tall rank grass, high as a man's head, which fringed the papyrus swamp, the two foremost lay down, while the last one, the one I had floored with the Winchester, turned, and with nose outstretched began to come toward us. He was badly crippled, however, and with a soft-nosed bullet from my heavy Holland I knocked him down, this time for good. The other two then rose, and though each was again hit they reached the swamp, one of them to our right, the other to the left where the papyrus came out in a point.

We decided to go after the latter, and advancing very cautiously toward the edge of the swamp, put in the three big dogs. A moment after, they gave tongue within the papyrus; then we heard the savage grunt of the buffalo and saw its form just within the reeds; and as the rifles cracked, down it went. But it was not dead, for we heard it grunt savagely, and the dogs bayed as loudly as ever. Heatley now mounted his trained shooting-pony and rode toward the place, while we covered him with our rifles, his plan being to run right across our front if the bull charged. The bull was past charging, lying just within the reeds, but he was still able to do damage, for in another minute one of the dogs came out by us and ran straight back to the farmhouse, where we found him dead on our return. He had been caught by the buffalo's horns when he went in too close. Heatley, a daring fellow, with great confidence in both his horse and his rifle, pushed forward as we came up, and saw the bull lying on the ground while the two other dogs bit and worried it; and he put a bullet through its head.

The remaining bull got off into the swamp, where a week later Heatley found his dead body. Fortunately the head proved to be in less good condition than any of the others, as one horn was broken off about halfway up; so that if any of the four had to escape, it was well that this should have been the one.

Our three bulls were fine trophies. The largest, with the largest horns, was the first killed, being the one that fell to my first bullet; yet it was the youngest of the three. The other two were old bulls. The second one killed had smaller horns than the other, but the bosses met in the middle of the forehead for a space of several inches, making a solid shield. I had just been reading a pamphlet by a German specialist who had divided the African buffalo into fifteen or twenty different species, based upon differences in various pairs of horns. The worth of such fine distinctions, when made on insufficient data, can be gathered from the fact that on the principles of specific division adopted in the pamphlet in question, the three bulls we had shot would have represented certainly two and possibly three different species.

Heller was soon on the ground with his skinning tent and skinners, and the Boer farmer went back to fetch the ox-wagon on which the skins and meat were brought in to camp. Laymen can hardly realize, and I certainly did not realize, what an immense amount of work is involved in preparing the skins of large animals such as buffalo, rhino, hippo, and above all, elephant, in hot climates. On this first five weeks' trip we got over seventy skins, including twenty-two species ranging in size from a dikdik to a rhino, and all of these Heller prepared and sent to the Smithsonian. Mearns and Loring were just as busy shooting birds and trapping small mammals. Often while Heller would be off for a few days with Kermit and myself, Mearns and Loring would be camped elsewhere, in a region better suited for the things they were after. While at Juja Farm they went down the Nairobi in a boat to shoot water-birds, and saw many more crocodiles and hippo than I did. Loring is a remarkably successful trapper of small mammals. I do not believe there is a better collector anywhere. Doctor Mearns, in addition to birds and plants, never let pass the opportunity to collect anything else from reptiles and fishes to land-shells. Moreover, he was the best shot in our party. He killed two great bustards with the rifle, and occasionally shot birds like vultures on the wing with a rifle. I do not believe that three better men than Mearns, Heller, and Loring, for such an expedition as ours, could be found anywhere.

It was three days later before we were again successful with buffalo. On this occasion we started about eight in the morning, having come to the conclusion that the herd was more apt to leave the papyrus late than early. Our special object was to get a cow. We intended to take advantage of a small half-dried water-course, an affluent of the Kamiti, which began a mile beyond where we had killed our bulls, and for three or four miles ran in a course generally parallel to the swamp, and at a distance which varied, but averaged perhaps a quarter of a mile. When we reached the beginning of this watercourse, we left our horses and walked along it. Like all such watercourses, it wound in curves. The banks were four or five feet high, the bottom was sometimes dry and sometimes contained reedy pools, while at intervals there were clumps of papyrus. Heatley went ahead, and just as we had about concluded that the buffalo would not come out, he came back to tell us that he had caught a glimpse of several, and believed that the main herd was with them. Cuninghame, a veteran hunter and first-class shot, than whom there could be no better man to have with one when after dangerous game, took charge of our further movements. We crept up the watercourse until about opposite the buffalo, which were now lying down. Cuninghame peered cautiously at them, saw there were two or three, and then led us on all fours toward them. There were patches where the grass was short, and other places where it was three feet high, and after a good deal of cautious crawling we had covered half the distance toward them, when one of them made us out, and several rose from their beds. They were still at least two hundred yards off—a long range for heavy rifles; but any closer approach was impossible, and we fired. Both the leading bulls were hit, and at the shots there rose from the grass not half a dozen buffalo, but seventy or eighty, and started at a gallop parallel to the swamp and across our front. In the rear were a number of cows and calves, and I at once singled out a cow and fired. She plunged forward at the shot and turned toward the swamp, going slowly and dead lame, for my bullet had struck the shoulder and had gone into the cavity of the chest. But at this moment our attention was distracted from the wounded cow by the conduct of the herd, which, headed by the wounded bulls, turned in a quarter-circle toward us, and drew up in a phalanx facing us with out-stretched heads. It was not a nice country in which to be charged by the herd, and for a moment things trembled in the balance. There was a perceptible motion of uneasiness among some of our followers. "Stand steady! Don't run!" I called out. "And don't shoot!" called out Cuninghame; for to do either would invite a charge. A few seconds passed, and then the unwounded mass of the herd resumed their flight, and after a little hesitation the wounded bulls followed. We now turned our attention to the wounded cow, which was close to the papyrus. She went down to our shots, but the reeds and marsh-grass were above our heads when we drew close to the swamp. Once again Heatley went in with his white horse, as close as it was even reasonably safe, with the hope either of seeing the cow, or of getting her to charge him and so give us a fair chance at her. But nothing happened and we loosed the two dogs. They took up the trail and went some little distance into the papyrus, where we heard them give tongue, and immediately afterward there came the angry grunt of the wounded buffalo. It had risen and gone off thirty yards into the papyrus, although mortally wounded—the frothy blood from the lungs was actually coming out of my first bullet-hole. Its anger now made it foolish, and it followed the dogs to the edge of the papyrus. Here we caught a glimpse of it. Down it went to our shots, and in a minute we heard the moaning bellow which a wounded buffalo often gives before dying. Immediately afterward we could hear the dogs worry-ing it, while it bellowed again. It was still living as I came up, and though it evidently could not rise, there was a chance of its damaging one of the dogs, so I finished it off with a shot from the Winchester. Heller reached it that afternoon, and the skin and meat were brought in by the porters before nightfall.

Cuninghame remained with the body while the rest of us

rode off and killed several different animals we wanted. In the afternoon I returned, having a vaguely uncomfortable feeling that as it grew dusk the buffalo might possibly make their appearance again. Sure enough, there they were. A number of them were in the open plain, although close to the swamp, a mile and a half beyond the point where the work of cutting up the cow was just being finished, and the porters were preparing to start with their loads. It seemed very strange that after their experience in the morning any of the herd should be willing to come into the open so soon. But there they were. They were grazing to the number of about a dozen. Looking at them through the glasses I could see that their attention was attracted to us. They gazed at us for quite a time, and then walked slowly in our direction for at least a couple of hundred yards. For a moment I was even doubtful whether they did not intend to come toward us and charge. But it was only curiosity on their part, and after having gazed their fill, they sauntered back to the swamp and disappeared. There was no chance to get at them, and moreover darkness was rapidly falling.

Next morning we broke camp. The porters, strapping grown-up children that they were, felt as much pleasure and excitement over breaking camp after a few days' rest as over reaching camp after a fifteen-mile march. On this occasion, after they had made up their loads, they danced in a ring for half an hour, two tin cans being beaten as tom-toms. Then off they strode in a long line with their burdens, following one another in Indian file, each greeting me with a smile and a deep "Yambo, Bwana!" as he passed. I had grown attached to them, and of course especially to my tent-boys, gun-bearers, and saises, who quite touched me by their evident pleasure in coming to see me and greet me if I happened to be away from them for two or three days.

Kermit and I rode off with Heatley to pass the night at his house. This was at the other end of his farm, in a totally different kind of country, a country of wooded hills, with glades and dells and long green grass in the valleys. It did not in the least resemble what one would naturally expect in equatorial Africa. On the contrary it reminded me of the beautiful rolling wooded country of middle Wisconsin. But of course everything was really different. There were monkeys and leopards in the forests, and we saw whydah-birds of a new kind, with red on the head and throat, and brilliantly colored woodpeckers, and black-and-gold weaver-birds. Indeed, the wealth of bird life was such that it cannot be described. Here, too, there were many birds with musical voices, to which we listened in the early morning. The best timber was yielded by the tall mahogo-tree, a kind of sandalwood. This was the tree selected by the wild fig for its deadly embrace. The wild fig begins as a huge parasitic vine, and ends as one of the largest and most stately, and also one of the greenest and most shady, trees in this part of Africa. It grows up the mahogo as a vine and gradually, by branching, and by the spreading of the branches, completely envelops the trunk and also grows along each limb, and sends out great limbs of its own. Every stage can be seen, from that in which the big vine has begun to grow up along the still flourishing mahogo, through that in which the tree looks like a curious composite, the limbs and thick foliage of the fig branching out among the limbs and scanty foliage of the still living mahogo, to the stage in which the mahogo is simply a dead skeleton seen here and there through the trunk or the foliage of the fig. Finally nothing remains but the fig, which grows to be a huge tree.

Heatley's house was charming, with its vine-shaded veranda, its summer-house and outbuildings, and the great trees clustered round about. He was fond of sport in the right way, that is, he treated it as a sport and not business, and did not allow it to interfere with his prime work of being a successful farmer. He had big stockyards for his cattle and swine, and he was growing all kinds of things of both the temperate and the tropic zones: wheat and apples, coffee and sugar-cane. The bread we ate and the coffee we drank were made from what he had grown on his own farm. There were roses in the garden and great bushes of heliotrope by the veranda, and the drive to his place was bordered by trees from Australia and beds of native flowers.

Next day we went into Nairobi, where we spent a most busy week, especially the three naturalists; for the task of getting into shape for shipment and then shipping the many hundreds of specimens—indeed, all told there were thousands of specimens—was of herculean proportions. Governor Jackson—a devoted ornithologist and probably the best living authority on East African birds, taking into account the standpoints of both the closet naturalist and the field naturalist—spent hours with Mearns, helping him to identify and arrange the species.

Nairobi is a very attractive town, and most interesting, with its large native quarter and its Indian colony. One of the streets consists of little except Indian shops and bazaars. Outside the business portion, the town is spread over much territory, the houses standing isolated, each by itself, and each usually bowered in trees, with vines shading the verandas, and pretty flower-gardens round about. Not only do I firmly believe in the future of East Africa for settlement as a white man's country, but I feel that it is an ideal playground alike for sportsmen, and for travellers who wish to live in health and comfort, and yet to see what is beautiful and unusual.

VII

TREKKING THROUGH THE THIRST TO THE SOTIK

ON June 5 we started south from Kijabe to trek through the thirst, through the waterless country which lies across the way to the Sotik.

The preceding Sunday, at Nairobi, I had visited the excellent French Catholic Mission, had been most courteously received by the fathers, had gone over their plantations and the school in which they taught the children of the settlers (much to my surprise, among them were three Parsee children, who were evidently put on a totally different plane from the other Indians, even the Goanese), and had been keenly interested in their account of their work and of the obstacles with which they met.

At Kijabe I spent several exceedingly interesting hours at the American Industrial Mission. Its head, Mr. Hurlburt, had called on me in Washington at the White House, in the preceding October, and I had then made up my mind that if the chance occurred I must certainly visit his mission. It is an interdenominational mission, and is carried on in a spirit which combines to a marked degree broad sanity and common sense with disinterested fervor. Of course such work, under the conditions which necessarily obtain in East Africa, can only show gradual progress; but I am sure that missionary work of the Kijabe kind will be an indispensable factor in the slow uplifting of the natives. There is full recognition of the fact that industrial training is a foundation-stone in the effort to raise ethical and moral standards. Industrial teaching must go hand in hand with moral teaching—and in both the mere force of example and the influence of firm, kindly sympathy and understanding count immeasurably. There is further recognition of the fact that in such a country the missionary should either already know how to, or else at once learn how to, take the lead himself in all kinds of industrial and mechanical work. Finally the effort is made consistently to teach the native how to live a more comfortable, useful, and physically and morally cleanly life, not under white conditions, but under the conditions which he will actually have to face when he goes back to his people, to live among them, and, if things go well, to be in his turn a conscious or unconscious missionary for good.

At lunch, in addition to the missionaries and their wives and children, there were half a dozen of the neighboring settlers, with their families. It is always a good thing to see the missionary and the settler working shoulder to shoulder. Many parts of East Africa can, and I believe will, be made into a white man's country; and the process will be helped, not hindered, by treating the black man well. At Kijabe, nearly under the equator, the beautiful scenery was almost northern in type; at night we needed blazing camp-fires and the days were as cool as September on Long Island or by the southern shores of the Great Lakes. It is a very healthy region; the children of the missionaries and settlers, of all ages, were bright and strong; those of Mr. and Mrs. Hurlburt had not been out of the country for eight years, and showed no ill effects whatever; on the contrary, I quite believed Mrs. Hurlburt when she said that she regarded the fertile wooded hills of Kijabe, with their forest and clear brooks, as forming a true health resort.

The northern look of the place was enhanced by the fact that the forests contained junipers; but they also contained monkeys, a small green monkey, and the big guerza, with its long silky hair and bold black-and-white coloring. Kermit, Heller, and Loring shot several. There were rhinoceros and buffalo in the neighborhood. A few days previously some buffalo had charged, unprovoked, a couple of the native boys of the mission, who had escaped only by their agility in tree-climbing. On one of his trips to an outlying mission station, Mr. Hurlburt had himself narrowly escaped a serious accident. Quite wantonly, a cow rhino, with a calf, charged the safari almost before they knew of its presence. It attacked Hurlburt's mule, which fortunately he was not riding, and tossed and killed it; it passed through the line, and then turned and again charged it, this time attacking one of the porters. The porter dodged behind a tree, and the rhino hit the tree, knocked off a huge flake of bark and wood, and galloped away.

The trek across "the thirst," as any waterless country is apt to be called by an Africander, is about sixty miles, by the road. On our horses we could have ridden it in a night; but on a serious trip of any kind loads must be carried, and laden porters cannot go fast, and must rest at intervals. We had rather more than our porters could carry, and needed additional transportation for the water for the safari; and we had hired four ox-wagons. They were under the lead of a fine young colonial Englishman named Ulyate, whose great-grandfather had come to South Africa in 1820, as part of the most important English emigration that ever went thither. His father and sisters had lunched with us at the missionary's the day before; his wife's baby was too young for her to come. It was the best kind of pioneer family; all the members, with some of their fellow colonials, had spent much of the preceding three years in adventurous exploration of the country in their ox-wagons, the wives and daughters as valiant as the men; one of the two daughters I met had driven one of the ox-wagons on the hardest and most dangerous trip they made, while her younger sister led the oxen. It was on this trip that they had pioneered the way across the waterless route I was to take. For those who, like ourselves, followed the path they had thus blazed, there was no danger to the men, and merely discomfort to the oxen; but the first trip was a real feat, for no one could tell what lay ahead, or what exact route would be practicable. The family had now settled on a big farm, but also carried on the business of "transport-riding," as freighting with wagons is called in Africa; and they did it admirably.

With Ulyate were three other white wagon-drivers, all colonials; two of them English, the third Dutch, or Boer. There was also a Cape boy, a Kaffir wagon-driver; utterly different from any of the East African natives, and dressed in ordinary clothes. In addition there were various natives—primitive savages in dress and habit, but coming from the cattle-owning tribes. Each ox-team was guided by one of these savages, who led the first yoke by a leathern thong, while the wagon-driver, with his long whip, stalked to and fro beside the line of oxen, or rode in the wagon. The huge wagons, with their white tops or "sails," were larger than those our own settlers and freighters used. Except one small one, to which there were but eight oxen, each was drawn by a span of seven or eight yoke; they were all native humped cattle.

We had one hundred and ninety-six porters, in addition to the aswaris, tent-boys, gun-bearers, and saises. The management of such a safari is a work of difficulty; but no better man for the purpose than Cuninghame could be found anywhere, and he had chosen his head men well. In the thirst, the march goes on by day and night. The longest halt is made in the day, for men and animals both travel better at night than under the blazing noon. We were fortunate in that it was just after the full of the moon, so that our night treks were made in good light. Of course on such a march the porters must be spared as much as possible; camp is not pitched, and each white man uses for the trip only what he wears, or carries on his horse—and the horse also must be loaded as lightly as possible. I took nothing but my army overcoat, rifle and cartridges, and three canteens of water. Kermit did the same.

The wagons broke camp about ten, to trek to the water, a mile and a half off, where the oxen would be outspanned to take the last drink for three days; stock will not drink early in the morning nearly as freely as if the march is begun later. We, riding our horses, followed by the long line of burdened porters, left at half past twelve, and in a couple of hours overtook the wagons. The porters were in high spirits. In the morning, before the start, they twice held regular dances, the chief musician being one of their own number who carried an extraordinary kind of native harp; and after their loads were allotted they marched out of camp singing and blowing their horns and whistles. Three askaris brought up the rear to look after laggards, and see that no weak or sick man fell out without our knowing or being able to give him help.

The trail led first through open brush, or low, dry forest, and then out on the vast plains, where the withered grass was dotted here and there with low, scantily leaved thorn-trees, from three to eight feet high. Hour after hour we drew slowly ahead under the shimmering sunlight. The horsemen walked first, with the gun-bearers, saises, and usually a few very energetic and powerful porters; then came the safari in single file; and then the lumbering white-topped wagons, the patient oxen walking easily, each team led by a half-naked savage with frizzed hair and a spear or throwing-stick in his hand, while at intervals the long whips of the drivers cracked like rifles. The dust rose in clouds from the dry earth, and soon covered all of us; in the distance herds of zebra and hartbeest gazed at us as we passed, and we saw the old spoor of rhino, beasts we hoped to avoid, as they often charge such a caravan.

Slowly the shadows lengthened; the light waned, the glare of the white, dusty plain was softened, and the bold outlines of the distant mountains grew dim. Just before nightfall we halted on the farther side of a dry watercourse. The safari came up singing and whistling, and the men put down their loads, lit fires, and with chatter and laughter prepared their food. The crossing was not good, the sides of the watercourse being steep; and each wagon was brought through by a double span, the whips cracking lustily as an accompaniment to the shouts of the drivers, as the thirty oxen threw their weight into the yokes by which they were attached to the long trek tow. The horses were fed. We had tea, with bread and cold meat—and a most delicious meal it was—and then lay dozing or talking beside the bush-fires. At half past eight, the moon having risen, we were off again. The safari was still in high spirits, and started with the usual chanting and drumming.

We pushed steadily onward across the plain, the dust rising in clouds under the spectral moonlight. Sometimes we rode, sometimes we walked to ease our horses. The Southern Cross was directly ahead, not far above the horizon. Higher and higher rose the moon, and brighter grew the flood of her light. At intervals the barking call of zebras was heard on either hand. It was after midnight when we again halted. The porters were tired, and did not sing as they came up; the air was cool, almost nipping, and they at once huddled down in their blankets, some of them building fires. We, the white men, after seeing our horses staked out, each lay down in his overcoat or jacket and slicker, with his head on his saddle, and his rifle beside him, and had a little over two hours' sleep. At three we were off again, the shivering porters making no sound as they started; but once under way the more irrepressible spirits speedily began a kind of intermittent chant, and most of the rest by degrees joined in the occasional grunt or hum that served as chorus.

For four hours we travelled steadily, first through the moonlight, and then through the reddening dawn. Jackals shrieked, and the plains plover wailed and scolded as they circled round us. When the sun was well up, we halted; the desolate flats stretched far and wide on every side and rose into lofty hills ahead of us. The porters received their water and food, and lay down to sleep, some directly in the open, others rigging little sun shelters under the scattering thorn-bushes. The horses were fed, were given half a pail of water apiece, and were turned loose to graze with the oxen; this was the last time the oxen would feed freely, unless there was rain; and this was to be our longest halt. We had an excellent breakfast, like our supper the night before, and then slept as well as we could.

Noon came, and soon afterward we again started. The country grew hilly, and brushy. It was too dry for much game, but we saw a small herd of giraffe, which are independent of water. Now riding our horses, now leading them, we travelled until nearly sunset, when we halted at the foot of a steep divide, beyond which our course lay across slopes that gradually fell to the stream for which we were heading. Here the porters had all the food and water they wished, and so did the horses; and, each with a double span of oxen, the wagons were driven up the slope, the weary cattle straining hard in the yokes.

Black clouds had risen and thickened in the west, boding rain. Three-fourths of our journey was over; and it was safe to start the safari and then leave it to come on by itself, while the ox-wagons followed later. At nine, before the moon struggled above the hill crests to our left, we were off. Soon we passed the wagons, drawn up abreast, a lantern high on a pole, while the tired oxen lay in their yokes, attached to the trek tow. An hour afterward we left the safari behind, and rode ahead, with only our saises and gun-bearers. Gusts of rain blew in our faces, and gradually settled into a steady, gentle downpour. Our horses began to slip in the greasy soil; we knew the rain would refresh the cattle, but would make the going harder.

At one we halted, in the rain, for a couple of hours' rest. Just before this we heard two lions roaring, or rather grunting, not far in front of us; they were after prey. Lions are bold on rainy nights; and we did not wish to lose any of our horses; so a watch was organized, and we kept ready for immediate action, but the lions did not come. The native boys built fires, and lay close to them, relieving one another, and us, as sentinels. Kermit and I had our army overcoats, which are warm and practically water-proof; the others had coats almost as good. We lay down in the rain, on the drenched grass, with our saddle-cloths over our feet, and our heads on our saddles, and slept comfortably for two hours.

At three we mounted and were off again, the rain still falling. There were steep ravines to cross, slippery from the wet; but we made good time, and soon after six off-saddled on the farther side of a steep drift or ford in the little Suavi River. It is a rapid stream flowing between high, well-wooded banks; it was an attractive camp site, and, as we afterward found, the nights were so cool as to make great camp-fires welcome. At half past ten the safari appeared, in excellent spirits, the flag waving, to an accompaniment of chanting and horn-blowing; and, to their loudly expressed satisfaction, the porters were told that they should have an extra day's rations, as well as a day's rest. Camp was soon pitched; and all, of every rank, slept soundly that night, though the lions moaned near by. The wagons did not get in until ten the following morning. By that time the oxen had been nearly three days without water, so, by dawn, they were unyoked and driven down to drink before the drift was attempted, the wagons being left a mile or two back. The approaches to the drift were steep and difficult, and, with two spans to each, the wagons swayed and plunged over the twisted boulder-choked trails down into the river-bed, crossed it, and, with lurching and straining, men shouting and whips cracking, drew slowly up the opposite bank.

After a day's rest, we pushed on, in two days' easy travelling, to the Guaso Nyero of the south. Our camps were pleasant, by running streams of swift water; one was really beautiful, in a grassy bend of a rapid little river, by huge African yew-trees, with wooded cliffs in front. It was cool, rainy weather, with overcast skies and misty mornings, so that it seemed strangely unlike the tropics. The country was alive with herds of Masai cattle, sheep, and donkeys. The Masai, herdsmen by profession and warriors by preference, with their great spears and ox-hide shields, were stalwart savages, and showed the mixture of types common to this part of Africa, which is the edge of an ethnic whirlpool. Some of them were of seemingly pure negro type; others except in their black skin had little negro about them, their features being as clear cut as those of ebony Nilotic Arabs. They were dignified, but friendly and civil, shaking hands as soon as they came up to us.

On the Guaso Nyero was a settler from South Africa, with his family; and we met another settler travelling with a big flock of sheep which he had bought for trading purposes. The latter, while journeying over our route with cattle, a month before, had been attacked by lions one night. They seized his cook as he lay by the fire, but fortunately grabbed his red blanket, which they carried off, and the terrified man escaped; and they killed a cow and a calf. Ulyate's brother-in-law, Smith, had been rendered a hopeless cripple for life, six months previously, by a lioness he had wounded. Another settler while at one of our camping-places lost two of his horses, which were killed although within a boma. One night lions came within threatening neighborhood of our ox-wagons; and we often heard them moaning in the early part of the night, roaring when full fed toward morning; but we were not molested.

The safari was in high feather, for the days were cool, the work easy, and we shot enough game to give them meat. When we broke camp, after breakfast, the porters would all stand ranged by their loads; then Tarlton would whistle, and a chorus of whistles, horns, and tom-toms would answer, as each porter lifted and adjusted his burden, fell into his place, and then joined in some shrill or guttural chorus as the long line swung off at its marching pace. After nightfall the camp-fires blazed in the cool air, and as we stood or sat around them each man had tales to tell: Cuninghame and Tarlton of elephant-hunting in the Congo and of perilous adventures hunting lion and buffalo; Mearns of long hikes and fierce fighting in the steaming Philippine forests; Loring and Heller of hunting and collecting in Alaska, in the Rockies, and among the deserts of the Mexican border; and always our talk came back to strange experiences with birds and beasts, both great and small, and to the ways of the great game. The three naturalists revelled in the teeming bird life, with its wealth of beauty and color— nor was the beauty only of color and shape, for at dawn the bird songs made real music. The naturalists trapped many small mammals: big-eared mice looking like our white-footed mice, mice with spiny fur, mice that lived in trees, rats striped like our chipmunks, rats that jumped like jerboas, big cane-rats, dormice, and tiny shrews. Meercats, things akin to a small mongoose, lived out in the open plains, burrowing in companies like prairie-dogs, very spry and active, and looking like picket-pins when they stood up on end to survey us. I killed a nine-foot python which had swallowed a rabbit. Game was not plentiful, but we killed enough for the table. I shot a wildebeest bull one day, having edged up to it on foot, after missing it standing; I broke it down with a bullet through the hips as it galloped across my front at three hundred yards. Kermit killed our first topi, a bull; a beautiful animal, the size of a hartbeest, its glossy coat, with a satin sheen, varying from brown to silver and purple.

By the Guaso Nyero we halted for several days; and we arranged to leave Mearns and Loring in a permanent camp, so that they might seriously study and collect the birds and small mammals while the rest of us pushed wherever we wished after the big game. The tents were pitched, and the ox-wagons drawn up on the southern side of the muddy river, by the edge of a wide plain, on which we could see the game grazing as we walked around camp. The alluvial flats bordering the river, and some of the higher plains, were covered with an open forest growth, the most common tree looking exactly like a giant sage-brush, thirty feet high; and there were tall aloes and cactus and flat-topped mimosa. We found a wee hedgehog, with much white about it. He would cuddle up in my hand snuffing busily with his funny little nose. We did not have the heart to turn the tame, friendly little fellow over to the naturalists, and so we let him go. Birds abounded. One kind of cuckoo called like a whippoorwill in the early morning and late evening, and after nightfall. Among our friendly visitors were the pretty, rather strikingly colored little chats —Livingstone's wheatear—which showed real curiosity in coming into camp. They were nesting in burrows on the open plains round about. Mearns got a white egg and a nest at the end of a little burrow two feet long; wounded, the birds ran into holes or burrows. They sang attractively on the wing, often at night. The plover-like coursers, very pretty birds, continually circled round us with querulous clamor. Gorgeously colored, diminutive sunbirds, of many different kinds, were abundant; they had an especial fondness for the gaudy flowers of the tall mint which grew close to the river. We got a small cobra, less than eighteen inches long; it had swallowed another snake almost as big as itself; unfortunately the head of the swallowed snake was digested, but the body looked like that of a young puff-adder.

The day after reaching this camp I rode off for a hunt, accompanied by my two gun-bearers and with a dozen porters following, to handle whatever I killed. One of my original gun-bearers, Mahomet, though a good man in the field, had proved in other respects so unsatisfactory that he had been replaced by another, a Wakamba heathen named Gouvimali —I could never remember his name until, as a mnemonic aid, Kermit suggested that I think of Gouverneur Morris, the old Federalist statesman, whose life I had once studied. He was a capital man for the work.

Half a mile from camp I saw a buck tommy with a good head, and as we needed his delicious venison for our own table, I dismounted and after a little care killed him as he faced me at two hundred and ten yards. Sending him back by one of the porters, I rode on toward two topi we saw far in front. But there were zebra, hartbeest, and wildebeest in between, all of which ran; and the topi proved wary. I was still walking after them when we made out two eland bulls ahead and to our left. The ground was too open to admit the possibility of a stalk; but leaving my horse and the porters to follow slowly, the gun-bearers and I walked quartering toward them. They hesitated about going, and when I had come as close as I dared, I motioned to the two gun-bearers to continue walking, and dropped on one knee. I had the little Springfield, and was anxious to test the new sharp-pointed military bullet on some large animal. The biggest bull was half facing me, just two hundred and eighty yards off; I fired a little bit high and a trifle to the left; but the tiny ball broke his back and the splendid beast, heavy as a prize steer, came plunging and struggling to the ground. The other bull started to run off, but after I had walked a hundred yards forward, he actually trotted back toward his companion; then halted, turned, and galloped across my front at a distance of a hundred and eighty yards; and him too I brought down with a single shot. The little full-jacketed, sharp-pointed bullet made a terrific rending compared with the heavier, ordinary-shaped bullet of the same composition.

I was much pleased with my two prizes, for the National Museum particularly desired a good group of eland. They were splendid animals, like beautiful heavy cattle; and I could not sufficiently admire their sleek, handsome, striped coats, their shapely heads, fine horns, and massive bodies. The big bull, an old one, looked blue at a distance; he was very heavy and his dewlap hung down just as with cattle. His companion, although much less heavy, was a full-grown bull in his prime, with longer horns; for the big one's horns had begun to wear down at the tips. In their stomachs were grass blades and, rather to my surprise, aloe-leaves.

We had two canvas cloths with us, which Heller had instructed me to put over anything I shot in order to protect it from the sun; so, covering both bulls, I left a porter with them, and sent in another to notify Heller—who came out with an ox-wagon to bring in the skins and meat. I had killed these two eland bulls, as well as the buck gazelle (bringing down each with a single bullet) within three-quarters of an hour after leaving camp.

I wanted a topi, and continued the hunt. The country swarmed with the herds and flocks of the Masai, who own a wealth of live stock. Each herd of cattle and donkeys or flock of sheep was guarded by its herdsmen; bands of stalwart, picturesque warriors, with their huge spears and ox-hide shields, occasionally strolled by us; and we passed many bomas, the kraals where the stock is gathered at night, with the mud huts of the owners ringing them. Yet there was much game in the country also, chiefly zebra and hartbeest; the latter, according to their custom, continually jumping up on ant-hills to get a clearer view of me, and sometimes standing on them motionless for a considerable time, as sentries to scan the country around.

At last we spied a herd of topi, distinguishable from the hartbeest at a very long distance by their dark coloring, the purples and browns giving the coat a heavy shading which when far off, in certain lights, looks almost black. Topi, hartbeest, and wildebeest belong to the same group, and are specialized, and their peculiar physical and mental traits developed, in the order named. The wildebeest is the least normal and most grotesque and odd-looking of the three, and his idiosyncrasies of temper are also the most marked. The hartbeest comes next, with his very high withers, long face, and queerly shaped horns; while the topi, although with a general hartbeest look, has the features of shape and horn less pronounced, and bears a greater resemblance to his more ordinary kinsfolk. In the same way, though it will now and then buck and plunge when it begins to run after being startled, its demeanor is less pronounced in this respect. The topi's power of leaping is great; I have seen one when frightened bound clear over a companion, and immediately afterward over a high ant-hill.

The herd of topi we saw was more shy than the neighboring zebra and hartbeest. There was no cover and I spent an hour trying to walk up to them by manœuvring in one way and another. They did not run clear away, but kept standing and letting me approach to distances varying from 450 to 600 yards; tempting me to shoot, while nevertheless I could not estimate the range accurately, and was not certain whether I was over or under shooting. So I fired more times than I care to mention before I finally got my topi—at just 520 yards. It was a handsome cow, weighing 260 pounds; for topi are somewhat smaller than kongoni. The beauty of its coat, in texture and coloring, struck me afresh as I looked at the sleek creature stretched out on the grass. Like the eland, it was free from ticks; for the hideous pests do not frequent this part of the country in any great numbers.

I reached camp early in the afternoon, and sat down at the mouth of my tent to enjoy myself. It was on such occasions that the "Pigskin Library" proved itself indeed a blessing. In addition to the original books we had picked up one or two old favorites on the way: "Alice's Adventures," for instance, and Fitzgerald—I say Fitzgerald, because reading other versions of Omar Khayyam always leaves me with the feeling that Fitzgerald is the major partner in the book we really like. Then there was a book I had not read, Dumas's "Louves de Machecoul." This was presented to me at Port Said by M. Jusserand, the brother of an old and valued friend, the French ambassador at Washington—the vice-president of the "Tennis Cabinet." We had been speaking of Balzac, and I mentioned regretfully that I did not at heart care for his longer novels excepting the "Chouans;" and, as John Hay once told me, in the eye of all true Balzacians to like the "Chouans" merely aggravates the offense of not liking the novels which they deem really great. M. Jusserand thereupon asked me if I knew Dumas's Vendean novel; being a fairly good Dumas man, I was rather ashamed to admit that I did not; whereupon he sent it to me, and I enjoyed it to the full.

The next day was Kermit's red-letter day. We were each out until after dark; I merely got some of the ordinary game, taking the skins for the naturalists, the flesh for our following; he killed two cheetahs, and a fine maned lion, finer than any previously killed. There were three cheetahs together.

Kermit, who was with Tarlton, galloped the big male, and, although it had a mile's start, ran into it in three miles, and shot it as it lay under a bush. He afterward shot another, a female, who was lying on a stone koppie. Neither made any attempt to charge; the male had been eating a tommy. The lion was with a lioness, which wheeled to one side, as the horsemen galloped after her maned mate. He turned to bay after a run of less than a mile, and started to charge from a distance of two hundred yards; but Kermit's first bullet mortally wounded him and crippled him so that he could not come at any pace and was easily stopped before covering half the distance. Although nearly a foot longer than the biggest of the lions I had already killed, he was so gaunt—whereas they were very fat—that he weighed but little more, only 412 pounds.

The following day I was out by myself, after impala and Roberts's gazelle; and the day after I went out with Tarlton to try for lion. We were away from camp for over fifteen hours. Each was followed by his sais and gun-bearers, and we took a dozen porters also. The day may be worth describing, as a sample of the days when we did not start before dawn for a morning's hunt.

We left camp at seven, steering for a high, rocky hill, four miles off. We passed zebra and hartbeest, and on the hill came upon Chanler's reedbuck; but we wanted none of these. Continually, Tarlton stopped to examine some distant object with his glasses, and from the hill we scanned the country far and wide; but we saw nothing we desired and continued on our course. The day was windy and cool, and the sky often overcast. Slowly we walked across the stretches of brown grassland, sometimes treeless, sometimes scantily covered with an open growth of thorn-trees, each branch armed with long spikes, needle-sharp; and among the thorns here and there stood the huge cactus-like euphorbias, shaped like candelabra, groups of tall aloes, and gnarled wild olives of great age, with hoary trunks and twisted branches. Now and then there

would be a dry water-course, with flat-topped acacias bordering it, and perhaps some one pool of thick greenish water.
There was game always in view, and about noon we sighted
three rhinos, a bull, a cow, and a big calf, nearly a mile ahead
of us. We were travelling down-wind, and they scented us,
but did not charge, making off in a semicircle and halting when
abreast of us. We examined them carefully through the
glasses. The cow was bigger than the bull, and had fair horns,
but nothing extraordinary; and as we were twelve miles from
camp, so that Heller would have had to come out for the
night if we shot her, we decided to leave her alone. Then our
attention was attracted by seeing the game all grazing in one
direction, and we made out a hyena; I got a shot at it, at
three hundred yards, but missed. Soon afterward we saw
another rhino, but on approaching it proved to be about two-
thirds grown, with a stubby horn. We did not wish to shoot
it, and therefore desired to avoid a charge; and so we passed
three or four hundred yards to leeward, trusting to its bad
eyesight. Just opposite it, when it was on our right, we saw
another hyena on our left, about as far off as the rhino. I
decided to take a shot, and run the chance of disturbing the
rhino. So I knelt down and aimed with the little Springfield,
keeping the Holland by me to be ready for events. I never
left camp, on foot or on horseback, for any distance, no matter how short, without carrying one of the repeating rifles;
and when on a hunt my two gun-bearers carried, one the other
magazine rifle, and one the double-barrelled Holland.

Tarlton, whose eye for distance was good, told me the hyena
was over three hundred yards off; it was walking slowly to
the left. I put up the three-hundred-yard sight, and drew a
rather coarse bead; and down went the hyena with its throat
cut; the little sharp-pointed, full-jacketed bullet makes a slashing wound. The distance was just three hundred and ·fifty
long paces. As soon as I had pulled trigger I wheeled to watch
the rhino. It started round at the shot and gazed toward us
with its ears cocked forward, but made no movement to ad-

vance. While a couple of porters were dressing the hyena, I could not help laughing at finding that we were the centre of a thoroughly African circle of deeply interested spectators. We were in the middle of a vast plain, covered with sun-scorched grass and here and there a stunted thorn; in the background were isolated barren hills, and the mirage wavered in the distance. Vultures wheeled overhead. The rhino, less than half a mile away, stared steadily at us. Wildebeest—their heavy fore quarters and the carriage of their heads making them look like bison—and hartbeest were somewhat nearer, in a ring all round us, intent upon our proceedings. Four topi became so much interested that they approached within two hundred and fifty yards and stood motionless. A buck tommy came even closer, and a zebra trotted by at about the same distance, uttering its queer bark or neigh. It continued its course past the rhino, and started a new train of ideas in the latter's muddled reptilian brain; round it wheeled, gazed after the zebra, and then evidently concluded that everything was normal, for it lay down to sleep.

On we went, past a wildebeest-herd lying down; at a distance they looked exactly like bison as they used to lie out on the prairie in the old days. We halted for an hour and a half to rest the men and horses, and took our lunch under a thick-trunked olive-tree that must have been a couple of centuries old. Again we went on, ever scanning through the glasses every distant object which we thought might possibly be a lion, and ever being disappointed. A serval-cat jumped up ahead of us in the tall grass, but I missed it. Then, trotting on foot, I got ahead of two wart-hog boars, and killed the bigger; making a bad initial miss and then emptying my magazine at it as it ran. We sent it in to camp, and went on, following a donga, or small watercourse, fringed with big acacias. The afternoon was wearing away, and it was time for lions to be abroad.

The sun was near the horizon when Tarlton thought he saw something tawny in the watercourse ahead of us, behind a grassy ant-hill, toward which we walked after dismounting. Some buck were grazing peacefully beyond it, and for a moment we supposed that this was what he had seen. But as we stood, one of the porters behind called out "Simba;" and we caught a glimpse of a big lioness galloping down beside the trees, just beyond the donga; she was out of sight in an instant. Mounting our horses, we crossed the donga; she was not to be seen, and we loped at a smart pace parallel with the line of trees, hoping to see her in the open. But, as it turned out, as soon as she saw us pass, she crouched in the bed of the donga; we had gone by her a quarter of a mile when a shout from one of our followers announced that he had seen her, and back we galloped, threw ourselves from our horses, and walked toward where the man was pointing. Tarlton took his big double-barrel and advised me to take mine, as the sun had just set and it was likely to be close work; but I shook my head, for the Winchester 405 is, at least for me personally, the "medicine gun" for lions. In another moment up she jumped, and galloped slowly down the other side of the donga, switching her tail and growling; I scrambled across the donga, and just before she went round a clump of trees, eighty yards off, I fired. The bullet hit her fair, and going forward injured her spine. Over she rolled, growling savagely, and dragged herself into the watercourse; and running forward I finished her with two bullets behind the shoulder. She was a big, fat lioness, very old, with two cubs inside her; her lower canines were much worn and injured. She was very heavy, and probably weighed considerably over three hundred pounds.

The light was growing dim, and camp was eight or ten miles away. The porters—they are always much excited over the death of a lion—wished to carry the body whole to camp, and I let them try. While they were lashing it to a pole another lion began to moan hungrily half a mile away. Then we started; there was no moon, but the night was clear and we could guide ourselves by the stars. The porters staggered under their heavy load, and we made slow progress; most of

the time Tarlton and I walked, with our double-barrels in
our hands, for it was a dangerous neighborhood. Again and
again we heard lions, and twice one accompanied us for some
distance, grunting occasionally, while we kept the men closed.
Once the porters were thrown into a panic by a succession of
steam-engine-like snorts on our left, which announced the immediate proximity of a rhino. They halted in a huddle while
Tarlton and I ran forward and crouched to try to catch
the great beast's loom against the sky-line; but it moved off.
Four miles from camp was a Masai kraal, and we went toward
this when we caught the gleam of the fires; for the porters
were getting exhausted.

The kraal was in shape a big oval, with a thick wall of thorn-
bushes, eight feet high, the low huts standing just within this
wall, while the cattle and sheep were crowded into small bomas
in the centre. The fires gleamed here and there within, and
as we approached we heard the talking and laughing of men
and women, and the lowing and bleating of the pent-up herds
and flocks. We hailed loudly, explaining our needs. At first
they were very suspicious. They told us we could not bring
the lion within, because it would frighten the cattle, but after
some parley consented to our building a fire outside, and skinning the animal. They passed two brands over the thorn fence,
and our men speedily kindled a blaze, and drew the lioness
beside it. By this time the Masai were reassured, and a score
of their warriors, followed soon by half a dozen women, came
out through a small opening in the fence, and crowded close
around the fire, with boisterous, noisy good humor. They
showed a tendency to chaff our porters. One, the humorist
of the crowd, excited much merriment by describing, with
pantomimic accompaniment of gestures, how when the white
man shot a lion it might bite a Swahili, who thereupon would
call for his mother. But they were entirely friendly, and
offered me calabashes of milk. The men were tall, finely shaped
savages, their hair plastered with red mud, and drawn out into
longish ringlets; they were naked except for a blanket worn,

not round the loins, but over the shoulders; their ears were slit, and from them hung bone and wooden ornaments; they wore metal bracelets and anklets, and chains which passed around their necks, or else over one side of the neck and under the opposite arm. The women had pleasant faces, and were laden with metal ornaments—chiefly wire anklets, bracelets, and necklaces—of many pounds weight. The features of the men were bold and clear cut, and their bearing warlike and self-reliant; as the flame of the fire glanced over them, and brought their faces and bronze figures into lurid relief against the darkness, the likeness was striking, not to the West Coast negroes, but to the engravings on the tombs, temples, and palaces of ancient Egypt; they might have been soldiers in the armies of Thothmes or Rameses. They stood resting on their long staffs, and looked at me as I leaned on my rifle; and they laughed and jested with their women, who felt the lion's teeth and claws and laughed back at the men; our gun-bearers worked at the skinning, and answered the jests of their warlike friends with the freedom of men who themselves followed a dangerous trade; the two horses stood quiet just outside the circle; and over all the firelight played and leaped.

It was after ten when we reached camp, and I enjoyed a hot bath and a shave before sitting down to a supper of eland venison and broiled spur-fowl; and surely no supper ever tasted more delicious.

Next day we broke camp. My bag for the five days illustrates ordinary African shooting in this part of the continent. Of course I could have killed many other things; but I shot nothing that was not absolutely needed, both for scientific purposes and for food; the skin of every animal I shot was preserved for the National Museum. The bag included fourteen animals, of ten different species; one lioness, one hyena, one wart-hog boar, two zebra, two eland, one wildebeest, two topi, two impala, one Roberts's gazelle, one Thomson's gazelle. Except the lioness and one impala (both of which I shot running), all were shot at rather long ranges; seven were shot

standing, two walking, five running. The average distance
at which they were shot was a little over two hundred and
twenty yards. I used sixty-five cartridges, an amount which
will seem excessive chiefly to those who are not accustomed
actually to count the cartridges they expend, to measure the
distances at which they fire, and to estimate for themselves
the range, on animals in the field when they are standing or
running a good way off. Only one wounded animal got away;
and eight of the animals I shot had to be finished with one
bullet—two in the case of the lioness—as they lay on the
ground. Many of the cartridges expended really represented
range-finding.

CHAPTER VIII

HUNTING IN THE SOTIK

OUR next camp was in the middle of the vast plains, by some limestone springs, at one end of a line of dark acacias. There were rocky koppies two or three miles off on either hand. From the tents, and white-topped wagons, we could see the game grazing on the open flats, or among the scattered wizened thorns. The skies were overcast, and the nights cool; in the evenings the camp-fires blazed in front of the tents, and after supper we gathered round them, talking, or sitting silently, or listening to Kermit strumming on his mandolin.

The day after reaching this camp we rode out, hoping to get either rhino or giraffe; we needed additional specimens of both for the naturalists, who especially wanted cow giraffes. It was cloudy and cool, and the common game was shy; though we needed meat, I could not get within fair range of the wildebeest, hartbeest, topi, or big gazelle; however I killed a couple of tommies, one by a good shot, the other running, after I had missed him in rather scandalous fashion while he was standing.

An hour or two after leaving the tents we made out on the sky-line a couple of miles to our left some objects which scrutiny showed to be giraffe. After coming within a mile the others halted and I rode ahead on the tranquil sorrel, heading for a point toward which the giraffe were walking; stalking was an impossibility, and I was prepared either to manœuvre for a shot on foot, or to ride them, as circumstances might determine. I carried the little Springfield, being desirous of testing the small, solid, sharp-pointed army bullet on the big beasts. As I rode, a wildebeest bull played around me within two hundred yards, prancing, flourishing his tail, tossing his head and uttering his grunting bellow; it almost seemed as if he knew I would not shoot at him, or as if for the moment he had been infected with the absurd tameness which the giraffe showed.

There were seven giraffes, a medium-sized bull, four cows, and two young ones; and, funnily enough, the young ones were by far the shyest and most suspicious. I did not want to kill a bull unless it was exceptionally large; whereas I did want two cows and a young one, for the museum. When a quarter of a mile away I dismounted, threw the reins over Tranquillity's head—whereat the good placid old fellow at once began grazing—and walked diagonally toward the biggest cow, which was ahead of the others. The tall, handsome, ungainly creatures were nothing like as shy as the smaller game had shown themselves that morning, and of course they offered such big targets that three hundred yards was a fair range for them. At two hundred and sixty yards I fired at the big cow as she stood almost facing me, twisting and curling her tail. The bullet struck fair and she was off at a hurried, clumsy gallop. I gave her another bullet, but it was not necessary, and down she went. The second cow, a fine young heifer, was now cantering across my front, and with two more shots I got her; the sharp-pointed bullets penetrating well, and not splitting into fragments, but seeming to cause a rending shock.

I met with much more difficulty in trying to kill the young one I needed. I walked and trotted a mile after the herd. The old ones showed little alarm, standing again and again to look at me. Finally I shot one of the two young ones, at four hundred and ten long paces, while a cow stood much nearer, and the bull only three hundred yards off. But this was not all. The four survivors did not leave even after such experience, but stayed in the plain, not far off, for several hours, and thereby gave Kermit a chance to do something much better worth while than shooting them. His shoulder was sore, and he did not wish to use a rifle, and so was devoting

himself to his camera, which one of his men always carried.
With this, after the exercise of much patience, he finally managed to take a number of pictures of the giraffe, getting within fifty yards of the bull.

Nor were the giraffe the only animals that showed a tameness bordering on stupidity. Soon afterward we made out
three rhino, a mile away. They were out in the bare plain, alternately grazing and enjoying a noontide rest; the bull himself, the cow with her calf a quarter of a mile off. There was
not a scrap of cover, but we walked up-wind to within a hundred and fifty yards of the bull. Even then he did not seem
to see us, but the tick-birds, which were clinging to his back
and sides, gave the alarm, and he trotted to and fro, uncertain
as to the cause of the disturbance. If Heller had not had
his hands full with the giraffes I might have shot the bull
rhino; but his horn and bulk of body, though fair, were not
remarkable, and I did not molest him. He went toward the
cow, which left her calf and advanced toward him in distinctly
bellicose style; then she recognized him, her calf trotted up,
and the three animals stood together, tossing their heads, and
evidently trying to make out what was near them. But we
were down-wind, and they do not see well, with their little
twinkling pig's eyes. We were anxious not to be charged by
the cow and calf, as her horn was very poor, and it would
have been unpleasant to be obliged to shoot her, and so we
drew off.

Next day, when Kermit and I were out alone with our gun-
bearers we saw another rhino, a bull, with a stubby horn. This
rhino, like the others of the neighborhood, was enjoying his
noonday rest in the open, miles from cover; "Look at him,"
said Kermit, "standing there in the middle of the African
plain, deep in pre-historic thought." Indeed the rhinoceros
does seem like a survival from the elder world that has vanished; he was in place in the Pliocene; he would not have been
out of place in the Miocene; but nowadays he can only exist
at all in regions that have lagged behind, while the rest of

the world, for good or for evil, has gone forward.   Like other beasts rhinos differ in habits in different places.   This prehensile-lipped species is everywhere a browser, feeding on the twigs and leaves of the bushes and low trees; but in their stomachs I have found long grass stems mixed with the twig tips and leaves of stunted bush.   In some regions they live entirely in rather thick bush; whereas on the plains over which we were hunting the animals haunted the open by preference, feeding through thin bush, where they were visible miles away, and usually taking their rest, either standing or lying, out on the absolutely bare plains.   They drank at the small shallow rain-pools, seemingly once every twenty-four hours; and I saw one going to water at noon, and others just at dark; and their hours for feeding and resting were also irregular, though they were apt to lie down or stand motionless during the middle of the day.   Doubtless in very hot weather they prefer to rest under a tree; but we were hunting in cool weather, during which they paid no heed whatever to the sun.   Their sight is very bad, their scent and hearing acute.

On this day Kermit was shooting from his left shoulder, and did very well, killing a fine Roberts's gazelle, and three topi; I also shot a topi bull, as Heller wished a good series for the National Museum.   The topi and wildebeest I shot were all killed at long range, the average distance for the first shot being over three hundred and fifty yards; and in the Sotik, where hunters were few, the game seemed if anything shyer than on the Athi Plains, where hunters were many.   But there were wide and inexplicable differences in this respect among the animals of the same species.   One day I wished to get a doe tommy for the museum; I saw scores, but they were all too shy to let me approach within shot; yet four times I passed within eighty yards of bucks of the same species which paid hardly any heed to me.   Another time I walked for five minutes alongside a big party of Roberts's gazelles, within a hundred and fifty yards, trying in vain to pick out a buck worth shooting; half an hour afterward I came on another party which contained such a buck, but they would not let me get within a quarter of a mile.

Wildebeest are usually the shyest of all game. Each herd has its own recognized beat, to which it ordinarily keeps. Near this camp, there was a herd almost always to be found somewhere near the southern end of a big hill two miles east of us; while a solitary bull was invariably seen around the base of a small hill a couple of miles southwest of us. The latter was usually in the company of a mixed herd of Roberts's and Thomson's gazelles. Here, as everywhere, we found the different species of game associating freely with one another. One little party interested us much. It consisted of two Roberts's bucks, two Roberts's does, and one Thomson's doe, which was evidently a *maîtresse femme* of strongly individualized character. The four big gazelles had completely surrendered their judgment to that of the little tommy doe. She was the acknowledged leader; when she started they started and followed in whatever direction she led; when she stopped they stopped; if she found a given piece of pasture good, upon it they grazed contentedly. Around this camp the topi were as common as hartbeest; they might be found singly, or in small parties, perhaps merely of a bull, a cow, and a calf; or they might be mixed with zebra, wildebeest, and hartbeest. Like the hartbeest, but less frequently, they would mount ant-hills to get a better look over the country. The wildebeest were extraordinary tenacious of life, and the hartbeest and topi only less so. After wounded individuals of all three kinds I more than once had sharp runs on horseback. On one occasion I wounded a wildebeest bull a couple of miles from camp; I was riding my zebra-shaped brown pony, who galloped well; and after a sharp run through the bush I overhauled the wildebeest; but when I jumped off, the pony bolted for camp, and as he disappeared in one direction my game disappeared in the other.

At last a day came when I saw a rhino with a big body and a good horn. We had been riding for a couple of hours; the

game was all around us. Two giraffes stared at us with silly
curiosity rather than alarm; twice I was within range of the
bigger one. At last Bakhari, the gun-bearer, pointed to a gray
mass on the plain, and a glance through the glasses showed
that it was a rhino lying asleep with his legs doubled under him.
He proved to be a big bull, with a front horn nearly twenty-
six inches long. I was anxious to try the sharp-pointed bullets of the little Springfield rifle on him; and Cuninghame and
I, treading cautiously, walked up-wind straight toward him,
our horses following a hundred yards behind. He was waked
by the tick-birds, and twisted his head to and fro, but at first
did not seem to hear us, although looking in our direction.
When we were a hundred yards off he rose and faced us, huge
and threatening, head up and tail erect. But he lacked heart
after all. I fired into his throat, and instead of charging, he
whipped round and was off at a gallop, immediately disappearing over a slight rise. We ran back to our horses, mounted,
and galloped after him. He had a long start, and, though
evidently feeling his wound, was going strong; and it was
some time before we overtook him. I tried to gallop alongside, but he kept swerving; so jumping off (fortunately, I was
riding Tranquillity) I emptied the magazine at his quarters
and flank. Rapid galloping does not tend to promote accuracy
of aim; the rhino went on; and, remounting, I followed, overtook him, and repeated the performance. This time he wheeled
and faced round, evidently with the intention of charging, but
a bullet straight in his chest took all the fight out of him,
and he continued his flight. But his race was evidently run,
and when I next overtook him I brought him down. I had
put nine bullets in him; and though they had done their work
well, and I was pleased to have killed the huge brute with the
little sharp-pointed bullets of the Springfield, I was confirmed
in my judgment that for me personally the big Holland rifle
was the best weapon for heavy game, although I did not care
as much for it against lighter-bodied beasts like lions. In
all we galloped four miles after this wounded rhino bull.

We sent a porter to bring out Heller, and an ox-wagon on which to take the skin to camp. While waiting for them I killed a topi bull, at 260 yards with one bullet, and a wildebeest bull with a dozen; I crippled him with my first shot at 360 yards, and then walked and trotted after him a couple of miles, getting running and standing shots at from 300 to 500 yards. I hit him several times. As with everything else I shot, the topi and wildebeest were preserved as specimens for the museum, and their flesh used for food. Our porters had much to do, and they did it well, partly because they were fed well. We killed no game of which we did not make the fullest use. It would be hard to convey to those who have not seen it on the ground an accurate idea of its abundance. When I was walking up to this rhino, there were in sight two giraffes, several wildebeest bulls, and herds of hartbeest, topi, zebra, and the big and little gazelles.

In addition to being a mighty hunter, and an adept in the by no means easy work of handling a large safari in the wilderness, Cuninghame was also a good field naturalist and taxidermist; and at this camp we got so many specimens that he was obliged to spend most of his time helping Heller; and they pressed into the work at times even Tarlton. Accordingly Kermit and I generally went off by ourselves, either together or separately. Once however Kermit went with Tarlton, and was as usual lucky with cheetahs, killing two. Tarlton was an accomplished elephant, buffalo, and rhino hunter, but he preferred the chase of the lion to all other kinds of sport; and if lions were not to be found he liked to follow anything else he could gallop on horseback. Kermit was also a good and hard rider. On this occasion they found a herd of eland, and galloped into it. The big bull they overhauled at once, but saw that his horns were poor and left him. Then they followed a fine cow with an unusually good head. She started at a rattling pace, and once leaped clear over another cow that got in her way; but they rode into her after a mile's smart gallop—not a racing gallop by any means—and after that she was as manageable as a tame ox. Cantering and trotting within thirty yards of her on either quarter they drove her toward camp; but when it was still three-quarters of a mile distant they put up a cheetah, and tore after it; and they overtook and killed it just before it reached cover. A cheetah with a good start can only be overtaken by hard running. This one behaved just as did the others they ran down. For a quarter of a mile no animal in the world has a cheetah's speed; but he cannot last. When chased the cheetahs did not sprint, but contented themselves with galloping ahead of the horses; at first they could easily keep their distance, but after a mile or two their strength and wind gave out, and then they always crouched flat to the earth, and were shot without their making any attempt to charge. But a wart-hog boar which Kermit ran down the same day and shot with his revolver did charge, and wickedly.

While running one of his cheetahs Kermit put up two old wildebeests bulls, and they joined in the procession, looking as if they too were pursuing the cheetah; the cheetah ran first, the two bulls, bounding and switching their tails, came next, and Kermit, racing in the rear, gained steadily. Wildebeest are the oddest in nature and conduct, and in many ways the most interesting of all antelopes. There is in their temper something queer, fiery, eccentric, and their actions are abrupt and violent. A single bull will stand motionless with head raised to stare at an intruder until the latter is a quarter of a mile off; then down goes his head, his tail is lashed up and around, and off he gallops, plunging, kicking, and shaking his head. He may go straight away, he may circle round, or even approach nearer to, the intruder; and then he halts again to stare motionless, and perhaps to utter his grunt of alarm and defiance. A herd when approached, after fixed staring will move off, perhaps at a canter. Soon the leaders make a half wheel, and lead their followers in a semicircle; suddenly a couple of old bulls leave the rest, and at a tearing gallop describe a semicircle in exactly the opposite direction, racing by their comrades as these canter the other way. With one accord the whole troop may then halt and stare again at the object they suspected; then off they all go at a head-long run, kicking and bucking, tearing at full speed in one direction, then suddenly wheeling in semicircles so abrupt as to be almost zigzags, the dust flying in clouds; and two bulls may suddenly drop to their knees and for a moment or two fight furiously in their own peculiar fashion. By careful stalking Kermit got some good pictures of the wildebeest in spite of their wariness. Like other game they seem most apt to lie down during the heat of the day; but they may lie down at night too; at any rate, I noticed one herd of hartbeest which after feeding through the late afternoon lay down at nightfall.

After getting the bull rhino, Heller needed a cow and calf to complete the group; and Kermit and I got him what he needed, one day when we were out alone with our gun-bearers. About the middle of the forenoon we made out the huge gray bulk of the rhino, standing in the bare plain, with not so much as a bush two feet high within miles; and we soon also made out her calf beside her. Getting the wind right we rode up within a quarter of a mile, and then dismounted and walked slowly toward her. It seemed impossible that on that bare plain we could escape even her dull vision, for she stood with her head in our direction; yet she did not see us, and actually lay down as we walked toward her. Careful examination through the glasses showed that she was an unusually big cow, with thick horns of fair length—twenty-three inches and thirteen inches respectively. Accordingly we proceeded, making as little noise as possible. At fifty yards she made us out, and jumped to her feet with unwieldy agility. Kneeling I sent the bullet from the heavy Holland just in front of her right shoulder as she half faced me. It went through her vitals, lodging behind the opposite shoulder; and at once she began the curious death waltz which is often, though by no means always, the sign of immediate dissolution in a mortally wounded rhino. Kermit at once put a bullet from his Winchester behind her shoulder; for it is never safe to take chances with a rhino; and we shot the calf, which when dying uttered a screaming whistle, almost like that of a small steam-engine. In a few seconds both fell, and we walked up to them, examined them, and then continued our ride, sending in a messenger to bring Cuninghame, Heller, and an ox-wagon to the carcasses.

The stomach of this rhino contained some grass stems and blades, some leaves and twig tips of bushes, but chiefly the thick, thorny, fleshy leaves of a kind of euphorbia. As the juice of the euphorbia's cactus-like leaves is acrid enough to blister—not to speak of the thorns—this suffices to show what a rhino's palate regards as agreeably stimulating. This species of rhino, by the way, affords a curious illustration of how blind many men who live much of their lives outdoors may be to facts which stare them in the face. For years most South African hunters, and most naturalists, believed in the existence of two species of prehensile-lipped, or so-called "black," rhinoceros: one with the front horn much the longer, one with the rear horn at least equal to the front. It was Selous, a singularly clear-sighted and keen observer, who first proved conclusively that the difference was purely imaginary. Now, the curious thing is that these experienced hunters usually attributed entirely different temperaments to these two imaginary species. The first kind, that with the long front horn, they described as a miracle of dangerous ferocity, and the second as comparatively mild and inoffensive; and these veterans (Drummond is an instance) persuaded themselves that this was true, although they were writing in each case of identically the same animal!

After leaving the dead rhinos we rode for several miles, over a plain dotted with game, and took our lunch at the foot of a big range of hills, by a rapid little brook, running under a fringe of shady thorns. Then we rode back to camp. Lines of zebra filed past on the horizon. Ostriches fled while we were yet far off. Topi, hartbeest, wildebeest, and gazelle gazed at us as we rode by, the sunlight throwing their shapes

and colors into bold relief against the parched brown grass.
I had an hour to myself after reaching camp, and spent it
with Lowell's "Essays." I doubt whether any man takes
keener enjoyment in the wilderness than he who also keenly
enjoys many other sides of life; just as no man can relish
books more than some at least of those who also love horse
and rifle and the winds that blow across lonely plains and
through the gorges of the mountains.

Next morning a lion roared at dawn so near camp that
we sallied forth after him. We did not find him, but we enjoyed our three hours' ride through the fresh air before breakfast, with the game as usual on every hand. Some of the game
showed tameness, some wildness, the difference being not between species and species, but between given individuals of almost every species. While we were absent two rhinos passed
close by camp, and stopped to stare curiously at it; we saw
them later as they trotted away, but their horns were not good
enough to tempt us.

At a distance the sunlight plays pranks with the coloring
of the animals. Cock ostriches always show jet-black, and
are visible at a greater distance than any of the common game;
the neutral tint of the hens making them far less conspicuous.
Both cocks and hens are very wary, sharp-sighted, and hard
to approach. Next to the cock ostrich in conspicuousness comes
the wildebeest, because it shows black in most lights; yet when
headed away from the onlooker, the sun will often make the
backs of a herd look whitish in the distance. Wildebeest are
warier than most other game. Round this camp the topi were
as tame as the hartbeest; they look very dark in most lights,
only less dark than the wildebeest, and so are also conspicuous. The hartbeest change from a deep brown to a light foxy
red, according to the way they stand toward the sun; and when
a herd was feeding away from us, their white sterns showed
when a very long way off. The zebra's stripes cease to be
visible after he is three hundred yards off, but in many lights
he glistens white in the far distance, and is then very con-

spicuous; on this day I came across a mixed herd of zebra and eland in thin bush, and when still a long way off the zebras caught the eye, while their larger companions were as yet hardly to be made out without field-glasses. The gazelles usually show as sandy-colored, and are therefore rather less conspicuous than the others when still; but they are constantly in motion, and in some lights show up as almost white. When they are far off the sun-rays make any of these animals look very dark or very light. In fact all of them are conspicuous at long distances, and none of them make any effort to escape observation as do certain kinds that haunt dense bush and forest. But constant allowance must be made for the wide variations among individuals. Ordinarily tommies are the tamest of the game, with the big gazelle and the zebra next; but no two herds will behave alike; and I have seen a wildebeest bull look at me motionless within a hundred and fifty yards, while the zebras, tommies, and big gazelles which were his companions fled in panic; and I left him still standing, as I walked after the gazelles, to kill a buck for the table. The game is usually sensitive to getting the hunter's wind; but on these plains I have again and again seen game stand looking at us within fairly close range to leeward, and yet on the same day seen the same kind of game flee in mad fright when twice the distance to windward. Sometimes there are inexplicable variations between the conduct of beasts in one locality and in another. In East Africa the hyenas seem only occasionally to crunch the long bones of the biggest dead animals; whereas Cuninghame, who pointed out this fact to me, stated that in South Africa the hyenas, of the same kind, always crunched up the big bones, eating both the marrow and fragments of the bone itself.

Now and then the game will choose a tree as a rubbing-post, and if it is small will entirely destroy the tree; and I have seen them use for the same purpose an oddly shaped stone, one corner of which they had worn quite smooth. They have stamping-grounds, small patches of bare earth from which they have removed even the roots of the grass and bushes by the trampling of their hoofs, leaving nothing but a pool of dust. One evening I watched some zebras stringing slowly along in a line which brought them past a couple of these stamping-grounds. As they came in succession to each bare place half the herd, one after another, lay down and rolled to and fro, sending up spurts of dust so thick that the animal was hidden from sight; while perhaps a companion, which did not roll, stood near by, seemingly to enjoy the dust.

On this same evening we rode campward facing a wonderful sunset. The evening was lowering and overcast. The darkening plains stretched dim and vague into the far distance. The sun went down under a frowning sky, behind shining sheets of rain; and it turned their radiance to a angry splendor of gold and murky crimson.

At this camp the pretty little Livingstone's wheatears or chats were very familiar, flitting within a few yards of the tents. They were the earliest birds to sing. Just before our eyes could distinguish the first faint streak of dawn first one and then another of them would begin to sing, apparently either on the ground or in the air, until there was a chorus of their sweet music. Then they were silent again until the sun was about to rise. We always heard them when we made a very early start to hunt. By the way, with the game of the plains and the thin bush, we found that nothing was gained by getting out early in the morning; we were quite as apt to get what we wanted in the evening or indeed at high noon.

The last day at this camp Kermit, Tarlton, and I spent on a twelve hours' lion-hunt. I opened the day inauspiciously, close to camp, by missing a zebra, which we wished for the porters. Then Kermit, by a good shot, killed a tommy buck with the best head we had yet gotten. Early in the afternoon we reached our objective, some high koppies, broken by cliffs and covered with brush. There were klipspringers on these koppies, little rock-loving antelopes, with tiny hoofs and queer brittle hair; they are marvellous jumpers and continually utter a bleating whistle. I broke the neck of one as it ran at a distance of a hundred and fifty yards; but the shot was a fluke, and did not make amends for the way I had missed the zebra in the morning. Among the thick brush on these hills were huge euphorbias, aloes bearing masses of orange flowers, and a cactus-like ground plant with pretty pink blossoms. All kinds of game from the plains, even rhino, had wandered over these hilltops.

But what especially interested us was that we immediately found fresh beds of lions, and one regular lair. Again and again, as we beat cautiously through the bushes, the rank smell of the beasts smote our nostrils. At last, as we sat at the foot of one koppie, Kermit spied through his glasses a lion on the side of the koppie opposite, the last and biggest; and up it we climbed. On the very summit was a mass of cleft and broken boulders, and while on these Kermit put up two lions from the bushes which crowded beneath them. I missed a running shot at the lioness, as she made off through the brush. He probably hit the lion, and, very cautiously, with rifles at the ready, we beat through the thick cover in hopes to find it; but in vain. Then we began a hunt for the lioness, as apparently she had not left the koppie. Soon one of the gun-bearers, who was standing on a big stone, peering under some thick bushes, beckoned excitedly to me; and when I jumped up beside him he pointed at the lioness. In a second I made her out. The sleek sinister creature lay not ten paces off, her sinuous body following the curves of the rock as she crouched flat looking straight at me. A stone covered the lower part, and the left of the upper part, of her head; but I saw her two unwinking green eyes looking into mine. As she could have reached me in two springs, perhaps in one, I wished to shoot straight; but I had to avoid the rock which covered the lower part of her face, and moreover I fired a little too much to the left. The bullet went through the side of her head, and in between the neck and shoulder, inflicting a mortal, but not immediately fatal, wound. However it knocked her off the little ledge on which she was lying, and instead of charging she rushed uphill. We promptly followed, and again clambered up the mass of boulders at the top. Peering over the one on which I had climbed there was the lioness directly at its foot, not twelve feet away, lying flat on her belly; I could only see the aftermost third of her back. I at once fired into her spine; with appalling grunts she dragged herself a few paces downhill; and another bullet behind the shoulder finished her.

She was skinned as rapidly as possible; and just before sundown we left the koppie. At its foot was a deserted Masai cattle kraal and a mile from this was a shallow, muddy pool, fouled by the countless herds of game that drank thereat. Toward this we went, so that the thirsty horses and men might drink their fill. As we came near we saw three rhinoceros leaving the pool. It was already too dusk for good shooting, and we were rather relieved when, after some inspection, they trotted off and stood at a little distance in the plain. Our men and horses drank, and then we began our ten miles' march through the darkness to camp. One of Kermit's gun-bearers saw a puff-adder (among the most deadly of all snakes); with delightful nonchalance he stepped on its head, and then held it up for me to put my knife through its brain and neck. I slipped it into my saddle pocket, where its blood stained the pigskin cover of the little pocket "Nibelungenlied" which that day I happened to carry. Immediately afterward there was a fresh alarm from our friends the three rhinos; dismounting and crouching down, we caught the loom of their bulky bodies against the horizon; but a shot in the ground seemed to make them hesitate, and they finally concluded not to charge. So, with the lion-skin swinging behind two porters, a moribund puff-adder in my saddle pocket, and three rhinos threatening us in the darkness to one side, we marched campward through the African night.

Next day we shifted camp to a rush-fringed pool by a grove of tall, flat-topped acacias at the foot of a range of low, steep mountains. Before us the plain stretched, and in front of our tents it was dotted by huge candelabra euphorbias. I shot a buck for the table just as we pitched camp. There were Masai kraal and cattleherds near by, and tall warriors, pleasant and friendly, strolled among our tents, their huge razor-edged spears tipped with furry caps to protect the points. Kermit was off all day with Tarlton, and killed a magnificent lioness. In the morning, on some high hills, he obtained a good impala ram, after persevering hours of climbing and running—for only one of the gun-bearers and none of the whites could keep up with him on foot when he went hard. In the afternoon at four he and Tarlton saw the lioness. She was followed by three three-parts grown young lions, doubtless her cubs, and, without any concealment, was walking across the open plain toward a pool by which lay the body of a wildebeest bull she had killed the preceding night. The smaller lions saw the hunters and shrank back, but the old lioness never noticed them until they were within a hundred and fifty yards. Then she ran back, but Kermit crumpled her up with his first bullet. He then put another bullet in her, and as she seemed disabled walked up within fifty yards, and took some photos. By this time she was recovering, and switching her tail she gathered her hind quarters under her for a charge; but he stopped her with another bullet, and killed her outright with a fourth.

We heard that Mearns and Loring, whom we had left ten days before, had also killed a lioness. A Masai brought in word to them that he had marked her down taking her noonday rest near a kongoni she had killed; and they rode out, and Loring shot her. She charged him savagely; he shot her straight through the heart, and she fell literally at his feet. The three naturalists were all good shots, and were used to all the mishaps and adventures of life in the wilderness. Not only would it have been indeed difficult to find three better men for their particular work—Heller's work, for instance, with Cuninghame's help, gave the chief point to our big-game shooting—but it would have been equally difficult to find three better men for any emergency. I could not speak too highly of them; nor indeed of our two other companions, Cuninghame

and Tarlton, whose mastery of their own field was as noteworthy as the pre-eminence of the naturalists in their field.

The following morning the head men asked that we get the
porters some meat; Tarlton, Kermit, and I sallied forth accordingly. The country was very dry, and the game in our
immediate neighborhood was not plentiful and was rather shy.
I killed three kongoni out of a herd, at from 250 to 390 paces;
one topi at 330 paces, and a Roberts's gazelle at 270. Meanwhile the other two had killed a kongoni and five of the big
gazelles; wherever possible the game being hallalled in ortho-
dox fashion by the Mohammedans among our attendants, so
as to fit it for use by their coreligionists among the porters.
Then we saw some giraffes, and galloped them to see if there
was a really big bull in the lot. They had a long start, but
Kermit and Tarlton overtook them after a couple of miles,
while I pounded along in the rear. However, there was no
really good bull, Kermit and Tarlton pulled up, and we jogged
along toward the koppies where two days before I had shot
the lioness. I killed a big bustard, a very handsome, striking-
looking bird, larger than a turkey, by a rather good shot at
230 yards.

It was now midday, and the heat-waves quivered above the
brown plain. The mirage hung in the middle distance, and
beyond it the bold hills rose like mountains from a lake. In
mid-afternoon we stopped at a little pool, to give the men and
horses water; and here Kermit's horse suddenly went dead
lame, and we started it back to camp with a couple of men,
while Kermit went forward with us on foot, as we rode round
the base of the first koppies. After we had gone a mile loud
shouts called our attention to one of the men who had left with
the lame horse. He was running back to tell us that they had
just seen a big maned lion walking along in the open plain toward the body of a zebra he had killed the night before. Immediately Tarlton and I galloped in the direction indicated,
while the heart-broken Kermit ran after us on foot, so as not
to miss the fun; the gun-bearers and saises stringing out behind

him. In a few minutes Tarlton pointed out the lion, a splendid old fellow, a heavy male with a yellow-and-black mane; and after him we went. There was no need to go fast; he was too burly and too savage to run hard, and we were anxious that our hands should be reasonably steady when we shot; all told, the horses, galloping and cantering, did not take us two miles.

The lion stopped and lay down behind a bush; jumping off I took a shot at him at two hundred yards, but only wounded him slightly in one paw; and after a moment's sullen hesitation off he went, lashing his tail. We mounted our horses and went after him; Tarlton lost sight of him, but I marked him lying down behind a low grassy ant-hill. Again we dismounted at a distance of two hundred yards; Tarlton telling me that now he was sure to charge. In all East Africa there is no man, not even Cuninghame himself, whom I would rather have by me than Tarlton, if in difficulties with a charging lion; on this occasion, however, I am glad to say that his rifle was badly sighted, and shot altogether too low.

Again I knelt and fired; but the mass of hair on the lion made me think he was nearer than he was, and I undershot, inflicted a flesh wound that was neither crippling nor fatal. He was already grunting savagely and tossing his tail erect, with his head held low; and at the shot the great sinewy beast came toward us with the speed of a greyhound. Tarlton then, very properly, fired, for lion-hunting is no child's play, and it is not good to run risks. Ordinarily it is a very mean thing to experience joy at a friend's miss; but this was not an ordinary case, and I felt keen delight when the bullet from the badly sighted rifle missed, striking the ground many yards short. I was sighting carefully, from my knee, and I knew I had the lion all right; for though he galloped at a great pace, he came on steadily—ears laid back, and uttering terrific coughing grunts—and there was now no question of making allowance for distance, nor, as he was out in the open, for the fact that he had not before been distinctly visible. The bead of my foresight was exactly on the centre of his chest as I pressed the trigger, and the bullet went as true as if the place had been plotted with dividers. The blow brought him up all standing, and he fell forward on his head. The soft-nosed Winchester bullet had gone straight through the chest cavity, smashing the lungs and the big blood-vessels of the heart. Painfully he recovered his feet, and tried to come on, his ferocious courage holding out to the last; but he staggered, and turned from side to side, unable to stand firmly, still less to advance at a faster pace than a walk. He had not ten seconds to live; but it is a sound principle to take no chances with lions. Tarlton hit him with his second bullet, probably in the shoulder; and with my next shot I broke his neck. I had stopped him when he was still a hundred yards away; and certainly no finer sight could be imagined than that of this great maned lion as he charged. Kermit gleefully joined us as we walked up to the body; only one of our followers had been able to keep up with him on his two miles' run. He had had a fine view of the charge, from one side, as he ran up, still three hundred yards distant; he could see all the muscles play as the lion galloped in, and then everything relax as he fell to the shock of my bullet.

The lion was a big old male, still in his prime. Between uprights his length was nine feet four inches, and his weight 410 pounds, for he was not fat. We skinned him and started for camp, which we reached after dark. There was a thunderstorm in the southwest, and in the red sunset that burned behind us the rain-clouds turned to many gorgeous hues. Then daylight failed, the clouds cleared, and, as we made our way across the formless plain, the half-moon hung high overhead, strange stars shone in the brilliant heavens, and the Southern Cross lay radiant above the sky-line.

Our next camp was pitched on a stony plain, by a winding stream-bed still containing an occasional rush-fringed pool of muddy water, fouled by the herds and flocks of the numerous Masai. Game was plentiful around this camp. We killed what we needed of the common kinds, and in addition each of us killed a big rhino. The two rhinos were almost exactly alike, and their horns were of the so-called "Keitloa" type; the fore horn twenty-two inches long, the rear over seventeen. The day I killed mine I used all three of my rifles. We all went out together, as Kermit was desirous of taking photos of my rhino, if I shot one; he had not been able to get good ones of his on the previous day. We also took the small ox-wagon, so as to bring into camp bodily the rhino—if we got it— and one or two zebras, of which we wanted the flesh for the safari, the skeletons for the museum. The night had been cool, but the day was sunny and hot. At first we rode through a broad valley, bounded by high, scrub-covered hills. The banks of the dry stream were fringed with deep-green acacias, and here and there in relief against their dark foliage flamed the orange-red flowers of the tall aloe slumps. With the Springfield I shot a steinbuck and a lesser bustard. Then we came out on the vast rolling brown plains. With the Winchester I shot two zebra stallions, missing each standing, at long range, and then killing them as they ran; one after a two miles' hard gallop, on my brown pony, which had a good turn of speed. I killed a third zebra stallion with my Springfield, again missing it standing and killing it running. In mid-afternoon we spied our rhino, and getting near saw that it had good horns. It was in the middle of the absolutely bare plain, and we walked straight up to the dull-sighted, dull-witted beast; Kermit with his camera, I with the Holland double-barrel. The tick-birds warned it, but it did not make us out until we were well within a hundred yards, when it trotted toward us, head and tail up. At sixty yards I put the heavy bullet straight into its chest, and knocked it flat with the blow; as it tried to struggle to its feet I again knocked it flat, with the left-hand barrel; but it needed two more bullets before it died, screaming like an engine whistle. Before I fired my last shot I had walked up directly beside the rhino; and just then Tarlton pointed me out a great bustard, stalking along with unmoved composure at a distance of a hundred and fifty yards; I took the Springfield, and kneeling down beside the rhino's hind quarters I knocked over the bustard, and then killed the rhino. We rode into camp by moonilght. Both these rhinos had their stomachs filled with the closely chewed leaves and twig tips of short brush mixed with grass—rather thick-stemmed grass—and in one case with the pulpy, spiny leaves of a low, ground-creeping euphorbia.

At this camp we killed five poisonous snakes: a light-colored tree-snake, two puff-adders, and two seven-foot cobras. One of the latter three times "spat" or ejected its poison at us, the poison coming out from the fangs like white films or threads, to a distance of several feet. A few years ago the singular power of this snake, and perhaps of certain other African species, thus to eject the poison at the face of an assailant was denied by scientists; but it is now well known. Selous had already told me of an instance which came under his own observation; and Tarlton had once been struck in the eyes and for the moment nearly blinded by the poison. He found that to wash the eyes with milk was of much relief. On the bigger puff-adder, some four feet long, were a dozen ticks, some swollen to the size of cherries; apparently they were disregarded by their sluggish and deadly host. Heller trapped some jackals, of two species; and two striped hyenas, the first we had seen; apparently more timid and less noisy beasts than their bigger spotted brothers.

One day Kermit had our first characteristic experience with a honey-bird; a smallish bird, with its beak like a grosbeak's and its toes like a woodpecker's, whose extraordinary habits as a honey-guide are known to all the natives of Africa throughout its range. Kermit had killed an eland bull, and while he was resting, his gun-bearers drew his attention to the calling of the honey-bird in a tree near by. He got up, and as he approached the bird, it flew into another tree in front and again began its twitter. This was repeated again and again as Kermit walked after it. Finally the bird darted round behind his followers, in the direction from which they had come; and for a moment they thought it had played them false. But immediately afterward they saw that it had merely overshot its mark, and had now flown back a few rods to the honey-tree, round which it was flitting, occasionally twittering. When they came toward the tree it perched silent and motionless in another, and thus continued while they took some honey—a risky business, as the bees were vicious. They did not observe what the bird then did; but Cuninghame told me that in one instance where a honey-bird led him to honey he carefully watched it and saw it picking up either bits of honey and comb, or else, more probably, the bee grubs out of the comb, he could not be certain which.

To my mind no more interesting incident occurred at this camp.

IX

TO LAKE NAIVASHA

FROM this camp we turned north toward Lake Naivasha. The Sotik country through which we had hunted was sorely stricken by drought. The grass was short and withered and most of the water-holes were drying up, while both the game and the flocks and herds of the nomad Masai gathered round the watercourses in which there were still occasional muddy pools, and grazed their neighborhood bare of pasturage. It was an unceasing pleasure to watch the ways of the game and to study their varying habits. Where there was a river from which to drink, or where there were many pools, the different kinds of buck, and the zebra, often showed comparatively little timidity about drinking, and came boldly down to the water's edge, sometimes in broad daylight, sometimes in darkness; although even under those conditions they were very cautious if there was cover at the drinking-place. But where the pools were few they never approached one without feeling panic dread of their great enemy the lion, who, they knew well, might be lurking around their drinking-place. At such a pool I once saw a herd of zebras come to water at nightfall. They stood motionless some distance off; then they slowly approached, and twice on false alarms wheeled and fled at speed; at last the leaders ventured to the brink of the pool and at once the whole herd came jostling and crowding in behind them, the water gurgling down their throats; and immediately afterward off they went at a gallop, stopping to graze some hundreds of yards away. The ceaseless dread of the lion felt by all but the heaviest game is amply justified by his ravages among them. They are always in peril from him at the drinking-places; yet in my experience I found that in the great majority of cases they were killed while feeding or resting far from water, the lion getting them far more often by stalking than by lying in wait. A lion will eat a zebra (beginning at the hind quarters, by the way, and sometimes having, and sometimes not having, previously disembowelled the animal), or one of the bigger buck at least once a week—perhaps once every five days. The dozen lions we had killed would probably, if left alive, have accounted for seven or eight hundred buck, pig, and zebra within the next year. Our hunting was a net advantage to the harmless game.

The zebras were the noisiest of the game. After them came the wildebeest, which often uttered their queer grunt; sometimes a herd would stand and grunt at me for some minutes as I passed, a few hundred yards distant. The togi uttered only a kind of sneeze, and the hartbeest a somewhat similar sound. The so-called Roberts's gazelle was merely the Grant's gazelle of the Athi, with the lyrate shape of the horns tending to be carried to an extreme of spread and backward bend. The tommy bucks carried good horns; the horns of the does were usually aborted, and were never more than four or five inches long. The most notable feature about the tommies was the incessant switching of their tails, as if jerked by electricity. In the Sotik the togis all seemed to have calves of about the same age, as if born from four to six months earlier; the young of the other game were of every age. The males of all the antelope fought much among themselves. The gazelle bucks of both species would face one another, their heads between the fore legs and the horns level on the ground, and each would punch his opponent until the hair flew.

Watching the game, one was struck by the intensity and the evanescence of their emotions. Civilized man now usually passes his life under conditions which eliminate the intensity of terror felt by his ancestors when death by violence was their normal end, and threatened them during every hour of the day and night. It is only in nightmares that the average dweller in civilized countries now undergoes the hideous horror which was the regular and frequent portion of his ages-vanished forefathers, and which is still an every-day incident in the lives of most wild creatures. But the dread is short-lived, and its horror vanishes with instantaneous rapidity. In these wilds the game dreaded the lion and the other flesh-eating beasts rather than man. We saw innumerable kills of all the buck, and of zebra, the neck being usually dislocated, and it being evident that none of the lion's victims, not even the truculent wildebeest or huge eland, had been able to make any fight against him. The game is ever on the alert against this greatest of foes, and every herd, almost every individual, is in imminent and deadly peril every few days or nights, and of course suffers in addition from countless false alarms. But no sooner is the danger over than the animals resume their feeding, or love-making, or their fighting among themselves. Two bucks will do battle the minute the herd has stopped running from the foe that has seized one of its number, and a buck will cover a doe in the brief interval between the first and second alarm, from hunter or lion. Zebra will make much noise when one of their number has been killed; but their fright has vanished when once they begin their barking calls.

Death by violence, death by cold, death by starvation— these are the normal endings of the stately and beautiful creatures of the wilderness. The sentimentalists who prattle about the peaceful life of nature do not realize its utter mercilessness; although all they would have to do would be to look at the birds in the winter woods, or even at the insects on a cold morning or cold evening. Life is hard and cruel for all the lower creatures, and for man also in what the sentimentalists call a "state of nature." The savage of today shows us what the fancied age of gold of our ancestors was really like; it was an age when hunger, cold, violence, and iron cruelty were the ordinary accompaniments of life. If Matthew Arnold, when he expressed the wish to know the thoughts of Earth's "vigor-

ous, primitive" tribes of the past, had really desired an answer
to his question, he would have done well to visit the homes of
the existing representatives of his "vigorous, primitive" ancestors, and to watch them feasting on blood and guts; while
as for the "pellucid and pure" feelings of his imaginary primitive maiden, they were those of any meek, cow-like creature
who accepted marriage by purchase or of convenence, as a
matter of course.

It was to me a perpetual source of wonderment to notice
the difference in the behavior of different individuals of the
same species, and in the behavior of the same individual at
different times; as, for example, in the matter of wariness,
of the times for going to water, of the times for resting, and,
as regards dangerous game, in the matter of ferocity. Their
very looks changed. At one moment the sun would turn the
zebras of a mixed herd white, and the hartbeest straw-colored,
so that the former could be seen much farther off than the
latter; and again the conditions would be reversed when under
the light the zebras would show up gray, and the hartbeest
as red as foxes.

I had now killed almost all the specimens of the common
game that the museum needed. However, we kept the skin
or skeleton of whatever we shot for meat. Now and then,
after a good stalk I would get a boar with unusually fine tusks,
a big gazelle with unusually long and graceful horns, or a fine
old wildebeest bull, its horns thick and battered, its knees bare
and calloused from its habit of going down on them when
fighting or threatening fight.

On our march northward, we first made a long day's journey to what was called a salt marsh. An hour or two after
starting we had a characteristic experience with a rhino. It
was a bull, with poor horns, standing in a plain which was
dotted by a few straggling thorn-trees and wild olives. The
safari's course would have taken it to windward of the rhino,
which then might have charged in sheer irritable bewilderment;
so we turned off at right angles. The long line of porters

passed him two hundred yards away, while we gunmen stood between with our rifles ready; except Kermit, who was busy taking photos. The rhino saw us, but apparently indistinctly. He made little dashes to and fro, and finally stood looking at us, with his big ears cocked forward; but he did nothing more, and we left him standing, plunged in meditation—probably it would be more accurate to say, thinking of absolutely nothing, as if he had been a huge turtle. After leaving him we also passed by files of zebra and topi who gazed at us, intent and curious, within two hundred yards, until we had gone by and the danger was over; whereupon they fled in fright.

The so-called salt marsh consisted of a dry water-course, with here and there a deep muddy pool. The ground was impregnated with some saline substance, and the game licked it, as well as coming to water. Our camp was near two reedy pools, in which there were big yellow-billed ducks, while queer brown herons, the hammerhead, had built big nests of sticks in the tall acacias. Bush-cuckoos gurgled in the underbrush by night and day. Brilliant rollers flitted through the trees. There was much sweet bird music in the morning. Funny little elephant-shrews with long snouts, and pretty zebra-mice, evidently of diurnal habit, scampered among the bushes or scuttled into their burrows. Tiny dikdiks, antelopes no bigger than hares, with swollen muzzles, and their little horns half hidden by tufts of hair, ran like rabbits through the grass; the females were at least as large as the males. Another seven-foot cobra was killed. There were brilliant masses of red aloe flowers, and of yellow-blossomed vines. Around the pools the ground was bare, and the game trails leading to the water were deeply rutted by the hoofs of the wild creatures that had travelled them for countless generations.

The day after reaching this camp, Cuninghame and I hunted on the plains. Before noon we made out with our glasses two rhinos lying down, a mile off. As usual with these sluggish creatures we made our preparations in leisurely style, and with scant regard to the animal itself. Moreover we did not intend to kill any rhino unless its horns were out of the common. I first stalked and shot a buck Roberts's gazelle with a good head. Then we offsaddled the horses and sat down to lunch under a huge thorn-tree, which stood by itself, lonely and beautiful, and offered a shelter from the blazing sun. The game was grazing on every side; and I kept thinking of all the life of the wilderness, and of its many tragedies, which the great tree must have witnessed during the centuries since it was a seedling.

Lunch over, I looked to the loading of the heavy rifle, and we started toward the rhinos, well to leeward. But the wind shifted every which way; and suddenly my gun-bearers called my attention to the rhinos, a quarter of a mile off, saying: "He charging, he charging." Sure enough, they had caught our wind, and were rushing toward us. I jumped off the horse and studied the oncoming beasts through my field glass; but head on it was hard to tell about the horns. However, the wind shifted again, and when two hundred yards off they lost our scent, and turned to one side, tails in the air, heads tossing, evidently much wrought up. They were a large cow and a young heifer, nearly two-thirds grown. As they trotted sideways I could see the cow's horns, and her doom was sealed; for they were of good length, and the hind one (it proved to be two feet long) was slightly longer than the stouter front one; it was a specimen which the museum needed.

So after them we trudged over the brown plain. But they were uneasy, and kept trotting and walking. They never saw us with their dull eyes; but a herd of wildebeest galloping by renewed their alarm; it was curious to see them sweeping the ground with their long, ugly heads, endeavoring to catch the scent. A mile's rapid walk brought us within two hundred yards, and we dared not risk the effort for a closer approach lest they should break and run. The cow turned broadside to, and I hit her behind the shoulder; but I was not familiar with the heavy Holland rifle at that range, and my bullet went rather low. I think the wound would eventually have proved fatal; but both beasts went off at a gallop, the cow now and then turning from side to side in high dudgeon, trying to catch the wind of her foe. We mounted our horses, and after a couple of miles' canter overhauled our quarry. Cuninghame took me well to leeward, and ahead, of the rhinos, which never saw us; and then we walked to within a hundred yards, and I killed the cow. But we were now much puzzled by the young one, which refused to leave; we did not wish to kill it, for it was big enough to shift for itself; but it was also big enough to kill either of us. We drew back, hoping it would go away; but it did not. So when the gunbearers arrived we advanced and tried to frighten it; but this plan also failed. It threatened to charge, but could not quite make up its mind. Watching my chance I then creased its stern with a bullet from the little Springfield, and after some wild circular galloping it finally decided to leave.

Kermit, about this time, killed a heavy boar from horseback after a three miles' run. The boar charged twice, causing the horse to buck and shy. Finally, just as he was going into his burrow backward, Kermit raced by and shot him, firing his rifle from the saddle after the manner of the old-time Western buffalo-runners.

We now rejoined Mearns and Loring on the banks of the Guaso Nyero. They had collected hundreds of birds and small mammals, among them several new species. We had already heard that a Mr. Williams, whom we had met at McMillan's ranch, had been rather badly mauled by a lion, which he had mortally wounded, but which managed to charge home. Now we found that Doctor Mearns had been quite busily engaged in attending to cases of men who were hurt by lions. Loring nearly got in the category. He killed his lioness with a light automatic rifle, utterly unfit for use against African game. Though he actually put a bullet right through the beast's heart, the shock from the blow was so slight that she was not stopped even for a second; he hit her four times

in all, each shot being mortal—for he was an excellent marks-
man—and she died nearly at his feet, her charge carrying her
several yards by him.   Mearns had galloped into a herd of
wildebeest and killed the big bull of the herd, after first running clean through a mob of zebras, which, as he passed,
skinned their long yellow teeth threateningly at him, but made
no attempt actually to attack him.

A settler had come down to trade with the Masai during
our absence.   He ran into a large party of lions, killed two,
and wounded a lioness which escaped after mauling one of
his gun-bearers.   The gun-bearer rode into camp, and the
doctor treated his wounds.   Next day Mearns was summoned
to a Masai kraal sixteen miles off to treat the wounds of two
of the Masai; it appeared that a body of them had followed
and killed the wounded lioness, but that two of their number
had been much maltreated in the fight.   One, especially, had
been fearfully bitten, the lioness having pulled the flesh loose
from the bones with her fixed teeth.   The doctor attended to
all three cases.   The gun-bearer recovered; both the Masai
died, although the doctor did all in his power for the two gal-
lant fellows.   Their deaths did not hinder the Masai from
sending to him all kinds of cases in which men or boys had
met with accidents.   He attended to them all, and gained a
high reputation with the tribe; when the case was serious the
patient's kinsfolk would present him with a sheep or war-
spear, or something else of value.   He took a great fancy to
the Masai, as indeed all of us did.   They are a fine, manly set
of savages, bold and independent in their bearing.   They never
eat vegetables; subsisting exclusively on milk, blood, and flesh;
and are remarkably hardy and enduring.

Kermit found a cave which had recently been the abode of
a party of 'Ndorobo, the wild hunter-savages of the wilderness,
who are more primitive in their ways of life than any other
tribes of this region.   They live on honey and the flesh of
the wild beasts they kill; they are naked, with few and rude
arms and utensils; and, in short, carry on existence as our own

ancestors did at a very early period of paleolithic time. Around this cave were many bones. Within it were beds of grass, and a small roofed enclosure of thorn-bushes for the dogs. Fire-sticks had been left on the walls, to be ready when the owners' wanderings again brought them back to the cave; and also very curious soup-sticks, each a rod with one of the vertebræ of some animal stuck on the end, designed for use in stirring their boiled meat.

From our camp on the Guaso Nyero we trekked in a little over four days to a point on Lake Naivasha where we intended to spend some time. The first two days were easy travelling, the porters not being pressed and there being plenty of time in the afternoons to pitch camp comfortably; then the wagons left us with their loads of hides and skeletons and spare baggage. The third day we rose long before dawn, breakfasted, broke camp, and were off just at sunrise. There was no path; at one time we followed game trails, at another the trails made by the Masai sheep and catle, and again we might make our own trail. We had two Masai guides, tireless runners, as graceful and sinewy as panthers; they helped us; but Cuninghame had to do most of the pathfinding himself. It was a difficult country, passable only at certain points, which it was hard to place with exactness. We had seen that each porter had his water-bottle full before starting; but, though willing, good-humored fellows, strong as bulls, in forethought they are of the grass-hopper type; and all but a few exhausted their supply by mid-afternoon. At this time we were among bold mountain ridges, and here we struck the kraal of some Masai, who watered their cattle at some spring pools, three miles to one side, up a valley. It was too far for the heavily laden porters; but we cantered our horses thither and let them drink their fill; and then cantered along the trail left by the safari until we overtook the rear men just as they were going over the brink of the Mau escarpment. The scenery was wild and beautiful; in the open places the ground was starred with flowers of many colors;

we rode under vine-tangled archways through forests of strange trees.

Down the steep mountainside went the safari, and at its foot struck off nearly parallel to the high ridge. On our left the tree-clad mountainside hung above us; ravines, with mimosa clustering in them, sundered the foot-hills, and wound until they joined into what looked like rivers; the thick grass grew waist-high. It looked like a well-watered country; but it was of porous, volcanic nature, and the soil was a sieve. After nightfall we came to where we hoped to find water; but there was not a drop in the dried pools; and we had to make a water-less camp. A drizzling rain had set in, enough to wet every-thing, but not enough to give any water for drinking. It was eight o'clock before the last of the weary, thirsty burden-car-riers stumbled through the black, boulder-strewn ravine on, whose farther side we were camped, and threw down his load among his fellows, who were already clustered around the little fires they had started in the tall grass. We slept as we were, and comfortably enough; indeed, there was no hardship for us white men, with our heavy overcoats, and our food and water —which we shared with our personal attendants; but I was uneasy for the porters, as there was another long and ex-hausting day's march ahead. Before sunrise we started; and four hours later, in the bottom of a deep ravine, Cuninghame found a pool of green water in a scooped-out cavity in the rock. It was a pleasant sight to see the thirsty porters drink. Then they sat down, built fires and boiled their food; and went on in good heart.

Two or three times we crossed singularly beautiful ravines, the trail winding through narrow clefts that were almost tunnels, and along the brinks of sheer cliffs, while the green mat of trees and vines was spangled with many colored flowers. Then we came to barren ridges and bare, dusty plains; and at nightfall pitched camp near the shores of Lake Naivasha. It is a lovely sheet of water, surrounded by hills and mountains, the shores broken by rocky promontories, and indented by papyrus-fringed bays. Next morning we shifted camp four miles to a place on the farm, and near the house, of the Messrs. Attenborough, settlers on the shores of the lake, who treated us with the most generous courtesy and hospitality—as, indeed, did all the settlers we met. They were two brothers; one had lived twenty years on the Pacific coast, mining in the Sierras; and the other had just retired from the British navy, with the rank of commander; they were able to turn their hands to anything, and were just the men for work in a new country—for a new country is a poor place for the weak and incompetent, whether of body or mind. They had a steam-launch and a big heavy rowboat, and they most kindly and generously put both at our disposal for hippo-hunting.

At this camp I presented the porters with twenty-five sheep, as a recognition of their good conduct and hard work; whereupon they improvised long chants in my honor, and feasted royally.

We spent one entire day with the rowboat in a series of lagoons near camp, which marked an inlet of the lake. We did not get any hippo, but it was a most interesting day. A broad belt of papyrus fringed the lagoons and jutted out between them. The straight green stalks with their feathery heads rose high and close, forming a mass so dense that it was practically impenetrable save where the huge bulk of the hippos had made tunnels. Indeed, even for the hippos it was not readily penetrable. The green monotony of a papyrus swamp becomes wearisome after a while; yet it is very beautiful, for each reed is tall, slender, graceful, with its pale flowering crown; and they are typical of the tropics, and their mere sight suggests a vertical sun and hot, steaming swamps, where great marsh beasts feed and wallow and bellow, amidst a teeming reptilian life. A fringe of papyrus here and there adds much to the beauty of a lake, and also to the beauty of the river pools, where clumps of them grow under the shade of the vine-tangled tropical trees.

The open waters of the lagoons were covered with water-

lilies, bearing purple or sometimes pink flowers. Across the
broad lily-pads ran the curious "lily-trotters," or jacanas,
richly colored birds, with toes so long and slender that the
lily-pads support them without sinking. They were not shy,
and their varied coloring—a bright chestnut being the most
conspicuous hue—and singular habits made them very conspicuous. There was a wealth of bird life in the lagoons. Small
gulls, somewhat like our black-headed gull, but with their
hoods gray, flew screaming around us. Black and white kingfishers, tiny, red-billed kingfishers, with colors so brilliant
that they flashed like jewels in the sun, and brilliant green bee-
eaters with chestnut breasts perched among the reeds. Spur-
winged plover clamored as they circled overhead near the edges
of the water. Little rills and red-legged water-hens threaded
the edges of the papyrus, and grebes dived in the open water.
A giant heron, the Goliath, flew up at our approach; and
there were many smaller herons and egrets, white or parti-
colored. There were small, dark cormorants, and larger ones
with white throats; and African ruddy ducks, and teal and big
yellow-billed ducks, somewhat like mallards. Among the
many kinds of ducks was one which made a whistling noise
with its wings as it flew. Most plentiful of all were the
coots, much resembling our common baldpate coot, but
with a pair of horns or papillæ at the hinder end of the bare
frontal space.

There were a number of hippo in these lagoons. One afternoon after four o'clock I saw two standing half out of water
in a shallow, eating the water-lilies. They seemed to spend
the fore part of the day sleeping or resting in the papyrus
or near its edge; toward evening they splashed and waded
among the water-lilies, tearing them up with their huge jaws;
and during the night they came ashore to feed on the grass
and land plants. In consequence those killed during the day,
until the late afternoon, had their stomachs filled, not with
water-plants but with grasses which they must have obtained
in their night journeys on dry land. At night I heard the

bulls bellowing and roaring. They fight savagely among themselves, and, where they are not molested, and the natives are timid, they not only do great damage to the gardens and crops, trampling them down and shovelling basketfuls into their huge mouths, but also become dangerous to human beings, attacking boats or canoes in a spirit of wanton and ferocious mischief. At this place, a few weeks before our arrival, a young bull, badly scarred, and evidently having been mishandled by some bigger bull, came ashore in the daytime and actually attacked the cattle, and was promptly shot in consequence. They are astonishingly quick in their movements for such shapeless-looking, short-legged things. Of course they cannot swim in deep water with anything like the speed of the real swimming mammals, nor move on shore with the agility and speed of the true denizens of the land; nevertheless, by sheer muscular power and in spite of their shape, they move at an unexpected rate of speed both on dry land and in deep water; and in shallow water, their true home, they gallop very fast on the bottom, under water. Ordinarily only their heads can be seen, and they must be shot in the brain. If they are found in a pool with little cover, and if the shots can be taken close by, from firm ground, there is no sport whatever in killing them. But the brain is small and the skull huge, and if they are any distance off, and especially if the shot has to be taken from an unsteady boat, there is ample opportunity to miss.

On the day we spent with the big rowboat in the lagoons both Kermit and I had shots; each of us hit but neither of us got his game. My shot was at the head of a hippo facing me in a bay about a hundred yards off, so that I had to try to shoot very low between the eyes; the water was smooth, and I braced my legs well and fired offhand. I hit him, but was confident that I had missed the brain, for he lifted slightly, and then went under, nose last; and when a hippo is shot in the brain the head usually goes under nose first. An exasperating feature of hippo shooting is that, save in exceptional circumstances, where the water is very shallow, the animal sinks at once when killed outright, and does not float for one or two or three hours; so that one has to wait that length of time before finding out whether the game has or has not been bagged. On this occasion we never saw a sign of the animal after I fired, and as it seemed impossible that in that situation the hippo could get off unobserved, my companions thought I had killed him; I thought not, and unfortunately my judgment proved to be correct.

Another day, in the launch, I did much the same thing. Again the hippo was a long distance off, only his head appearing, but unfortunately not in profile, much the best position for a shot; again I hit him; again he sank and, look as hard as we could, not a sign of him appeared, so that every one was sure he was dead; and again no body ever floated. But on this day Kermit got his hippo. He hit it first in the head, merely a flesh wound; but the startled creature then rose high in the water and he shot it in the lungs. It now found difficulty in staying under, and continually rose to the surface with a plunge like a porpoise, going as fast as it could toward the papyrus. After it we went, full speed, for once in the papyrus we could not have followed it; and Kermit finally killed it, just before it reached the edge of the swamp, and, luckily, where the water was so shallow that we did not have to wait for it to float, but fastened a rope to two of its turtle-like legs, and towed it back forthwith.

There were otters in the lake. One day we saw two playing together near the shore; and at first we were all of us ceratin that it was some big water-snake. It was not until we were very close that we made out the supposed one big snake to be two otters; it was rather interesting, as giving one of the explanations of the stories that always appear about large water-snakes, or similar monsters, existing in almost every lake of any size in a wild country. On another day I shot another near shore; he turned over and over, splashing and tumbling; but just as we were about to grasp him, he partially recovered and dived to safety in the reeds.

On the second day we went out in the launch I got my hippo. We steamed down the lake, not far from the shore, for over ten miles, dragging the big, clumsy rowboat, in which Cuninghame had put three of our porters who knew how to row. Then we spied a big hippo walking entirely out of the water on the edge of the papyrus, at the farther end of a little bay which was filled with water-lilies. Thither we steamed, and when a few rods from the bay, Cuninghame steered, Kermit carried his camera, and I steadied myself in the bow with the little Springfield rifle. The hippo was a self-confident, truculent beast; it went under water once or twice, but again came out to the papyrus and waded along the edge, its body out of water. We headed toward it, and thrust the boat in among the water-lilies, finding that the bay was shallow, from three to six feet deep. While still over a hundred yards from the hippo, I saw it turn as if to break into the papyrus, and at once fired into its shoulder, the tiny pointed bullet smashing the big bones. Round spun the great beast, plunged into the water, and with its huge jaws open came straight for the boat, floundering and splashing through the thick-growing water-lilies. I think that its chief object was to get to deep water; but we were between it and the deep water, and instead of trying to pass to one side it charged straight for the boat, with open jaws, bent on mischief. But I hit it again and again with the little sharp-pointed bullet. Once I struck it between the neck and shoulder; once, as it rushed forward with its huge jaws stretched to their threatening utmost, I fired right between them, whereat it closed them with the clash of a sprung bear trap; and then, when under the punishment it swerved for a moment, I hit it at the base of the ear, a brain shot which dropped it in its tracks. Meanwhile Kermit was busily taking photos of it as it charged, and, as he mentioned afterward, until it was dead he never saw it except in the "finder" of his camera. The water was so shallow where

I had killed the hippo that its body projected slightly above the surface. It was the hardest kind of work getting it out from among the water-lilies; then we towed it to camp behind the launch.

The engineer of the launch was an Indian Moslem. The fireman and the steersman were two half-naked and much-ornamented Kikuyus. The fireman wore a blue-bead chain on one ankle, a brass armlet on the opposite arm, a belt of short steel chains, a dingy blanket (no loin-cloth), and a skull cap surmounted by a plume of ostrich feathers. The two Kikuyus were unconsciously entertaining companions. Without any warning they would suddenly start a song or chant, usually an impromptu recitative of whatever at the moment interested them. They chanted for half an hour over the feat of the "B'wana Makuba" (great master or chief, my name) in killing the hippo; laying especial stress upon the quantity of excellent meat it would furnish, and how very good the eating would be. Usually, one would improvise the chant, and the other join in the chorus. Sometimes they would solemnly sing complimentary songs to one another, each in turn chanting the manifold good qualities of his companion.

Around this camp were many birds. The most noteworthy was a handsome gray eagle-owl, bigger than our great horned owl, to which it is closely akin. It did not hoot or scream, its voice being a kind of grunt, followed in a second or two by a succession of similar sounds, uttered more quickly and in a lower tone. These big owls frequently came round camp after dark, and at first their notes completely puzzled me, as I thought they must be made by some beast. The bulbuls sang well. Most of the birds were in no way like our home birds.

Loring trapped quantities of mice and rats, and it was curious to see how many of them had acquired characters which caused them superficially to resemble American animals with which they had no real kinship. The sand-rats that burrowed in the dry plains were in shape, in color, eyes, tail, and paws strikingly like our pocket-gophers, which have similar habits. So the long-tailed gerbilles, or gerbille-like rats, resembled our kangaroo-rats; and there was a blunt-nosed, stubby-tailed little rat superficially hardly to be told from our rice-rat. But the most characteristic rodent, the big long-tailed, jumping springhaas, resembled nothing of ours; and there were tree-rats and spiny mice. There were gray monkeys in the trees around camp, which the naturalists shot.

Heller trapped various beasts; beautifully marked genets, and a big white-tailed mongoose which was very savage. But his most remarkable catch was a leopard. He had set a steel trap, fastened to a loose thorn-branch, for mongoose, civets, or jackals; it was a No. 2 Blake, such as in America we use for coons, skunks, foxes, and perhaps bobcats and coyotes. In the morning he found it gone, and followed the trail of the thorn-branch until it led into a dense thicket, from which issued an ominous growl. His native boy shouted "simba"; but it was a leopard, not a lion. He could not see into the thicket; so he sent back to camp for his rifle, and when it came he climbed a tree and endeavored to catch a glimpse of the animal. He could see nothing, however; and finally fired into the thicket rather at random. The answer was a furious growl, and the leopard charged out to the foot of the tree, much hampered by the big thorn-branch. He put a bullet into it, and back it went, only to come out and to receive another bullet; and he killed it. It was an old male, in good condition, weighing one hundred and twenty-six pounds. The trap was not big enough to contain his whole paw, and he had been caught firmly by one toe. The thorn-bush acted as a drag, which prevented him from going far, and yet always yielded somewhat when he pulled. A bear thus caught would have chewed up the trap or else pulled his foot loose, even at the cost of sacrificing the toe; but the cats are more sensitive to pain. This leopard was smaller than any full-grown male cougar I have ever killed, and yet cougars often kill game rather heavier than leopards usually venture upon; yet very few

cougars indeed would show anything like the pluck and ferocity shown by this leopard, and characteristic of its kind.

Kermit killed a water-buck of a kind new to us, the singsing. He also killed two porcupines and two baboons. The
porcupines are terrestrial animals, living in burrows to which
they keep during the daytime. They are much heavier than,
and in all their ways totally different from, our sluggish tree-
porcupines. The baboons are numerous around this camp,
living both among the rocks and in the tree-tops. They are
hideous creatures. They ravage the crops and tear open new-
born lambs to get at the milk inside them; and where the
natives are timid and unable to harm them, they become wantonly savage and aggressive and attack and even kill women
and children. In Uganda, Cuninghame had once been asked
by a native chief to come to his village and shoot the baboons,
as they had just killed two women, badly bitten several children, and caused such a reign of terror that the village would
be abandoned if they were not killed or intimidated. He himself saw the torn and mutilated bodies of the dead women;
and he stayed in the village a week, shooting so many baboons
that the remainder were thoroughly cowed. Baboons and
boars are the most formidable of all foes to the dogs that
hunt them—just as leopards are of all wild animals those
most apt to prey on dogs. A baboon's teeth and hands are
far more formidable weapons than those of any dog, and
only a very few wholly exceptional dogs of huge size, and great
courage and intelligence, can, single-handed, contend with an
old male. But we saw a settler whose three big terriers could
themselves kill a full-grown wart-hog boar; an almost unheard-
of feat. They backed up one another with equal courage and
adroitness, their aim being for two to seize the hind legs;
then the third, watching his chance, would get one foreleg,
when the bull was speedily thrown, and when weakened, killed
by bites in his stomach.

Hitherto we had not obtained a bull hippo, and I made up
my mind to devote myself to getting one, as otherwise the

group for the museum would be incomplete. Save in exceptional cases I do not think hippo-hunting, after the first one has been obtained, a very attractive sport, because usually one has to wait an hour before it is possible to tell whether or not a shot has been successful, and also because, a portion of the head being all that is usually visible, it is exceedingly difficult to say whether the animal seen is a bull or a cow. As the time allowed for a shot is very short, and any hesitation probably insures the animal's escape, this means that two or three hippo may be killed, quite unavoidably, before the right specimen is secured. Still there may be interesting and exciting incidents in a hippo-hunt. Cuninghame, the two Attenboroughs, and I started early in the launch, towing the big, clumsy rowboat, with as crew three of our porters who could row. We steamed down the lake some fifteen miles to a wide bay, indented by smaller bays, lagoons, and inlets, all fringed by a broad belt of impenetrable papyrus, while the beautiful purple lilies, with their leathery-tough stems and broad surface-floating leaves, filled the shallows. At the mouth of the main bay we passed a floating island, a mass of papyrus perhaps a hundred and fifty acres in extent which had been broken off from the shore somewhere, and was floating over the lake as the winds happened to drive it.

In an opening in the dense papyrus masses we left the launch moored, and Cuninghame and I started in the rowboat to coast the green wall of tall, thick-growing, feather-topped reeds. Under the bright sunshine the shallow flats were alive with bird life. Gulls, both the gray-hooded and the black-backed, screamed harshly overhead. The chestnut-colored lily-trotters tripped daintily over the lily-pads, and when they flew, had their long legs straight behind them, so that they looked as if they had tails like pheasants. Sacred ibis, white with naked black head and neck, stalked along the edge of the water, and on the bent papyrus small cormorants and herons perched. Everywhere there were coots and ducks, and crested grebes, big and little. Huge white pelicans floated on the water.

Once we saw a string of flamingoes fly by, their plumage a wonderful red.

Immediately after leaving the launch we heard a hippo, hidden in the green fastness on our right, uttering a meditative soliloquy, consisting of a succession of squealing grunts. Then we turned a point, and in a little bay saw six or eight hippo, floating with their heads above water. There were two much bigger than the others, and Cuninghame, while of course unable to be certain, thought these were probably males. The smaller ones, including a cow and her calf, were not much alarmed, and floated quietly, looking at us, as we cautiously paddled and drifted nearer; but the bigger ones dove and began to work their way past us toward deep water. We could trace their course by the twisting of the lily-pads. Motionless the rowers lay on their oars; the line of moving lily-pads showed that one of the big hippo was about to pass the boat; suddenly the waters opened close at hand and a monstrous head appeared. "Shoot," said Cuninghame; and I fired into the back of the head just as it disappeared. It sank out of sight without a splash, almost without a ripple, the lily-pads ceased twisting; a few bubbles of air rose to the surface; evidently the hippo lay dead underneath. Poling to the spot, we at once felt the huge body with our oar-blades. But, alas, when the launch came round, and we raised the body, it proved to be that of a big cow.

So I left Cuninghame to cut off the head for the museum, and started off by myself in the boat with two rowers, neither of whom spoke a word of English. For an hour we saw only the teeming bird life. Then, in a broad, shallow lagoon, we made out a dozen hippo, two or three very big. Cautiously we approached them, and when seventy yards off I fired at the base of the ear of one of the largest. Down went every head, and utter calm succeeded. I had marked the spot where the one at which I shot had disappeared, and thither we rowed. When we reached the place, I told one of the rowers to thrust a pole down and see if he could touch the dead body. He thrust accordingly, and at once shouted that he had found the hippo; in another moment his face altered, and he shouted much more loudly that the hippo was alive. Sure enough, bump went the hippo against the bottom of the boat, the jar causing us all to sit suddenly down—for we were standing. Another bump showed that we had again been struck; and the shallow, muddy water boiled, as the huge beasts, above and below the surface, scattered every which way. Their eyes starting, the two rowers began to back water out of the dangerous neighborhood, while I shot at an animal whose head appeared to my left, as it made off with frantic haste; for I took it for granted that the hippo at which I had first fired (and which was really dead) had escaped. This one disappeared as usual, and I had not the slightest idea whether or not I had killed it. I had small opportunity to ponder the subject, for twenty feet away the water bubbled and a huge head shot out facing me, the jaws wide open. There was no time to guess at its intentions, and I fired on the instant. Down went the head, and I felt the boat quiver as the hippo passed underneath. Just here the lily-pads were thick; so I marked its course, fired as it rose, and down it went. But on the other quarter of the boat a beast, evidently of great size— it proved to be a big bull—now appeared, well above water; and I put a bullet into its brain.

I did not wish to shoot again unless I had to, and stood motionless, with the little Springfield at the ready. A head burst up twenty yards off, with a lily-pad plastered over one eye, giving the hippo an absurd resemblance to a discomfited prize-fighter, and then disappeared with great agitation. Two half-grown beasts stupid from fright appeared, and stayed up for a minute or two at a time, not knowing what to do. Other heads popped up, getting farther and farther away. By degrees everything vanished, the water grew calm, and we rowed over to the papyrus, moored ourselves by catching hold of a couple of stems, and awaited events. Within an hour four dead hippos appeared: a very big bull and three big cows. Of course I would not have shot the latter if it could have been avoided; but under the circumstances I do not see how it was possible to help it. The meat was not wasted; on the contrary, it was a godsend, not only to our own porters, but to the natives round about, many of whom were on short commons on account of the drought.

Bringing over the launch, we worked until after dark to get the bull out of the difficult position in which he lay. It was nearly seven o'clock before we had him fixed for towing on one quarter, the rowboat towing on the other, by which time two hippos were snorting and blowing within a very few yards of us, their curiosity much excited as to what was going on. The night was overcast; there were drenching rainsqualls, and a rather heavy sea was running, and I did not get back to camp until after three. Next day the launch fetched in the rest of the hippo meat.

From this camp we went into Naivasha, on the line of the railway. In many places the road was beautiful, leading among the huge yellow trunks of giant thorn-trees, the ground rising sheer on our left as we cantered along the edge of the lake. We passed impala, tommies, zebra, and wart-hog; and in one place saw three water-buck cows feeding just outside the papyrus at high noon. They belonged to a herd that lived in the papyrus and fed on the grassy flats outside; and their feeding in the open exactly at noon was another proof of the fact that the custom of feeding in the early morning and late evening is with most game entirely artificial and the result of fear of man. Birds abounded. Parties of dark-colored ant-eating wheatear sang sweetly from trees and bushes, and even from the roofs of the settlers' houses. The tricolored starlings— black, white, and chestnut—sang in the air, as well as when perched on twigs. Stopping at the government farm (which is most interesting; the results obtained in improving the native sheep, goats, and cattle by the use of imported thoroughbred bulls and rams have been astonishingly successful) we saw the little long-tailed, red-billed, black-and-white whydahs flitting around the outbuildings as familiarly as sparrows. Water-birds of all kinds thronged the meadows bordering the papyrus, and swam and waded among the water-lilies; sacred ibis, herons, beautiful white spoonbills, darters, cormorants, Egyptian geese, ducks, coots, and water-hens. I got up within rifle range of a flock of the queer ibis stork, black-and-white birds with curved yellow bills, naked red faces, and wonderful purple tints on the edges and the insides of the wings; with the little Springfield I shot one on the ground and another on the wing, after the flock had risen.

That night Kermit and Doctor Mearns went out with lanterns and shotguns, and each killed one of the springhaas, the jumping hares, which abounded in the neighborhood. These big, burrowing animals, which progress by jumping like kangaroos, are strictly nocturnal, and their eyes shine in the glare of the lanterns.

Next day I took the Fox gun, which had already on ducks, guinea-fowl, and francolin shown itself an exceptionally hard-hitting and close-shooting weapon, and collected various water-birds for the naturalists; among others, a couple of Egyptian geese. I also shot a white pelican with the Springfield rifle; there was a beautiful rosy flush on the breast.

Here we again got news of the outside world. While on safari the only newspaper which any of us ever saw was the *Owego Gazette,* which Loring, in a fine spirit of neighborhood loyalty, always had sent to him in his mail. To the doctor, by the way, I had become knit in a bond of close intellectual sympathy ever since a chance allusion to "William Henry's Letters to His Grandmother" had disclosed the face that each of us, ever since the days of his youth, had preserved the bound volumes of *Our Young Folks,* and moreover firmly believed that there never had been its equal as a magazine, whether for old or young; even though the Plancus of our golden consulship was the not wholly happy Andrew Johnson.

CHAPTER X

ELEPHANT-HUNTING ON MOUNT KENIA

ON July 24, in order to ship our fresh accumulations of specimens and trophies, we once more went into Nairobi. It was a pleasure again to see its tree-bordered streets and charming houses bowered in vines and bushes, and to meet once more the men and women who dwelt in the houses. I wish it were in my power to thank individually the members of the many East African households of which I shall always cherish warm memories of friendship and regard.

At Nairobi I saw Selous, who had just returned from a two months' safari with McMillan, Williams, and Judd. Their experience shows how large the element of luck is in lion-hunting. Selous was particularly anxious to kill a good lion; there is nowhere to be found a more skilful or more hard-working hunter; yet he never even got a shot. Williams, on the other hand, came across three. Two he killed easily. The third charged him. He was carrying a double-barrelled 450, but failed to stop the beast; it seized him by the leg, and his life was saved by his Swahili gun-bearer, who gave the lion a fatal shot as it stood over him He came within an ace of dying; but when I saw him, at the hospital, he was well on the road to recovery. One day Selous while on horseback saw a couple of lionesses, and galloped after them, followed by Judd, seventy or eighty yards behind. One lioness stopped and crouched under a bush, let Selous pass, and then charged Judd. She was right alongside him, and he fired from the hip; the bullet went into her eye; his horse jumped and swerved at the shot, throwing him off, and he found himself sitting on the ground, not three yards from the dead lioness. Nothing more was seen of the other.

Continually I met men with experiences in their past lives which showed how close the country was to those primitive conditions in which warfare with wild beasts was one of the main features of man's existence. At one dinner my host and two of my fellow guests had been within a year or eighteen months severely mauled by lions. All three, by the way, informed me that the actual biting caused them at the moment no pain whatever; the pain came later. On meeting Harold Hill, my companion on one of my Kapiti Plains lion-hunts, I found that since I had seen him he had been roughly handled by a dying leopard. The government had just been obliged to close one of the trade routes to native caravans because of the ravages of a man-eating lion, which carried men away from the camps. A safari which had come in from the north had been charged by a rhino, and one of the porters tossed and killed, the horn being driven clean through his loins. At Heatley's farm three buffalo (belonging to the same herd from which we had shot five) rushed out of the papyrus one afternoon at a passing buggy, which just managed to escape by a breakneck run across the level plain, the beasts chasing it for a mile. One afternoon, at Government House, I met a government official who had once succeeded in driving into a corral seventy zebras, including more stallions than mares; their misfortune in no way abated their savagery toward one another, and as the limited space forbade the escape of the weaker, the stallions fought to the death with teeth and hoofs during the first night, and no less than twenty were killed outright or died of their wounds.

Most of the time in Nairobi we were the guests of ever-hospitable McMillan, in his low, cool house, with its broad, vine-shaded veranda, running around all four sides, and its garden, fragrant and brilliant with innumerable flowers. Birds abounded, singing beautifully; the bulbuls were the most noticeable singers, but there were many others. The dark ant-eating chats haunted the dusky roads on the outskirts of the town, and were interesting birds; they were usually found in parties, flirted their tails up and down as they sat on bushes or roofs or wires, sang freely in chorus until after dusk, and then retired to holes in the ground for the night. A tiny owl with a queer little voice called continually not only after night-fall, but in the bright afternoons. Shrikes spitted insects on the spines of the imported cactus in the gardens.

It was race week, and the races, in some of which Kermit rode, were capital fun. The white people—army officers, government officials, farmers from the country round about, and their wives—rode to the races on ponies or even on camels, or drove up in rickshaws, in gharries, in bullock tongas, occasionally in automobiles, most often in two-wheel carts or rickety hacks drawn by mules and driven by a turbaned Indian or a native in a cotton shirt. There were Parsees, and Goanese dressed just like the Europeans. There were many other Indians, their picturesque womenkind gaudy in crimson, blue, and saffron. The constabulary, Indian and native, were in neat uniforms and well set up, though often barefooted. Straight, slender Somalis with clear-cut features were in attendance on the horses. Native negroes, of many different tribes, flocked to the race-course and its neighborhood. The Swahilis, and those among the others who aspired toward civilization, were well clad, the men in half-European costume, the women in flowing, parti-colored robes. But most of them were clad, or unclad, just as they always had been. Wakamba, with filed teeth, crouched in circles on the ground. Kikuyu passed, the men each with a blanket hung round the shoulders, and girdles of chains, and armlets and anklets of solid metal; the older women bent under burdens they carried on the back, half of them in addition with babies slung somewhere round them, while now and then an unmarried girl would have her face painted with ochre and vermilion. A small party of Masai warriors kept close together, each clutching his shining, long-bladed war spear, their hair daubed red and twisted into strings. A large band of Kavirondo, stark naked, with shield and spear and head-dress of nodding plumes, held a dance near the race-track. As for the races themselves, they were carried on in the most sporting spirit, and only the Australian poet Patterson could adequately write of them.

On August 4 I returned to Lake Naivasha, stopping on the way at Kijabe to lay the corner-stone of the new mission building. Mearns and Loring had stayed at Naivasha and had collected many birds and small mammals. That night they took me out on a springhaas-hunt. Thanks to Kermit we had discovered that the way to get this curious and purely nocturnal animal was by "shining" it with a lantern at night, just as in our own country deer, coons, owls, and other creatures can be killed. Springhaas live in big burrows, a number of them dwelling together in one community, the holes close to one another, and making what in the West we would call a "town" in speaking of prairie-dogs. At night they come out to feed on the grass. They are as heavy as a big jack-rabbit, with short fore legs, and long hind legs and tail, so that they look and on occasion move like miniature kangaroos, although, in addition to making long hops or jumps, they often run almost like an ordinary rat or rabbit. They are pretty creatures, fawn-colored above, and white beneath, with the terminal half of the tail very dark. In hunting them we simply walked over the flats for a couple of hours, flashing the bull's-eye lantern on all sides, until we saw the light reflected back by a springhaas's eyes. Then I would approach to within range, and hold the lantern in my left hand so as to shine both on the sight and on the eyes in front, resting my gun on my left wrist. The No. 3 shot, in the Fox double-barrel, would always do the business, if I held straight enough. There was nothing but the gleam of the eyes to shoot at; and this might suddenly be raised or lowered as the intently watching animal crouched on all fours or raised itself on its hind legs. I shot half a dozen, all that the naturalists wanted. Then I tried to shoot a fox; but the moon had risen from behind a cloud bank; I had to take a long shot and missed; but my companions killed several, and found that they were a new species of the peculiar African long-eared fox.

While waiting for the safari to get ready, Kermit went off on a camping trip and shot two bushbuck, while I spent a couple of days trying for singsing water-buck on the edge of the papyrus. I missed a bull, and wounded another which I did not get. This was all the more exasperating because interspersed with the misses were some good shots: I killed a fine water-buck cow at a hundred yards and a buck tommy for the table at two hundred and fifty; and, after missing a handsome black-and-white, redbilled and redlegged jabiru, or saddlebilled stork, at a hundred and fifty yards, as he stalked through the meadow after frogs, I cut him down on the wing at a hundred and eighty, with the little Springfield rifle. The water-buck spent the daytime outside, but near the edge of, the papyrus; I found them grazing or resting, in the open, at all times between early morning and late afternoon. Some of them spent most of the day in the papyrus, keeping to the watery trails made by the hippos and by themselves; but this was not the general habit, unless they had been persecuted. When frightened they often ran into the papyrus, smashing the dead reeds and splashing the water in their rush. They are noble-looking antelope, with long, shaggy hair, and their chosen haunts beside the lake were very attractive. Clumps of thorn-trees and flowering bushes grew at the edge of the tall papyrus here and there, and often formed a matted jungle, the trees laced together by creepers, many of them brilliant in their bloom. The climbing morning-glories sometimes completely covered a tree with their pale-purple flowers; and other blossoming vines spangled the green over which the sprays were flung with masses of bright yellow.

Four days' march from Naivasha, where we again left Mearns and Loring, took us to Neri. Our line of march lay across the high plateaus and mountain chains of the Aberdare range. The steep, twisting trail was slippery with mud. Our last camp, at an altitude of about ten thousand feet, was so cold that the water froze in the basins, and the shivering porters slept in numbed discomfort. There was constant fog and rain, and on the highest plateau the bleak landscape, shrouded in driving mist, was northern to all the senses. The ground was rolling, and through the deep valleys ran brawling brooks of clear water; one little foaming stream, suddenly tearing down a hillside, might have been that which Childe Roland crossed before he came to the dark tower.

There was not much game, and it generally moved abroad by night. One frosty evening we killed a duiker by shining its eyes. We saw old elephant tracks. The high, wet levels swarmed with mice and shrews, just as our arctic and alpine meadows swarm with them. The species were really widely different from ours, but many of them showed curious analogies in form and habits; there was a short-tailed shrew much like our mole-shrew, and a long-haired, short-tailed rat like a very big meadow-mouse. They were so plentiful that we frequently saw them, and the grass was cut up by their runways. They were abroad during the day, probably finding the nights too cold, and in an hour Heller trapped a dozen or two individuals belonging to seven species and five different genera. There were not many birds so high up. There were deer-ferns; and Spanish moss hung from the trees and even from the bamboos. The flowers included utterly strange forms, as for instance giant lobelias ten feet high. Others we know in our gardens; geraniums and red-hot pokers, which in places turned the glades to a fire color. Yet others either were like, or looked like, our own wild flowers: orange lady-slippers, red gladiolas on stalks six feet high, pansy-like violets, and blackberries and yellow raspberries. There were stretches of bushes bearing masses of small red or large white flowers shaped somewhat like columbines, or like the garden balsam; the red flower bushes were under the bamboos, the white at a lower level. The crests and upper slopes of the mountains were clothed in the green uniformity of the bamboo forest, the trail winding dim under its dark archway of tall, close-growing stems. Lower down were junipers and yews, and then many other trees, with among them tree-ferns and strange dragon-trees with lily-like frondage. Zone succeeded zone from top to bottom, each marked by a different plant life.

In this part of Africa, where flowers bloom and birds sing all the year round, there is no such burst of bloom and song as in the northern spring and early summer. There is nothing like the mass of blossoms which carpet the meadows of the high mountain valleys and far northern meadows, during their brief high tide of life, when one short joyous burst of teeming and vital beauty atones for the long death of the iron fall and winter. So it is with the bird songs. Many of them are beautiful, though to my ears none quite as beautiful as the best of our own bird songs. At any rate there is nothing that quite corresponds to the chorus that during May and June moves northward from the Gulf States and southern California to Maine, Minnesota, and Oregon, to Ontario and Saskatchewan; when there comes the great vernal burst of bloom and song; when the may-flower, bloodroot, wake-robin, anemone, adder's-tongue, liverwort, shadblow, dogwood, redbud, gladden the woods; when mocking-birds and cardinals sing in the magnolia-groves of the South, and hermit-thrushes, winter wrens, and sweetheart sparrows in the spruce and hemlock forests of the North; when bobolinks in the East and meadowlarks East and West sing in the fields; and water-ousels by the cold streams of the Rockies, and canyon-wrens in their sheer gorges; when from the Atlantic seaboard to the Pacific woodthrushes, veeries, rufous-backed thrushes, robins, bluebirds, orioles, thrashers, catbirds, house-finches, song-sparrows—some in the East, some in the West, some both East and West—and many, many other singers thrill the gardens at sunrise; until the long days begin to shorten, and tawny lilies burn by the roadside, and the indigo-buntings trill from the tops of little trees throughout the hot afternoons.

We were in the Kikuyu country. On our march we met several parties of natives. I had been much inclined to pity the porters, who had but one blanket apiece; but when I saw the Kikuyus, each with nothing but a smaller blanket, and without the other clothing and the tents of the porters, I realized how much better off the latter were simply because they were on a white man's safari. At Neri boma we were greeted with the warmest hospitality by the district commissioner, Mr. Browne. Among other things, he arranged a great Kikuyu dance in our honor. Two thousand warriors, and many women, came in; as well as a small party of Masai moran. The warriors were naked, or half-naked; some carried gaudy blankets, others girdles of leopard-skin; their ox-hide shields were colored in bold patterns, their long-bladed spears quivered and gleamed. Their faces and legs were painted red and yellow; the faces of the young men who were about to undergo the rite of circumcision were stained a ghastly white, and their bodies fantastically painted. The warriors wore bead necklaces and waist-belts and armlets of brass and steel, and spurred anklets of monkey-skin. Some wore head-dresses made out of a lion's mane or from the long black-and-white fur of the Colobus monkey; others had plumes stuck in their red-daubed hair. They chanted in unison a deep-toned chorus, and danced rhythmically in rings, while the drums throbbed and the horns blared; and they danced by us in column, springing and chanting. The women shrilled applause, and danced in groups by themselves. The Masai circled and swung in a panther-like dance of their own, and the measure, and their own fierce singing and calling, maddened them until two of their number, their eyes staring, their faces working, went into fits of berserker frenzy, and were disarmed at once to prevent mischief. Some of the tribesmen held wilder dances still in the evening, by the light of fires that blazed in a grove where their thatched huts stood.

The second day after reaching Neri the clouds lifted and we dried our damp clothes and blankets. Through the bright sunlight we saw in front of us the high rock peaks of Kenia, and shining among them the fields of everlasting snow which feed her glaciers; for beautiful, lofty Kenia is one of the glacier-bearing mountains of the equator. Here Kermit and Tarlton went northward on a safari of their own, while Cuninghame, Heller, and I headed for Kenia itself. For two days we travelled through a well-peopled country. The fields of corn—always called mealies in Africa—of beans, and sweet potatoes, with occasional plantations of bananas, touched one another in almost uninterrupted succession. In most of them we saw the Kikuyu women at work with their native hoes; for among the Kikuyus, as among other savages, the woman is the drudge and beast of burden. Our trail led by clear, rushing streams, which formed the headwaters of the Tana; among the trees fringing their banks were graceful palms, and there were groves of tree-ferns here and there on the sides of the gorges.

On the afternoon of the second day we struck upward among the steep foot-hills of the mountain, riven by deep ravines. We pitched camp in an open glade, surrounded by the green wall of tangled forest, the forest of the tropical mountainsides. The trees, strange of kind and endless in variety, grew tall and close, laced together by vine and creeper, while underbrush crowded the space between their mossy trunks, and covered the leafy mould beneath. Toward dusk crested ibis flew overhead with harsh clamor, to seek their night roosts; parrots chattered, and a curiously homelike touch was given by the presence of a thrush in color and shape almost exactly like our robin. Monkeys called in the depths of the forest, and after dark tree-frogs piped and croaked, and the tree-hyraxes uttered their wailing cries.

Elephants dwelt permanently in this mountainous region of heavy woodland. On our march thither we had already seen their traces in the "shambas," as the cultivated fields of the

natives are termed; for the great beasts are fond of raiding
the crops at night, and their inroads often do serious damage.
In this neighborhood their habit is to live high up in the
mountains, in the bamboos, while the weather is dry; the cows
and calves keeping closer to the bamboos than the bulls.   A
spell of wet weather, such as we had fortunately been having,
drives them down in the dense forest which covers the lower
slopes.   Here they may either pass all their time, or at night
they may go still farther down, into the open valley where
the shambas lie; or they may occasionally still do what they
habitually did in the days before the white hunters came,
and wander far away, making migrations that are sometimes
seasonal, and sometimes irregular and unaccountable.

No other animal, not the lion himself, is so constant a theme
of talk, and a subject of such unflagging interest round the
camp-fires of African hunters and in the native villages of
the African wilderness, as the elephant.   Indeed the elephant
has always profoundly impressed the imagination of mankind.
It is, not only to hunters, but to naturalists, and to all people
who possess any curiosity about wild creatures and the wild
life of nature, the most interesting of all animals.   Its huge
bulk, its singular form, the value of its ivory, its great intelligence—in which it is only matched, if at all, by the highest
apes, and possibly by one or two of the highest carnivora—
and its varied habits, all combine to give it an interest such as
attaches to no other living creature below the rank of man.
In line of descent and in physical formation it stands by itself,
wholly apart from all the other great land beasts, and differing
from them even more widely than they differ from one another.   The two existing species—the African, which is the
larger and finer animal, and the Asiatic—differ from one another as much as they do from the mammoth and similar extinct forms which were the contemporaries of early man in
Europe and North America.   The carvings of our paleolithic
forefathers, etched on bone by cavern-dwellers, from whom
we are sundered by ages which stretch into an immemorial

past, show that in their lives the hairy elephant of the North played the same part that his remote collateral descendant now plays in the lives of the savages who dwell under a vertical sun beside the tepid waters of the Nile and the Congo.

In the first dawn of history, the sculptured records of the kings of Egypt, Babylon, and Ninevah show the immense importance which attached in the eyes of the mightiest monarchs of the then world to the chase and the trophies of this great strange beast. The ancient civilization of India boasts as one of its achievements the taming of the elephant; and in the ancient lore of that civilization the elephant plays a distinguished part.

The elephant is unique among the beasts of great bulk in the fact that his growth in size has been accompanied by growth in brain-power. With other beasts growth in bulk of body has not been accompanied by similar growth of mind. Indeed, sometimes there seems to have been mental retrogression. The rhinoceros, in several different forms, is found in the same regions as the elephant, and in one of its forms it is in point of size second only to the elephant among terrestrial animals. Seemingly the ancestors of the two creatures, in that period, separated from us by uncounted hundreds of thousands of years, which we may conveniently designate as late Miocene or early Pliocene, were substantially equal in brain development. But in one case increase in bulk seems to have induced lethargy and atrophy of brain-power, while in the other case brain and body have both grown. At any rate the elephant is now one of the wisest and the rhinoceros one of the stupidest of big mammals. In consequence the elephant outlasts the rhino, although he is the largest, carries infinitely more valuable spoils, and is far more eagerly and persistently hunted. Both animals wandered freely over the open country of East Africa thirty years ago. But the elephant learns by experience infinitely more readily than the rhinoceros. As a rule, the former no longer lives in the open plains, and in many places now even crosses them if possible only at night.   But those rhinoceros which formerly dwelt in the plains for the most part continued to dwell there until killed out.   So it is at the present day.   Not the most foolish elephant would under similar conditions behave as the rhinos that we studied and hunted by Kilimakiu and .in the Sotik behaved.   No elephant, in regions where they have been much persecuted by hunters, would habitually spend its days lying or standing in the open plain; nor would it, in such places, repeatedly, and in fact uniformly, permit men to walk boldly up to it without heeding them until in its immediate neighborhood.   The elephant's sight is bad, as is that of the rhinoceros; but a comparatively brief experience with rifle-bearing man usually makes the former take refuge in regions where scent and hearing count for more than sight; while no experience has any such effect on the rhino.   The rhinos that now live in the bush are the descendants of those which always lived in the bush; and it is in the bush that the species will linger long after it has vanished from the open; and it is in the bush that it is most formidable.

Elephant and rhino differ as much in their habits as in their intelligence.   The former is very gregarious, herds of several hundred being sometimes found, and is of a restless, wandering temper, often shifting his abode and sometimes making long migrations.   The rhinoceros is a lover of solitude; it is usually found alone, or a bull and cow, or cow and calf may be in company; very rarely are as many as half a dozen found together.   Moreover, it is comparatively stationary in its habits, and as a general thing stays permanently in one neighborhood, not shifting its position for very many miles unless for grave reasons.

The African elephant has recently been divided into a number of subspecies; but as within a century its range was continuous over nearly the whole continent south of the Sahara, and as it was given to such extensive occasional wanderings, it is probable that the examination of a sufficient series of specimens would show that on their confines these

races grade into one another. In its essentials the beast is
almost everywhere the same, although, of course, there must
be variation of habits with any animal which exists throughout
so wide and diversified a range of territory; for in one place
it is found in high mountains, in another in a dry desert, in
another in low-lying marshes or wet and dense forests.

In East Africa the old bulls are usually found singly or in
small parties by themselves. These have the biggest tusks;
the bulls in the prime of life, the herd bulls or breeding bulls,
which keep in herds with the cows and calves, usually have
smaller ivory. Sometimes, however, very old but vigorous
bulls are found with the cows; and I am inclined to think
that the ordinary herd bulls at times also keep by themselves,
or at least in company with only a few cows, for at certain
seasons, generally immediately after the rains, cows, most of
them with calves, appear in great numbers at certain places,
where only a few bulls are ever found. Where undisturbed,
elephant rest, and wander about at all times of the day and
night, and feed without much regard to fixed hours. Morning or evening, noon or midnight, the herd may be on the
move, or its members may be resting; yet, during the hottest
hours of noon they seldom feed, and ordinarily stand almost
still, resting—for elephant very rarely lie down unless sick.
Where they are afraid of man, their only enemy, they come
out to feed in thinly forested plains, or cultivated fields, when
they do so at all, only at night, and before daybreak move
back into the forest to rest. Elsewhere they sometimes spend
the day in the open, in grass or low bush. Where we were, at
this time, on Kenia, the elephants sometimes moved down at
night to feed in the shambas, at the expense of the crops of
the natives, and sometimes stayed in the forest, feeding by
day or night on the branches they tore off the trees, or, occasionally, on the roots they grubbed up with their tusks. They
work vast havoc among the young or small growth of a forest,
and the readiness with which they uproot, overturn, or break
off medium-sized trees conveys a striking impression of their

enormous strength. I have seen a tree a foot in diameter thus uprooted and overturned.

The African elephant has never, like his Indian kinsman, been trained to man's use. There is still hope that the feat may be performed; but hitherto its probable economic usefulness has for various reasons seemed so questionable that there has been scant encouragement to undergo the necessary expense and labor. Up to the present time the African elephant has yielded only his ivory as an asset of value. This, however, has been of such great value as well-nigh to bring about the mighty beast's utter extermination. Ivory-hunters and ivory-traders have penetrated Africa to the haunts of the elephant since centuries before our era, and the elephant boundaries have been slowly receding throughout historic time; but during the century just passed its process has been immensely accelerated, until now there are but one or two out-of-the-way nooks of the Dark Continent to the neighborhood of which hunter and trader have not penetrated. Fortunately the civilized powers which now divide dominion over Africa have waked up in time, and there is at present no danger of the extermination of the lord of all four-footed creatures. Large reserves have been established on which various herds of elephants now live what is, at least for the time being, an entirely safe life. Furthermore, over great tracts of territory outside the reserves regulations have been promulgated which, if enforced as they are now enforced, will prevent any excessive diminution of the herds. In British East Africa, for instance, no cows are allowed to be shot save for special purposes, as for preservation in a museum, or to safeguard life and property; and no bulls with tusks weighing less than thirty pounds apiece. This renders safe almost all the females and an ample supply of breeding males. Too much praise cannot be given the governments and the individuals who have brought about this happy result; the credit belongs especially to England and to various Englishmen. It would be a veritable and most tragic calamity if the lordly elephant, the giant among existing four-footed creatures, should be permitted to vanish from the face of the earth.

But of course protection is not permanently possible over the greater part of that country which is well fitted for settlement; nor anywhere, if the herds grow too numerous. It would be not merely silly, but worse than silly, to try to stop all killing of elephants. The unchecked increase of any big and formidable wild beast, even though not a flesh-eater, is incompatible with the existence of man when he has emerged from the state of lowest savagery. This is not a matter of theory, but of proved fact. In place after place in Africa where protection has been extended to hippopotamus or buffalo, rhinoceros or elephant, it has been found necessary to withdraw it because the protected animals did such damage to property, or became such menaces to human life. Among all four species cows with calves often attack men without provocation, and old bulls are at any time likely to become infected by a spirit of wanton and ferocious mischief and apt to become man-killers. I know settlers who tried to preserve the rhinoceros which they found living on their big farms, and who were obliged to abandon the attempt, and themselves to kill the rhinos because of repeated and wanton attacks on human beings by the latter. Where we were by Neri, a year or two before our visit, the rhinos had become so dangerous, killing one white man and several natives, that the district commissioner who preceded Mr. Browne was forced to undertake a crusade against them, killing fifteen. Both in South Africa and on the Nile protection extended to hippopotamus has in places been wholly withdrawn because of the damage done by the beasts to the crops of the natives, or because of their unprovoked assaults on canoes and boats. In one instance a last surviving hippo was protected for years, but finally grew bold because of immunity, killed a boy in sheer wantonness, and had to be himself slain. In Uganda the buffalo were for years protected, and grew so bold, killed so many natives, and ruined so many villages, that they are now classed as vermin and their destruction in every way encouraged.   In the very neighborhood where I was hunting at Kenia but six weeks before my coming, a cow buffalo had wandered down into the plains and run amuck, had attacked two villages, had killed a man and a boy, and had then been mobbed to death by the spearmen.   Elephant, when in numbers, and when not possessed of the fear of man, are more impossible neighbors than hippo, rhino, or buffalo; but they are so eagerly sought after by ivory-hunters that it is only rarely that they get the chance to become really dangerous to life, although in many places their ravages among the crops are severely felt by the unfortunate natives who live near them.

The chase of the elephant, if persistently followed, entails more fatigue and hardship than any other kind of African hunting.   As regards risk, it is hard to say whether it is more or less dangerous than the chase of the lion and the buffalo. Both Cuninghame and Tarlton, men of wide experience, ranked elephant-hunting, in point of danger, as nearly on the level with lion-hunting, and as more dangerous than buffalo-hunting; and all three kinds as far more dangerous than the chase of the rhino.   Personally, I believe the actual conflict with a lion, where the conditions are the same, to be normally the more dangerous sport; though far greater demands are made by elephant-hunting on the qualities of personal endurance and hardihood and resolute perseverance in the face of disappointment and difficulty.   Buffalo, seemingly, do not charge as freely as elephant, but are more dangerous when they do charge.   Rhino when hunted, though at times ugly customers, seem to me certainly less dangerous than the other three; but from sheer stupid truculence they are themselves apt to take the offensive in unexpected fashion, being far more prone to such aggression than are any of the others—man-eating lions always excepted.

Very few of the native tribes in Africa hunt the elephant systematically.   But the 'Ndorobo, the wild bush people of East Africa, sometimes catch young elephants in the pits they dig with slow labor, and very rarely they kill one with a kind of harpoon. The 'Ndorobo are doubtless in part descended from some primitive bush people, but in part also derive their blood from the more advanced tribes near which their wandering families happen to live; and they grade into the latter, by speech and through individuals who seem to stand halfway between. Thus we had with us two Masai 'Ndorobo, true wild people, who spoke a bastard Masai; who had formerly hunted with Cuninghame, and who came to us because of their ancient friendship with him. These shy wood creatures were afraid to come to Neri by daylight, when we were camped there, but after dark crept to Cuninghame's tent. Cuninghame gave them two fine red blankets, and put them to sleep in a little tent, keeping their spears in his own tent, as a matter of precaution to prevent their running away. The elder of the two, he informed me, would certainly have a fit of hysterics when we killed our elephant! Cuninghame was also joined by other old friends of former hunts, Kikuyu 'Ndorobo these, who spoke Kikuyu like the people who cultivated the fields that covered the river-bottoms and hillsides of the adjoining open country, and who were, indeed, merely outlying, forest-dwelling members of the lowland tribes. In the deep woods we met one old Dorobo, who had no connection with any more advanced tribe, whose sole belongings were his spear, skin cloak, and fire-stick, and who lived purely on honey and game; unlike the bastard 'Ndorobo, he was ornamented with neither paint nor grease. But the 'Ndorobo who were our guides stood farther up in the social scale. The men passed most of their time in the forest, but up the mountainsides they had squalid huts on little clearings, with shambas, where their wives raised scanty crops. To the 'Ndorobo, and to them alone, the vast, thick forest was an open book; without their aid as guides both Cuninghame and our own gun-bearers were at fault, and found their way around with great difficulty and slowness. The bush people had nothing in the way of clothing save a blanket over the shoulders, but wore the usual paint and grease and ornaments; each carried a spear which might have a long and narrow, or short and broad blade; two of them wore head-dresses *of tripe*—skull-caps made from the inside of a sheep's stomach.

For two days after reaching our camp in the open glade on the mountainside it rained. We were glad of this, because it meant that the elephants would not be in the bamboos, and Cuninghame and the 'Ndorobo went off to hunt for fresh signs. Cuninghame is as skilful an elephant-hunter as can be found in Africa, and is one of the very few white men able to help even the wild bushmen at their work. By the afternoon of the second day they were fairly well satisfied as to the whereabouts of the quarry.

The following morning a fine rain was still falling when Cuninghame, Heller, and I started on our hunt; but by noon it had stopped. Of course we went in single file and on foot; not even a bear-hunter from the cane-brakes of the lower Mississippi could ride through that forest. We left our home camp standing, taking blankets and a coat and change of underclothing for each of us, and two small Whymper tents, with enough food for three days; I also took my wash kit and a book from the Pigskin Library. First marched the 'Ndorobo guides, each with his spear, his blanket round his shoulders, and a little bundle of corn and sweet potato. Then came Cuninghame, followed by his gun-bearer. Then I came, clad in khaki-colored flannel shirt and khaki trousers buttoning down the legs, with hobnailed shoes and a thick slouch-hat; I had intended to wear rubber-soled shoes, but the soaked ground was too slippery. My two gun-bearers followed, carrying the Holland and the Springfield. Then came Heller, at the head of a dozen porters and skinners; he and they were to fall behind when we actually struck fresh elephant spoor, but to follow our trail by the help of a Dorobo who was left with them.

For three hours our route lay along the edge of the woods. We climbed into and out of deep ravines in which groves of tree-ferns clustered. We waded through streams of swift

water, whose course was broken by cataract and rapid. We
passed through shambas, and by the doors of little hamlets of
thatched behive huts. We met flocks of goats and hairy, fat-
tailed sheep guarded by boys; strings of burden-bearing women
stood meekly to one side to let us pass; parties of young men
sauntered by, spear in hand.

Then we struck into the great forest, and in an instant the
sun was shut from sight by the thick screen of wet foliage. It
was a riot of twisted vines, interlacing the trees and bushes.
Only the elephant paths, which, of every age, crossed and
recrossed it hither and thither, made it passable. One of the
chief difficulties in hunting elephants in the forest is that it is
impossible to travel, except very slowly and with much noise,
off these trails, so that it is sometimes very difficult to take
advantage of the wind; and although the sight of the elephant
is dull, both its sense of hearing and its sense of smell are
exceedingly acute.

Hour after hour we worked our way onward through
tangled forest and matted jungle. There was little sign of
bird or animal life. A troop of long-haired black-and-white
monkeys bounded away among the tree-tops. Here and there
brilliant flowers lightened the gloom. We ducked under vines
and climbed over fallen timber. Poisonous nettles stung our
hands. We were drenched by the wet boughs which we
brushed aside. Mosses and ferns grew rank and close. The
trees were of strange kinds. There were huge trees with little
leaves, and small trees with big leaves. There were trees with
bare, fleshy limbs, that writhed out through the neighboring
branches, bearing sparse clusters of large frondage. In places
the forest was low, the trees thirty or forty feet high, the
bushes, that choked the ground between, fifteen or twenty feet
high. In other places mighty monarchs of the wood, straight
and tall, towered aloft to an immense height; among them were
trees whose smooth, round boles were spotted like sycamores,
while far above our heads their gracefully spreading branches
were hung with vines like mistletoe and draped with Spanish

moss; trees whose surfaces were corrugated and knotted as if they were made of bundles of great creepers; and giants whose buttressed trunks were four times a man's length across.

Twice we got on elephant spoor, once of a single bull, once of a party of three. Then Cuninghame and the 'Ndorobo redoubled their caution. They would minutely examine the fresh dung; and above all they continually tested the wind, scanning the treetops, and lighting matches to see from the smoke what the eddies were near the ground. Each time after an hour's stealthy stepping and crawling along the twisted trail a slight shift of the wind in the almost still air gave our scent to the game, and away it went before we could catch a glimpse of it; and we resumed our walk. The elephant paths led up hill and down—for the beasts are wonderful climbers—and wound in and out in every direction. They were marked by broken branches and the splintered and shattered trunks of the smaller trees, especially where the elephant had stood and fed, trampling down the bushes for many yards around. Where they had crossed the marshy valleys they had punched big round holes, three feet deep, in the sticky mud.

As evening fell we pitched camp by the side of a little brook at the bottom of a ravine, and dined ravenously on bread, mutton, and tea. The air was keen, and under our blankets we slept in comfort until dawn. Breakfast was soon over and camp struck; and once more we began our cautious progress through the dim, cool archways of the mountain forest.

Two hours after leaving camp we came across the fresh trail of a small herd of perhaps ten or fifteen elephant cows and calves, but including two big herd bulls. At once we took up the trail. Cuninghame and his bush people consulted again and again, scanning every track and mark with minute attention. The signs showed that the elephants had fed in the shambas early in the night, had then returned to the mountain, and stood in one place resting for several hours, and had left this sleeping-ground some time before we reached it. After we had followed the trail a short while we made the experiment of trying to force our own way through the jungle, so as to get the wind more favorable; but our progress was too slow and noisy, and we returned to the path the elephants had beaten. Then the 'Ndorobo went ahead, travelling noiselessly and at speed. One of them was clad in a white blanket, and another in a red one, which were conspicuous; but they were too silent and cautious to let the beasts see them, and could tell exactly where they were and what they were doing by the sounds. When these trackers waited for us they would appear before us like ghosts; once one of them dropped down from the branches above, having climbed a tree with monkey-like agility to get a glimpse of the great game.

At last we could hear the elephants, and under Cuninghame's lead we walked more cautiously than ever. The wind was right, and the trail of one elephant led close alongside that of the rest of the herd, and parallel thereto. It was about noon. The elephants moved slowly, and we listened to the boughs crack, and now and then to the curious internal rumblings of the great beasts. Carefully, every sense on the alert, we kept pace with them. My double-barrel was in my hands, and, whenever possible, as I followed the trail, I stepped in the huge footprints of the elephant, for where such a weight had pressed there were no sticks left to crack under my feet. It made our veins thrill thus for half an hour to creep stealthily along, but a few rods from the herd, never able to see it, because of the extreme denseness of the cover, but always hearing first one and then another of its members, and always trying to guess what each one might do, and keeping ceaselessly ready for whatever might befall. A flock of hornbills flew up with noisy clamor, but the elephants did not heed them.

At last we came in sight of the mighty game. The trail took a twist to one side, and there, thirty yards in front of us, we made out part of the gray and massive head of an elephant resting his tusks on the branches of a young tree. A couple of minutes passed before, by cautious scrutiny, we were able to tell whether the animal was a cow or a bull, and whether, if a bull, it carried heavy enough tusks. Then we saw that it was a big bull with good ivory. It turned its head in my direction and I saw its eye; and I fired a little to one side of the eye, at a spot which I thought would lead to the brain. I struck exactly where I aimed, but the head of an elephant is enormous and the brain small, and the bullet missed it. However, the shock momentarily stunned the beast. He stumbled forward, half falling, and as he recovered I fired with the second barrel, again aiming for the brain. This time the bullet sped true, and as I lowered the rifle from my shoulder, I saw the great lord of the forest come crashing to the ground.

But at that very instant, before there was a moment's time in which to reload, the thick bushes parted immediately on my left front, and through them surged the vast bulk of a charging bull elephant, the matted mass of tough creepers snapping like packthread before his rush. He was so close that he could have touched me with his trunk. I leaped to one side and dodged behind a tree trunk, opening the rifle, throwing out the empty shells, and slipping in two cartridges. Meanwhile Cuninghame fired right and left, at the same time throwing himself into the bushes on the other side. Both his bullets went home, and the bull stopped short in his charge, wheeled, and immediately disappeared in the thick cover. We ran forward, but the forest had closed over his wake. We heard him trumpet shrilly, and then all sounds ceased.

The 'Ndorobo, who had quite properly disappeared when this second bull charged, now went forward, and soon returned with the report that he had fled at speed, but was evidently hard hit, as there was much blood on the spoor. If we had been only after ivory we should have followed him at once; but there was no telling how long a chase he might lead us; and as we desired to save the skin of the dead elephant entire, there was no time whatever to spare. It is a formidable task, occupying many days, to preserve an elephant for mounting in a museum, and if the skin is to be properly saved, it must be taken off without an hour's unnecessary delay.

So back we turned to where the dead tusker lay, and I felt proud indeed as I stood by the immense bulk of the slain monster and put my hand on the ivory. The tusks weighed a hundred and thirty pounds the pair. There was the usual scene of joyful excitement among the gun-bearers—who had behaved excellently—and among the wild bush people who had done the tracking for us; and, as Cuninghame had predicted, the old Masai Dorobo, from pure delight, proceeded to have hysterics on the body of the dead elephant. The scene was repeated when Heller and the porters appeared half an hour later. Then, chattering like monkeys, and as happy as possible, all, porters, gun-bearers, and 'Ndorobo alike, began the work of skinning and cutting up the quarry, under the leadership and supervision of Heller and Cuninghame, and soon they were all splashed with blood from head to foot. One of the trackers took off his blanket and squatted stark naked inside the carcass the better to use his knife. Each laborer rewarded himself by cutting off strips of meat for his private store, and hung them in red festoons from the branches round about. There was no let-up in the work until it was stopped by darkness.

Our tents were pitched in a small open glade a hundred yards from the dead elephant. The night was clear, the stars shone brightly, and in the west the young moon hung just above the line of tall tree-tops. Fires were speedily kindled and the men sat around them, feasting and singing in a strange minor tone until late in the night. The flickering light left them at one moment in black obscurity, and the next brought into bold relief their sinewy crouching figures, their dark faces, gleaming eyes and flashing teeth. When they did sleep, two of the 'Ndorobo slept so close to the fire as to burn themselves; an accident to which they are prone, judging from the many scars of old burns on their legs. I toasted slices of elephant's heart on a pronged stick before the fire, and found it delicious; for I was hungry, and the night was cold. We talked of our success and exulted over it, and made our plans for the morrow;

and then we turned in under our blankets for another night's sleep.

Next morning some of the 'Ndorobo went off on the trail of Cuninghame's elephant to see if it had fallen, but found that it had travelled steadily, though its wounds were probably mortal. There was no object in my staying, for Heller and Cuninghame would be busy for the next ten days, and would ultimately have to use all the porters in taking off and curing the skin, and transporting it to Neri; so I made up my mind to go down to the plains for a hunt by myself. Taking one porter to carry my bedding, and with my gun-bearers and a Dorobo as guide, I struck off through the forest for the main camp, reaching it early in the afternoon. Thence I bundled off a safari to Cuninghame and Heller, with food for a week, and tents and clothing; and then enjoyed the luxury of a shave and a warm bath. Next day was spent in writing and in making preparations for my own trip. A Kikuyu chief, clad in a cloak of hyrax-skins and carrying his war spear, came to congratulate me on killing the elephant and to present me with a sheep. Early the following morning everything was in readiness; the bull-necked porters lifted their loads, I stepped out in front, followed by my led horse, and in ten hours' march we reached Neri boma with its neat buildings, its trees, and its well-kept flower-beds.

My hunting and travelling during the following fortnight will be told in the next chapter. On the evening of September 6 we were all together again at Meru boma, on the northeastern slopes of Kenia—Kermit, Tarlton, Cuninghame, Heller, and I. Thanks to the unfailing kindness of the commissioner, Mr. Horne, we were given full information of the elephant in the neighborhood. He had no 'Ndorobo, but among the Wa-Meru, a wild martial tribe, who lived close around him, there were a number of hunters, or at least of men who knew the forest and the game, and these had been instructed to bring in any news.

We had, of course, no idea that elephant would be found

close at hand. But next morning, about eleven, Horne came to our camp with four of his black scouts, who reported that three elephants were in a patch of thick jungle beside the shambas, not three miles away, Horne said that the elephants were cows, that they had been in the neighborhood some days, devastating the shambas, and were bold and fierce, having charged some men who sought to drive them away from the cultivated fields; it is curious to see how little heed these elephants pay to the natives. I wished a cow for the museum, and also another bull. So off we started at once, Kermit carrying his camera. I slipped on my rubber-soled shoes, and had my gun-bearers accompany me bare-footed, with the Holland and Springfield rifles. We followed footpaths among the fields until we reached the edge of the jungle in which the elephants stood.

This jungle lay beside the forest, and at this point separated it from the fields. It consisted of a mass of rank-growing bushes, allied to the cotton-plant, ten or twelve feet high, with only here and there a tree. It was not good ground in which to hunt elephant, for the tangle was practically impenetrable to a hunter save along the elephant trails, whereas the elephants themselves could move in any direction at will, with no more difficulty than a man would have in a hay-field. The bushes in most places rose just above their backs, so that they were completely hid from the hunter even a few feet away. Yet the cover afforded no shade to the mighty beasts, and it seemed strange that elephants should stand in it at midday with the sun out. There they were, however, for, looking cautiously into the cover from behind the bushes on a slight hill crest a quarter of a mile off, we could just make out a huge ear now and then as it lazily flapped.

On account of the wind we had to go well to one side before entering the jungle. Then in we went in single file, Cuninghame and Tarlton leading, with a couple of our naked guides. The latter showed no great desire to get too close, explaining that the elephants were "very fierce." Once in the jungle, we trod as quietly as possible, threading our way along the elephant trails, which crossed and recrossed one another. Evidently it was a favorite haunt, for the sign was abundant, both old and new. In the impenetrable cover it was quite impossible to tell just where the elephants were, and twice we sent one of the savages up a tree to locate the game. The last time the watcher, who stayed in the tree, indicated by signs that the elephant were not far off; and his companions wished to lead us round to where the cover was a little lower and thinner. But to do so would have given them our wind, and Cuninghame refused, taking into his own hands the management of the stalk. I kept my heavy rifle at the ready, and on we went, in watchful silence, prepared at any moment for a charge. We could not tell at what second we might catch our first glimpse at very close quarters of "the beast that hath between his eyes the serpent for a hand," and, when thus surprised, the temper of "the huge earth-shaking beast" is sometimes of the shortest.

Cuninghame and Tarlton stopped for a moment to consult; Cuninghame stooped, and Tarlton mounted his shoulders and stood upright, steadying himself by my hand. Down he came and told us that he had seen a small tree shake seventy yards distant; although upright on Cuninghame's shoulders he could not see the elephant itself. Forward we stole for a few yards, and then a piece of good luck befell us, for we came on the trunk of a great fallen tree, and scrambling up, we found ourselves perched in a row six feet above the ground. The highest part of the trunk was near the root, farthest from where the elephants were; and though it offered precarious footing, it also offered the best lookout. Thither I balanced, and looking over the heads of my companions I at once made out the elephant. At first I could see nothing but the shaking branches, and one huge ear occasionally flapping. Then I made out the ear of another beast, and then the trunk of a third was uncurled, lifted, and curled again; it showered its back with earth. The watcher we had left behind in the tree-top coughed; the elephants stood motionless, and up went the biggest elephant's trunk, feeling for the wind; the watcher coughed again, and then the bushes and saplings swayed and parted as three black bulks came toward us. The cover was so high that we could not see their tusks, only the tops of their heads and their backs being visible. The leader was the biggest, and at it I fired when it was sixty yards away, and nearly broadside on, but heading slightly toward me. I had previously warned every one to kneel. The recoil of the heavy rifle made me rock, as I stood unsteadily on my perch, and I failed to hit the brain. But the bullet, only missing the brain by an inch or two, brought the elephant to its knees; as it rose I floored it with the second barrel. The blast of the big rifle, by the way, was none too pleasant for the other men on the log and made Cuninghame's nose bleed. Reloading, I fired twice at the next animal, which was now turning. It stumbled and nearly fell, but at the same moment the first one rose again, and I fired both barrels into its head, bringing it once more to the ground. Once again it rose—an elephant's brain is not an easy mark to hit under such conditions—but as it moved slowly off, half stunned, I snatched the little Springfield rifle, and this time shot true, sending the bullet into its brain. As it fell I took another shot at the wounded elephant, now disappearing in the forest, but without effect.

On walking up to our prize it proved to be not a cow, but a good-sized adult (but not old) herd bull, with thick, short tusks weighing about forty pounds apiece. Ordinarily, of course, a bull, not a cow, is what one desires, although on this occasion I needed a cow to complete the group for the National Museum. However, Heller and Cuninghame spent the next few days in preserving the skin, which I afterward gave to the University of California; and I was too much pleased with our luck to feel inclined to grumble. We were back in camp five hours after leaving it. Our gun-bearers usually felt it incumbent on them to keep a dignified bearing while in our company. But the death of an elephant is always a great event; and one of the gun-bearers, as they walked ahead of us campward, soon began to improvise a song, reciting the success of the hunt, the death of the elephant, and the power of the rifles; and gradually, as they got farther ahead, the more light-hearted among them began to give way to their spirits and they came into camp frolicking, gambolling, and dancing as if they were still the naked savages that they had been before they became the white man's followers.

Two days later Kermit got his bull. He and Tarlton had camped about ten miles off in a magnificent forest, and late the first afternoon received news that a herd of elephants was in the neighborhood. They were off by dawn, and in a few hours came on the herd. It consisted chiefly of cows and calves, but there was one big master-bull, with fair tusks. It was open forest with long grass. By careful stalking they got within thirty yards of the bull, behind whom was a line of cows. Kermit put both barrels of his heavy double 450 into the tusker's head, but without even staggering him; and as he walked off Tarlton also fired both barrels into him, with no more effect; then, as he slowly turned, Kermit killed him with a shot in the brain from the 405 Winchester. Immediately the cows lifted their ears, and began trumpeting and threatening; if they had come on in a body at that distance, there was not much chance of turning them or of escaping from them; and after standing stock-still for a minute or two, Kermit and Tarlton stole quietly off for a hundred yards, and waited until the anger of the cows cooled and they had moved away, before going up to the dead bull. Then they followed the herd again, and Kermit got some photos which, as far as I know, are better than any that have ever before been taken of wild elephant. He took them close up, at imminent risk of a charge.

The following day the two hunters rode back to Meru, making a long circle. The elephants they saw were not worth shooting, but they killed the finest rhinoceros we had yet seen. They saw it in an open space of tall grass, surrounded by lantana brush, a flowering shrub with close-growing stems, perhaps twenty feet high and no thicker than a man's thumb; it forms a favorite cover for elephants and rhinoceros, and is well-nigh impenetrable to hunters. Fortunately this particular rhino was outside it, and Kermit and Tarlton got up to about twenty-five yards from him. Kermit then put one bullet behind his shoulder, and as he whipped round to charge, another bullet on the point of his shoulder; although mortally wounded, he showed no signs whatever of being hurt, and came at the hunters with great speed and savage desire to do harm. Then an extraordinary thing happened. Tarlton fired, inflicting merely a flesh wound in one shoulder, and the big, fearsome brute, which had utterly disregarded the two fatal shots, on receiving this flesh wound, wheeled and ran. Both firing, they killed him before he had gone many yards. He was a bull, with a thirty-inch horn.

By this time Cuninghame and Heller had finished the skin and skeleton of the bull they were preserving. Near the carcass Heller trapped an old male leopard, a savage beast; its skin was in fine shape, but it was not fat, and weighed just one hundred pounds. Now we all joined, and shifted camp to a point eight or nine miles distant from Meru boma, and fifteen hundred feet lower among the foot-hills. It was much hotter at this lower level; palms were among the trees that bordered the streams. On the day we shifted camp Tarlton and I rode in advance to look for elephants, followed by our gun-bearers and half a dozen wild Meru hunters, each carrying a spear or a bow and arrows. When we reached the hunting-grounds, open country with groves of trees and patches of jungle, the Meru went off in every direction to find elephant. We waited their return under a tree by a big stretch of cultivated ground. The region was well peopled, and all the way down the path had led between fields which the Meru women were tilling with their adze-like hoes, and banana-plantations where among the bananas other trees had been planted and the yam-vines trained up their trunks. These cool, shady banana-plantations, fenced in with tall hedges and bordered by rapid brooks, were really very attractive. Among them were scattered villages of

conical thatched huts, and level places plastered with cow dung
on which the grain was threshed; it was then stored in huts
raised on posts.   There were herds of cattle and flocks of
sheep and goats, and among the burdens the women bore we
often saw huge bottles of milk.   In the shambas there were
platforms and sometimes regular thatched huts placed in the
trees; these were for the watchers who were to keep the elephants out of the shambas at night.   Some of the natives wore
girdles of banana-leaves, looking, as Kermit said, much like
the pictures of savages in Sunday-school books.

Early in the afternoon some of the scouts returned with
news that three bull elephants were in a piece of forest a
couple of miles distant, and thither we went.   It was an open
grove of heavy thorn timber beside a strip of swamp; among
the trees the grass grew tall, and there were many thickets of
abutilon, a flowering shrub a dozen feet high.   On this the
elephant were feeding.   Tarlton's favorite sport was lion-hunting, but he was also a first-class elephant-hunter, and he brought
me up to these bulls in fine style.   Although only three hundred yards away, it took us two hours to get close to them.
Tarlton and the "shenzis"—wild natives, called in Swahili (a
kind of African chinook) "wa-shenzi"—who were with us,
climbed tree after tree, first to place the elephants, and then
to see if they carried ivory heavy enough to warrant my shooting them.   At last Tarlton brought me to within fifty yards
of them.   Two were feeding in bush which hid them from
view, and the third stood between, facing us.   We could only
see the top of his head and back, and not his tusks, and could
not tell whether he was worth shooting.   Much puzzled, we
stood where we were, peering anxiously at the huge, half-
hidden game.   Suddenly there was a slight eddy in the wind,
up went the elephant's trunk, twisting to and fro in the air;
evidently he could not catch a clear scent; but in another moment we saw the three great dark forms moving gently off
through the bush.   As rapidly as possible, following the trails
already tramped by the elephants, we walked forward, and

after a hundred yards Tarlton pointed to a big bull with good
tusks standing motionless behind some small trees seventy yards
distant. As I aimed at his head he started to move off; the
first bullet from the heavy Holland brought him to his knees,
and as he rose I knocked him flat with the second. He struggled to rise; but, both firing, we kept him down; and I finished
him with a bullet in the brain from the little Springfield. Although rather younger than either of the bulls I had already
shot, it was even larger. In its stomach were beans from the
shambas, abutilon tips, and bark, and especially the twigs,
leaves, and white blossoms of the smaller shrub. The tusks
weighed a little over a hundred pounds the pair.

We still needed a cow for the museum; and a couple of days
later, at noon, a party of natives brought in word that they
had seen two cows in a spot five miles away. Piloted by a
naked spearman, whose hair was done into a cue, we rode
toward the place. For most of the distance we followed old
elephant trails, in some places mere tracks beaten down through
stiff grass which stood above the head of a man on horseback,
in other places paths rutted deep into the earth. We crossed
a river where monkeys chattered among the tree-tops. On an
open plain we saw a rhinoceros cow trotting off with her calf.
At last we came to a hilltop with, on the summit, a noble fig-
tree, whose giant limbs were stretched over the palms that
clustered beneath. Here we left our horses and went forward
on foot, crossing a palm-fringed stream in a little valley. From
the next rise we saw the backs of the elephants as they stood
in a slight valley where the rank grass grew ten or twelve feet
high. It was some time before we could see the ivory so as to
be sure of exactly what we were shooting. Then the biggest
cow began to move slowly forward, and we walked nearly
parallel to her, along an elephant trail, until from a slight knoll
I got a clear view of her at a distance of eighty yards. As she
walked leisurely along, almost broadside to me, I fired the
right barrel of the Holland into her head, knocking her flat
down with the shock; and when she rose I put a bullet from

the left barrel through her heart, again knocking her completely off her feet; and this time she fell permanently. She was a very old cow, and her ivory was rather better than in the average of her sex in this neighborhood, the tusks weighing about eighteen pounds apiece. She had been ravaging the shambas overnight—which accounted in part for the natives being so eager to show her to me—and in addition to leaves and grass, her stomach contained quantities of beans. There was a young one—just out of calfhood, and quite able to take care of itself—with her; it ran off as soon as the mother fell.

Early next morning Cuninghame and Heller shifted part of the safari to the stream near where the dead elephant lay, intending to spend the following three days in taking off and preparing the skin. Meanwhile Tarlton, Kermit, and I were to try our luck in a short hunt on the other side of Meru boma, at a little crater lake called Lake Ingouga. We could not get an early start, and reached Meru too late to push on to the lake the same day.

The following morning we marched to the lake in two hours and a half. We spent an hour in crossing a broad tongue of woodland that stretched down from the wonderful mountain forest lying higher on the slopes. The trail was blind in many places because elephant paths of every age continually led along and across it, some of them being much better marked than the trail itself as it twisted through the sun-flecked shadows underneath the great trees. Then we came out on high downs, covered with tall grass and littered with volcanic stones and broken by ravines which were choked with dense underbrush. There were high hills, and to the left of the downs, toward Kenia, these were clad in forest. We pitched our tents on a steep cliff overlooking the crater lake—or pond, as it might more properly be called. It was bordered with sedge, and through the water-lilies on its surface we saw the reflection of the new moon after nightfall. Here and there thick forest came down to the brink, and through this, on opposite sides of the pond, deeply worn elephant paths, evidently travelled for ages, wound down to the water.

That evening we hunted for bushbuck but saw none. While sitting on a hillock at dusk, watching for game, a rhino trotted up to inspect us, with ears cocked forward and tail erect. A rhino always has something comic about it, like a pig, formidable though it at times is. This one carried a poor horn, and therefore we were pleased when at last it trotted off without obliging us to shoot it. We saw new kinds of whydahbirds, one with a yellow breast, one with white in its tail; at this altitude the cocks were still in full plumage, although it was just past the middle of September; whereas at Naivasha they had begun to lose their long tail-feathers nearly two months previously.

On returning to camp we received a note from Cuninghame saying that Heller had been taken seriously sick, and Tarlton had to go to them. This left Kermit and me to take our two days' hunt together.

One day we got nothing. We saw game on the open downs, but it was too wary, and though we got within twenty-five yards of eland in thick cover, we could only make out a cow, and she took fright and ran without our ever getting a glimpse of the bull that was with her. Late in the afternoon we saw an elephant a mile and a half away, crossing a corner of the open downs. We followed its trail until the light grew too dim for shooting, but never overtook it, although at the last we could hear it ahead of us breaking the branches; and we made our way back to camp through the darkness.

The other day made amends. It was Kermit's turn to shoot an elephant, and mine to shoot a rhinoceros; and each of us was to act as the backing gun for the other. In the forenoon, we saw a bull rhino with a good horn walking over the open downs. A convenient hill enabled us to cut him off without difficulty, and from its summit we killed him at the base, fifty or sixty yards off. His front horn was nearly twenty-nine inches long; but though he was an old bull, his total length, from tip of nose to tip of tail, was only twelve feet, and he was, I should guess, not more than two-thirds the bulk of the big bull I killed in the Sotik.

We rested for an hour or two at noon, under the shade of a very old tree with glossy leaves and orchids growing on its gnarled, hoary limbs, while the unsaddled horses grazed, and the gun-bearers slept near by, the cool mountain air, although this was midday under the equator, making them prefer the sunlight to the shade. When we moved on it was through a sea of bush ten or fifteen feet high, dotted here and there with trees and riddled in every direction by the trails of elephant, rhinoceros, and buffalo. Each of these animals frequents certain kinds of country to which the other two rarely or never penetrate; but here they all three found ground to their liking. Except along their winding trails, which were tunnels where the jungle was tall, it would have been practically impossible to traverse the thick and matted cover in which they had made their abode.

We could not tell what moment we might find ourselves face to face with some big beast at such close quarters as to insure a charge, and we moved in cautious silence, our rifles in our hands. Rhinoceros were especially plentiful, and we continually came across not only their tracks, but the dusty wallows in which they rolled, and where they came to deposit their dung. The fresh sign of elephant, however, distracted our attention from the lesser game, and we followed the big footprints eagerly, now losing the trail, now finding it again. At last near a clump of big trees we caught sight of three huge, dark bodies ahead of us. The wind was right, and we stole toward them, Kermit leading, and I immediately behind. Through the tangled branches their shapes loomed in vague outline; but we saw that one had a pair of long tusks, and our gun-bearers unanimously pronounced it a big bull, with good ivory. A few more steps gave Kermit a chance at its head, at about sixty yards, and with a bullet from his 405 Winchester he floored the mighty beast. It rose, and we both fired in unison, bringing it down again; but as we came up, it struggled to get on its feet, roaring savagely, and once more we both fired together. This finished it. We were disappointed at finding that it was not a bull, but it was a large cow, with tusks over five feet long—a very unusual length for a cow—one weighing twenty-five and the other twenty-two pounds.

Our experience had convinced us that both the Wincheser 405, and the Springfield 300 would do good work with elephants; although I kept to my belief that, for such very heavy game, my Holland 500–450 was an even better weapon.

Not far from where this elephant fell Tarlton had, the year before, witnessed an interesting incident. He was watching a small herd of elephants, cows and calves, which were in the open, when he saw them begin to grow uneasy. Then, with a shrill trumpet, a cow approached a bush, out of which bounded a big lion. Instantly all the cows charged him, and he fled as fast as his legs could carry him for the forest, two hundred yards distant. He just managed to reach the cover in safety; and then the infuriated cows, in their anger at his escape, demolished the forest for several rods in every direction.

XI

THE GUASO NYERO; A RIVER OF THE EQUATORIAL DESERT

WHEN I reached Neri, after coming down from killing my first elephant on Kenia, I was kept waiting two or three days before I could gather enough Kikuyu porters. As I could not speak a word of their language, I got a couple of young Scotch settlers, very good fellows, to take charge of the safari out to where I intended to hunt. There was a party of the King's African Rifles camped at Neri; the powerful-looking enlisted men were from the south, chiefly from one of the northern-most tribes of Zulu blood, and their two officers were of the best Kipling-soldier type. Then there was another safari, that of Messrs. Kearton and Clark, who were taking some really extraordinary photographs of birds and game. Finally, Governor and Mrs. Jackson arrived from a trip they had been making round Kenia; and I was much pleased to be able to tell the governor, who had helped me in every way, about my bull elephant, and to discuss with him some of the birds we had seen and the mammals we had trapped. A great ingowa, a war-dance of the natives, was held in his honor, and the sight was, as always, one of interest and of a certain fascination. There was an Indian trader at Neri from whom we had obtained donkeys to carry to our elephant camp "posho," or food for the porters. He announced that they were all in readiness in a letter to Cuninghame, which was meant to be entirely respectful, but which sounded odd, as it was couched in characteristic Baboo English. The opening lines ran: "Dear K-ham, the donkeys are altogether deadly."

At last fifty Kikuyus assembled—they are not able to carry the loads of regular Swahili porters—and I started that moment, though it was too late in the afternoon to travel more than three or four miles. The Kikuyus were real savages, naked save for a dingy blanket, usually carried round the neck. They formed a picturesque safari; but it was difficult to make the grasshopper-like creatures take even as much thought for the future as the ordinary happy-go-lucky porters take. At night if it rained they cowered under the bushes in drenched and shivering discomfort; and yet they had to be driven to make bough shelters for themselves. Once these shelters were up, and a little fire kindled at the entrance of each, the moping, spiritlesss wretches would speedily become transformed into beings who had lost all remembrance of ever having been wet or cold. After their posho had been distributed and eaten they would sit, huddled and cheerful, in their shelters, and sing steadily for a couple of hours. Their songs were much wilder than those of the regular porters, and were often warlike. Occasionally, some "chantey-man," as he would be called on shipboard, improvised or repeated a kind of story in short sentences or strophes; but the main feature of each song was the endless repetition of some refrain, musically chanted in chorus by the whole party. This repetition of a short sentence or refrain is a characteristic of many kinds of savage music; I have seen the Pawnees grow almost maddened by their triumph song, or victory song, which consisted of nothing whatever but the fierce, barking, wolf-like repetition of the words "In the morning the wolves feasted."

Our first afternoon's march was uneventful; but I was amused at one of our porters and the "safari" ants. These safari ants are so called by the natives because they go on foraging expeditions in immense numbers. The big-headed warriors are able to inflict a really painful bite. In open spaces, as where crossing a path, the column makes a little sunken way through which it streams uninterruptedly. Whenever we came to such a safari ant column, in its sunken way, crossing our path, the porter in question laid two twigs on the ground as a peace-offering to the ants. He said that they were on safari, just as we were, and that it was wise to propitiate them.

That evening we camped in a glade in the forest. At night-fall dozens of the big black-and-white hornbill, croaking harsh-ly, flew overhead, their bills giving them a curiously top-heavy look. They roosted in the trees near by.

Next day we came out on the plains, where there was no cultivation, and instead of the straggling thatch and wattle, unfenced villages of the soil-tilling Kikuyus, we found our-selves again among the purely pastoral Masai, whose tem-porary villages are arranged in a ring or oval, the cattle being each night herded in the middle, and the mud-daubed, cowdung-plastered houses so placed that their backs form a nearly con-tinuous circular wall, the spaces between being choked with thorn-bushes. I killed a steinbuck, missed a tommy, and at three hundred yards hit a Jackson's hartbeest too far back, and failed in an effort to ride it down.

The day after we were out on plains untenanted by human beings, and early in the afternoon struck water by which to pitch our tents. There was not much game, and it was shy; but I thought that I could kill enough to keep the camp in meat, so I sent back the two Scotchmen and their Kikuyus, after having them build a thorn boma, or fence, round the camp. One of the reasons why the Masai had driven their herds and flocks off this plain was because a couple of lions had turned man-eaters, and had killed a number of men and women. We saw no sign of lions, and believed they had fol-lowed the Masai; but there was no use in taking needless chances.

The camp was beside a cold, rapid stream, one of the head-waters of the Guaso Nyero. It was heavily fringed with thorn timber. To the east the crags and snow-fields of Kenia rose from the slow swell of the mountain's base. It should have been the dry season, but there were continual heavy rains, which often turned into torrential downpours. In the overcast mornings as I rode away from camp, it was as cool as if I were riding through the fall weather at home; at noon, if the sun came out, straight overhead, the heat was blazing; and we generally returned to camp at nightfall, drenched with the cold rain. The first heavy storm, the evening we pitched camp, much excited all my followers. Ali came rushing into the tent to tell me that there was "a big snake up high." This certainly seemed worth investigating, and I followed him outside where everybody was looking at the "snake," which proved to be a huge, funnel-shaped, whirling cloud, careering across the darkened sky. It was a kind of waterspout or cyclone; fortunately it passed to one side of camp.

The first day I hunted I shot only a steinbuck for the table. The country alternated between bare plains and great stretches of sparse, stunted thorns. We saw zebra, and two or three bands of oryx; big, handsome antelope strongly built and boldly colored, with long, black, rapier-like horns. They were very wary, much more so than the zebra with which they associated, and we could not get anywhere near them.

Next day I hunted along the edges of a big swamp. We saw water-buck, but were unable to get within shot. However, near the farther end of the swamp, in an open swale, we found four eland feeding. The eland is the king of antelope; and not only did I desire meat for camp, but I wished the head of a good bull as a trophy for myself, the eland I had hitherto shot being for the National Museum. The little band included a big bull, a small bull, and two cows; at a distance the big bull looked slaty blue. The great, sleek, handsome creatures were feeding in the long grass just like cattle, switching their long tails at the flies. The country looked like a park, with clumps of thorn-trees scattered over the grassy sward. Carefully I crept on all fours from tree clump to tree clump, trying always to move when the elands' heads were down grazing. At last I was within three hundred yards, when one of the cows caught a glimpse of me and alarmed the others. They were startled, but puzzled, and after trotting a few rods turned to stare at the half-seen object of their alarm. Rising to my knee I shot the big bull in the throat as with head erect he gazed in my direction. Off he went with a rush, the others bounding and leaping as they accompanied him, and we followed on the blood spoor. Bakhari and Gouvimali trotted fast on the trail, and in order to be fresh for the shot I mounted Tranquillity. Suddenly out bounced the wounded bull from some bushes close by, and the horse nearly had a fit; I could hardly get off in time to empty my magazine at long range—fortunately with effect. It was a magnificent bull of the variety called Patterson's eland, with a fine head. Few prize oxen would be as heavy, and in spite of its great size, its finely moulded limbs and beautiful coat gave it a thoroughly game look.

Oryx were now what I especially wished, and we devoted all of the following day to their pursuit. We saw three bands, two of them accompanying herds of zebra, after the manner of kongoni. Both species were found indifferently on the bare, short-grass flats and among the thin, stunted thorn-trees which covered much of the plains. After a careful stalk, the latter part on all fours, I got to within about three hundred yards of a mixed herd, and put a bullet into one oryx as it faced me, and hit another as it ran. The first, from its position, I thought I would surely kill if I hit it at all, and both of the wounded beasts were well behind the herd when it halted a mile away on the other side of the plain. But as we approached they all went off together, and I can only hope the two I hit recovered, at any rate, after we had followed them for miles, the tough beasts were still running as strongly as ever.

All the morning I manœuvred and tramped hard, in vain. At noon, I tried a stalk on a little band of six, who were standing still, idly switching their tails, out in a big flat. They saw me, and at four hundred yards I missed the shot. By this time I felt rather desperate, and decided for once to abandon legitimate proceedings and act on the Ciceronian theory, that he who throws the javelin all day must hit the mark some time.

Accordingly I emptied the magazines of both my rifles at the oryx, as they ran across my front, and broke the neck of a fine cow, at four hundred and fifty yards. Six or seven hundred yards off the survivors stopped, and the biggest bull, evidently much put out, uttered loud bawling grunts and drove the others round with his horns. Meanwhile I was admiring the handsome dun gray coat of my prize, its long tail and long, sharp, slender horns, and the bold black-and-white markings on its face. Hardly had we skinned the carcass before the vultures lit on it; with them were two marabou storks, one of which I shot with a hard bullet from the Springfield.

The oryx, like the roan and sable, and in striking contrast to the eland, is a bold and hard fighter, and when cornered will charge a man or endeavor to stab a lion. If wounded it must be approached with a certain amount of caution. The eland, on the other hand, in spite of its huge size, is singularly mild and inoffensive, an old bull being as inferior to an oryx in the will and power to fight as it is in speed and endurance. "Antelope," as I have said, is a very loose term, meaning simply any hollow-horned ruminant that isn't an ox, a sheep, or a goat. The eland is one of the group of tragelaphs, which are as different from the true antelopes, such as the gazelles, as they are from the oxen. One of its kinsfolk is the handsome little bushbuck, about as big as a whitetail deer; a buck of which Kermit had killed two specimens. The bushbuck is a wicked fighter, no other buck of its size being as dangerous; which makes the helplessness and timidity of its huge relative all the more striking.

I had kept four Kikuyu with me to accompany me on my hunts and carry in the skins and meat. They were with me on this occasion; and it was amusing to see how my four regular attendants, Bakhari and Gouvimali the gun-bearers, Simba the sais, and Kibobo the skinner, looked down on their wild and totally uncivilized brethren. They would not associate with the "shenzis," as they called them; that is, savages or bush people. But the "shenzis" always amused and interested me;

and this was especially true on the afternoon in question. Soon after we had started campward with the skin and meat of the oryx, we encountered a succession of thunder-storms. The rain came down in a deluge, so that the water stood ankle-deep on the flats, the lightning flashed continuously on every side, and the terrific peals of thunder made one continuous roll. At first it maddened my horse; but the uninterrupted blaze and roar, just because uninterrupted, ended by making him feel there was nothing to be done, and he plodded stolidly forward through the driving storm. My regular attendants accepted it with an entire philosophy, which was finally copied by the Kikuyus, who at first felt frightened. One of them had an old umbrella which he shared with a crony. He himself was carrying the marabou stork; his crony had long strips of raw oryx meat wound in a swollen girdle about his waist; neither had a stitch on save the blankets which were wrapped round their throats; and they clasped each other in a tight embrace as they walked along under the battered old umbrella.

In this desolate and lonely land the majesty of the storms impressed on the beholder a sense of awe and solemn exaltation. Tossing their crests, and riven by lightning, they gathered in their wrath from every quarter of the heavens, and darkness was before and under them; then, in the lull of a moment, they might break apart, while the sun turned the rain to silver and the rainbows were set in the sky; but always they gathered again, menacing and mighty—for the promise of the bow was never kept, and ever the clouds returned after the rain. Once as I rode facing Kenia the clouds tore asunder, to right and left, and the mountain towered between, while across its base was flung a radiant arch. But almost at once the many-colored glory was dimmed; for in splendor and terror the storm strode in front, and shrouded all things from sight in thunder-shattered sheets of rain.

These days alone in the wilderness went by very pleasantly, and, as it was for not too long, I thoroughly enjoyed being entirely by myself, so far as white men were concerned. By

AFRICAN GAME TRAILS
232

this time I had become really attached to my native followers,
who looked after my interest and comfort in every way; and
in return I kept them supplied with plenty of food, saw that
they were well clothed, and forced them to gather enough fire-
wood to keep their tents dry and warm at night—for cold,
rainy weather is always hard upon them.

Ali, my faithful head tent-boy, and Shemlani his assistant
—poor Bill the Kikuyu had left because of an intricate row
with his fellows—were both, as they proudly informed me,
Arabs. On the East African coast the so-called Arabs almost
all have native blood in them and speak Swahili; the curious,
newly created language of the descendants of the natives whom
the Arabs originally enslaved, and who themselves may have in
their veins a little Arab blood; in fact, the dividing line between
Swahili and Arab bcomes impracticable for an outsider to draw
where, as is generally the case, it is patent that the blood of
both races is mixed to a degree at which it is only possible
to guess. Ali spoke some English; and he and Shemlani were
devoted and efficient servitors. Bakhari the gun-bearer was a
Swahili, quite fearless with dangerous game, rather sullen,.
and unmoved by any emotion that I could ever discover. He
spoke a little English, but it could not be called idiomatic. One
day we saw two ostriches, a cock and a hen, with their chicks,
and Bakhari with some excitement said: "Look, sah! ostrich!
bull, cow, and pups!" The other gun-bearer, Gouvimali, in
some ways an even better hunter, and always good-tempered,
knew but one English phrase; regularly every afternoon or
evening, after cleaning the rifle he had carried, he would say,
as he left the tent, his face wreathed in smiles: "G-o-o-d-e-bye!"
Gouvimali was a Wakamba, as were Simba and my other
sais, M'nyassa, who had taken the place of Hamisi (Hamisi
had broken down in health, his legs, as he assured me, becom-
ing "very sick"). The cook, Roberti, was a mission boy, a
Christian; we had several Christians with the safari, one being
a head man, and all did excellently. I mention this because one
so often hears it said that mission boys turn out worthless.

Most of our men were heathens; and of course many, both of the Christians and the Mohammedans, were rather thinly veneered with the religions they respectively professed.

When in the morning we started on our hunt my gun-bearers and sais, and the skinners, if any were along, walked silently behind me, on the lookout for game. Returning, they were apt to get in front, to pilot me back to camp. If, as at this time was generally the case, we returned with our heads bent to the rushing rain, they trudged sturdily ahead in dripping silence. If the weather was clear the spirits of the stalwart fellows were sure to rise until they found some expression. The Wakamba might break into song; or they might all talk together in Swahili, recounting the adventures of the day, and chaffing one another with uproarious laughter about any small misadventure: a difference of opinion as to the direction of camp being always a subject, first for earnest discussion, and then for much mirth at the expense of whomever the event proved mistaken.

My two horses, when I did not use them, grazed contentedly throughout the day near the little thorn boma which surrounded our tents; and at nightfall the friendly things came within it of their own accord to be given their feed of corn and be put in their own tent. When the sun was hot they were tormented by biting flies; but their work was easy, and they were well treated and throve. In the daytime vultures, kites, and white-necked ravens came round camp, and after nightfall jackals wailed and hyenas uttered their weird cries as they prowled outside the thorn walls. Twice, at midnight, we heard the ominous sighing or moaning of a hungry lion, and I looked to my rifle, which always stood, loaded, at the head of my bed. But on neither occasion did he come near us. Every night a fire was kept burning in the entrance to the boma, and the three askaris watched in turn, with instructions to call me if there was any need.

I easily kept the camp in meat, as I had guessed that I could do. My men feasted on oryx and eland, while I reserved the tongues and tenderloins for myself. Each day I hunted for

eight or ten hours, something of interest always happening. I
would not shoot at the gazelles; and the game I did want was
so shy that almost all my shots were at long range, and conse-
quently a number of them did not hit. However, I came on
my best oryx in rather thick bush, and killed it at a hundred
and twenty-five yards, as it turned with a kind of sneeze of
alarm or curiosity, and stood broadside to me, the sun glinting
on its handsome coat and polished black horns. One of my
Kikuyu followers packed the skin entire to camp. I had more
trouble with another oryx, wounding it one evening at three
hundred and fifty yards, and next morning following the trail
and after much hard work and a couple of misses killing it
with a shot at three hundred yards. On September 2 I found
two newly born oryx calves. The color of the oryx made
them less visible than hartbeest when a long way off on the
dry plains. I noticed that whenever we saw them mixed in a
herd with zebra, it was the zebra that first struck our eyes.
But in bright sunlight, in bush, I also noticed that the zebra
themselves were hard to see.

One afternoon, while skirting the edge of a marsh teeming
with waders and water-fowl, I came across four stately Kavirondo cranes, specimens of which bird the naturalists had been
particularly anxious to secure. They were not very shy for
cranes, but they would not keep still, and I missed a shot with
the Springfield as they walked along about a hundred and fifty
yards ahead of me. However, they were unwise enough to
circle round me when they rose, still keeping the same distance,
and all the time uttering their musical call, while their great
wings flapped in measured beats. Wing-shooting with the rifle,
even at such large birds of such slow and regular flight, is never
easy, and they were rather far off; but with the last cartridge
in my magazine—the fifth—I brought one whirling down
through the air, the bullet having pierced its body. It was a
most beautiful bird, black, white, and chestnut, with an erect
golden crest, and long, lanceolate gray feathers on the throat
and breast.

There were water-buck and impala in this swamp. I tried to get a bull of the former but failed. Several times I was within fifty yards of doe impala and cow water-buck, with their young, and watched them as they fed and rested, quite unconscious of my presence. Twice I saw steinbuck, on catching sight of me, lie down, hoping to escape observation. The red coat of the steinbuck is rather conspicuous, much more so than the coat of the duiker; yet it often tries to hide from possible foes.

Late in the afternoon of September 3, Cuninghame and Heller, with the main safari, joined me, and I greeted them joyfully; while my men were equally pleased to see their fellows, each shaking hands with his especial friends. Next morning we started toward Meru, heading northeast, toward the foot-hills of Kenia. The vegetation changed its character as we rose. By the stream where we had camped grew the great thorn-trees with yellow-green trunks which we had become accustomed to associate with the presence of herds of game. Out on the dry flats were other thorns, weazened little trees, or mere scrawny bushes, with swellings like bulbs on the branches and twigs, and the long thorns far more conspicuous than the scanty foliage; though what there was of this foliage, now brilliant green, was exquisite in hue and form, the sprays of delicate little leaves being as fine as the daintiest lace. On the foot-hills all these thorn-trees vanished. We did not go as high as the forest belt proper (here narrow, while above it the bamboos covered the mountainside), but tongues of juniper forest stretched down along the valleys which we crossed, and there were large patches of coarse deerfern, while among many unknown flowers we saw blue lupins, ox-eyed daisies, and clover. That night we camped so high that it was really cold, and we welcomed the roaring fires of juniper logs.

We rose at sunrise. It was a glorious morning, clear and cool, and as we sat at breakfast, the table spread in the open on the dew-drenched grass, we saw in the southeast the peak of Kenia, and through the high, transparent air the snow-fields seemed so close as almost to dazzle our eyes. To the north and west we looked far out over the wide, rolling plains to a wilderness of mountain ranges, barren and jagged. All that day and the next we journeyed eastward, almost on the equator. At noon the overhead sun burned with torrid heat; but with the twilight—short compared to the long northern twilights, but not nearly as short as tropical twilights are often depicted—came the cold, and each night the frost was heavy. The country was untenanted by man. In the afternoon of the third day we began to go downhill, and hour by hour the flora changed. At last we came to a broad belt of woodland, where the strange trees of many kinds grew tall and thick. Among them were camphor-trees, and trees with gouty branch tips, bearing leaves like those of the black walnut, and panicles of lilac flowers, changing into brown seed-vessels; and other trees, with clusters of purple flowers, and the seeds or nuts enclosed in hard pods or seed-vessels like huge sausages.

On the other side of the forest we came suddenly out on the cultivated fields of the Wa-Meru, who, like the Kikuyu, till the soil; and among them, farther down, was Meru boma, its neat, picturesque buildings beautifully placed among green groves and irrigated fields, and looking out from its cool elevation over the hot valleys beneath. It is one of the prettiest spots in East Africa. We were more than hospitably received by the commissioner, Mr. Horne, who had been a cow-puncher in Wyoming for seven years—so that naturally we had much in common. He had built the station himself, and had tamed the wild tribes around by mingled firmness and good treatment; and he was a mighty hunter, and helped us in every way.

Here we met Kermit and Tarlton, and heard all about their hunt. They had been away from us for three weeks and a half, along the Guaso Nyero, and had enjoyed first-rate luck. Kermit had been particularly interested in a caravan they had met, consisting of wild spear-bearing Borani, people like Somalis, who were bringing down scores of camels and hundreds of small horses to sell at Nairobi. They had come from the north, near the outlying Abyssinian lands, and the caravan was commanded by an Arab of stately and courteous manners. Such an extensive caravan journey was rare in the old days before English rule; but one of the results of the "Pax Europaica," wherever it obtains in German, French, or English Africa, is a great increase of intercourse, commercial and social, among the different tribes, even where widely separated. This caravan had been followed by lions; and a day or two afterward Kermit and Tarlton ran into what were probably these very lions. There were eleven of them: a male with a heavy mane, three lionesses, and seven cubs, some of them about half grown. As Kermit and Tarlton galloped after them, the lion took the lead, the cubs coming in the middle, while three lionesses loped along in the rear, guarding their young. The lion cared little for his wives and offspring, and gradually drew ahead of them, while the two horsemen, riding at full speed, made a wide détour round the others in order to reach him; so that at last they got between him and the ten lionesses and cubs, the big lion coming first, the horsemen next, and then the lesser lions, all headed the same way. As the horse-hoofs thundered closer the lion turned to bay. Kermit—whose horse had once fallen with him in the chase—and Tarlton leaped off their horses, and Kermit hit the lion with his first shot, and, as it started to charge, mortally wounded it with a second bullet. It turned and tried to reach cover, and Tarlton stopped it with a third shot; for there was no time to lose, as they wished to tackle the other lions. After a sharp gallop they rounded up the lioness and cubs. Kermit killed one large cub, which they mistook for a lioness; wounded a lioness which for the time being escaped; killed another with a single bullet from his 30–40 Winchester—for the others he used his 405 Winchester—and hit the third as she crouched facing him at two hundred yards. She at once came in at full speed, making a most determined charge. Kermit and Tarlton were standing near their horses. The lioness came on with great bounds so that Kermit missed her twice, but broke her shoulder high up when she was but thirty yards off. She fell on her head and, on rising, galloped, not at the men, but at the horses, who, curiously enough, paid no heed to her. Tarlton stopped her with a bullet in the nick of time, just before she reached them, and with another bullet Kermit killed her. Two days later they came on the remaining cubs and the wounded lioness, and Kermit killed the latter; but they let the cubs go, feeling it unsportsmanlike to kill them—a feeling which I am by no means certain I share, for lions are scourges not only to both wild and tame animals but to man himself.

Kermit also rode down and killed two cheetahs and a serval, and got a bad tumble while chasing a jackal, his horse turning a complete somersault through a thorny bush. This made seven cheetahs that he had killed, a record unequalled for any other East African trip of the same length; and the finding and galloping down of these cheetahs—going at breakneck speed over any and every kind of ground, and then shooting them either from foot or horseback—made one of the noteworthy features of our trip. One of these two cheetahs had just killed a steinbuck. The serval was with its mate and Kermit watched them for some time through his glasses before following them. There was one curious feature of their conduct. One of them was playing about, now near the other, now leaving it; and near by was a bustard, which it several times pretended to stalk, crawling toward it a few yards, and then standing up and walking away. The bustard paid no heed to it; and, more singular still, two white-necked ravens lit close to it, within a few yards on either side; the serval sitting erect between them, seemingly quite unconcerned for a couple of minutes, and then strolling off without making any effort to molest them. I can give no explanation of the incident; it illustrates afresh the need of ample and well-recorded observations by trustworthy field naturalists, who shall go into the wilderness before the big game, the big birds, and the beasts of prey vanish. Those pages of the book of nature which are best worth reading can best be read far from the dwellings of civilized man; and for their full interpretation we need the services, not of one man, but of many men, who in addition to the gift of accurate observation shall if possible possess the power fully, accurately, and with vividness to write about what they have observed.

Kermit shot many other animals, among them three fine oryx, one of which he rode down on horseback, manœuvring so that at last it galloped fairly closely across his front, whereupon he leaped off his horse for the shot; an aardwolf (a miniature hyena with very weak teeth) which bolted from its hole at his approach; gerenuk, small antelope with necks relatively as long as giraffes', which are exceedingly shy and difficult to obtain; and the Grevy's zebra, as big as a small horse. Most of his hunting was done alone, either on foot or on horseback; on a long run or all-day tramp no other member of our outfit, black or white, could quite keep up with him. He and Tarlton found where a leopard had killed and partly eaten a nearly full-grown individual of this big zebra. He also shot a twelve-foot crocodile. The ugly, formidable brute had in its belly sticks, stones, the claws of a cheetah, the hoofs of an impala, and the big bones of an eland, together with the shell plates of one of the large river-turtles; evidently it took toll indifferently from among its fellow denizens of the river, and from among the creatures that came to drink, whether beasts of pasture or the flesh-eaters that preyed upon them.

He also shot three buffalo bulls, Tarlton helping him to finish them off, for they are tough animals, tenacious of life and among the most dangerous of African game. One turned to charge, but was disabled by the bullets of both of them before he could come on. Tarlton, whose experience in the hunting-field against dangerous game had been large, always maintained that, although lion-hunting was the most dangerous sport, because a hunted lion was far more apt to charge than any other animal, yet when a buffalo bull did charge he was more dangerous than a lion, because harder to kill or turn. Where zebra and other game are abundant, as on the Athi

Plains, lion do not meddle with such formidable quarry as buffalo; on Heatley's farm lions sometimes made their lairs in the same papyrus swamp with the buffalo, but hardly ever molested them. In many places, however, the lion preys largely, and in some places chiefly, on the buffalo. The hunters of wide experience with whom I conversed, men like Tarlton, Cuninghame, and Horne, were a unit in stating that where a single lion killed a buffalo they had always found that the buffalo was a cow or immature bull, and that whenever they had found a full-grown bull thus killed, several lions had been engaged in the job. Horne had once found the carcass of a big bull which had been killed and eaten by lions, and near by lay a dead lioness with a great rip in her side, made by the buffalo's horn in the fight in which he succumbed. Even a buffalo cow, if fairly pitted against a single lion, would probably stand an even chance; but of course the fight never is fair, the lion's aim being to take his prey unawares and get a death grip at the outset; and then, unless his hold is broken, he cannot be seriously injured.

Twenty years ago the African buffalo were smitten with one of those overwhelming disasters which are ever occurring and recurring in the animal world. Africa is not only the land, beyond all others, subject to odious and terrible insect plagues of every conceivable kind, but is also peculiarly liable to cattle murrains. About the year 1889, or shortly before, a virulent form of rinderpest started among the domestic cattle and wild buffalo almost at the northern border of the buffalo's range, and within the next few years worked gradually southward to beyond the Zambesi. It wrought dreadful havoc among the cattle, and in consequence decimated by starvation many of the cattle-owning tribes; it killed many of the large bovine antelopes, and it well-nigh exterminated the buffalo. In many places the buffalo-herds were absolutely wiped out, the species being utterly destroyed throughout great tracts of territory, notably in East Africa; in other places the few survivors did not represent the hundredth part of those that had died. For years the East African buffalo ceased to exist as a beast of the chase. But all the time it was slowly regaining the lost ground, and during the last decade its increase has been rapid. Unlike the slow-breeding elephant and rhinoceros, buffalo multiply apace, like domestic cattle, and in many places the herds have now become too numerous. Their rapid recovery from a calamity so terrific is interesting and instructive.* Doubtless for many years after man, in recognizably human form, appeared on this planet, he played but a small part in the destruction of big animals, compared to plague, to insect pests and microbes, to drought, flood, earth upheaval, and change of temperature. But during the geological moment covering the few thousand years of recorded history man has been not merely the chief, but practically the sole factor in the extermination of big mammals and birds.

At and near Meru boma we spent a fortnight hunting elephant and rhinoceros, as described in the preceding chapter. While camped by the boma white-necked vulturine ravens and black-and-white crows came familiarly around the tents. A young eland bull, quite as tame as a domestic cow, was picketed, now here, now there, about us. Horne was breaking it to drive in a cart.

During our stay another district commissioner, Mr. Piggott, came over on a short visit; it was he who the preceding year, while at Neri, had been obliged to undertake the crusade against the rhinos, because, quite unprovoked, they had killed various natives. He told us that at the same time a man-eating leopard made its appearance, and killed seven children. It did not attack at night, but in the daytime, its victims being the little boys who were watching the flocks of goats; sometimes it took a boy and sometimes a goat. Two old men killed it with spears on the occasion of its taking the last victim. It was a big male, very old, much

---

* On our trip along the Guaso Nyero we heard that there had been a fresh outbreak of rinderpest among the buffalo; I hope it will not prove such a hideous disaster.

emaciated, and the teeth worn to stumps.   Horne told us
that a month or two before our arrival at Meru a leopard
had begun a career of woman-killing.   It killed one woman
by a bite in the throat, and ate the body.   It sprang on
and badly wounded another, but was driven off in time to
save her life.   This was probably the leopard Heller trapped
and shot, in the very locality where it had committed its
ravages; it was an old male, but very thin, with worn teeth.
In these cases the reason for the beast's action was plain:
in each instance, a big savage male had found his powers
failing, and had been driven to prey on the females and
young of the most helpless of animals, man.   But another
attack, of which Piggott told us, was apparently due to the
queer individual freakishness always to be taken into account
in dealing with wild beasts.   A Masai chief, with two or
three followers, was sitting eating under a bush, when, absolutely without warning, a leopard sprang on him, clawed him
on the head and hand, without biting him, and as instantly
disappeared.   Piggott attended to the wounded man.

In riding in the neighborhood, through the tall dry grass,
which would often rattle in the wind, I was amused to find
that if I suddenly heard the sound I was apt to stand alertly
on guard, quite unconsciously and instinctively, because it
suggested the presence of a rattlesnake.   During the years I
lived on a ranch in the West I was always hearing and killing
rattlesnakes, and although I knew well that no African snake
carries a rattle, my subconscious senses always threw me
to attention if there was a sound resembling that made by
a rattler.   Tarlton, by the way, told me an interesting anec-
dote of a white-tailed mongoose and a snake.   The mongoose
was an inmate of the house where he dwelt with his brother
and was quite tame.   One day they brought in a rather small
puff-adder, less than two feet long, put it on the floor, and
showed it to the mongoose.   Instantly the latter sprang toward
the snake, every hair in its body and tail on end, and halted
five feet away, while the snake lay in curves like the thong

of a whip, its head turned toward the mongoose. Both were motionless for a moment. Then suddenly the mongoose seemed to lose all its excitement; its hair smoothed down; and it trotted quietly up to the snake, seized it by the middle of the back—it always devoured its food with savage voracity—and settled comfortably down to its meal. Like lightning the snake's head whipped round. It drove its fangs deep into the snout or lip of the mongoose, hung on for a moment, and then repeated the blow. The mongoose paid not the least attention, but went on munching the snake's body, severed its back-bone at once, and then ate it all up, head, fangs, poison, and everything; and it never showed a sign of having received any damage in the encounter. I had always understood that the mongoose owed its safety to its agility in avoiding the snake's stroke, and I can offer no explanation of this particular incident.

There were eland on the high downs not far from Meru, apparently as much at home in the wet, cold climate as on the hot plains. Their favorite gait is the trot. An elephant moves at a walk or rather rack; a giraffe has a very peculiar leisurely looking gallop, both hind legs coming forward nearly at the same time, outside the fore legs; rhino and buffalo trot and run. Eland when alarmed bound with astonishing agility for such large beasts—a trait not shown by other large antelope, like oryx—and then gallop for a short distance; but the big bulls speedily begin to trot, and the cows and younger bulls gradually also drop back into the trot. In fact, their gaits are in essence those of the wapiti, which also prefer the trot, although wapiti never make the bounds that eland do at the start. The moose, however, is more essentially a trotter than either eland or wapiti; a very old and heavy moose never, when at speed, goes at any other gait than a trot, except that under the pressure of great and sudden danger it may perhaps make a few bounds.*

* A perfectly trustworthy Maine hunter informed me that in the spring he had once seen in the snow where a bear had sprung at two big moose,

While at Meru boma I received a cable, forwarded by native runners, telling me of Peary's wonderful feat in reaching the North Pole. Of course we were all overjoyed, and in particular we Americans could not but feel a special pride in the fact that it was a fellow countryman who had performed the great and noteworthy achievement. A little more than a year had passed since I said good-by to Peary as he started on his arctic quest; after leaving New York in the *Roosevelt,* he had put into Oyster Bay to see us, and we had gone aboard the *Roosevelt,* had examined with keen interest how she was fitted for the boreal seas and the boreal winter, and had then waved farewell to the tall, gaunt explorer, as he stood looking toward us over the side of the stout little ship.*

On September 21, Kermit and Tarlton started southwest, toward Lake Hannington, and Cuninghame and I north toward the Guaso Nyero. Heller was under the weather, and we left him to spend a few days at Meru boma, and then to take in the elephant-skins and other museum specimens to Nairobi.

As Cuninghame and I were to be nearly four weeks in a country with no food-supplies, we took a small donkey safari to carry the extra food for our porters—for in these remote places the difficulty of taking in many hundred pounds of salt, as well as skin tents, and the difficulty of bringing out the skeletons and skins of the big animals collected, make such an expedition as ours, undertaken for scientific purposes, far more cumbersome and unwieldy than a mere hunting

and they had bounded for several rods before settling into the tremendous trot which is their normal gait when startled. I have myself seen signs that showed where a young moose had galloped for some rods under similar circumstances; and I have seen big moose calves, or half-grown moose, in captivity gallop a few yards in play, although rarely. But the normal, and under ordinary circumstances the only, gait of the moose is the trot.

* When I reached Neri I received from Peary the following cable: "Your farewell was a royal mascot. The Pole is ours.—PEARY."

trip, or even than a voyage of exploration, and trebles the labor.

A long day's march brought us down to the hot country. That evening we pitched our tents by a rapid brook, bordered by palms, whose long, stiff fronds rustled ceaselessly in the wind. Monkeys swung in the tree-tops. On the march I shot a Kavirondo crane on the wing with the little Springfield, almost exactly repeating my experience with the other crane which I had shot three weeks before, except that on this occasion I brought down the bird with my third bullet, and then wasted the last two cartridges in the magazine at his companions. At dusk the donkeys were driven to a fire within the camp, and they stood patiently round it in a circle throughout the night, safe from lions and hyenas.

Next day's march brought us to another small tributary of the Guaso Nyero, a little stream twisting rapidly through the plain, between sheer banks. Here and there it was edged with palms and beds of bulrushes. We pitched the tents close to half a dozen flat-topped thorn-trees. We spent several days at this camp. Many kites came around the tents, but neither vultures nor ravens. The country was a vast plain bounded on almost every hand by chains of far-off mountains. In the southwest, just beyond the equator, the snows of Kenia lifted toward the sky. To the north the barren ranges were grim with the grimness of the desert. The flats were covered with pale, bleached grass which waved all day long in the wind; for though there were sometimes calms, or changes in the wind, on most of the days we were out it never ceased blowing from some point in the south. In places the parched soil was crumbling and rotten; in other places it was thickly strewn with volcanic stones; there were but few tracts over which a horse could gallop at speed, although neither the rocks nor the rotten soil seemed to hamper the movements of the game. Here and there were treeless stretches. Elsewhere there were occasional palms; and trees thirty or forty feet high, seemingly cactus or aloes, which looked even more like candelabra than the euphorbia which is thus named; and a scattered growth of thorn-trees and bushes. The thorn-trees were of many kinds. One bore only a few leathery leaves, the place of foliage being taken by the mass of poisonous-looking, fleshy spines which, together with the end of the branches, were bright green. The camel-thorn was completely armed with little, sharply hooked thorns which tore whatever they touched, whether flesh or clothes. Then there were the mimosas, with long, straight thorn spikes; they are so plentiful in certain places along the Guaso Nyero that almost all the lions have festering sores in their paws because of the spikes that have broken off in them. In these thorn-trees the weaver-birds had built multitudes of their straw nests, each with its bottle-shaped mouth toward the north, away from the direction of the prevailing wind. Each morning we were up at dawn, and saw the heavens redden and the sun flame over the rim of the world. All day long we rode and walked across the endless flats, save that at noon, when the sky was like molten brass, we might rest under the thin half-shade of some thorn-tree. As the shadows lengthened and the harsh, pitiless glare softened, we might turn campward; or we might hunt until the sun went down, and the mountains in the far-off west, and the sky above them, grew faint and dim with the hues of fairy-land. Then we would ride back through the soft, warm beauty of the tropic night, the stars blazing overhead and the silver moonlight flooding the reaches of dry grass; it was so bright that our shadows were almost as black and clear-cut as in the day. On reaching camp I would take a cup of tea with crackers or gingersnaps, and after a hot bath and a shave I was always eager for dinner.

Scattered over these flats were herds of zebra, oryx, and gazelle. The gazelle, the most plentiful and much the tamest of the game, were the northern form of the Grant's gazelle, with straighter horns which represented the opposite extreme when compared with the horns of the Roberts's type which we got on the Sotik. They seemed to me somewhat less in size than the big gazelle of the Kapiti Plains. One of the bucks I shot, an adult of average size (I was not able to weigh my biggest one), weighed one hundred and fifteen pounds; a very big true Grant's buck which I shot on the Kapiti Plains weighed one hundred and seventy-one pounds; doubtless there is complete intergradation, but the Guaso Nyero form seemed slimmer and lighter, and in some respects seemed to tend toward the Somaliland gazelles. I marked no difference in the habits, except that these northern gazelle switched their tails more jerkily, more like tommies, than was customary with the true Grant's gazelles. But the difference may have been in my observation. At any rate, the gazelles in this neighborhood, like those elsewhere, went in small parties, or herds of thirty or forty individuals, on the open plains or where there were a few scattered bushes, and behaved like those in the Sotik or on the Athi Plains. A near kinsman of the gazelle, the gerenuk, a curious creature with a very long neck, which the Swahilis call "little giraffe," was scattered singly or in small parties through the brush, and was as wild and wary as the common gazelle was tame. It seemed to prefer browsing, while the common gazelle grazes.

The handsome oryx, with their long horns carried by both sexes, and their coloring of black, white, and dun gray, came next to the gazelle in point of numbers. They were generally found in herds of from half a dozen to fifty individuals, often mixed with zebra herds. There were also solitary bulls, probably turned out of the herds by more vigorous rivals, and often one of these would be found with a herd of zebras, more merciful to it than its own kinsfolk. All this game of the plains is highly gregarious in habit, and the species associate freely with one another. The oryx cows were now generally accompanied by very young calves, for, unlike what we found to be the case with the hartbeest on the Athi, the oryx on the Guaso Nyero seem to have a definite calving time —September.* I shot only bulls (there was no meat, either for

* Of course this represents only one man's experience. I wish there were many such observations. On the Athi in May I found new-born

the porters or ourselves, except what I got with the rifle), and they were so wary that almost all those I killed were shot at ranges between three hundred and five hundred yards; and at such ranges I need hardly say that I did a good deal of missing. One wounded bull which, the ground being favorable, I galloped down, turned to bay and threatened to charge the horse. We weighed one bull; it tipped the scales at four hundred pounds. The lion kills we found in this neighborhood were all oryx and zebra; and evidently the attack was made in such fashion that the oryx had no more chance to fight than the zebra.

The zebra were of both species, the smaller or Burchell's, and the Grevy's, which the porters called kangani. Each animal went in herds by itself, and almost as frequently we found them in mixed herds containing both species. But they never interbreed, and associate merely as each does with the oryx. The kangani is a fine zeast, much bigger than its kinsman; it is as large as a polo-pony. It is less noisy than the common zebra, the bonte quagga of the Boers, and its cry is totally different. Its gaits are a free, slashing trot and gallop. When it stands facing one the huge fringed ears make it instantly recognizable. The stripes are much narrower and more numerous than those on the small zebra, and in consequence cease to be distinguishable at a shorter distance; the animal then looks gray, like a wild ass. When the two zebras are together the coloring of the smaller kind is more conspicuous. In scanning a herd with the glasses we often failed to make out the species until we could catch the broad black-and-white stripes on the rump of the common bonte quagga. There were many young foals with the kangani; I happened not to see any with the Burchell's. I found the kangani even more wary and more difficult to shoot than the oryx. The first one I killed was shot at a range of four hundred yards; the next I wounded

wildebeest and hartbeest calves, and others several months old. In June in the Sotik I saw new-born eland calves, and topi calves several months old. In September on the Guaso Nyero all the oryx calves were new-born. The zebra foals were also very young.

at that distance, and had to ride it down, at the cost of a hard gallop over very bad country and getting torn by the "wait-a-bit" thorns.

There were a number of rhinos on the plains, dull of wit and senses, as usual. Three times we saw cows with calves trotting at their heels. Once, while my men were skinning an oryx, I spied a rhino less than half a mile off. Mounting my horse I cantered down, and examined it within a hundred yards. It was an old bull with worn horns, and never saw me. On another occasion, while we were skinning a big zebra, there were three rhinoceros, all in different places, in sight at the same time.

There were also ostriches. I saw a party of cocks, with wings spread and necks curved backward, strutting and dancing. Their mincing, springy run is far faster than, when the bird is near by, it seems. The neck is held back in running, and when at speed the stride is twenty-one feet. No game is more wary or more difficult to approach. I killed both a cock and a hen—which I found the naturalists valued even more than a cock. We got them by stumbling on the nest, which contained eleven huge eggs, and was merely a bare spot in the sand, surrounded by grass two feet high; the bird lay crouched, with the neck flat on the ground. When we accidentally came across the nest the cock was on it, and I failed to get him as he ran. The next day we returned, and dismounted before we reached the near neighborhood of the nest. Then I advanced, cautiously, my rifle at the ready. It seemed impossible that so huge a bird could lie hidden in such scanty cover, but not a sign did we see until, when we were sixty yards off, the hen, which this time was on the nest, rose, and I killed her at sixty yards. Even this did not make the cock desert the nest; and on a subsequent day I returned, and after missing him badly, I killed him at eighty-five yards; and glad I was to see the huge black-and-white bird tumble in the dust. He weighed two hundred and sixty-three pounds and was in fine plumage. The hen weighed two hundred and forty pounds. Her stomach and gizzard, in addition to small, white quartz pebbles, contained a mass of vegetable substance; the bright-green leaves and twig tips of a shrub, a kind of rush with jointed stem and tuberous root, bean pods from different kinds of thorn-trees, and the leaves and especially the seed-vessels of a bush, the seed-vessels being enclosed in cases or pods so thorny that they pinched our fingers, and made us wonder at the bird's palate. Cock and hen brood the eggs alternately. We found the heart and liver of the ostrich excellent eating; the eggs were very good also. As the cock died it uttered a kind of loud, long-drawn grunting boom that was almost a roar. Its beautiful white wing-plumes were almost unworn. A full-grown wild ostrich is too wary to fall into the clutches of a lion or leopard, save by accident, and it will master any of the lesser carnivora; but the chicks are preyed on by jackals and wildcats, and of course by the larger beasts of prey also; and the eggs are eagerly sought by furred and feathered foes alike. Seemingly trustworthy settlers have assured me that vultures break the tough shells with stones. The cock and hen will try to draw their more formidable foes away from the nest or the chicks by lingering so near as to lure them into pursuit; and anything up to the size of a hyena they will attack and drive away, or even kill. The terrific downward stroke of an ostrich's leg is as dangerous as the kick of a horse; the thump will break a rib or back-bone of any ordinary animal, and in addition to the force of the blow itself the big nails may make a ghastly rip. Both cock and hen lead about the young brood and care for it. The two ostriches I shot were swarming with active parasitic flies, a little like those that were on the lions I shot in the Sotik. Later the porters brought us in several ostrich chicks. They also brought two genet kittens, which I tried to raise, but failed. They were much like ordinary kittens, with larger ears, sharper noses, and longer tails, and loved to perch on my shoulder or sit on my lap while I stroked them. They made dear little pets, and I was very sorry when they died.

On the day that I shot the cock ostrich I also shot a giraffe. The country in which we were hunting marks the southern limit of the "reticulated" giraffe, a form or species entirely distinct from the giraffe we had already obtained in the country south of Kenia. The southern giraffe is blotched with dark on a light ground, whereas this northern or north-eastern form is of a uniform dark color on the back and sides, with a network or reticulation of white lines placed in a large pattern on this dark background. The naturalists were very anxious to obtain a specimen of this form from its southern limit of distribution, to see if there was any in-tergradation with the southern form, of which we had already shot specimens near its northern, or at least northeastern, limit. The distinction proved sharp.

On the day in question we breakfasted at six in the morning, and were off immediately afterward; and we did not eat anything again until supper at quarter to ten in the evening. In a hot climate a hunter does not need lunch; and though in a cold climate a simple lunch is permissible, anything like an elaborate or luxurious lunch is utterly out of place if the man is more than a parlor or drawing-room sportsman. We saw no sign of giraffe until late in the afternoon. Hour after hour we plodded across the plain, now walking, now riding, in the burning heat. The withered grass was as dry as a bone, for the country had been many months without rain; yet the oryx, zebra, and gazelle evidently throve on the harsh pasturage. There were innumerable game trails leading hither and thither, and, after the fashion of game trails, usually fad-ing out after a few hundred yards. But there were certain trails which did not fade out. These were the ones which led to water. One such we followed. It led across stretches of grass-land, through thin bush, thorny and almost leafless, over tracts of rotten soil, cracked and crumbling, and over other tracts where the unshod horses picked their way gingerly among the masses of sharp-edged volcanic stones. Other trails joined in, and it grew more deeply marked. At last it led to a bend in a little river, where flat shelves of lime-stone bordered a kind of pool in the current where there were beds of green rushes and a fringe of trees and thorn thickets. This was evidently a favorite drinking-place. Many trails converged toward it, and for a long distance round the ground was worn completely bare by the hoofs of the countless herds of thirsty game that had travelled thither from time imme-morial. Sleek, handsome, long-horned oryx, with switching tails, were loitering in the vicinity, and at the water-hole itself we surprised a band of gazelles not fifty yards off; they fled panic-struck in every direction. Men and horses drank their fill; and we returned to the sunny plains and the endless reaches of withered, rustling grass.

At last, an hour or two before sunset, when the heat had begun a little to abate, we spied half a dozen giraffes scat-tered a mile and a half ahead of us, feeding on the tops of the few widely separated thorn-trees. Cuninghame and I started toward them on foot, but they saw us when we were a mile away, and after gazing a short while, turned and went off at their usual rocking-horse canter, twisting and screw-ing their tails. We mounted and rode after them. I was on my zebra-shaped brown horse, which was hardy and with a fair turn of speed, and which by this time I had trained to be a good hunting-horse. On the right were two giraffe which eventually turned out to be a big cow followed by a nearly full-grown young one; but Cuninghame, scanning them through his glasses, and misled by the dark coloration, pro-nounced them a bull and cow; and after the big one I went. By good luck we were on one of the rare pieces of the country which was fitted for galloping. I rode at an angle to the giraffe's line of flight, thus gaining considerably; and when it finally turned and went straight away I followed it at a fast run, and before it was fully awake to the danger I was but a hundred yards behind. We were now getting into bad coun-try, and jumping off I opened fire and crippled the great beast.

Mounting, I overtook it again in a quarter of a mile and killed it.

In half an hour the skinners and porters came up—one of the troubles of hunting as a naturalist is that it necessitates the presence of a long tail of men to take off and carry in the big skins, in order that they may ultimately appear in museums. In an hour and a half the giraffe's skin, with the head and the leg bones, was slung on two poles; eight porters bore it, while the others took for their own use all the meat they could carry. They were in high good humor, for an abundant supply of fresh meat always means a season of rejoicing, and they started campward singing loudly under their heavy burdens. While the giraffe was being skinned we had seen a rhinoceros feeding near our line of march campward, and had watched it until the light grew dim. By the time the skin was ready night had fallen, and we started under the brilliant moon. It lit up the entire landscape; but moonlight is not sunlight, and there was the chance of our stumbling on the rhino unawares, and of its charging; so I rode at the head of the column with full-jacketed bullets in my rifle. However, we never saw the rhino, nor had we any other adventure; and the ride through the moonlight, which softened all the harshness, and gave a touch of magic and mystery to the landscape, was so pleasant that I was sorry when we caught the gleam of the camp-fires.

Next day we sent our porters to bring in the rest of the giraffe meat and the ostrich eggs. The giraffe's heart was good eating. There were many ticks on the giraffe, as on all the game hereabouts, and they annoyed us a little also, although very far from being the plague they were on the Athi Plains. Among the flies which at times tormented the horses and hung around the game were big gadflies with long wings folded longitudinally down the back, not in the ordinary fly fashion; they were akin to the tsetse flies, one species of which is fatal to domestic animals, and another, the sleeping-sickness fly, to man himself. They produce death by means of the fatal microbes introduced into the blood by their bite; whereas another African fly, the seroot, found more to the north, in the Nile countries, is a scourge to man and beast merely because of its vicious bite, and where it swarms may drive the tribes that own herds entirely out of certain districts.

One afternoon, while leading my horse because the ground was a litter of sharp-edged stones, I came out on a plain which was crawling with zebra. In every direction there were herds of scores or of hundreds. They were all of the common or small kind, except three individuals of the big kangani, and were tame, letting me walk by within easy shot. Other game was mixed in with them. Soon, walking over a little ridge of rocks, we saw a rhino sixty yards off. To walk forward would give it our wind; I did not wish to kill it; and I was beginning to feel about rhino the way Alice did in Looking-Glass country, when the elephants "did bother so." Having spied us the beast at once cocked its ears and tail, and assumed its usual absurd resemblance to a huge and exceedingly alert and interested pig. But with a rhino tragedy sometimes treads on the heels of comedy, and I watched it sharply, my rifle cocked, while I had all the men shout in unison to scare it away. The noise puzzled it much; with tail erect and head tossing and twisting, it made little rushes hither and thither, but finally drew off. Next day, in shifting camp, Cuninghame and I were twice obliged to dismount and keep guard over the safari while it marched by within a hundred yards of a highly puzzled rhino, which trotted to and fro in the bush, evidently uncertain whether or not to let its bewilderment turn into indignation.

The camp to which we thus shifted was on the banks of the Guaso Nyero, on the edge of an open glade in a shady grove of giant mimosas. It was a beautiful camp, and in the soft tropic nights I sat outside my tent and watched the full moon rising through and above the tree-tops. There was absolutely no dew at night, by the way. The Guaso Nyero runs across and along the equator, through a desert country, eastward into the dismal Lorian swamp, where it disappears, save in very wet seasons, when it continues to the Tana. At our camp it was a broad, rapid, muddy stream infested with crocodiles. Along its banks grew groves of ivorynut palms, their fronds fan-shaped, their tall trunks forked twenty or thirty feet from the ground, each stem again forking—something like the antlers of a blacktail buck. In the frond of a small palm of this kind we found a pale-colored, very long-tailed tree-mouse, in its nest, which was a ball of chopped straw. Spur-fowl and francolin abounded, their grating cries being heard everywhere; I shot a few as well as one or two sand-grouse; and with the rifle I knocked off the heads of two guinea-fowls. The last feat sounds better in the narration than it was in the performance; for I wasted nearly a beltful of cartridges in achieving it, as the guineas were shy and ran rapidly through the tall grass. I also expended a large number of cartridges before securing a couple of gerenuk; the queer, long-legged, long-necked antelope were wary, and as soon as they caught a glimpse of me off they would go at a stealthy trot or canter through the bushes, with neck outstretched. They had a curious habit of rising on their hind legs to browse among the bushes; I do not remember seeing any other antelope act in this manner. There were water-buck along the river-banks, and I shot a couple of good bulls; they belonged to the southern and eastern species, which has a light-colored ring around the rump; whereas the western form, which I saw at Naivasha, has the whole rump light-colored. They like the neighborhood of lakes and rivers. I have seen parties of them resting in the open plains during the day, under trees which yielded little more shade than telegraph-poles. The handsome, shaggy-coated water-buck has not the high withers which mark the oryx, wildebeest, and hartbeest, and he carries his head and neck more like a stag or a wapiti bull.

One day we went back from the river after giraffe. It must have been a year since any rain had fallen. The surface of the baked soil was bare and cracked, the sparse tussocks of grass were brittle straw, and the trees and bushes were leafless; but instead of leaves they almost all carried thorns, the worst being those of the wait-a-bit, which tore our clothes, hands, and faces. We found the giraffe three or four miles away from the river, in an absolutely waterless region, densely covered with these leafless wait-a-bit thorn-bushes. Hanging among the bare bushes, by the way, we roused two or three of the queer, diurnal, golden-winged, slate-colored bats; they flew freely in the glare of the sunlight, minding it as little as they did the furnace-like heat. We found the really dense wait-a-bit thorn thickets quite impenetrable, whereas the giraffe moved through them with utter unconcern. But the giraffe's indifference to thorns is commonplace compared to its indifference to water. These particular giraffe were not drinking either at the river or at the one or two streams which were running into it; and in certain places giraffe will subsist for months without drinking at all. How the waste and evaporation of moisture from their huge bodies is supplied is one of the riddles of biology.

We could not get a bull giraffe, and it was only a bull that I wanted. I was much interested, however, in coming up to a cow asleep. She stood with her neck drooping slightly forward, occasionally stamping or twitching an ear, like a horse when asleep standing. I saw her legs first, through the bushes, and finally walked directly up to her in the open, until I stood facing her at thirty yards. When she at last suddenly saw me, she came nearer to the execution of a gambol than any other giraffe I have ever seen.

Another day we went after buffalo. We left camp before sunrise, riding along parallel to the river to find the spoor of a herd which had drunk and was returning to the haunts, away from the river, in which they here habitually spent the day. Two or three hours passed before we found what we sought; and we at once began to follow the trail. It was in open thorn-bush, and the animals were evidently feeding. Before we had followed the spoor half an hour we ran across a rhinoceros. As the spoor led above wind, and as we did not wish to leave it for fear of losing it, Cuninghame stayed where he was, and I moved round to within fifty yards of the rhino, and, with my rifle ready, began shouting, trying to keep the just mean as regards noise, so as to scare him, and yet not yell so loudly as to reach the buffalo if they happened to be near by. At last I succeeded, and he trotted sullenly off, tacking and veering, and not going far. On we went, and in another half-hour came on our quarry. I was the first to catch a glimpse of the line of bulky black forms, picked out with white where the sun glinted on the horn bosses. It was ten o'clock, a hot, windless morning on the equator, with the sun shining from a cloudless sky; yet these buffalo were feeding in the open, miles from water or dense cover. They were greedily cropping the few tufts of coarse herbage that grew among the sparse thorn-bushes, which here were not more than two feet high. In many places buffalo are purely nocturnal feeders, and do not come into the hot, bare plains in the scorching glare of daylight; and our experience with this herd illustrates afresh the need of caution in generalizing about the habits of game.

We crept toward them on all fours, having left the porters hidden from sight. At last we were within rather long range —a buffalo's eyesight is good, and cannot be trifled with as if he were a rhino or elephant—and cautiously scrutinized the herd through our glasses. There were only cows and perhaps one or two young bulls with horns no bigger than those of cows. I would have liked another good bull's head for myself; but I also wished another cow for the museum. Before I could shoot, however, a loud yelling was heard from among the porters in our rear; and away went the buffalo. Full of wrath, we walked back to inquire. We found that one porter had lost his knife, and had started back to look for it, accompanied by two of his fellows, which was absolutely against orders. They had come across a rhino, probably the one I had frightened from our path, and had endeavored to avoid him; but he had charged them, whereupon they scattered. He overtook one and tossed him, goring him in the thigh; whereupon they came back, the two unwounded ones supporting the other, and all howling like lost souls. I had some crystals of permanganate, an antiseptic, and some cotton in my saddle pocket; Cuninghame tore some of the lining out of his sleeve for a bandage; and we fixed the man up and left him with one companion, while we sent another in to camp to fetch out a dozen men with a ground-sheet and some poles, to make a litter in which the wounded man could be carried. While we were engaged in this field surgery another rhino was in sight half a mile off.

Then on we went on the trail of the herd. It led straight across the open, under the blazing sun; and the heat was now terrific. At last, almost exactly at noon, Cuninghame, who was leading, stopped short. He had seen the buffalo, which had halted, made a half-bend backward on their tracks, and stood for their noonday rest among some scattered, stunted thorn-trees, leafless and yielding practically no shade whatever. A cautious stalk brought me to within a hundred and fifty yards. I merely wounded the one I first shot at, but killed another as the herd started to run. Leaving the skinners to take care of the dead animal, a fine cow, Cuninghame and I started after the herd, to see if the wounded one had fallen out. After a mile the trail led into some scant cover. Here the first thing we did was to run into another rhinoceros. It was about seventy yards away, behind a thorn-tree, and began to move jerkily and abruptly to and fro, gazing toward us. "Oh, you malevolent old idiot!" I muttered, facing it with rifle cocked; then, as it did not charge, I added to Cuninghame: "Well, I guess it will let us by, all right." And let us by it did. We were anxious not to shoot it, both because in a country with no settlers a rhino rarely does harm, and I object to anything like needless butchery, and furthermore because we desired to avoid alarming the buffalo. Half a mile farther on we came on the latter, apparently past their fright. We looked them carefully over with our glasses; the wounded one was evidently not much hurt, and therefore I did not wish to kill her, for I did not need another cow; and there was no adult bull. So we did not molest them; and after a while they got our wind and went off at a lumbering gallop. Returning to the dead cow, we found the skin ready and marched back to camp, reaching it just as the moon rose, at seven; we had been away thirteen hours, with nothing to eat and only the tepid water in our canteens to drink.

We were in the country of the Samburu, and several of their old men and warriors visited us at this camp. They are cattle-owning nomads like the Masai; but in addition to cattle, sheep, and goats they own herds of camels, which they milk but do not use as beasts of burden. In features they are more like Somalis than negroes.

Near this camp was the remains of the boma or home camp of Arthur Neuman, once the most famous elephant-hunter between Tana and Lake Rudolf. Neuman, whose native name was Nyama Yango, was a strange moody man who died by his own hand. He was a mighty hunter, of bold and adventure-loving temper. With whites he was unsocial, living in this far-off region exactly like a native, and all alone among the natives; living in some respects too much like a native. But, from the native standpoint, and without making any effort to turn the natives into anything except what they were, he did them good, and left a deep impression on their minds. They talked to us often about him, in many different places; they would not believe that he was dead; and when assured it was so they showed real grief. At Meru boma, when we saw the Meru tribesmen dance, one of the songs they sung was, "Since Nyama Yango came, our sheep graze untouched by the Samburu," and, rather curiously, the Samburu sing a similar song, reciting how he saved them from the fear of having their herds raided by the nomads farther north.

After leaving this camp we journeyed up the Guaso Nyero for several days. The current was rapid and muddy, and there were beds of reeds and of the tall, graceful papyrus. The country round about was a mass of stony, broken hills, and the river wound down among these, occasionally cutting its way through deep gorges, and its course being continually broken by rapids. Whenever on our hunts we had to cross it, we shouted and splashed and even fired shots, to scare the crocodiles. I shot one on a sand-bar in the river. The man the rhino had wounded was carried along on a litter with the safari.

Sometimes I left camp with my sais and gun-bearer before dawn, starting in the light of the waning moon, and riding four or five hours before halting to wait for the safari; on the way I had usually shot something for the table—a water-buck, impala, or gazelle. On other occasions Cuninghame and I would spend the day hunting in the waterless country back of the river, where the heat at midday was terrific. We might not reach camp until after nightfall. Once as we came to it in the dark it seemed as if ghostly arms stretched above it; for on this evening the tents had been pitched under trees up which huge rubber-vines had climbed, and their massive dead-white trunks and branches glimmered pale and ghostly in the darkness.

Twice my gun-bearers tried to show me a cheetah; but my eyes were too slow to catch the animal before it bounded off in safety among the bushes. Another time after an excellent bit of tracking, the gun-bearers brought me up to a buffalo bull, standing for his noonday rest in the leafless thorns a mile from the river. I thought I held the heavy Holland straight for his shoulder, but I must have fired high; for though he fell to the shot he recovered at once. We followed the blood spoor for an hour, the last part of the time when the trail wandered among and through the heavy thickets under the trees on the river-banks; here I walked beside the tracker with my rifle at full cock, for we could not tell what instant we might be charged. But his trail finally crossed the river, and as he was going stronger and stronger we had to abandon the chase. In the waterless country, away from the river, we found little except herds of zebra, of both kinds, occasionally oryx and eland, and a few giraffe. A stallion of the big kangani zebra which I shot stood fourteen hands high at the withers and weighed about eight hundred and thirty pounds,* according to the Seton beam. I shot another kangani just at nightfall, a mile or so from camp, as it drank in a wild, tree-clad gorge of the river. I was alone, strolling quietly through the dusk, along the margin of the high banks by the stream, and saw a mixed herd of zebras coming down to a well-worn drinking-place, evidently much used by game, on the opposite side of the river. They were alert and nervous, evidently on the lookout for both lions and crocodiles. I singled out the largest, the leader of the troop, and shot it across the stream; I have rarely taken a shot among more picturesque surroundings.

At our final camp on the river, before leaving it on our week's steady trek southward to Neri, we found a spot in which game abounded. It was about ten miles back from the river, a stretch of plain sparsely covered with thorn-trees, broken by koppies, and bounded by chains of low, jagged mountains, with an occasional bold, isolated peak. The crags and cliff walls were fantastically carved and channelled by the weathering of ages in that dry climate. It was a harsh, unlovely spot in the glare of the hot daylight; but at sunset it was very lovely, with a wild and stern beauty.

Here the game abounded, and was not wary. Before starting out on our week's steady marching I wished to give the safari a good feed; and one day I shot them five zebra and an oryx bull, together with a couple of gazelle for ourselves

---

* The aggregate of the weights of the different pieces was seven hundred and seventy-eight pounds; the loss of blood and the drying of the pieces of flesh in the intense heat of the sun we thought certainly accounted for fifty pounds more. The stallion was not fat. At any rate it weighed between eight hundred and eight hundred and fifty pounds. Its testicles, though fully developed, had not come down out of the belly skin; one of those shot by Kermit showed the same peculiarity; Cuninghame says it is a common occurrence with this species. Moreover the stallions did not have their canine teeth developed.

and our immediate attendants—enough of the game being hallalled to provide for the Mohammedans in the safari. I also shot an old bull giraffe of the northern form, after an uneventful stalk which culminated in a shot with the Winchester at a hundred and seventy yards. In most places this particular stretch of country was not suitable for galloping, the ground being rotten, filled with holes, and covered with tall, coarse grass. One evening we saw two lions half a mile away; I tried to ride them, but my horse fell twice in the first hundred and fifty yards and I could not even keep them in sight. Another day we got a glimpse of two lions, quarter of a mile off, gliding away among the thorns. They went straight to the river and swam across it. More surprising was the fact that a monkey, which lost its head when we surprised it in a tree by the river, actually sprang plump into the stream, and swam, easily and strongly, across it.

One day we had a most interesting experience with a cow giraffe. We saw her a long way off and stalked to within a couple of hundred yards before we could make out her sex. She was standing under some thorn-trees, occasionally shifting her position for a few yards, and then again standing motionless with her head thrust in among the branches. She was indulging in a series of noon naps. At last, when she stood and went to sleep again, I walked up to her, Cuninghame and our two gun-bearers, Bakhari and Kongoni, following a hundred yards behind. When I was within forty yards, in plain sight, away from cover, she opened her eyes and looked drowsily at me; but I stood motionless and she dozed off again. This time I walked up to within ten feet of her. Nearer I did not care to venture, as giraffe strike and kick very hard with their hoofs, and, moreover, occasionally strike with the head, the blow seemingly not being delivered with the knobby, skin-covered horns, but with the front teeth of the lower jaw. She waked, looked at me, and then, rearing slightly, struck at me with her left fore leg, the blow falling short. I laughed and leaped back, and the other men ran up shouting. But the giraffe would not run away. She stood within twenty feet of us, looking at us peevishly, and occasionally pouting her lips at us, as if she were making a face. We kept close to the tree, so as to dodge round it, under the branches, if she came at us; for we would have been most reluctant to shoot her. I threw a stick at her, hitting her in the side, but she paid no attention; and when Bakhari came behind her with a stick she turned sharply on him and he made a prompt retreat. We were laughing and talking all the time. Then we pelted her with sticks and clods of earth, and, after having thus stood within twenty feet of us for three or four minutes, she cantered slowly off for fifty yards, and then walked away with leisurely unconcern. She was apparently in the best of health and in perfect condition. She did not get our wind; but her utter indifference to the close presence of four men is inexplicable.*

On each of the two days we hunted this little district we left camp at sunrise, and did not return until eight or nine in the evening, fairly well tired, and not a little torn by the thorns into which we blundered during the final two hours' walk in the darkness. It was hot, and we neither had nor wished for food, and the tepid water in the canteens lasted us through. The day I shot the giraffe the porters carrying the skin fell behind, and never got in until next morning. Coming back in the late twilight a party of the big zebra, their forms shadowy and dim, trotted up to us, evidently attracted by the horses, and accompanied us for some rods; and a hedgehog, directly in our path, kept bleating loudly, like an antelope kid.

The day we spent in taking care of the giraffe-skin we, of course, made no hunt. However, in the afternoon I sauntered upstream a couple of miles to look for crocodiles. I

---

*After writing the above account I read it over to Mr. Cuninghame so as to be sure that it was accurate in all its details. All the game was tame in this locality, even the giraffe, but no other giraffe allowed us to get within two hundred yards, and most of them ran long before that distance was reached, even when we were stalking carefully.

saw none, but I was much interested in some zebra and water-buck. The zebra were on the opposite side of the river, standing among some thorns, and at three, mid-afternoon, they came down to drink; up to this time I had generally found zebra drinking in the evening or at night. Then I saw some water-buck, also on the opposite bank, working their way toward the river, and seeing a well-marked drinking-place ahead I hastened toward it, and sat down in the middle of the broad game trail leading down to the water on my side. I sat perfectly still, and my clothes were just the color of the ground, and the water-buck never noticed me, though I was in plain view when they drank, just opposite me, and only about fifty yards off. There were four cows and a bull. It was four o'clock in the afternoon. The cows came first, one by one, and were very alert and suspicious. Each continually stopped and stood motionless, or looked in every direction, and gave little false starts of alarm. When they reached the green grass by the water's edge each cropped a few mouthfuls, between times nervously raising its head and looking in every direction, nostrils and ears twitching. They were not looking for crocodiles, but for land foes, lions or leopards. Each in turn drank, skipping up to the top of the bank after a few mouthfuls, and then returning to the water. The bull followed with rather less caution, and before he had finished drinking, the cows scurried hurriedly back to the thorn-trees and the open country. We had plenty of meat in camp, and I had completed my series of this species of water-buck for the museum; and I was glad there was no need to molest them.

The porters were enjoying the rest and the abundance of meat. They were lying about camp or were scattered up and down stream fishing. When, walking back, I came to the outskirts of camp, I was attracted by the buzzing and twanging of the harp; there was the harper and two friends, all three singing to his accompaniment. I called "Yambo" (greeting), and they grinned and stood up, shouting "Yambo" in return. In camp a dozen men were still at work at the giraffe-skin, and they were all singing loudly, under the lead of my gun-bearer, Gouvimali, who always acted as chantey-man, or improvisatore, on such occasions.

For a week we now trekked steadily south across the equator, heel and toe marching, to Neri. Our first day's journey took us to a gorge riven in the dry mountain. Half-way up it, in a side pocket, was a deep pool, at the foot of a sloping sheet of rock, down which a broad, shallow dent showed where the torrent swept during the rains. In the trees around the pool black drongo shrikes called in bell-like tones, and pied horn-bills flirted their long tails as they bleated and croaked. The water was foul; but in a dry country one grows gratefully to accept as water anything that is wet. Klipspringers and baboons were in the sheer hills around; and among the rocks were hyraxes (looking like our Rocky Mountain conies or Little Chief hares), queer diurnal rats, and bright blue-green lizards with orange heads. Rhinos drank at this pool; we frequently saw them on our journey, but always managed to avoid wounding their susceptibilities, and so escaped an encounter. Each day we endeavored to camp a couple of hours before sundown so as to give the men plenty of chance to get fire-wood, pitch the tents, and put everything in order. Sometimes we would make an early start; in which case we would breakfast in the open, while in the east the crescent of the dying moon hung over the glow that heralded the sunrise.

As we reached the high, rolling downs the weather grew cooler, and many flowers appeared; those of the aloes were bright red, standing on high stalks above the clump of fleshy, spined leaves, which were handsomely mottled, like a snake's back. As I rode at the head of the safari I usually, in the course of the day, shot a buck of some kind for the table. I had not time to stalk, but simply took the shots as they came, generally at long range. One day I shot an eland, an old blue bull. We needed the skin for the museum, and as there was water near by we camped where we were; I had already shot a water-buck that morning, and this and the eland together gave the entire safari a feast of meat.

On another occasion an eland-herd afforded me fun, although no profit. I was mounted on Brownie, the zebra-shaped pony. Brownie would still occasionally run off when I dismounted to shoot (a habit that had cost me an eland bull); but he loved to gallop after game. We came on a herd of eland in an open plain; they were directly in our path. We were in the country where the ordinary or Livingstone's eland grades into the Patterson's; and I knew that the naturalists wished an additional bull's head for the museum. So I galloped toward the herd; and for the next fifteen or twenty minutes I felt as if I had renewed my youth and was in the cow camps of the West, a quarter of a century ago. Eland are no faster than range cattle. Twice I rounded up the herd—just as once in the Yellowstone Park I rounded up a herd of wapiti for John Burroughs to look at—and three times I cut out of the herd a big animal, which, however, in each case, proved to be a cow. There were no big bulls, only cows and young stock; but I enjoyed the gallop.

From Neri we marched through mist and rain across the cold Aberdare table-lands, and in the forenoon of October 20 we saw from the top of the second Aberdare escarpment the blue waters of beautiful Lake Naivasha. On the next day we reached Nairobi.

XII

TO THE UASIN GISHU

AT Nairobi Kermit joined me, having enjoyed a notably successful hunt during the month since we had parted, killing both Neuman's hartbeest and koodoo. The great koodoo, with its spiral horns and striped coat, is the stateliest and handsomest antelope in the world. It is a shy creature, fond of bush and of rocky hills, and is hard to get.

After leaving me at Meru, Kermit and Tarlton had travelled hard to Rumeruti. They had intended to go to Lake Hannington, but finding that this was in the reserve they went three days toward the northwest, stopping a score of miles east of Barengo. The country, which showed many traces of volcanic action, was rough, rocky, and dry; the hunting was exhausting, and Kermit was out from morning to night. Tarlton had been very sick on the Guaso Nyero, and although he was better he was in no shape to accompany Kermit, who therefore hunted only with his gun-boys, taking them out alternately so as to spare them as much as possible. It took three days' steady work before he got his first koodoo. On the third day he hunted fruitlessly all the morning, came back to camp, picked up a fresh gun-bearer, Juma Yohari, and started out again. At four in the afternoon he came to the brink of a great hollow a mile across, perhaps an extinct crater, and looking from the rim-rock, spied a koodoo bull in the bottom. The steep sides of the hollow were covered with a tangled growth of thorn-scrub and cactus, traversed by rhinoceros paths. The bottom was more open, strewn with bushy mounds or hillocks, and on one of these stood a noble koodoo bull. He stood with his massive spiral horns thrown back, and they shifted slowly as he turned his head from side to side. Kermit stole down one of the rhino paths, save for which the scrub would have been practically impenetrable; it was alive with rhinos; Kermit heard several, and Juma, who followed some distance behind, saw three. The stalk took time; and the sun was on the horizon and the light fading when, at over two hundred yards, Kermit took his shot. The first bullet missed, but as for a moment the bull paused and wheeled, Kermit fired again and the second bullet went home. The wounded beast ran, Kermit, with Juma, hard on the trail; and he overtook and killed it just as darkness fell. Then back to camp they stumbled and plunged through the darkness, Kermit tearing the sole completely off one shoe. They reached camp at ten and Juma, who had only been working half the day, took out some porters to the dead bull, which they skinned, and then slept by until morning. Later, on his birthday, he killed a cow, which completed the group; the two koodoo cost him ten days' steady labor. The koodoo were always found on steep, rocky hills; their stomachs contained only grass, for both beasts when shot were grazing (I do not know whether or not they also browse). The midday hours, when the heat was most intense, they usually spent resting; but once Kermit came on two which were drinking in a stream exactly at noon.

From the koodoo camp the two hunters went to Lake Hannington, a lovely lake, with the mountains rising sheer from three of its sides. The water was saline, abounding with crocodiles and hippos; and there were myriads of flamingoes. They were to be seen swimming by thousands on the lake, and wading and standing in the shallows; and when they rose they looked like an enormous pink cloud; it was a glorious sight. They were tame; and Kermit had no difficulty in killing the specimens needed for the museum. Here Kermit also killed an impala ram which had met with an extraordinary misadventure. It had been fighting with another ram, which had stabbed it in the chest with one horn. The violent strain and shock, as the two vigorous beasts bounded together, broke off the horn, leaving the broken part, ten inches long, embedded in the other buck's chest; about three inches of the point being fixed firmly in the body of the buck, while the rest stuck out like a picket-pin. Yet the buck seemed well and strong.

Two days after leaving Lake Hannington they camped near the ostrich-farm of Mr. London, an American from Baltimore. He had been waging war on the lions and leopards, because they attacked his ostriches. He had killed at least a score of each, some with the rifle, some with poison or steel traps. The day following their arrival London went out hunting with Kermit and Tarlton. They saw nothing until evening, when Kermit's gun-bearer, Kassitura, spied a leopard coming from the carcass of a zebra which London had shot to use as bait for his traps. The leopard saw them a long way off and ran; Kermit ran after it and wounded it badly, twice; then Tarlton got a shot and hit it; and then London came across the dying beast at close quarters and killed it just as it was gathering itself to spring at him.

Thence they went to Nakuru, where Kermit killed two Neuman's hartbeest. They were scarce and wild, and Kermit obtained his two animals by long shots after following them for hours; following them until, as he expressed it, they got used to him, became a little less quick to leave, and gave him his chance.

While on this trip Kermit passed his twentieth birthday. While still nineteen he had killed all the kinds of African dangerous game—lion, leopard, elephant, buffalo, and rhino.

Heller also rejoined us, entirely recovered. He had visited Mearns and Loring at their camp high up on Mount Kenia, where they had made a thoroughly biological survey of the mountain. He had gone to the line of perpetual snow, where the rock peak rises abruptly from the swelling downs, and had camped near a little glacial lake, whose waters froze every night. The zones of plant and animal life were well marked; but there are some curious differences between the zones on these equatorial African snow mountains and those on similar mountains in the northern hemisphere, especially America. In the high mountains of North America the mammals are apt to be, at least in part, of totally different kinds from those found in the adjacent warm or hot plains, because they represent a fauna which was once spread over the land, but which has retreated northward, leaving faunal islands on the summits of the taller mountains. In this part of Africa, however, there has been no faunal retreat of this type, no survivals on the peaks of an ancient fauna which in the plains and valleys has been replaced by another fauna; here the mammals of the high mountains and table-lands are merely modified forms of the mammals of the adjacent lowlands, which have gradually crept up the slopes, changing in the process. High on Mount Kenia, for instance, are hyraxes, living among the snow-fields, much bigger than their brethren of the forests and rocky hills below; and light-colored mole-rats, also much bigger than those of the lower country. Moreover, the lack of seasonal change is probably accountable for differences in the way that the tree zones are delimited. The mountain conifers of America are huge trees on the middle slopes, but higher up gradually dwindle into a thick, low scrub, composed of sprawling, dwarfed individuals of the same species. On Mount Kenia the tree zone ceases much more abruptly and with much less individual change among the different kinds of trees. Above this zone are the wet, cold downs and moors, with a very peculiar vegetation, plants which we know only as small flowering things having become trees. The giant groundsel, for instance, reaches a height of twenty feet, with very thick trunk and limbs which, though hollow, make good firewood; and this is only one example of the kind.

At Nairobi we learned, as usual, of incident after incident, which had happened among our friends and acquaintances, of exactly the type which would occur were it possible in North America or Europe suddenly to mix among existing conditions the men and animals that died out some hundreds of thousands of years ago. In a previous chapter I mentioned on one occa-

sion meeting at dinner three men, all of whom had been mauled
by lions; one being our host, Mr. F. A. Ward, who had served
as a captain in the South African War, and was now one of
the heads of the Boma Trading Company. Among our fellow
guests at this dinner was Captain Douglas Pennant of the British army. When we went north to Kenia he went south to
the Sotik. There he made a fine bag of lions; but having
wounded a leopard and followed it into cover it suddenly sprang
on him, apparently from a tree. His life was saved by his
Somali gun-bearer who blew out the leopard's brains as it bore
him to the ground, so that it had time to make only one bite;
but this bite just missed crushing in the skull, broke the jaw,
tore off one ear, and caused ghastly wreck. He spent some
weeks in the hospital at Nairobi, and then went for further
treatment to England; his place in the hospital being taken by
another man who had been injured by a leopard.

There had been quite a plague of wild beasts in Nairobi
itself. One family had been waked at midnight by a leopard
springing on the roof of the house and thence to an adjacent
shed; it finally spent a couple of hours on the veranda. A
lion had repeatedly wandered at night through the outlying
(the residential) portion of the town. Doctor Milne, the
head of the government medical department, had nearly run
into it on his bicycle, and, as a measure of precaution, guests
going out to dinner usually carried spears or rifles. One night
I dined with the provincial commissioner, Mr. Hobley, and
the next with the town clerk, Captain Sanderson. In each case
the hostess, the host, and the house were all delightful, and
the evening just like a very pleasant evening spent anywhere
in civilization; the houses were only half a mile apart; and
yet on the road between them a fortnight previously a lady
on a bicycle, wheeling down to a rehearsal of "Trial by Jury,"
had been run into and upset by a herd of frightened zebras.
One of my friends, Captain Smith, director of surveys in the
protectorate, had figured in another zebra incident to which
only Mark Twain could do justice. Captain Smith lived on

the outskirts of the town, and was much annoyed by the zebras tearing through his ground and trampling down his vegetables and flowers. So one night, by his direction, his Masai servant sallied out and speared a zebra which was tangled in a wire fence. But the magistrate, a rigid upholder of the letter of the law, fined the Masai for killing game without a license! (A touch quite worthy of comparison with Mark Twain's account of how, when he called for assistance while drowning, he was arrested for disturbing the peace.) Captain Smith decided that next time there should be no taint of illegality about his behavior, so he got ropes ready, and when the zebras returned he and his attendants again chased them toward the wire fences, and tied up one which got caught therein; and then with much difficulty he led it downtown, *put it in the pound,* and notified Captain Sanderson, the town clerk, what he had done. This proceeding was entirely regular; and so was all that followed. For seven days the zebra was kept in the pound, while the authorities solemnly advertised for a highly improbable owner; then it was sold at auction, being brought to the sale, bucking, rolling, and fighting, securely held by ropes in the hands of various stalwart natives, and disposed of to the only bidder for five rupees. The court records are complete. The district court criminal register, under date of February 1, 1909, contains the entry of the prosecution by the crown through "Mutwa Wa. Najaka A.N." of the Masai for "killing zebra without a license (under section 4/35 Game Regulations of 15th April, 1906)," and of the infliction of a fine of twenty rupees. The sequel appears in the Nairobi Municipality Pound Book under date of August 6, 1909. In the column headed "Description of Animal" is the entry "1 zebra"; under the heading "By whom impounded" is the entry "Major Smith, R.E."; under the heading "Remarks" is the entry "Sold by Public Auctioneers Raphael & Coy on 24/8/09."

We had with us several recent books on East African big game; Chapman's "On Safari," dealing alike with the hunting and the natural history of big game; Powell Cotton's accounts of his noteworthy experiences both in hunting and in bold exploration; Stigand's capital studies of the spoor and habits of big game (it is to be regretted that he was too modest to narrate some of his own really extraordinary adventures in the chase of dangerous beasts); and Buxton's account of his two African trips. Edward North Buxton's books ought to be in the hands of every hunter everywhere, and especially of every young hunter, because they teach just the right way in which to look at the sport. With Buxton big-game hunting is not a business but a pastime, not allowed to become a mania or in any way to interfere with the serious occupations of life, whether public or private; and yet as he has carried it on it is much more than a mere pastime, it is a craft, a pursuit of value in exercising and developing hardihood of body and the virile courage and resolution which necessarily lie at the base of every strong and manly character. He has not a touch of the game-butcher in him; nor has he a touch of that craving for ease and luxury the indulgence in which turns any sport into a sham and a laughing-stock. Big-game hunting, pursued as he has pursued it, stands at the opposite pole from those so-called sports carried on primarily either as money-making exhibitions, or, what is quite as bad—though the two evils are usually found in different social strata—in a spirit of such luxurious self-indulgence as to render them at best harmless extravagances, and at worst forces which positively tend to the weakening of moral and physical fibre.

On October 26, Tarlton, Kermit, Heller, and I started from the railroad-station of Londiani, for the Uasin Gishu plateau and the 'Nzoi River, which flows not far from the foot of Mount Elgon. This stretch of country has apparently received its fauna from the shores of Lake Victoria Nyanza, and contains several kinds of antelope, and a race or variety of giraffe, the five-horned, which are not found to the eastward, in the region where we had already hunted.

On the 27th we were marching hard, and I had no chance

to hunt; I would have liked to take a hunt, because it was my birthday. The year before I had celebrated my fiftieth birthday by riding my jumping horse, Roswell, over all the jumps in Rock Creek Park, at Washington. Roswell is a safe and good jumper, and a very easy horse to sit at a jump; he took me, without hesitation or error, over everything, from the water jump to the stone wall, the rails, and the bank, including a brush-hurdle just over five feet and a half high.

For the first four days our route led among rolling hills and along valleys and ravines, the country being so high that the nights were actually cold, although we crossed and re-crossed the equator. The landscape in its general effect called to mind southern Oregon and northern California rather than any tropical country. Some of the hills were bald, others wooded to the top; there were wet meadows, and hillsides covered with tussocks of rank, thick-growing grass, alternating with stretches of forest; and the chief trees of the forest were stately cedars, yews, and tall laurel-leaved olives. All this was, at least in superficial aspect, northern enough; but now and then we came to patches of the thoroughly tropical bamboo, which in East Africa, however, one soon grows to associate with cold, rainy weather, for it only grows at high altitudes. In this country, high, cold, rainy, there were several kinds of buck, but none in any numbers. The most interesting were the roan antelope, which went in herds. Their trails led everywhere, across the high, rolling hill pastures of coarse grass, and through the tangled tree groves and the still, lifeless bamboo jungle. They were found in herds and lived in the open, feeding on the bare hillsides and in the wet valleys at all hours; but they took cover freely, and when the merciless gales blew they sought shelter in woodland and jungle. Usually they grazed, but once I saw one browsing. Both on our way in and on our way back, through this hill-country, we shot several roan, for, though their horns are poor, they form a distinct subspecies, peculiar to the region. The roan is a big antelope, nearly as tall, although by no means as bulky, as an eland, with curved scimitar-like horns, huge ears, and face markings as sharply defined as those of an oryx. It is found here and there, in isolated localities, throughout Africa south of the Sahara, and is of bold, fierce temper. One of those which Kermit shot was only crippled by the first bullet, and charged the gun-bearers, squealing savagely, in addition to using its horns; an angry roan, like a sable, is said sometimes to bite with its teeth. Kermit also killed a ratel or honey-badger, in a bamboo thicket; an interesting beast; its back snow-white and the rest of its body jet-black.

As on the Aberdares and the slopes of Kenia, the nights among these mountains were cold; sometimes so cold that I was glad to wear a mackinaw, a lumberman's jacket, which had been given me by Jack Greenway, and which I certainly never expected to wear in Africa.

The porters always minded cold, especially if there was rain, and I was glad to get them to the Uasin Gishu, where the nights were merely cool enough to make one appreciate blankets, while the days were never oppressively hot. Although the Swahilis have furnished the model for all East African safari work, and supply the lingua franca for the country, they no longer compose the bulk of the porters. Of our porters at this time about two-fifths were stalwart M'nuwezi from German East Africa, two-fifths were Wakamba, and the remainder Swahilis with half a dozen Kavirondos and Kikuyus. The M'nuwezi are the strongest of all, and make excellent porters. They will often be as much as two or three years away from their homes; for safari work is very attractive to the best type of natives, as they live much better than if travelling on their own account, and as it offers almost the only way in which they can earn money. The most severe punishment that can be inflicted on a gun-bearer, tent-boy, sais, or porter is to dismiss him on such terms as to make it impossible for him again to be employed on a safari. In camp the men of each tribe group themselves together in parties, each man sharing any unwonted delicacy with his cronies.

Very rarely did we have to take such long marches as to exhaust our strapping burden-bearers; usually they came into camp in high good humor, singing and blowing antelope horns; and in the evening, after the posho had been distributed, cooked, and eaten, the different groups would gather each around its camp-fire, and the men would chant in unison while the flutes wailed and the buzzing harps twanged. Of course individuals were all the time meeting with accidents or falling sick, especially when they had the chance to gorge themselves on game that we had killed; and then Cuninghame or Tarlton—than whom two stancher and pleasanter friends, keener hunters, or better safari managers are not to be found in all Africa—would have to add the functions of a doctor to an already multifarious round of duties. Some of the men had to be watched lest they should malinger; others were always complaining of trifles; others never complained at all. Gosho, our excellent head man, came in the last category. On this Uasin Gishu trip we noticed him limping one evening; and inquiry developed the fact that the previous night, while in his tent, he had been bitten by a small poisonous snake. The leg was much swollen, and looked angry and inflamed; but Gosho never so much as mentioned the incident until we questioned him, and in a few days was as well as ever. Heller's chief feeling, by the way, when informed what had happened, was one of indignation because the offending snake, after paying the death penalty, had been thrown away instead of being given to him as a specimen.

The roans were calving in early November; whereas, when we went thirty miles on, at an elevation a thousand feet less, we at first saw no very young fawns accompanying the hartbeests, and no very young foals with the zebras. These hartbeests, which are named after their discoverer, Governor Jackson, are totally different from the hartbeests of the Athi and the Sotik countries, and are larger and finer in every way. One bull I shot weighed, in pieces, four hundred and seventy pounds. No allowance was made for the spilt blood, and, inasmuch as he had been hallalled, I think his live weight would have been nearly four hundred and ninety pounds. He was a big, full-grown bull, but not of extraordinary size; later I killed much bigger ones, unusually fine specimens, which must have weighed well over five hundred pounds. The horns, which are sometimes two feet long, are set on great bony pedicels, so that the face seems long and homely even for a hartbeest. The first two or three of these hartbeests which I killed were shot at long range, for, like all game, they are sometimes exceedingly wary; but we soon found that normally they were as tame as they were plentiful. We frequently saw them close by the herds of the Boer settlers. They were the common game of the plains. At times of course they were difficult to approach; but again and again, usually when we were riding, we came upon not only individuals but herds, down wind and in plain view, which permitted us to approach to within a hundred yards before they definitely took flight. Their motions look ungainly until they get into their full-speed stride. They utter no sound save the usual hartbeest sneeze.

There were bohor reedbuck also, pretty creatures, about the size of a whitetail deer, which lay close in the reed beds, or in hollows among the tall grass, and usually offered rather difficult running shots or very long standing shots. Still prettier were the little oribi. These are grass antelopes, frequenting much the same places as the duiker and steinbuck and not much larger. Where the grass was long they would lie close, with neck flat along the ground, and dart off when nearly stepped on, with a pig-like rush like that of a reedbuck or duiker in similar thick cover. But where the grass was short, and especially where it was burned, they did not trust to lying down and hiding; on the contrary, in such places they were conspicuous little creatures, and trusted to their speed and alert vigilance for their safety. They run very fast, with great bounds, and when they stand—usually at a hundred and fifty or two hundred yards—they face the hunter, the forward-thrown ears being the most noticeable thing about them. We found that each oribi bagged cost us an unpleasantly large number of cartridges.

One day we found where a large party of hyenas had established their day lairs in the wet seclusion of some reed beds. We beat through these reed beds, and, in the words once used by an old plains friend in describing the behavior of a family of black bears under similar circumstances, the hyenas "came bilin' out." As they bolted, Kermit shot one and I another; he bit savagely at a stick with which one of the gun-bearers poked it. It is difficult at first glance to tell the sex of a hyena, and our followers stoutly upheld the wide-spread African belief that they are bisexual, being male or female as they choose. A wounded or trapped hyena will of course bite if seized, but shows no sign of the ferocious courage which marks the leopard under such circumstances; for the hyena is as cowardly as it is savage, although its size and the tremendous power of its jaws ought to make it as formidable as the fierce spotted cat.

The day after this incident we came on a herd of giraffe. It was Kermit's turn for a giraffe; and just as the herd got under way he wounded the big bull. Away went the tall creatures, their tails twisting and curling, as they cantered along over the rough velt and among the thorn-bushes, at that gait of theirs which looks so leisurely and which yet enables them to cover so much ground. After them we tore, Kermit and Tarlton in the lead; and a fine chase we had. It was not until we had gone two or three miles that the bull lagged behind the herd. I was riding the tranquil sorrel, not a speedy horse; and by this time my weight was telling on him. Kermit and his horse had already turned a somersault, having gone into an ant-bear hole, which the tall grass concealed; but they were up and off in an instant. All of Tranquillity's enthusiasm had vanished, and only by constant thumping with heels and gun butt could I keep him at a slow hand-gallop, and in sight of the leaders. We came to a slight rise, where the rank grass grew high and thick; and Tranquillity put both his fore legs into an ant-bear hole, and with obvious relief rolled gently over on his side. It was not really a tumble; he hailed the ant-bear burrow as offering a way out of a chase in which he had grown to take less than no interest. Besides, he really was winded, and when we got up I could barely get him into a canter; and I saw no more of the run. Meanwhile Kermit and Tarlton raced alongside the wounded bull, one on each flank, and started him toward camp, which was about five miles from where the hunt began. Two or three times he came to a standstill, and turned first toward one and then toward the other of his pursuers, almost as if he meditated a charge; but they shouted at him and he resumed his flight. They brought him within three hundred yards of camp, and then Kermit leaped off and finished him.

This bull was a fine specimen, colored almost exactly like the giraffes of the Athi and Sotik, but with much more horn development. I doubt whether this five-horned kind is more than a local race. The bulls have been described as very dark; but the one thus shot, a big and old master-bull, was unusually light, and in the herd there were individuals of every shade, much the darkest being a rather small cow. Indeed, in none of the varieties of giraffe did we find that the old bulls were markedly darker than the others; many of them were dark, but some of the biggest were light-colored, and the darkest individuals in a herd were often cows. Giraffes, by the way, do sometimes lie down to sleep, but not often.*

In order that Heller might take care of the giraffe-skin, we had to spend a couple of days where we were then camped.

* This is just one of the points as to which no one observer should dogmatize or try to lay down general laws with no exceptions. Moreover, the personal equation of even the most honest observer must always be taken into account in considering not merely matters like this, but even such things as measurements. For example, Neuman, in his "Elephant Hunting," gives measurements of the height of both elephants and Grevy's zebra; our measurements made the elephants taller, and the big zebras less tall, than he found them. Measurements of the lengths of lions, made by different observers, are for this reason rarely of much value for purposes of comparison.

The tents were pitched near a spring of good water, beside a slight valley in which there were marshy spots and reed beds. The country was rolling, and covered with fine grass, unfortunately so tall as to afford secure cover for lions. There were stretches bare of trees, and other stretches with a sparse, scattered growth of low thorns or of the big, glossy-leaved bush which I have spoken of as the African jessamine because of the singularly sweet and jessamine-like fragrance of its flowers. Most of these bushes were in full bloom, as they had been six months before on the Athi and three months before near Kenia; some bore berries, of which it is said that the wild elephant-herds are fond.

It is hard to lay down general rules as to the blossoming-times of plants or breeding-times of animals in equatorial Africa. Before we left the Uasin Gishu table-land some of the hartebeest cows appeared with new-born calves. Some of the acacias had put forth their small, globular, yellow blossoms, just as the acacias on the Athi Plains were doing in the previous May. The blue lupins were flowering, for it is a cool, pleasant country.

Our camp here was attractive, and Kermit and I took advantage of our leisure to fill out the series of specimens of the big hartebeest and the oribi which Heller needed for the National Museum. The flesh of the oribis was reserved for our own table; that of the kongonis—which had been duly hallalled by the Moslems among our gun-bearers—was turned over to what might be called the officers' mess of the safari proper, the head man, cooks, tent-boys, gun-bearers, and saises; while of course the skinners and porters who happened to be out with us when any animal was slain got their share of the meat. We also killed two more hyenas; one, a dog, weighed one hundred and twenty pounds, being smaller than those Heller had trapped while skinning the first bull elephant I shot in the Kenia forest.

Good Ali, my tent-boy, kept bowls of the sweet-scented jessamine on our dining-table; now that there were four of us

together again we used the dining tent, which I had discarded
on the Guaso Nyero trip. Bakhari had been rather worn
down by the work on the Guaso Nyero, and in his place I
had taken Kongoni, a Wakamba, with filed teeth, like my second gun-bearer, Gouvimali, but a Moslem—although his Mos-
lemism did not go very deep. Kongoni was the best gun-bearer
I had yet had, very willing, and excellent both at seeing and
tracking game. Kermit's two gun-bearers were Juma Yohari,
a coal-black Wahili Moslem, and Kassitura, a Christian negro
from Uganda. Both of them were as eager to do everything
for Kermit as mine were to render me any service great or
small; and in addition they were capital men for their special
work. Juma was always smiling and happy, and was a high
favorite among his fellows; at lunch, when we had any, if I
gave my own followers some of the chocolate, or whatever
else it was that I had put in my saddle pocket, I always noticed
that they called up Yohari to share it. He it was who would
receive the colored cards from my companions' tobacco-pouches,
or from the packages of chocolate, and after puzzling over them
until he could himself identify the brilliantly colored ladies,
gentlemen, little girls, and wild beasts, would volubly explain
them to the others. Kassitura, quite as efficient and hard-
working, was a huge, solemn black man, as faithful and
uncomplaining a soul as I ever met. Kermit had picked
him out from among the porters to carry his camera, and
had then promoted him to be gun-bearer. In his place he
had taken as camera-bearer an equally powerful porter, a
heathen M'nuwezi named Mali. His tent-boy had gone
crooked; and one evening some months later after a long
and trying march he found Mali, whose performance of his
new duties he had been closely watching, the only man up;
and Mali, always willing, turned in of his own accord to help
get Kermit's tent in shape; so Kermit suddenly told him
he would promote him to be tent-boy. At first Mali did not
quite understand; then he pondered a moment or two, and
suddenly leaped into the air exclaiming in Swahili, "Now I

am a big man." And he faithfully strove to justify his promotion. In similar fashion Kermit picked out on the Nairobi race-track a Kikuyu sais named Magi, and brought him out with us. Magi turned out the best sais in the safari; and besides doing his own duty so well he was always exceedingly interested in everything that concerned his own Bwana, Kermit, or me—from the proper arrangement of our sun-pads to the success of our shooting.

From the giraffe camp we went two days' journey to the 'Nzoi River. Until this Uasin Gishu trip we had been on waters which either vanished in the desert or else flowed into the Indian Ocean. Now we had crossed the divide, and were on the Nile side of the watershed. The 'Nzoi, a rapid muddy river, passing south of Mount Elgon, empties into the Victoria Nyanza. Our route to its bank led across a rolling country, covered by a dense growth of tall grass, and in most places by open thorn-scrub, while here and there, in the shallow valleys or depressions, were swamps. There were lions, and at night we heard them; but in such long grass it was well-nigh hopeless to look for them. Evidently troops of elephants occasionally visited these plains, for the tops of the little thorn-trees were torn off and browsed down by the mighty brutes. How they can tear off and swallow such prickly dainties as these thorn branches, armored with needle-pointed spikes, is a mystery. Tarlton told me that he had seen an elephant, while feeding greedily on the young top of a thorn-tree, prick its trunk until it uttered a little scream or whine of pain; and it then in a fit of pettishness revenged itself by wrecking the thorn-tree.

Game abounded on the plains. We saw a couple of herds of giraffes. The hartbeests were the most plentiful and the least shy; time after time a small herd loitered until we were within a hundred yards before cantering away. Once or twice we saw topi among them; and often there were mixed herds of zebras and hartbeests. Oribi were common, and sometimes uttered a peculiar squealing whistle when they

first saw us. The reedbuck also whistled, but their whistle
was entirely distinct. It was astonishing how close the reedbuck lay. Again and again we put them up within a few feet
of us from patches of reeds or hollows in the long grass.
A much more singular habit is the way in which they share
these retreats with dangerous wild beasts; a trait common also
to the cover-loving bushbuck. From one of the patches of
reeds in which Kermit and I shot two hyenas a reedbuck
doe immediately afterward took flight. She had been reposing
peacefully during the day within fifty yards of several hyenas!
Tarlton had more than once found both reedbuck and bushbuck in comparatively small patches of cover which also held
lions.

It is, by the way, a little difficult to know what names to use
in distinguishing between the sexes of African game. The
trouble is one which obtains in all new countries, where the
settlers have to name new beasts; and is, of course, primarily
due to the fact that the terms already found in the language
originally applied only to domestic animals and to European
beasts of the chase. Africanders, whether Dutch or English,
speak of all antelope, of either sex, as "buck." Then they call
the males and females of the larger kinds bulls and cows, just
as Americans do when they speak of moose, wapiti, and cari-
bou; and the males and females of the smaller kinds they
usually speak of as rams and ewes.

While on safari to the 'Nzoi I was even more interested in
honey-birds which led us to honey than I was in the game.
Before starting for Africa John Burroughs had especially
charged me to look personally into this extraordinary habit
of the honey-bird; a habit so extraordinary that he was inclined to disbelieve the reality of its existence. But it unquestionably does exist. Every experienced hunter and every
native who lives in the wilderness has again and again been
an eye-witness of it. Kermit, in addition to his experience in
the Sotik, had been led by a honey-bird to honey in a rock,
near Lake Hannington. Once while I was tracking game a

honey-bird made his appearance, chattering loudly and flying beside us; I let two of the porters follow it, and it led them to honey. On the morning of the day we reached the 'Nzoi, a honey-bird appeared beside the safari, behaving in the same manner. Some of the men begged to be allowed to follow it; while they were talking to me the honey-bird flew to a big tree fifty yards off, and called loudly as it flitted to and fro in the branches; and sure enough there was honey in the tree. I let some of the men stay to get the honey; but they found little except comb filled with grubs. Some of this was put aside for the bird, which ate the grubs. The natives believe that misfortune will follow any failure on their part to leave the honey-bird its share of the booty. They also insist that sometimes the honey-bird will lead a man to a serpent or wild beast; and sure enough Doctor Mearns was once thus led up to a rhinoceros. While camped on the 'Nzoi the honey-birds were almost a nuisance; they were very common, and were continually accompanying us as we hunted, flying from tree to tree, and never ceasing their harsh chatter. Several times we followed birds, which in each case led us to bee-trees, and then perched quietly by until the gun-bearers and porters (Gouvimali shone on such occasions) got out the honey—which we found excellent eating, by the way.

Our camp here was in a beautiful country, and game, for the most part Uganda kob and singsing water-buck, often fed in sight of the tents. The kob is a small, short-haired water-buck, with slightly different horns. It is a chunky antelope, with a golden-red coat; I weighed one old buck which I shot and it tipped the beam at two hundred and twenty pounds; Kermit killed a bigger one, weighing two hundred and forty pounds, but its horns were poorer. In their habits the kob somewhat resemble impala, the does being found in bands of twenty or thirty with a single master-buck; and they sometimes make great impala-like bounds. They fed, at all hours of the day, in the flats near the river, and along the edges of the swamps, and were not very wary. They never tried to hide, and were always easily seen; in utter contrast to the close-lying, skulking, bohor reedbuck, which lay like a rabbit in the long grass or reeds. The kob, on the contrary, were always anxious themselves to see round about, and, like water-buck and hartbeest, frequently used the ant-heaps as lookout stations. It was a pretty sight to see a herd of the bright-red creatures clustered on a big ant-hill, all the necks outstretched, and all the ears thrown forward. The females are hornless. By the middle of November we noticed an occasional new-born calf.

The handsome, shaggy-coated, singsing water-buck had much the same habits as the kob. Like the kob they fed at all hours of the day; but they were more wary and more apt to be found in country where there were a good many bushes or small trees. Water-buck and kob sometimes associated together.

The best singsing bull I got I owed to Tarlton's good eyesight and skill in tracking and stalking. The herd of which he was master-bull were shy, and took the alarm just as we first saw them. Tarlton followed their trail for a couple of miles, and then stalked them to an inch, by the dexterous use of a couple of bushes and an ant-hill; the ant-hill being reached after a two-hundred-yards' crawl, first on all fours and then flat on the ground, which resulted in my getting a good offhand shot at a hundred and eighty yards. At this time, about the middle of November, some of the cows had new-born calves. One day I shot a hartbeest bull, with horns twenty-four inches long, as it stood on the top of an ant-heap. On going up to it we noticed something behind a little bush, sixty yards off. We were puzzled what it could be, but finally made out a water-buck cow; and a minute or two later away she bounded to safety, followed by a wee calf. The porters much appreciated the flesh of the water-buck. We did not. It is the poorest eating of African antelope—and among the big antelope only the eland is good as a steady diet.

One day we drove a big swamp, putting a hundred porters across it in line, while Kermit and I walked a little ahead of them along the edges, he on one side and I on the other. I shot a couple of bushbuck, a ewe and a young ram; and after the drive was over he shot a female leopard as she stood on the side of an ant-hill.

There were a number of both reedbuck and bushbuck in the swamp. The reedbuck were all ewes, which we did not want. There were one or two big bushbuck rams, but they broke back through the beaters; and so did two bushbuck ewes and one reedbuck ewe, one of the bushbuck ewes actually knocking down a beater. They usually either cleared out while the beaters were still half a mile distant, or else waited until they were almost trodden on. The bushbuck rams were very dark-colored; the hornless ewes, and the young, were a brilliant red, the belly, the under side and edges of the conspicuous fluffy tail, and a few dim spots on the cheeks and flanks, being white. Although these buck frequent thick cover, forest, or swamp, and trust for their safety to hiding, and to eluding observation by their stealthy, skulking ways, their coloration has not the smallest protective value, being on the contrary very conspicuous in both sexes, but especially in the females and young, who most need protection. Bushbuck utter a loud bark. The hoofs of those we shot were very long, as is often the case with water-loving, marsh-frequenting species. There is a curious collar-like space around the neck on which there is no hair. Although if anything smaller than our whitetail deer, the bushbuck is a vicious and redoubtable fighter, and will charge a man without hesitation.

The last day we were at the 'Nzoi the porters petitioned for one ample meal of meat; and we shot a dozen buck for them —kongoni, kob, and singsing. One of the latter, a very fine bull, fairly charged Kermit and his gun-bearer when they got within a few yards of it, as it lay wounded. This bull grunted loudly as he charged; the grunt of an oryx under similar circumstances is almost a growl. On this day both Kermit and I were led to bee-trees by honey-birds and took some of the honey for lunch. Kermit stayed after his boys had left the tree, so as to see exactly what the honey-bird did. The boys had smoked out the bees, and when they left the tree was still smoking. Throughout the process the honey-bird had stayed quietly in a neighboring tree, occasionally uttering a single bubbling cluck. As soon as the boys left, it flew straight for the smoking bee-tree, uttering a long trill, utterly different from the chattering noise made while trying to attract the attention of the men and lead them to the tree; and not only did it eat the grubs, but it also ate the bees that were stupefied by the smoke.

Next day we moved camp to the edge of a swamp about five miles from the river. Near the tents was one of the trees which, not knowing its real name, we called "sausage-tree"; the seeds or fruits are encased in a kind of hard gourd, the size of a giant sausage, which swings loosely at the end of a long tendril. The swamp was half or three-quarters of a mile across, with one or two ponds in the middle, from which we shot ducks. Francolins—delicious eating, as the ducks were also—uttered their grating calls near by; while oribi and hart-beest were usually to be seen from the tents. The hartbeest, by the way, in its three forms, is much the commonest game animal of East Africa.

A few miles beyond this swamp we suddenly came on a small herd of elephants in the open. There were eight cows and two calves, and they were moving slowly, feeding on the thorny tops of the scattered mimosas, and of other bushes which were thornless. The eyesight of elephants is very bad; I doubt whether they see more clearly than a rather near-sighted man; and we walked up to within seventy yards of these, slight though the cover was, so that Kermit could try to photograph them. We did not need to kill another cow for the National Museum, and so after we had looked at the huge, interesting creatures as long as we wished, we croaked and whistled, and they moved off with leisurely indifference. There is always a fascination about watching elephants; they are such giants, they are so intelligent—much more so than any other game, except perhaps the lion, whose intelligence has a very sinister bent—and they look so odd with their great ears flapping and their trunks lifting and curling. Elephants are rarely absolutely still for any length of time; now and then they flap an ear, or their bodies sway slightly, while at intervals they utter curious internal rumblings, or trumpet gently. These were feeding on saplings of the mimosas and other trees, apparently caring nothing for the thorns of the former; they would tear off branches, big or little, or snap a trunk short off if the whim seized them. They swallowed the leaves and twigs of these trees; but I have known them merely chew and spit out the stems of certain bushes.

After leaving the elephants we were on our way back to camp when we saw a white man in the trail ahead; and on coming nearer whom should it prove to be but Carl Akeley, who was out on a trip for the American Museum of Natural History in New York. We went with him to his camp, where we found Mrs. Akeley, Clark, who was assisting him, and Messrs. McCutcheon and Stevenson, who were along on a hunting trip. They were old friends and I was very glad to see them. McCutcheon, the cartoonist, had been at a farewell lunch given me by Robert Collier just before I left New York, and at the lunch we had been talking much of George Ade, and the first question I put to him was, "*Where* is George Ade?" for if one unexpectedly meets an American cartoonist on a hunting trip in mid-Africa there seems no reason why one should not also see his crony, an American playwright. A year previously Mr. and Mrs. Akeley had lunched with me at the White House, and we had talked over our proposed African trips. Akeley, an old African wanderer, was going out with the especial purpose of getting a group of elephants for the American Museum, and was anxious that I should shoot one or two of them for him. I had told him that I certainly would if it were a possibility; and on learning that we had just seen a herd of cows he felt—as I did—that the chance had come for me to fulfil my promise. So we decided

that he should camp with us that night, and that next morning we would start with a light outfit to see whether we could
not overtake the herd.

An amusing incident occurred that evening. After dark
some of the porters went through the reeds to get water from
the pond in the middle of the swamp. I was sitting in my
tent when a loud yelling and screaming rose from the swamp,
and in rushed Kongoni to say that one of the men, while
drawing water, had been seized by a lion. Snatching up a
rifle I was off at a run for the swamp, calling for lanterns;
Kermit and Tarlton joined me, the lanterns were brought, and
we reached the meadow of short marsh-grass which surrounded
the high reeds in the middle. No sooner were we on this
meadow than there were loud snortings in the darkness ahead
of us, and then the sound of a heavy animal galloping across
our front. It now developed that there was no lion in the
case at all, but that the porters had been chased by a hippo.
I should not have supposed that a hippo would live in such
a small, isolated swamp; but there he was on the meadow in
front of me, invisible, but snorting, and galloping to and fro.
Evidently he was much interested in the lights, and we thought
he might charge us; but he did not, retreating slowly as we
advanced, until he plunged into the little pond. Hippos are
sometimes dangerous at night, and so we waded through the
swamp until we came to the pool at which the porters filled
their buckets, and stood guard over them until they were
through; while the hippo, unseen in the darkness, came closer
to us, snorting and plunging—possibly from wrath and inso-
lence, but more probably from mere curiosity.

Next morning Akeley, Tarlton, Kermit, and I started on
our elephant-hunt. We were travelling light. I took nothing
but my bedding, wash-kit, spare socks, and slippers, all in
a roll of water-proof canvas. We went to where we had seen
the herd and then took up the trail, Kongoni and two or three
other gun-bearers walking ahead as trackers. They did their
work well. The elephants had not been in the least alarmed.

Where they had walked in single file it was easy to follow their trail; but the trackers had hard work puzzling it out where the animals had scattered out and loitered along feeding. The trail led up and down hills and through open thornscrub, and it crossed and recrossed the wooded watercourses in the bottoms of the valleys. At last, after going some ten miles we came on signs where the elephants had fed that morning, and four or five miles farther on we overtook them. That we did not scare them into flight was due to Tarlton. The trail went nearly across wind; the trackers were leading us swiftly along it, when suddenly Tarlton heard a low trumpet ahead and to the right hand. We at once doubled back, left the horses, and advanced toward where the noise indicated that the herd was standing.

In a couple of minutes we sighted them. It was just noon. There were six cows, and two well-grown calves—these last being quite big enough to shift for themselves or to be awkward antagonists for any man of whom they could get hold. They stood in a clump, each occasionally shifting its position or lazily flapping an ear; and now and then one would break off a branch with its trunk, tuck it into its mouth, and withdraw it stripped of its leaves. The wind blew fair, we were careful to make no noise, and with ordinary caution we had nothing to fear from their eyesight. The ground was neither forest nor bare plain; it was covered with long grass and a scattered open growth of small scantily leaved trees, chiefly mimosas, but including some trees covered with gorgeous orange-red flowers. After careful scrutiny we advanced behind an anthill to within sixty yards, and I stepped forward for the shot.

Akeley wished two cows and a calf. Of the two best cows one had rather thick, worn tusks; those of the other were smaller, but better shaped. The latter stood half facing me, and I put the bullet from the right barrel of the Holland through her lungs, and fired the left barrel for the heart of the other. Tarlton, and then Akeley and Kermit, followed suit. At once the herd started diagonally past us, but half halted and

faced toward us when only twenty-five yards distant, an unwounded cow beginning to advance with her great ears cocked
at right angles to her head; and Tarlton called "Look out; they
are coming for us." At such a distance a charge from half
a dozen elephant is a serious thing; I put a bullet into the
forehead of the advancing cow, causing her to lurch heavily
forward to her knees; and then we all fired. The heavy rifles
were too much even for such big beasts, and round they spun
and rushed off. As they turned I dropped the second cow
I had wounded with a shot in the brain, and the cow that had
started to charge also fell, though it needed two or three more
shots to keep it down as it struggled to rise. The cow at
which I had first fired kept on with the rest of the herd, but
fell dead before going a hundred yards. After we had turned
the herd Kermit with his Winchester killed a bull calf, necessary to complete the museum group; we had been unable to
kill it before because we were too busy stopping the charge
of the cows. I was sorry to have to shoot the third cow,
but with elephant starting to charge at twenty-five yards the
risk is too great, and the need of instant action too imperative,
to allow of any hesitation.

We pitched camp a hundred yards from the elephants and
Akeley, working like a demon, and assisted by Tarlton, had
the skins off the two biggest cows and the calf by the time
night fell; I walked out and shot an oribi for supper. Soon
after dark the hyenas began to gather at the carcasses and to
quarrel among themselves as they gorged. Toward morning
a lion came near and uttered a kind of booming, long-drawn
moan, an ominous and menacing sound. The hyenas answered with an extraordinary chorus of yelling, howling,
laughing, and chuckling, as weird a volume of noise as any
to which I ever listened. At dawn we stole down to the
carcasses in the faint hope of a shot at the lion. However,
he was not there; but as we came toward one carcass a hyena
raised its head seemingly from beside the elephant's belly, and
I brained it with the little Springfield. On walking up it ap-

peared that I need not have shot at all. The hyena, which was swollen with elephant meat, had gotten inside the huge body, and had then bitten a hole through the abdominal wall of tough muscle and thrust his head through. The wedge-shaped head had slipped through the hole all right, but the muscle had then contracted, and the hyena was fairly caught, with its body inside the elephant's belly, and its head thrust out through the hole. We took several photos of the beast in its queer trap.

After breakfast we rode back to our camp by the swamp. Akeley and Clark were working hard at the elephant-skins; but Mrs. Akeley, Stevenson, and McCutcheon took lunch with us at our camp. They had been having a very successful hunt; Mrs. Akeley had to her credit a fine maned lion and a bull elephant with enormous tusks. This was the first safari we had met while we were out in the field; though in Nairobi, and once or twice at outlying bomas, we had met men about to start on, or returning from, expeditions; and as we marched into Meru we encountered the safari of an old friend, William Lord Smith—"Tiger" Smith—who, with Messrs. Brooks and Allen, was on a trip which was partly a hunting trip and partly a scientific trip undertaken on behalf of the Cambridge Museum.

From the 'Nzoi we made a couple days' march to Lake Sergoi, which we had passed on our way out; a reed-fringed pond, surrounded by rocky hills which marked about the limit to which the Boer and English settlers who were taking up the country had spread. All along our route we encountered herds of game; sometimes the herd would be of only one species; at other times we would come across a great mixed herd, the red hartbeest always predominating; while among them might be zebras, showing silvery white or dark gray in the distance, topis with beautifully colored coats, and even water-buck. We shot what hartbeests, topis, and oribis were needed for food. All over the uplands we came on the remains of a race of which even the memory has long since vanished. These remains consist of large, nearly circular walls of stones, which are sometimes roughly squared. A few of these circular enclosures contain more than one chamber. Many of them, at least, are not cattle kraals, being too small, and built round hollows; the walls are so low that by themselves they could not serve for shelter or defense, and must probably have been used as supports for roofs of timber or skins. They were certainly built by people who were in some respects more advanced than the savage tribes who now dwell in the land; but the grass grows thick on the earth mounds into which the ancient stone walls are slowly crumbling, and not a trace of the builders remains. Barbarians they doubtless were; but they have been engulfed in the black oblivion of a lower barbarism, and not the smallest tradition lingers to tell of their craft or their cruelty, their industry or prowess, or to give us the least hint as to the race from which they sprang.

We had with us an ox-wagon, with the regulation span of sixteen oxen, the driver being a young Colonial Englishman from South Africa—for the Dutch and English Africanders are the best ox-wagon drivers in the world. On the way back to Sergoi he lost his oxen, which were probably run off by some savages from the mountains; so at Sergoi we had to hire another ox-wagon, the South African who drove it being a Dutchman named Botha. Sergoi was as yet the limit of settlement; but it was evident that the whole Uasin Gishu country would soon be occupied. Already many Boers from South Africa, and a number of English Africanders had come in; and no better pioneers exist to-day than these South Africans, both Dutch and English. Both are so good that I earnestly hope they will become indissolubly welded into one people; and the Dutch Boer has the supreme merit of preferring the country to the town and of bringing his wife and children—plenty of children—with him to settle on the land. The home-maker is the only type of settler of permanent value; and the cool, healthy, fertile Uasin Gishu region is an ideal land for the right kind of pioneer home-maker, whether he hopes to make his living by raising stock or by growing crops.

At Sergoi Lake there is a store kept by Mr. Kirke, a South African of Scotch blood. With a kind courtesy which I cannot too highly appreciate he, with the equally cordial help of another settler, Mr. Skally—also a South African, but of Irish birth—and of the district commissioner, Mr. Corbett, had arranged for a party of Nandi warriors to come over and show me how they hunted the lion. Two Dutch farmers, Boers, from the neighborhood, had also come; they were Messrs. Mouton and Jordaan, fine fellows both, the former having served with De Wet during the war. Mr. and Mrs. Corbett—who were hospitality itself—had also come to see the sport; and so had Captain Chapman, an English army officer who was taking a rest after several years' service in Northern Nigeria.

The Nandi are a warlike pastoral tribe, close kin to the Masai in blood and tongue, in weapons and in manner of life. They have long been accustomed to kill with the spear lions which become man-eaters or which molest their cattle overmuch; and the peace which British rule has imposed upon them—a peace so welcome to the weaker, so irksome to the predatory, tribes—has left lion killing one of the few pursuits in which glory can be won by a young warrior. When it was told them that if they wished they could come to hunt lions at Sergoi, eight hundred warriors volunteered, and much heartburning was caused in choosing the sixty or seventy who were allowed the privilege. They stipulated, however, that they should not be used merely as beaters, but should kill the lion themselves, and refused to come unless with this understanding.

The day before we reached Sergoi they had gone out, and had killed a lion and lioness; the beasts were put up from a small covert and despatched with the heavy throwing spears on the instant, before they offered, or indeed had the chance to offer, any resistance. The day after our arrival there was mist and cold rain, and we found no lions. Next day, November 20, we were successful.

We started immediately after breakfast. Kirke, Skally, Mouton, Jordaan, Mr. and Mrs. Corbett, Captain Chapman, and our party were on horseback; of course we carried our rifles, but our duty was merely to round up the lion and hold him, if he went off so far in advance that even the Nandi runners could not overtake him. We intended to beat the country toward some shallow, swampy valleys twelve miles distant.

In an hour we overtook the Nandi warriors, who were advancing across the rolling, grass plains in a long line, with intervals of six or eight yards between the men. They were splendid savages, stark naked, lithe as panthers, the muscles rippling under their smooth dark skins; all their lives they had lived on nothing but animal food, milk, blood, and flesh, and they were fit for any fatigue or danger. Their faces were proud, cruel, fearless; as they ran they moved with long springy strides. Their head-dresses were fantastic; they carried ox-hide shields painted with strange devices; and each bore in his right hand the formidable war spear, used both for strapping and for throwing at close quarters. The narrow spear heads of soft iron were burnished till they shone like silver; they were four feet long, and the point and edges were razor-sharp. The wooden haft appeared for but a few inches; the long butt was also of iron, ending in a spike, so that the spear looked almost solid metal. Yet each sinewy warrior carried his heavy weapon as if it were a toy, twirling it till it glinted in the sun-rays. Herds of game, red hartebeests and striped zebra and wild swine, fled right and left before the advance of the line.

It was noon before we reached a wide, shallow valley, with beds of rushes here and there in the middle, and on either side high grass and dwarfed and scattered thorn-trees. Down this we beat for a couple of miles. Then, suddenly, a maned lion rose a quarter of a mile ahead of the line and galloped off through the high grass to the right; and all of us on horse-back tore after him.

He was a magnificent beast, with a black and tawny mane; in his prime, teeth and claws perfect, with mighty thews, and savage heart. He was lying near a hartbeest on which he had been feasting; his life had been one unbroken career of rapine and violence; and now the maned master of the wilderness, the terror that stalked by night, the grim lord of slaughter, was to meet his doom at the hands of the only foes who dared molest him.

It was a mile before we brought him to bay. Then the Dutch farmer, Mouton, who had not even a rifle, but who rode foremost, was almost on him; he halted and turned under a low thorn-tree, and we galloped past him to the opposite side, to hold him until the spearmen could come. It was a sore temptation to shoot him; but of course we could not break faith with our Nandi friends. We were only some sixty yards from him, and we watched him with our rifles ready, lest he should charge either us, or the first two or three spearmen, before their companions arrived.

One by one the spearmen came up, at a run, and gradually began to form a ring around him. Each, when he came near enough, crouched behind his shield, his spear in his right hand, his fierce, eager face peering over the shield rim. As man followed man, the lion rose to his feet. His mane bristled, his tail lashed, he held his head low, the upper lip now drooping over the jaws, now drawn up so as to show the gleam of the long fangs. He faced first one way and then another, and never ceased to utter his murderous grunting roars. It was a wild sight; the ring of spearmen, intent, silent, bent on blood, and in the centre the great man-killing beast, his thunderous wrath growing ever more dangerous.

At last the tense ring was complete, and the spearmen rose and closed in. The lion looked quickly from side to side, saw where the line was thinnest, and charged at his topmost speed. The crowded moment began. With shields held steady,

and quivering spears poised, the men in front braced themselves for the rush and the shock; and from either hand the
warriors sprang forward to take their foe in flank. Bounding
ahead of his fellows, the leader reached throwing distance;
the long spear flickered and plunged; as the lion felt the wound
he half turned, and then flung himself on the man in front.
The warrior threw his spear; it drove deep into the life, for
entering at one shoulder it came out of the opposite flank,
near the thigh, a yard of steel through the great body. Rearing, the lion struck the man, bearing down the shield, his back
arched; and for a moment he slaked his fury with fang and
talon. But on the instant I saw another spear driven clear
through his body from side to side; and as the lion turned
again the bright spear blades darting toward him were flashes
of white flame. The end had come. He seized another man,
who stabbed him and wrenched loose. As he fell he gripped
a spear head in his jaws with such tremendous force that he
bent it double. Then the warriors were round and over him,
stabbing and shouting, wild with furious exultation.

From the moment when he charged until his death I doubt
whether ten seconds had elapsed, perhaps less; but what a
ten seconds! The first half-dozen spears had done the work.
Three of the spear blades had gone clear through the body, the
points projecting several inches; and these, and one or two
others, including the one he had seized in his jaws, had been
twisted out of shape in the terrible death-struggle.

We at once attended to the two wounded men. Treating
their wounds with antiseptic was painful, and so, while the
operation was in progress, I told them, through Kirke, that I
would give each a heifer. A Nandi prizes his cattle rather
more than his wives; and each sufferer smiled broadly at the
news, and forgot all about the pain of his wounds.

Then the warriors, raising their shields above their heads,
and chanting the deep-toned victory song, marched with a slow,
dancing step around the dead body of the lion; and this savage

dance of triumph ended a scene of as fierce interest and excitement as I ever hope to see.

The Nandi marched back by themselves, carrying the two wounded men on their shields. We rode to camp by a roundabout way, on the chance that we might see another lion. The afternoon waned and we cast long shadows before us as we rode across the vast lonely plain. The game stared at us as we passed; a cold wind blew in our faces, and the tall grass waved ceaselessly; the sun set behind a sullen cloud bank; and then, just at nightfall, the tents glimmered white through the dusk.

Tarlton's partner, Newland—also an Australian, and as fine a fellow as Tarlton himself—once had a rather eerie adventure with a man-eating lion. He was camped near Kilimakiu, and after nightfall the alarm was raised that a lion was near by. He came out of his tent, more wood was thrown on the fire, and he heard footsteps retreating, but could not make out whether they were those of a lion or a hyena. Going back to his tent he lay down on his bed with his face turned toward the tent wall. Just as he was falling to sleep the canvas was pushed almost into his face by the head of some creature outside; immediately afterward he heard the sound of a heavy animal galloping, and then the scream of one of his porters whom the lion had seized and was dragging off into the darkness. Rushing out with his rifle he fired toward the sounds, shooting high; the lion let go his hold and made off, and the man ultimately recovered.

It has been said that lions are monogamous and that they mate for life. If this were so they would almost always be found in pairs, a lion and a lioness. They are sometimes so found; but it is much more common to come across a lioness and her cubs, an old lion with several lionesses and their young (for they are often polygamous), a single lion or lioness, or a couple of lions or lionesses, or a small troop, either all lions or all lionesses, or of mixed sexes. These facts are not compatible with the romantic theory in question.

We tried to get the Nandi to stay with us for a few days and beat for lions; but this they refused to do, unless they were also to kill them; and I did not care to assist as a mere spectator at any more lion-hunts, no matter how exciting—though to do so once was well worth while. So we moved on by ourselves, camping in likely places. In the swamps, living among the reeds, were big handsome cuckoos, which ate mice. Our first camp was by a stream bordered by trees like clove-trees; at evening multitudes of yellow-billed pigeons flew up its course. They were feeding on olives, and were good for the table; and so were the yellow-billed mallards, which were found in the occasional pools. Everything we shot at this time went into the pot—except a hyena. The stomachs of the reedbuck and oribi contained nothing but grass; but the stomachs of the duikers were filled with berries from a plant which looked like the deadly nightshade. On the burned ground, by the way, the oribi, which were very plentiful, behaved precisely like tommies, except that they did not go in as large troops; they made no effort to hide as they do in thick grass; and as duikers, steinbucks, and reedbucks always do. We saw, but could not get a shot at, one topi with a white or blazed face, like a South African blesbok. While beating one swamp a lion appeared for an instant at its edge, a hundred and fifty yards off. I got a snap-shot, and ought to have hit him, but didn't. We tried our best to get him out of the swamp, finally burning all of it that was not too wet; but we never saw him again.

We recrossed the high hill-country, through mists and driving rains, and were back at Londiani on the last day of November. Here, with genuine regret, we said good-by to our safari; for we were about to leave East Africa, and could only take a few of our personal attendants with us into Uganda and the Nile Valley. I was really sorry to see the last of the big, strong, good-natured porters. They had been with us over seven months, and had always behaved well—though this, of course, was mainly owing to Cuninghame's and Tarlton's management. We had not lost a single man by death. One had been tossed by a rhino, one clawed by a leopard, and several had been sent to hospital for dysentery, smallpox, or fever; but none had died. While on the Guaso Nyero trip we had run into a narrow belt of the dreaded tsetse fly, whose bite is fatal to domestic animals. Five of our horses were bitten, and four of them died, two not until we were on the Uasin Gishu; the fifth, my zebra-shaped brown, although very sick, ultimately recovered, to the astonishment of the experts. Only three of our horses lasted in such shape that we could ride them in to Londiani; one of them being Tranquillity, and another Kermit's white pony, Huan Daw, who was always dancing and curveting, and whom in consequence the saises had christened "merodadi," the dandy.

The first ten days of December I spent at Njoro, on the edge of the Mau escarpment, with Lord Delamere. It is a beautiful farming country; and Lord Delamere is a practical and successful farmer, and the most useful settler, from the standpoint of the all-round interests of the country, in British East Africa. Incidentally, the home-ranch was most attractive—especially the library, the room containing Lady Delamere's books. Delamere had been himself a noted big-game hunter, his bag including fifty-two lions; but instead of continuing to be a mere sportsman, he turned his attention to stock-raising and wheat-growing, and became a leader in the work of taming the wilderness, of conquering for civilization the world's waste spaces. No career can be better worth following.

During his hunting years Delamere had met with many strange adventures. One of the lions he shot mauled him, breaking his leg, and also mauling his two Somali gunbearers. The lion then crawled off into some bushes fifty yards away, and camp was pitched where the wounded men were lying. Soon after nightfall the hyenas assembled in numbers and attacked, killed, and ate the mortally wounded lion, the noise made by the combatants being ear-rending. On another occasion he had heard a leopard attack some baboons in the rocks, a tremendous row following as the big dog baboons hastened to the assistance of the one who had been seized and drove off the leopard. That evening a leopard, evidently the same one, very thin and hungry, came into camp and was shot; it was frightfully bitten, the injuries being such as only baboons inflict, and would unquestionably have died of its wounds. The leopard wherever possible takes his kill up a tree, showing extraordinary strength in the performance of this feat. It is undoubtedly due to fear of interference from hyenas. The 'Ndorobo said that no single hyena would meddle with a leopard, but that three or four would without hesitation rob it of its prey. Some years before this time, while hunting north of Kenia Lord Delamere had met a Doctor Kolb, who was killed by a rhino immediately afterward. Doctor Kolb was fond of rhinoceros liver, and killed scores of the animals for food; but finally a cow, with a half-grown calf, which he had wounded charged him and thrust her horn right through the middle of his body.

We spent several days vainly hunting bongo in the dense mountain forests, with half a dozen 'Ndorobo. These were true 'Ndorobo, who never cultivate the ground, living in the deep forests on wild honey and game. It has been said that they hunt but little, and only elephant and rhino; but this is not correct as regards the 'Ndorobo in question. They were all clad in short cloaks of the skin of the tree-hyrax; hyrax, monkey, bongo, and forest hog, the only game of the dense, cool, wet forest, were all habitually killed by them. They also occasionally killed rhino and buffalo, finding the former, because it must occasionally be attacked in the open, the more dangerous of the two; twice Delamere had come across small communities of 'Ndorobo literally starving because the strong man, the chief hunter, the bread-winner, had been killed by a rhino which he had attacked. The head man of those with us, who was named Mel-el-lek, had himself been fearfully injured by a wounded buffalo; and the father of another one

who was with us had been killed by baboons which had ral-
lied to the aid of one which he was trying to kill with his
knobkerry. Usually they did not venture to meddle with the
lions which they found on the edge of the forest, or with
the leopards which occasionally dwelt in the deep woods; but
once Mel-el-lek killed a leopard with a poisoned arrow from
a tree, and once a whole party of them attacked and killed
with their poisoned arrows a lion which had slain a cow
buffalo near the forest. On another occasion a lion in its turn
killed two of their hunters. In fact they were living just as
paleolithic man lived in Europe, ages ago.

Their arms were bows and arrows, the arrows being carried
in skin quivers, and the bows, which were strung with zebra
gut, being swathed in strips of hide. When resting they often
stood on one leg, like storks. Their eyesight was marvellous,
and they were extremely skilful alike in tracking and in seeing
game. They threaded their way through the forest noiselessly and at speed, and were extraordinary climbers. They
were continually climbing trees to get at the hyrax, and once
when a big black-and-white Colobus monkey which I had
shot lodged in the top of a giant cedar one of them ascended
and brought it down with matter-of-course indifference. He
cut down a sapling, twenty-five feet long, with the stub of
a stout branch left on as a hook, and for a rope used a section of vine which he broke and twisted into flexibility. Then,
festooned with all his belongings, he made the ascent. There
was a tall olive, sixty or eighty feet high, close to the cedar,
and up this he went. From its topmost branches, where only
a monkey or a 'Ndorobo could have felt at home, he reached
his sapling over to the lowest limb of the giant cedar, and
hooked it on; and then crawled across on this dizzy bridge.
Up he went, got the monkey, recrossed the bridge, and climbed
down again, quite unconcerned.

The big black-and-white monkeys ate nothing but leaves,
and usually trusted for safety to ascending into the very tops
of the tallest cedars. Occasionally they would come in a flying

leap down to the ground, or to a neighboring tree; when on the ground they merely dashed toward another tree, being less agile than the ordinary monkeys, whether in the tree-tops or on solid earth. They are strikingly handsome and conspicuous creatures. Their bold coloration has been spoken of as "protective"; but it is protective only to town-bred eyes. A non-expert finds any object, of no matter what color, difficult to make out when hidden among the branches at the top of a tall tree; but the black-and-white coloration of this monkey has not the slightest protective value of any kind. On the contrary, it is calculated at once to attract the eye. The 'Ndorobo were a unit in saying that these monkeys were much more easy to see than their less brightly colored kinsfolk who dwell in the same forests; and this was my own experience.

When camped in these high forests the woods after nightfall were vocal with the croaking and wailing of the tree-hyraxes. They are squat, woolly, funny things, and to my great amusement I found that most of the settlers called them "Teddy bears." They are purely arboreal and nocturnal creatures, living in hollows high up in the big trees, by preference in the cedars. At night they are very noisy, the call consisting of an opening series of batrachian-like croaks, followed by a succession of quavering wails—eerie sounds enough, as they come out of the black stillness of the midnight. They are preyed on now and then by big owls and by leopards, and the white-tailed mongoose is their especial foe, following them everywhere among the tree-tops. This mongoose is both terrestrial and arboreal in habits, and is hated by the 'Ndorobo because it robs their honey buckets.

The bongo and the giant hog were the big game of these deep forests, where a tangle of undergrowth filled the spaces between the trunks of the cedar, the olive, and the yew or yellowwood, while where the bamboos grew they usually choked out all other plants. Delamere had killed several giant hogs with his half-breed hounds; but on this occasion the hounds would not follow them. On three days we came across bongo;

once a solitary bull, on both the other occasions herds. We never saw them, although we heard the solitary bull crash off through the bamboos; for they are very wary and elusive, being incessantly followed by the 'Ndorobo. They are as large as native bullocks, with handsomely striped skins, and both sexes carry horns. On each of the three days we followed them all day long, and it was interesting to trace so much as we could of their habits. Their trails are deeply beaten, and converge toward the watercourses, which run between the steep, forest-clad spurs of the mountains. They do not graze, but browse, cropping the leaves, flowers, and twigs of various shrubs, and eating thistles; they are said to eat bark, but this our 'Ndorobo denied. They are also said to be nocturnal, feeding at night, and lying up in the daytime; but this was certainly not the case with those we came across. Both of the herds, which we followed patiently and cautiously for hours without alarming them, were feeding as they moved slowly along. One herd lay down for a few hours at noon; the other kept feeding until mid-afternoon, when we alarmed it; and the animals then went straight up the mountain over the rim-rock. It was cold rainy weather, and the dark of the moon, which may perhaps have had something to do with the bongo being on the move and feeding during the day; but the 'Ndorobo said that they never fed at night—I of course know nothing about this personally. Leopards catch the young bongo and giant hog, but dare not meddle with those that are full grown. The forest which they frequent is so dense, so well-nigh impenetrable, that half the time no man can follow their trails save by bending and crawling, and cannot make out an object twenty yards ahead. It is extraordinary to see the places through which the bongo pass, and which are their chosen haunts.

While Lord Delamere and I were hunting in vain Kermit was more fortunate. He was the guest of Barclay Cole, Delamere's brother-in-law. They took eight porters and went into the forest accompanied by four 'Ndorobo. They marched straight up to the bamboo and yellowwood forest near the top of the Mau escarpment. They spent five days hunting. The procedure was simply to find the trail of a herd, to follow it through the tangled woods as rapidly and noiselessly as possible until it was overtaken, and then to try to get a shot at the first patch of reddish hide of which they got a glimpse —for they never saw more than such a patch, and then only for a moment. The first day Kermit, firing at such a patch, knocked over the animal; but it rose and the tracks were so confused that even the keen eyes of the wild men could not pick out the right one. Next day they again got into a herd; this time Kermit was the first to see the game—all that was visible being a patch of reddish, the size of a man's two hands, with a white stripe across it. Firing he killed the animal; but it proved to be only half grown. Even the 'Ndorobo now thought it useless to follow the herd; but Kermit took one of them and started in pursuit. After a couple of hours' trailing the herd was again overtaken, and again Kermit got a glimpse of the animals. He hit two; and selecting the trail with most blood they followed it for three or four miles, until Kermit overtook and finished off the wounded bongo, a fine cow.

Kermit always found them lying up during the middle of the day and feeding in the morning and afternoon; otherwise his observations of their habits coincided with mine.

The next ten days Kermit spent in a trip to the coast, near Mombasa, for sable—the most beautiful antelope next to the koodoo. The cows and bulls are red, the very old bulls (of the typical form) jet-black, all with white bellies; like the roan, both sexes carry scimitar-shaped horns, but longer than the roans. He was alone with his two gun-bearers, and some Swahili porters; he acted as head man himself. They marched from Mombasa, being ferried across the harbor of Kilindini in a dhow, and then going some fifteen miles south. Next day they marched about ten miles to a Nyika village, where they arrived just in the middle of a funeral-dance which was being held in honor of a chief's son who had died. Kermit was much amused to find that this death-dance had more life and go to it than any dance he had yet seen, and the music —the dirge music—had such swing and vivacity that it almost reminded him of a comic opera. The dancers wore tied round their legs queer little wickerwork baskets, with beans inside, which rattled in the rhythm of their dancing. Camp was pitched under a huge baobab-tree, in sight of the Indian Ocean; but in the middle of the night the ants swarmed in and drove everybody out; and next day, while Kermit was hunting, camp was shifted on about an hour's march to a little grove of trees by a brook. It was a well-watered country, very hilly, with palm-bordered streams in each valley. These wild palms bore ivorynuts, the fruit tasting something like an apple. Each village had a grove of cocoanut-palms, and Kermit found the cool cocoanut milk delicious after the return from a long day's hunting.

Each morning he was off before daylight, and rarely returned until after nightfall; and tired though he was he enjoyed to the full the walks campward in the bright moonlight among the palm-groves beside the rushing streams, while the cicadas cried like katydids at home. The grass was long. The weather was very hot, and almost every day there were drenching thunder-storms, and the dews were exceedingly heavy, so that Kermit was wet almost all the time, although he kept in first-rate health. There were not many sable and they were shy. About nine or ten o'clock they would stop feeding and leave their pasture-grounds of long grass, taking refuge in some grove of trees and thick bushes, not coming out again until nearly five o'clock.

On the second day's hunting Juma spied a little band of sable just entering a grove. A long and careful stalk brought the hunters to the grove, but after reaching it they at first saw nothing of the game. Then Kermit caught a glimpse of a head, fired, and brought down the beast in its tracks. It proved to be a bull, just changing from the red to the black coat; the horns were fair—in this northern form they never reach the length of those borne by the sable bulls of South Africa. He also killed a cow, not fully grown. He therefore still needed a full-grown cow, which he obtained three days later; this animal when wounded was very savage, and tried to charge.

We now went to Nairobi, where Cuninghame, Tarlton, and the three naturalists were already preparing for the Uganda trip and shipping the stuff hitherto collected. Working like beavers we got everything ready—including additions to the Pigskin Library, which included, among others, Cervantes, Goethe's "Faust," Molière, Pascal, Montaigne, St. Simon, Darwin's "Voyage of the Beagle," and Huxley's "Essays" —and on December 18 started for Lake Victoria Nyanza.

XIII

UGANDA, AND THE GREAT NYANZA LAKES

WHEN we left Nairobi it was with real regret that we said good-by to the many friends who had been so kind to us; officials, private citizens, almost every one we had met—including Sir Percy Girouard, the new governor. At Kijabe the men and women from the American mission—and the children too—were down at the station to wish us good luck; and at Nakuru the settlers from the neighborhood gathered on the platform to give us a farewell cheer. The following morning we reached Kisumu on Lake Victoria Nyanza. It is in the Kavirondo country, where the natives, both men and women, as a rule go absolutely naked, although they are peaceable and industrious. In the native market they had brought in baskets, iron spade heads, and food, to sell to the native and Indian traders who had their booths round about; the meat-market, under the trees, was especially interesting.

At noon we embarked in a smart little steamer, to cross the lake. Twenty-four hours later we landed at Entebbe, the seat of the English governor of Uganda. Throughout our passage the wind hardly ruffled the smooth surface of the lake. As we steamed away from the eastern shore the mountains behind us and on our right hand rose harsh and barren, yet with a kind of forbidding beauty. Dark clouds hung over the land we had left, and a rainbow stretched across their front. At nightfall, as the red sunset faded, the lonely waters of the vast inland sea stretched, ocean-like, west and south into a shoreless gloom. Then the darkness deepened, the tropic stars blazed overhead, and the light of the half moon drowned in silver the embers of the sunset.

Next morning we steamed along and across the equator; the last time we were to cross it, for thenceforth our course lay northward. We passed by many islands, green with meadow and forest, beautiful in the bright sunshine, but empty with the emptiness of death. A decade previously these islands were thronged with tribes of fisherfolk; their villages studded the shores, and their long canoes, planks held together with fibre, furrowed the surface of the lake. Then, from out of the depths of the Congo forest came the dreadful scourge of the sleeping sickness, and smote the doomed peoples who dwelt beside the Victorian Nile, and on the coasts of the Nyanza Lakes and in the lands between. Its agent was a biting fly, brother to the tsetse whose bite is fatal to domestic animals. This fly dwells in forests, beside lakes and rivers; and wherever it dwells after the sleeping sickness came it was found that man could not live. In this country, between, and along the shores of, the great lakes, two hundred thousand people died in slow torment, before the hard-taxed wisdom and skill of medical science and governmental administration could work any betterment whatever in the situation. Men still die by thousands, and the disease is slowly spreading into fresh districts. But it has proved possible to keep it within limits in the regions already affected; yet only by absolutely abandoning certain districts, and by clearing all the forest and brush in tracts which serve as barriers to the fly, and which permit passage through the infected belts. On the western shores of Victoria Nyanza, and in the islands adjacent thereto, the ravages of the pestilence were such, the mortality it caused was so appalling, that the government was finally forced to deport all the survivors inland, to forbid all residence beside or fishing in the lake, and with this end in view to destroy the villages and the fishing-fleets of the people. The teeming lake-fish were formerly a main source of food-supply to all who dwelt near by; but this has now been cut off, and the myriads of fish are left to themselves, to the hosts of water-birds, and to the monstrous man-eating crocodiles of the lake, on whose blood the fly also feeds, and whence it is supposed by some that it draws the germs so deadly to humankind.

When we landed there was nothing in the hot, laughing, tropical beauty of the land to suggest the grisly horror that brooded so near. In green luxuriance the earth lay under a cloudless sky, yielding her increase to the sun's burning caresses, and men and women were living their lives and doing their work well and gallantly.

At Entebbe, we stayed with the acting governor, Mr. Boyle, at Kampalla with the district commissioner, Mr. Knowles; both of them veteran administrators, and the latter also a mighty hunter; and both of them showed us every courtesy, and treated us with all possible kindness. Entebbe is a pretty little town of English residents, chiefly officials; with well-kept roads, a golf-course, tennis-courts, and an attractive club-house. The whole place is bowered in flowers, on tree, bush, and vine, of every hue—masses of lilac, purple, yellow, blue, and fiery crimson. Kampalla is the native town, where the little King of Uganda, a boy, lives, and his chiefs of state, and where the native councils meets; and it is the headquarters of the missions, both Church of England and Roman Catholic.

Kampalla is an interesting place; and so is all Uganda. The first explorers who penetrated thither, half a century ago, found in this heathen state, of almost pure negroes, a veritable semicivilization, or advanced barbarism, comparable to that of the little Arab-negro or Berber-negro sultanates strung along the southern edge of the Sahara, and contrasting sharply with the weltering savagery which surrounded it, and which stretched away without a break for many hundreds of miles in every direction. The people were industrious tillers of the soil, who owned sheep, goats, and some cattle; they wore decent cloth-ing, and hence were styled "womanish" by the savages of the upper Nile region, who prided themselves on the nakedness of their men as a proof of manliness; they were unusually intelligent and ceremoniously courteous; and, most singular of all, although the monarch was a cruel despot, of the usual African (whether Mohammedan or heathen) type, there were certain excellent governmental customs, of binding observance, which in the aggregate might almost be called an unwritten constitution. Alone among the natives of tropical Africa the people of Uganda have proved very accessible to Christian teaching, so that the creed of Christianity is now dominant among them. For their good fortune, England has established a protectorate over them. Most wisely the English Government officials, and as a rule the missionaries, have bent their energies to developing them along their own lines, in government, dress, and ways of life, constantly striving to better them and bring them forward, but not twisting them aside from their natural line of development, nor wrenching them loose from what was good in their past, by attempting the impossible task of turning an entire native population into black Englishmen at one stroke.

The problem set to the governing caste in Uganda is totally different from that which offers itself in British East Africa. The highlands of East Africa form a white man's country, and the prime need is to build up a large, healthy population of true white settlers, white home-makers, who shall take the land as an inheritance for their children's children. Uganda can never be this kind of white man's country; and although planters and merchants of the right type can undoubtedly do well there—to the advantage of the country as well as of themselves—it must remain essentially a black man's country, and the chief task of the officials of the intrusive and masterful race must be to bring forward the natives, to train them, and above all to help them train themselves, so that they may advance in industry, in learning, in morality, in capacity for self-government—for it is idle to talk of "giving" a people self-government; the gift of the forms, when the inward spirit is lacking, is mere folly; all that can be done is patiently to help a people acquire the necessary qualities—social, moral,

intellectual, industrial, and lastly political—and meanwhile to
exercise for their benefit, with justice, sympathy, and firmness,
the governing ability which as yet they themselves lack. The
widely spread rule of a strong European race in lands like
Africa gives, as one incident thereof, the chance for nascent
cultures, nascent semicivilizations, to develop without fear of
being overwhelmed in the surrounding gulfs of savagery;
and this aside from the direct stimulus to development conferred by the consciously and unconsciously exercised influence
of the white man, wherein there is much of evil, but much
more of ultimate good. In any region of wide-spread savagery, the chances for the growth of each self-produced civilization are necessarily small, because each little centre of
effort toward this end is always exposed to destruction from
the neighboring masses of pure savagery; and therefore progress is often immensely accelerated by outside invasion and
control. In Africa the control and guidance is needed as
much in the things of the spirit as in the things of the body.
Those who complain of or rail at missionary work in Africa,
and who confine themselves to pointing out the undoubtedly
too numerous errors of the missionaries and shortcomings of
their flocks, would do well to consider that even if the light
which has been let in is but feeble and gray it has at least
dispelled a worse than Stygian darkness. As soon as native
African religions—practically none of which have hitherto
evolved any substantial ethical basis—develop beyond the most
primitive stage they tend, notably in middle and western Africa,
to grow into malign creeds of unspeakable cruelty and im-
morality, with a bestial and revolting ritual and ceremonial.
Even a poorly taught and imperfectly understood Christianity,
with its underlying foundation of justice and mercy, represents an immeasurable advance on such a creed.

Where, as in Uganda, the people are intelligent and the
missionaries unite disinterestedness and zeal with common
sense, the result is astounding. The majority of the people
of Uganda are now Christian, Protestant or Catholic; and

many thousands among them are sincerely Christian and show their Christianity in practical fashion by putting conduct above ceremonial and dogma. Most fortunately, Protestant and Catholic seem now to be growing to work in charity together, and to show rivalry only in healthy effort against the common foe; there is certainly enough evil in the world to offer a target at which all good men can direct their shafts, without expending them on one another.

We visited the Church of England mission, where we were received by Bishop Tucker, and the two Catholic missions, where we were received by Bishops Hanlon and Streicher; we went through the churches and saw the schools with the pupils actually at work. In all the missions we were received with American and British flags and listened to the children singing the "Star-Spangled Banner." The Church of England mission has been at work for a quarter of a century; what has been accomplished by Bishop Tucker and those associated with him makes one of the most interesting chapters in all recent missionary history; I saw the high school, where the sons of the chiefs are being trained in large numbers for their future duties, and I was especially struck by the admirable medical mission, and by the handsome cathedral, built by the native Christians themselves without outside assistance in either money or labor. At dinner at Mr. Knowles's, Bishop Tucker gave us exceedingly interesting details of his past experiences in Uganda, and of the progress of the missionary work. He had been much amused by an American missionary who had urged him to visit America, saying that he would "find the latch-string outside the door"; to an American who knows the country districts well the expression seems so natural that I had never even realized that it was an Americanism.

At Bishop Hanlon's mission, where I lunched with the bishop, there was a friend, Mother Paul, an American; before I left America I had promised that I would surely see her, and look into the work which she, and the sisters associated with her, were doing. It was delightful seeing her; she not merely spoke my language but my neighborhood dialect. She informed me that she had just received a message of good-will for me in a letter from two of "the finest"—of course I felt at home when in mid-Africa, under the equator, I received in such fashion a message from two of the men who had served under me in the New York police.* She had been teaching her pupils to sing some lines of the "Star-Spangled Banner," in English, in my especial honor; and, of course, had been obliged in writing it out to use spelling far more purely phonetic than I had ever dreamed of using. The first lines ran as follows: (Some of our word sounds have no equivalent in Uganda.)

"O se ka nyu sı bai di · mo   nseli laiti
(O say can you see by the morn's † early light)

 Wati so pulauli wi eli adi twayi laiti   silasi giremi"
(What so proudly we hailed at the twilight's last gleaming.)

After having taught the children the first verse in this manner, Mother Paul said that she stopped to avoid brain fever.

In addition to scholastic exercises Mother Paul and her associates were training their school-children in all kinds of industrial work, taking especial pains to develop those industries that were natural to them and would be of use when they returned to their own homes. Both at Bishop Hanlon's mission, and at Bishop Streicher's, the mission of the White Fathers—originally a French organization, which has established churches and schools in almost all parts of Africa— the fathers were teaching the native men to cultivate coffee, and various fruits and vegetables.

* For the benefit of those who do not live in the neighborhood of New York I may explain that all good, or typical, New Yorkers invariably speak of their police force as "the finest"; and if any one desires to know what a "good" or "typical" New Yorker is, I shall add, on the authority of either Brander Matthews or the late H. C. Bunner—I forget which— that when he isn't a Southerner or of Irish or German descent he is usually a man born out West of New England parentage.
 † sic.

I called on the little king, who is being well trained by his English tutor—few tutors perform more exacting or responsible duties—and whose comfortable house was furnished in English fashion. I met his native advisers, shrewd, powerful-looking men; and went into the council-chamber, where I was greeted by the council, substantial-looking men, well dressed in the native fashion, and representing all the districts of the kingdom. When we visited the king it was after dark, and we were received by smart-looking black soldiers in ordinary khaki uniform, while accompanying them were other attendants dressed in the old-time native fashion; men with flaming torches, and others with the big Uganda drums which they beat to an accompaniment of wild cries. These drums are characteristic of Uganda; each chief has one, and beats upon it his own peculiar tattoo. The king, and all other people of consequence, white, Indian, or native, went round in rickshaws, one man pulling in the shafts and three others pushing behind. The rickshaw men ran well, and sang all the time, the man in the shafts serving as chantey-man, while the three behind repeated in chorus every second or two a kind of clanging note; and this went on without a break, hour after hour. The natives looked well and were dressed well; the men in long flowing garments of white, the women usually in brown cloth made in the old native style out of the bark of the bark-cloth tree. The clothes of the chiefs were tastefully ornamented. All the people, gentle and simple, were very polite and ceremonious both to one another and to strangers. Now and then we met parties of Sikh soldiers, tall, bearded, fine-looking men with turbans; and there were Indian and Swahili and even Arab and Persian traders.

The houses had mud walls and thatched roofs. The gardens were surrounded by braided cane fences. In the gardens and along the streets were many trees; among them bark-cloth trees, from which the bark is stripped every year for cloth; great incense-trees, the sweet-scented gum oozing through wounds in the bark; and date-palms, in the fronds of which hung the nests of the golden weaver-birds, now breeding. White cow-herons, tamer than barnyard fowls, accompanied the cattle, perching on their backs, or walking beside them. Beautiful Kavirondo cranes came familiarly round the houses. It was all strange and attractive. Birds sang everywhere. The air was heavy with the fragrance of flowers of many colors; the whole place was a riot of lush-growing plants. Every day there were terrific thunder-storms. At Kampalla three men had been killed by lightning within six weeks; a year or two before our host, Knowles, had been struck by lightning and knocked senseless, a huge zigzag mark being left across his body, and the links of his gold watch-chain being fused; it was many months before he completely re-covered.

Knowles arranged a situtunga-hunt for us. The situtunga is closely related to the bushbuck but is bigger, with very long hoofs, and shaggy hair like a water-buck. It is exclusively a beast of the marshes, making its home in the thick reed beds, where the water is deep; and it is exceedingly shy, so that very few white men have shot, or even seen, it. Its long hoofs enable it to go over the most treacherous ground, and it swims well; in many of its haunts, in the thick papyrus, the water is waist-deep on a man. Through the papyrus, and the reeds and marsh-grass, it makes well-beaten paths. Where it is in any danger of molestation it is never seen abroad in the day-time, venturing from the safe cover of the high reeds only at night; but fifty miles inland, in the marsh-grass on the edge of a big papyrus swamp, Kermit caught a glimpse of half a dozen feeding in the open, knee-deep in water, long after sun-rise. On the hunt in question a patch of marsh was driven by a hundred natives, while the guns were strung along the likely passes which led to another patch of marsh. A fine situtunga buck came to Kermit's post, and he killed it as it bolted away. It had stolen up so quietly through the long marsh-grass that he only saw it when it was directly on him.

Its stomach contained not grass, but the leaves and twig tips of a shrub which grows in and alongside of the marshes.

The day after this hunt our safari started on its march northwestward to Lake Albert Nyanza. We had taken with us from East Africa our gun-bearers, tent-boys, and the men whom the naturalists had trained as skinners. The porters were men of Uganda; the askaris were from the constabulary, and widely different races were represented among them, but all had been drilled into soldierly uniformity. The porters were well-clad, well-behaved, fine-looking men, and did their work better than the "shenzis," the wild Meru of Kikiu tribesmen, whom we had occasionally employed in East Africa; but they were not the equals of the regular East African porters. I think this was largely because of their inferior food, for they ate chiefly yams and plantains; in other words inferior sweet potatoes and bananas. They were quite as fond of singing as the East African porters, and in addition were cheered on the march by drum and fife; several men had fifes, and one carried nothing but one of the big Uganda drums, which he usually bore at the head of the safari, marching in company with the flag-bearer. Every hour or two the men would halt, often beside one of the queer little wickerwork booths in which native hucksters disposed of their wares by the roadside.

Along the road we often met wayfarers; once or twice bullock-carts; more often men carrying rolls of hides or long bales of cotton on their heads; or a set of Bahima herdsmen, with clear-cut features, guarding their herds of huge-horned Angola cattle.

All greeted us most courteously, frequently crouching or kneeling, as is their custom when they salute a superior; and we were scrupulous to acknowledge their salutes, and to return their greetings in the native fashion, with words of courtesy and long-drawn e-h-h-s and a-a-h-s. Along the line of march the chiefs had made preparations to receive us. Each afternoon, as we came to the spot where we were to camp for the night, we found a cleared space strewed with straw and surrounded by a plaited reed fence. Within this space cane houses, with thatched roofs of coarse grass, had been erected, some for our stores, one for a kitchen, one, which was always decked with flowers, as a rest-house for ourselves; the latter with open sides, the roof upheld by cane pillars, so that it was cool and comfortable, and afforded a welcome shelter either from the burning sun if the weather was clear, or from the pelting, driving tropical storms if there was rain. The moon was almost full when we left Kampalla, and night after night it lent a half unearthly beauty to the tropical landscape.

Sometimes in the evenings the mosquitoes bothered us; more often they did not; but in any event we slept well under our nettings. Usually at each camp we found either the head chief of the district, or a sub-chief, with presents; eggs, chickens, sheep, once or twice a bullock, always pineapples and bananas. The chief was always well dressed in flowing robes, and usually welcomed us with dignity and courtesy (sometimes, however, permitting the courtesy to assume the form of servility); and we would have him in to tea, where he was sure to enjoy the bread and jam. Sometimes he came in a rickshaw, sometimes in a kind of wickerwork palanquin, sometimes on foot. When we left his territory we made him a return gift.

We avoided all old camping-grounds, because of the spirillum tick. This dangerous fever tick is one of the insect scourges of Uganda, for its bite brings on a virulent spirillum fever which lasts intermittently for months, and may be accompanied by partial paralysis. It is common on old camping-grounds, and in native villages. The malarial mosquitoes also abound in places; and repeated attacks of malaria pave the way for black-water fever, which is often fatal.

The first day's march from Kampalla led us through shambas, the fields of sweet potatoes and plantations of bananas being separated by hedges or by cane fences. Then for two or three days we passed over low hills and through swampy valleys, the whole landscape covered by a sea of elephant-grass, the close-growing, coarse blades more than twice the height of a man on horseback.   Here and there it was dotted with groves of strange trees; in these groves monkeys of various kinds—some black, some red-tailed, some auburn—chattered as they raced away among the branches; there were brilliant rollers and bee-eaters; little green and yellow parrots, and gray parrots with red tails; and many colored butterflies.   Once or twice we saw the handsome, fierce, short-tailed eagle, the bateleur eagle, and scared one from a reedbuck fawn it had killed.   Among the common birds there were black drongos. and musical bush-shrikes; small black magpies with brown tails; white-headed kites and slate-colored sparrow-hawks; palm-swifts, big hornbills; blue and mottled kingfishers, which never went near the water, and had their upper mandibles red and their under ones black; barbets, with swollen, saw-toothed bills, their plumage iridescent purple above and red below; bulbuls, also dark purple above and red below, which whistled and bubbled incessantly as they hopped among the thick bushes, behaving much like our own yellow-breasted chats; and a multitude of other birds, beautiful or fantastic.   There were striped squirrels too, reminding us of the big Rocky Mountain chipmunk or Say's chipmunk, but with smaller ears and a longer tail.

Christmas Day we passed on the march.   There is not much use in trying to celebrate Christmas unless there are small folks to hang up their stockings on Christmas Eve, to rush gleefully in at dawn next morning to open the stockings, and after breakfast to wait in hopping expectancy until their elders throw open the doors of the room in which the big presents are arranged, those for each child on a separate table.

Forty miles from the coast the elephant-grass began to disappear.   The hills became somewhat higher, there were thorn-trees, and stately royal palms of great height, their stems swollen and bulging at the top, near the fronds.   Parasitic ferns, with leaves as large as cabbage-leaves, grew on the branches of the acacias. One kind of tree sent down from its branches to the ground roots which grew into thick trunks. There were wide, shallow marshes, and although the grass was tall it was no longer above a man's head. Kermit and I usually got two or three hours' hunting each day. We killed singing water-buck, bushbuck, and bohor reedbuck. The reedbuck differed slightly from those of East Africa; in places they were plentiful, and they were not wary. We also killed several hartbeests; a variety of the Jackson's hartbeest, being more highly colored, with black markings. I killed a very handsome harnessed bushbuck ram. It was rather bigger than a good-sized whitetail buck, its brilliant red coat beautifully marked with rows of white spots, its twisted black horns sharp and polished. It seemed to stand about half-way between the dark-colored bushbuck rams of East and South Africa and the beautifully marked harnessed antelope rams of the west coast forests. The ewes and young rams showed the harness markings even more plainly; and, as with all bushbuck, were of small size compared to the old rams. These bushbuck were found in tall grass, where the ground was wet, instead of in the thick bush where their East African kinsfolk spend the daytime.

At the bushbuck camp we met a number of porters returning from the Congo, where they had been with an elephant-poacher named Busherri—at least that was as near the name as we could make out. He had gone into the Congo to get ivory, by shooting and trading; but the wild forest people had attacked him, and had killed him and seven of his followers, and the others were straggling homeward. In Kampalla we had met an elephant-hunter named Quin who had recently lost his right arm in an encounter with a wounded tusker. Near one camp the head chief pointed out two places, now over-grown with jungle, where little villages had stood less than a year before. In each case elephants had taken to feeding at night in the shambas, and had steadily grown bolder and bolder until the natives, their crops ruined by the depredations and their lives in danger, had abandoned the struggle, and shifted to some new place in the wilderness.

We were soon to meet elephants ourselves. The morning of the 28th was rainy; we struck camp rather late, and the march was long, so that it was mid-afternoon when Kermit and I reached our new camping-place. Soon afterward word was brought us that some elephants were near by; we were told that the beasts were in the habit of devastating the shambas, and were bold and truculent, having killed a man who had tried to interfere with them. Kermit and I at once started after them, just as the last of the safari came in, accompanied by Cuninghame, who could not go with us as he was recovering from a bout of fever.

In half an hour we came on fresh sign, and began to work cautiously along it. Our guide, a wild-looking savage with a blunt spear, went first, followed by my gun-bearer, Kongoni, who is excellent on spoor; then I came, followed by Kermit, and by the other gun-bearers. The country was covered with tall grass, and studded with numerous patches of jungle and small forest. In a few minutes we heard the elephants, four or five of them, feeding in thick jungle where the vines that hung in tangled masses from the trees and that draped the bushes made dark caves of greenery. It was difficult to find any space clear enough to see thirty yards ahead. Fortunately there was no wind whatever. We picked out the spoor of a big bull and for an hour and a half we followed it, Kongoni usually in the lead. Two or three times, as we threaded our way among the bushes, as noiselessly as possible, we caught glimpses of gray, shadowy bulks, but only for a second at a time, and never with sufficient distinctness to shoot. The elephants were feeding, tearing down the branches of a rather large-leaved tree with bark like that of a scrub-oak and big pods containing beans; evidently these beans were a favorite food. They fed in circles and zig-zags, but toward camp, until they were not much more than half a mile from it, and the noise made by the porters in talking and gathering wood was plainly audible; but the elephants paid no heed to it, being evidently too much accustomed to the natives to have much fear of man. We continually heard them breaking branches, and making rumbling or squeaking sounds. They then fed slowly along in the opposite direction, and got into rather more open country; and we followed faster in the big footprints of the bull we had selected. Suddenly in an open glade Kongoni crouched and beckoned to me, and through a bush I caught the loom of the tusker. But at that instant he either heard us, saw us, or caught a whiff of our wind, and without a moment's hesitation he himself assumed the offensive. With his huge ears cocked at right angles to his head, and his trunk hanging down, he charged full tilt at us, coming steadily, silently, and at a great pace, his feet swishing through the long grass; and a formidable monster he looked. At forty yards I fired the right barrel of the Holland into his head, and though I missed the brain the shock dazed him and brought him to an instant halt. Immediately Kermit put a bullet from the Winchester into his head; as he wheeled I gave him the second barrel between the neck and shoulder, through his ear; and Kermit gave him three more shots before he slewed round and disappeared. There were not many minutes of daylight left, and we followed hard on his trail, Kongoni leading. At first there was only an occasional gout of dark blood; but soon we found splashes of red froth from the lungs; then we came to where he had fallen, and then we heard him crashing among the branches in thick jungle to the right. In we went after him, through the gathering gloom, Kongoni leading and I close behind, with the rifle ready for instant action; for though his strength was evidently fast failing, he was also evidently in a savage temper, anxious to wreak his vengeance before he died. On we went, following the bloody trail through the dim, cavernous windings in the dark, vine-covered jungle; we heard him smash the branches but a few yards ahead, and fall and rise; and stealing forward Kermit and I slipped up to within a dozen feet of him as he stood on the other side of some small twisted trees, hung with a mat of creepers. I put a bullet into his heart, Kermit fired, each of us fired again on the instant; the mighty bull threw up his trunk, crashed over backward, and lay dead on his side among the bushes. A fine sight he was, a sight to gladden any hunter's heart, as he lay in the twilight, a giant in death.

At once we trotted back to camp, reaching it as darkness fell; and next morning all of us came out to the carcass. He was full grown, and was ten feet nine inches high. The tusks were rather short, but thick, and weighed a hundred and ten pounds the pair. Out of the trunk we made excellent soup.

Several times while following the trail of this big bull we could tell he was close by the strong elephant smell. Most game animals have a peculiar scent, often strong enough for the species to be readily recognizable before it is seen, if in forest or jungle. On the open plains, of course, one rarely gets close enough to an animal to smell it before seeing it; but I once smelled a herd of hartbeest, when the wind was blowing strongly from them, although they were out of sight over a gentle rise. Water-buck have a very strong smell. Buffalo smell very much like domestic cattle, but old bulls are rank. More than once, in forest, my nostrils have warned me before my eyes that I was getting near the quarry whose spoor I was on.

After leaving the elephant camp we journeyed through country for the most part covered with an open forest growth. The trees were chiefly acacias. Among them were interspersed huge candelabra euphorbias, all in bloom, and now and then one of the brilliant red flowering trees, which never seem to carry many leaves at the same time with their gaudy blossoms. At one place for miles the open forest was composed of the pod-bearing, thick-leaved trees on which we had found the elephants feeding; their bark and manner of growth gave them somewhat the look of jack-oaks; where they made up the forest, growing well apart from one another, it reminded us of the cross-timbers of Texas and Oklahoma. The grass was everywhere three or four feet high; here and there were patches of the cane-like elephant-grass, fifteen feet high.

It was pleasant to stride along the road in the early mornings, followed by the safari, and we saw many a glorious sunrise. But as noon approached it grew very hot, under the glare of the brazen equatorial sun, and we were always glad when we approached our new camp, with its grass-strewn ground, its wickerwork fence, and cool, open rest-house. The local subchief and his elders were usually drawn up to receive me at the gate, bowing, clapping their hands, and uttering their long-drawn e-h-h-s; and often banana saplings or branches would be stuck in the ground to form avenues of approach, and the fence and rest-house might be decorated with flowers of many kinds. Sometimes we were met with music, on instruments of one string, of three strings, of ten strings—rudimentary fiddles and harps; and there was a much more complicated instrument, big and cumbrous, made of bars of wood placed on two banana-stems, the bars being struck with a hammer, as if they were keys; its tones were deep and good. Along the road we did not see habitations or people; but continually there led away from it, twisting through the tall grass and the bush jungles, native paths, the earth beaten brown and hard by countless bare feet; and these, crossing and recrossing in a network, led to plantation after plantation of bananas and sweet potatoes, and clusters of thatched huts.

In the afternoon, as the sun began to get well beyond the meridian, we usually sallied forth to hunt, under the guidance of some native who had come in to tell us where he had seen game that morning. The jungle was so thick in places and the grass was everywhere so long, that without such guidance there was little successful hunting to be done in only two or three hours. We might come back with a buck, or with two or three guinea-fowl, or with nothing.

There were a good many poisonous snakes; I killed a big puff-adder with thirteen eggs inside it; and we also killed a squat, short-tailed viper, beautifully mottled, not eighteen

inches long, but with a wide, flat head and a girth of body
out of all proportion to its length; and another very poisonous
and vicious snake, apparently of colubrine type, long and slender. The birds were an unceasing pleasure. White wagtails
and yellow wagtails walked familiarly about us within a few
feet, wherever we halted and when we were in camp. Long-
tailed, crested colys, with all four of their red toes pointed forward, clung to the sides of the big fruits at which they picked.
White-headed swallows caught 'flies and gnats by our heads.
There were large plantain-eaters; and birds like small jays
with yellow wattles round the eyes. There were boat-tailed
birds, in color iridescent green and purple, which looked like
our grackles, but were kin to the bulbuls; and another bird,
related to the shrikes, with bristly feathers on the rump, which
was colored like a red-winged blackbird, black with red shoulders. Vultures were not plentiful, but the yellow-billed kites,
true camp scavengers, were common and tame, screaming as
they circled overhead, and catching bits of meat which were
thrown in the air for them. The shrews and mice which
the naturalists trapped around each camping-place were kin
to the species we had already obtained in East Africa, but
in most cases there was a fairly well-marked difference; the
gerbilles, for instance, had shorter tails, more like ordinary
rats. Frogs with queer voices abounded in the marshes. Among
the ants was one arboreal kind which made huge nests, shaped
like beehives or rather like big gray bells, in the trees. Near
the lake, by the way, there were Goliath beetles, as large as
small rats.

Ten days from Kampalla we crossed the little Kafu River,
the black, smooth current twisting quickly along between beds
of plumed papyrus Beyond it we entered the native kingdom
of Unyoro. It is part of the British protectorate of Uganda,
but is separate from the native kingdom of Uganda, though
its people in ethnic type and social development seem much
the same. We halted for a day at Hoima, a spread-out little
native town, pleasantly situated among hills, and surrounded

by plantations of cotton, plantains, yams, millet, and beans. It is the capital of Unyoro, where the king lives, as well as three or four English officials, and Episcopalian and Roman Catholic missionaries. The king, accompanied by his prime minister and by the English commissioner, called on me, and I gave him five-o'clock tea; he is a Christian, as are most of his chiefs and head men, and they are sending their children to the mission schools.

A heron, about the size of our night-heron but with a longer neck, and with a curiously crow-like voice, strolled about among the native houses at Hoima; and the kites almost brushed us with their wings as they swooped down for morsels of food. The cheerful, confiding little wagtails crossed the threshold of the rest-house in which we sat. Black-and-white crows and vultures came around camp; and handsome, dark hawks, with white on their wings and tails, and with long, conspicuous crests, perched upright on the trees. There were many kinds of doves; one pretty little fellow was but six inches long. At night the jackals wailed with shrill woe among the gardens.

From Hoima we entered a country covered with the tall, rank elephant-grass. It was traversed by papyrus-bordered streams, and broken by patches of forest. The date-palms grew tall, and among the trees were some with orange-red flowers like trumpetflowers, growing in grape-shaped clusters; and both the flowers and the seed-pots into which they turned stood straight up in rows above the leafy tops of the trees that bore them.

The first evening, as we sat in the cool, open cane rest-house, word was brought us that an elephant was close at hand. We found him after ten minutes' walk; a young bull, with very small tusks, not worth shooting. For three-quarters of an hour we watched him, strolling about and feeding, just on the edge of a wall of high elephant-grass. Although we were in plain sight, ninety yards off, and sometimes moved about, he never saw us; for an elephant's eyes are very bad.

He was feeding on some thick, luscious grass, in the usual leisurely elephant fashion, plucking a big tuft, waving it nonchalantly about in his trunk, and finally tucking it into his mouth; pausing to rub his side against a tree, or to sway to and fro as he stood; and continually waving his tail and half cocking his ears.

At noon on January 5, 1910, we reached Butiaba, a sandpit and marsh on the shores of Lake Albert Nyanza. We had marched about one hundred and sixty miles from Lake Victoria. We camped on the sandy beach by the edge of the beautiful lake, looking across its waters to the mountains that walled in the opposite shore. At midday the whole landscape trembled in the white, glaring heat; as the afternoon waned a wind blew off the lake, and the west kindled in ruddy splendor as the sun went down.

At Butiaba we took boats to go down the Nile to the Lado country. The head of the water transportation service in Uganda, Captain Hutchinson, R.N.R., met us, having most kindly decided to take charge of our flotilla himself. Captain Hutchinson was a mighty hunter, and had met with one most extraordinary experience while elephant-hunting; in Uganda the number of hunters who have been killed or injured by elephants and buffalos is large. He wounded a big bull in the head, and followed it for three days. The wound was serious and on the fourth day he overtook the elephant. It charged as soon as it saw him. He hit it twice in the head with his 450 double-barrel as it came on, but neither stopped nor turned it; his second rifle, a double 8 bore, failed to act; and the elephant seized him in its trunk. It brandished him to and fro in the air several times, and then planting him on the ground knelt and stabbed at him with its tusks. Grasping one of its fore legs he pulled himself between them in time to avoid the blow; and as it rose he managed to seize a hind leg and clung to it. But the tusker reached round and plucked him off with its trunk, and once more brandished him high in the air, swinging him violently about. He fainted from pain and dizziness. When he came to he was lying on the ground; one of his attendants had stabbed the elephant with a spear, whereupon the animal had dropped the white man, vainly tried to catch his new assailant, and had then gone off for some three miles and died. Hutchinson was frightfully bruised and strained, and it was six months before he recovered.

XIV

THE GREAT RHINOCEROS OF THE LADO

THE region of which I speak is a dreary region in Libya, by the borders of the river Zaire. And there is no quiet there nor silence. The waters of the river have a saffron hue, and for many miles on either side of the river's oozy bed is a pale desert of gigantic water-lilies . . . and I stood in the morass among the tall lilies and the lilies sighed one unto the other in the solemnity of their desolation. And all at once the moon arose through the thin ghastly mist, and was crimson in color. . . . And the man looked out upon the dreary river Zaire, and upon the yellow ghastly waters, and upon the pale legions of the water-lilies. . . . Then I went down into the recess of the morass, and waded afar in among the wilderness of the lilies, and called unto the hippopotami which dwelt among the fens in the recesses of the morass." I was reading Poe, on the banks of the upper Nile; and surely his "fable" does deserve to rank with the "tales in the volumes of the Magi—in the ironbound, melancholy volumes of the Magi."

We had come down through the second of the great Nyanza lakes. As we sailed northward, its waters stretched behind us beyond the ken of vision, to where they were fed by streams from the Mountains of the Moon. On our left hand rose the frowning ranges on the other side of which the Congo forest lies like a shroud over the land. On our right we passed the mouth of the Victorian Nile, alive with monstrous crocodiles, and its banks barren of human life because of the swarms of the fly whose bite brings the torment which ends in death. As night fell we entered the White Nile, and

steamed and drifted down the mighty stream. Its current
swirled in long curves between endless ranks of plumed papyrus. White and blue and red, the floating water-lilies covered
the lagoons and the still inlets among the reeds; and here and
there the lotus lifted its leaves and flowers stiffly above the
surface. The brilliant tropic stars made lanes of light on the
lapping water as we ran on through the night. The river-
horses roared from the reed beds, and snorted and plunged
beside the boat, and crocodiles slipped sullenly into the river
as we glided by. Toward morning a mist arose and through
it the crescent of the dying moon shone red and lurid. Then
the sun flamed aloft and soon the African landscape, vast,
lonely, mysterious, stretched on every side in a shimmering
glare of heat and light; and ahead of us the great, strange
river went twisting away into the distance.

At midnight we had stopped at the station of Koba, where
we were warmly received by the district commissioner, and
where we met half a dozen of the professional elephant-hunters, who for the most part make their money, at hazard of
their lives, by poaching ivory in the Congo. They are a hard-
bit set, these elephant-poachers; there are few careers more
adventurous, or fraught with more peril, or which make
heavier demands upon the daring, the endurance, and the
physical hardihood of those who follow them. Elephant-
hunters face death at every turn, from fever, from the
assaults of warlike native tribes, from their conflicts with
their giant quarry; and the unending strain on their health
and strength is tremendous.

At noon the following day we stopped at the deserted station of Wadelai, still in British territory. There have been
outposts of white mastery on the upper Nile for many years,
but some of them are now abandoned, for as yet there has
been no successful attempt at such development of the region
as would alone mean permanency of occupation. The natives
whom we saw offered a sharp contrast to those of Uganda;
we were again back among wild savages. Near the landing

at Wadelai was a group of thatched huts surrounded by a fence; there were small fields of mealies and beans, cultivated by the women, and a few cattle and goats; while big wicker-work fish-traps showed that the river also offered a means of livelihood. Both men and women were practically naked; some of the women entirely so except for a few beads. Here we were joined by an elephant-hunter, Quentin Grogan, who was to show us the haunts of the great square-mouthed rhinoceros, the so-called white rhinoceros, of the Lado, the only kind of African heavy game which we had not yet obtained. We were allowed to hunt in the Lado, owing to the considerate courtesy of the Belgian Government, for which I was sincerely grateful.

After leaving Wadelai we again went downstream. The river flowed through immense beds of papyrus. Beyond these on either side were rolling plains gradually rising in the distance into hills or low mountains. The plains were covered with high grass, dry and withered; and the smoke here and there showed that the natives, according to their custom, were now burning it. There was no forest; but scattered over the plains were trees, generally thorns, but other kinds also, among them palms and euphorbias.

The following morning, forty-eight hours after leaving Butiaba, on Lake Albert Nyanza, we disembarked from the little flotilla which had carried us—a crazy little steam-launch, two sailboats, and two big rowboats. We made our camp close to the river's edge, on the Lado side, in a thin grove of scattered thorn-trees. The grass grew rank and tall all about us. Our tents were pitched, and the grass huts of the porters built, on a kind of promontory, the main stream running past one side, while on the other was a bay. The nights were hot, and the days burning; the mosquitoes came with darkness, sometimes necessitating our putting on head nets and gloves in the evenings, and they would have made sleep impossible if we had not had mosquito biers. Nevertheless it was a very pleasant camp, and we thoroughly enjoyed it. It was a wild,

lonely country, and we saw no human beings except an occasional party of naked savages armed with bows and poisoned
arrows.   Game was plentiful, and a hunter always enjoys a
permanent camp in a good game country; for while the expedition is marching, his movements must largely be regulated
by those of the safari, whereas at a permanent camp he is
foot-loose.

There was an abundance of animal life, big and little, about
our camp. In the reeds, and among the water-lilies of the bay,
there were crocodiles, monitor lizards six feet long, and many
water-birds—herons, flocks of beautiful white egrets, clamor-
ous spur-winged plover, sacred ibis, noisy purple ibis, saddlebilled storks, and lily-trotters which ran lightly over the lily-
pads. There were cormorants and snake-birds. Fish-eagles
screamed as they circled around; very handsome birds, the
head, neck, tail, breast, and fore part of the back white, the rest
of the plumage black and rich chestnut. There was a queer
little eagle-owl with inflamed red eyelids. The black-and-red
bulbuls sang noisily. There were many kingfishers, some no
larger than chippy sparrows, and many of them brilliantly
colored; some had, and others had not, the regular kingfisher
voice; and while some dwelt by the river-bank and caught fish,
others did not come near the water and lived on insects. There
were paradise flycatchers with long, wavy white tails; and
olive-green pigeons with yellow bellies. Red-headed, red-
tailed lizards ran swiftly up and down the trees. The most
extraordinary birds were the nightjars; the cocks carried in
each wing one very long, waving plume, the pliable quill being
twice the length of the bird's body and tail, and bare except
for a patch of dark feather webbing at the end. The two
big, dark plume tips were very conspicuous, trailing behind
the bird as it flew, and so riveting the observer's attention as
to make the bird itself almost escape notice. When seen flying, the first impression conveyed was of two large, dark
moths or butterflies fluttering rapidly through the air; it was
with a positive effort of the eye that I fixed the actual bird.

The big slate and yellow bats were more interesting still. There were several kinds of bats at this camp; a small dark kind that appeared only when night had fallen and flew very near the ground all night long, and a somewhat larger one, lighter beneath, which appeared late in the evening and flew higher in the air. Both of these had the ordinary bat habits of continuous, swallow-like flight. But the habits of the slate and yellow bats were utterly different. They were very abundant, hanging in the thinly leaved acacias around the tents, and, as everywhere else, were crepuscular, indeed to a large extent actually diurnal, in habit. They saw well and flew well by daylight, passing the time hanging from twigs. They became active before sunset. In catching insects they behaved not like swallows but like flycatchers. Except that they perched upside down so to speak, that is, that they hung from the twigs instead of sitting on them, their conduct was precisely that of a phœbe-bird or a wood-pewee. Each bat hung from its twig until it espied a passing insect, when it swooped down upon it, and after a short flight returned with its booty to the same perch or went on to a new one close by; and it kept twitching its long ears as it hung head downward devouring its prey.

There were no native villages in our immediate neighborhood, and the game was not shy. There were many buck: water-buck, kob, hartbeest, bushbuck, reedbuck, oribi, and duiker. Every day or two Kermit or I would shoot a buck for the camp. We generally went out together with our gunbearers, Kermit striding along in front, with short trousers and leggings, his knees bare. Sometimes only one of us would go out. The kob and water-buck were usually found in bands, and were perhaps the commonest of all. The buck seemed to have no settled time for feeding. Two oribi which I shot were feeding right in the open, just at noon, utterly indifferent to the heat. There were hippo both in the bay and in the river. All night long we could hear them splashing, snorting, and grunting; they were very noisy, sometimes uttering a strange, long-drawn bellow, a little like the exhaust of a giant steam-pipe, once or twice whinnying or neighing; but usually making a succession of grunts, or bubbling squeals through the nostrils. The long grass was traversed in all directions by elephant trails, and there was much fresh signs of the huge beasts—their dung, and the wrecked trees on which they had been feeding; and there was sign of buffalo also. In Middle Africa, thanks to wise legislation, and to the very limited size of the areas open to true settlement, there has been no such reckless, wholesale slaughter of big game as that which has brought the once wonderful big-game fauna of South Africa to the verge of extinction. In certain small areas of Middle Africa, of course, it has gone; but as a whole it has not much diminished, some species have actually increased, and none is in danger of immediate extinction, unless it be the white rhinoceros. During the last decade, for instance, the buffalo have been recovering their lost ground throughout the Lado, Uganda, and British East Africa, having multiplied many times over. During the same period, in the same region, the elephant have not greatly diminished in aggregate numbers, although the number of bulls carrying big ivory has been very much reduced; indeed the reproductive capacity of the herds has probably been very little impaired, the energies of the hunters having been almost exclusively directed to the killing of the bulls with tusks weighing over thirty pounds apiece; and the really big tuskers, which are most eagerly sought after, are almost always past their prime, and no longer associate with the herd.

But this does not apply to the great beast which was the object of our coming to the Lado, the square-mouthed or, as it is sometimes miscalled, the white, rhinoceros. Africa is a huge continent, and many species of the big mammals inhabiting it are spread over a vast surface; and some of them offer strange problems for inquiry in the discontinuity of their distribution. The most extraordinary instance of this discontinuity is that offered by the distribution of the square-mouthed rhinoceros. It is almost as if our bison had never been known within historic times except in Texas and Ecuador. This great rhinoceros was formerly plentiful in South Africa south of the Zambesi, where it has been completely exterminated except for a score or so of individuals on a game reserve. North of the Zambesi it was and is utterly unknown, save that during the last ten years it has been found to exist in several localities on the left bank of the upper Nile, close to the river, and covering a north and south extension of about two hundred miles. Even in this narrow ribbon of territory the square-mouthed rhinoceros is found only in certain localities, and although there has not hitherto been much slaughter of the mighty beast, it would certainly be well if all killing of it were prohibited until careful inquiry has been made as to its numbers and exact distribution. It is a curious animal, on the average distinctly larger than, and utterly different from, the ordinary African rhinoceros. The spinal processes of the dorsal vertebræ are so developed as to make a very prominent hump over the withers, while forward of this is a still higher and more prominent fleshy hump on the neck. The huge, mis-shapen head differs in all respects as widely from the head of the common or so-called black rhinoceros as the head of a moose differs from that of a wapiti.

The morning after making camp we started on a rhinoceros-hunt. At this time in this neighborhood, the rhinoceros seemed to spend the heat of the day in sleep, and to feed in the morning and evening, and perhaps throughout the night; and to drink in the evening and morning, usually at some bay or inlet of the river. In the morning they walked away from the water for an hour or two, until they came to a place which suited them for the day's sleep. Unlike the ordinary rhinoceros, the square-mouthed rhinoceros feeds exclusively on grass. Its dung is very different; we only occasionally saw it deposited in heaps, according to the custom of its more common cousin. The big, sluggish beast seems fond of nosing the ant-hills of red earth, both with its horn and with its square muzzle; it may be that it licks them for some saline substance. It is apparently of less solitary nature than the prehensile-lipped rhino, frequently going in parties of four or five or half a dozen individuals.

We did not get an early start. Hour after hour we plodded on, under the burning sun, through the tall, tangled grass, which was often higher than our heads. Continually we crossed the trails of elephant and more rarely of rhinoceros, but the hard, sun-baked earth and stiff, tinder-dry long grass made it a matter of extreme difficulty to tell if a trail was fresh, or to follow it. Finally, Kermit and his gun-bearer, Kassitura, discovered some unquestionably fresh footprints which those of us who were in front had passed over. Immediately we took the trail, Kongoni and Kassitura acting as trackers, while Kermit and I followed at their heels. Once or twice the two trackers were puzzled, but they were never entirely at fault; and after half an hour Kassitura suddenly pointed toward a thorn-tree about sixty yards off. Mounting a low ant-hill I saw rather dimly through the long grass a big gray bulk, near the foot of the tree; it was a rhinoceros lying asleep on its side, looking like an enormous pig. It heard something and raised itself on its fore legs, in a sitting posture, the big ears thrown forward. I fired for the chest, and the heavy Holland bullet knocked it clean off its feet. Squealing loudly it rose again, but it was clearly done for, and it never got ten yards from where it had been lying.

At the shot four other rhino rose. One bolted to the right, two others ran to the left. Firing through the grass Kermit wounded a bull and followed it for a long distance, but could not overtake it; then days later,* however, he found the carcass, and saved the skull and horns. Meanwhile I killed a calf, which was needed for the museum; the rhino I had already shot was a full-grown cow, doubtless the calf's

---

* Kermit on this occasion was using the double-barrelled rifle which had been most kindly lent him for the trip by Mr. John Jay White, of New York.

mother. As the rhino rose I was struck by their likeness to the picture of the white rhino in Cornwallis Harris's folio of the big game of South Africa seventy years ago. They were totally different in look from the common rhino, seeming to stand higher and to be shorter in proportion to their height, while the hump and the huge, ungainly, square-mouthed head added to the dissimilarity. The common rhino is in color a very dark slate gray; these were a rather lighter slate gray; but this was probably a mere individual peculiarity, for the best observers say that they are of the same hue. The muzzle is broad and square, and the upper lip without a vestige of the curved, prehensile development which makes the upper lip of a common rhino look like the hook of a turtle's beak. The stomachs contained nothing but grass; it is a grazing, not a browsing, animal.

There were some white egrets—not, as is usually the case with both rhinos and elephants, the cow-heron, but the slender, black-legged, yellow-toed egret—on the rhinos, and the bodies and heads of both the cow and calf looked as though they had been splashed with streaks of whitewash. One of the egrets returned after the shooting and perched on the dead body of the calf.

The heat was intense, and our gun-bearers at once began skinning the animals, lest they should spoil; and that afternoon Cuninghame and Heller came out from camp with tents, food and water, and Heller cared for the skins on the spot, taking thirty-six hours for the job. The second night he was visited by a party of lions, which were after the rhinoceros meat and came within fifteen feet of the tents.

On the same night that Heller was visited by the lions we had to fight fire in the main camp. At noon we noticed two fires come toward us, and could soon hear their roaring. The tall, thick grass was like tinder; and if we let the fires reach camp we were certain to lose everything we had. So Loring, Mearns, Kermit, and I, who were in camp, got out the porters and cut a lane around our tents and goods; and then started a back-fire, section after section, from the other side of this lane. We kept every one ready, with branches and wet gunny sacks, and lit each section in turn, so that we could readily beat out the flames at any point where they threatened. The air was still, and soon after nightfall our back-fire had burnt fifty or a hundred yards away from camp, and the danger was practically over. Shortly afterward one of the fires against which we were guarding came over a low hill crest into view, beyond the line of our back-fire. It was a fine sight to see the long line of leaping, wavering flames advance toward one another. An hour or two passed before they met, half a mile from camp. Wherever they came together there would be a moment's spurt of roaring, crackling fire, and then it would vanish, leaving at that point a blank in the circle of flame. Gradually the blanks in the lines extended, until the fire thus burnt itself out, and darkness succeeded the bright red glare.

The fires continued to burn in our neighborhood for a couple of days. Finally one evening the great beds of papyrus across the bay caught fire. After nightfall it was splendid to see the line of flames, leaping fifty feet into the air as they worked across the serried masses of tall papyrus. When they came toward the water they kindled the surface of the bay into a ruddy glare, while above them the crimson smoke clouds drifted slowly to leeward. The fire did not die out until toward morning; and then, behind it, we heard the grand booming chorus of a party of lions. They were full-fed, and roaring as they went to their day-beds; each would utter a succession of roars which grew louder and louder until they fairly thundered, and then died gradually away, until they ended in a succession of sighs and grunts.

As the fires burned to and fro across the country, birds of many kinds came to the edge of the flames to pick up the insects which were driven out. There were marabou storks, kites, hawks, ground-hornbills, and flocks of beautiful egrets and cow-herons, which stalked sedately through the grass, and now and then turned a small tree nearly white by all perching in it. The little bank-swallows came in myriads; exactly the same, by the way, as our familiar home friends, for the bank-swallow is the most widely distributed of all birds. The most conspicuous attendants of the fires, however, were the bee-eaters, the largest and handsomest we had yet seen, their plumage, every shade of blended red and rose, varied with brilliant blue and green. The fires seemed to bother the bigger animals hardly at all. The game did not shift their haunts, or do more than move in quiet, leisurely fashion out of the line of advance of the flames. I saw two oribi which had found a patch of short grass that split the fire, feeding there-on, entirely undisturbed, although the flames were crackling by some fifty yards on each side of them. Even the mice and shrews did not suffer much, probably because they went into holes. Shrews, by the way, were very plentiful, and Loring trapped four kinds, two of them new. It was always a surprise to me to find these tiny shrews swarming in equa-torial Africa just as they swarm in arctic America.

In a little patch of country not far from this camp there were a few sleeping-sickness fly, and one or two of us were bitten, but, seemingly, the fly were not infected, although at this very time eight men were dying of sleeping sickness at Wadelai where we had stopped. There were also some ordinary tsetse fly, which caused us uneasiness about our mule. We had brought four little mules through Uganda, riding them occasionally on safari; and had taken one across into the Lado, while the other three, with the bulk of the porters, marched on the opposite bank of the Nile from Koba, and were to join us at Nimule.

It was Kermit's turn for the next rhino; and by good luck it was a bull, giving us a complete group of bull, cow, and calf for the National Museum. We got it as we had gotten our first two. Marching through likely country—burnt, this time—we came across the tracks of three rhino, two big and one small, and followed them through the black ashes. It was an intricate and difficult piece of tracking, for the trail wound hither and thither and was crisscrossed by others; but Kongoni and Kassitura gradually untangled the maze, found where the beasts had drunk at a small pool that morning, and then led us to where they were lying asleep under some thorn-trees. It was about eleven o'clock. As the bull rose Kermit gave him a fatal shot with his beloved Winchester. He galloped full speed toward us, not charging, but in a mad panic of terror and bewilderment; and with a bullet from the Holland I brought him down in his tracks only a few yards away. The cow went off at a gallop. The calf, a big creature, half grown, hung about for some time, and came up quite close, but was finally frightened away by shouting and hand-clapping. Some cow-herons were round these rhino; and the head and body of the bull looked as if it had been splashed with whitewash.

It was an old bull, with a short, stubby, worn-down horn. It was probably no heavier than a big ordinary rhino bull such as we had shot on the Sotik, and its horns were no larger, and the front and rear ones were of the same proportions relatively to each other. But the misshaped head was much larger, and the height seemed greater because of the curious hump. This fleshy hump is not over the high dorsal vertebræ, but just forward of them, on the neck itself, and has no connection with the spinal column. The square-mouthed rhinoceros of South Africa is always described as being very much bigger than the common prehensile-lipped African rhinoceros, and as carrying much longer horns. But the square-mouthed rhinos we saw and killed in the Lado did not differ from the common kind in size and horn development as much as we had been led to expect; although on an average they were undoubtedly larger, and with bigger horns, yet there was in both respects overlapping, the bigger prehensile-lipped rhinos equalling or surpassing the smaller individuals of the other kind. The huge, square-muzzled head, and the hump, gave the Lado rhino an utterly different look, however, and its habits are also in some important respects different. Our gun-bearers were all East Africans, who had never before been in the Lado. They had been very sceptical when told that the rhinos were different from those they knew, remarking that "all rhinos were the same"; and the first sight of the spoor merely confirmed them in their belief; but they at once recognized the dung as being different; and when the first animal was down they examined it eagerly and proclaimed it as a rhinoceros with a hump, like their own native cattle, and with the mouth of a hippopotamus.

On the way to camp, after the death of this bull rhino, I shot a water-buck bull with finer horns than any I had yet obtained. Herds of water-buck and of kob stared tamely at me as I walked along; whereas a little party of hartbeest were wild and shy. On other occasions I have seen this conduct exactly reversed, the hartbeest being tame, and the water-buck and kob shy. Heller, as usual, came out and camped by this rhino, to handle the skin and skeleton. In the middle of the night a leopard got caught in one of his small steel traps, which he had set out with a light drag. The beast made a terrific row and went off with the trap and drag. It was only caught by one toe; a hyena similarly caught would have wrenched itself loose; but the leopard, though a far braver and more dangerous beast, has less fortitude under pain than a hyena. Heller tracked it up in the morning, and shot it as, hampered by the trap and drag, it charged the porters.

On the ashes of the fresh burn the footprints of the game showed almost as distinctly as on snow. One morning we saw where a herd of elephant, cows and calves, had come down the night before to drink at a big bay of the Nile, three or four miles north of our camp. Numerous hippo tracks showed that during the darkness these beasts wandered freely a mile or two inland. They often wandered back of our camp at night. Always beside these night trails we found withered remnants of water-cabbage and other aquatic plants which they had carried inland with them; I suppose accidentally on

their backs. On several occasions where we could only make
out scrapes on the ground the hippo trails puzzled us, being so
far inland that we thought they might be those of rhinos;
until we would come on some patch of ashes or of soft soil
where we could trace the four toe-marks. The rhino has but
three toes, the one in the middle being very big; it belongs,
with the tapir and horse, to the group of ungulates which
tends to develop one digit of each foot at the expense of all
the others; a group which in a long-past geological age was
the predominant ungulate group of the world. The hippo,
on the contrary, belongs with such cloven-hoofed creatures as
the cow and pig, in the group of ungulates which has developed equally two main digits in each foot; a group much
more numerously represented than the other in the world
of today.

As the hippos grew familiar with the camp they became
bolder and more venturesome after nightfall. They grunted
and brayed to one another throughout the night, splashed
and wallowed among the reeds, and came close to the tents
during their dry-land rambles in the darkness. One night,
in addition to the hippo chorus, we heard the roaring of
lions and the trumpeting of elephants. We were indeed in
the heart of the African wilderness.

Early in the morning after this concert we started for
a day's rhino-hunt, Heller and Cuninghame having just finished the preparation, and transport to camp, of the skin of
Kermit's bull. Loring, who had not hitherto seen either elephant or rhino alive, went with us; and by good luck he saw
both.

A couple of miles from camp we were crossing a wide,
flat, swampy valley in which the coarse grass grew as tall
as our heads. Here and there were kob, which leaped up
on the ant-hills to get a clear view of us. Suddenly our attention was attracted by the movements of a big flock of
cow-herons in front of us, and then watching sharply we
caught a glimpse of some elephants, about four hundred yards

off. We now climbed an ant-hill ourselves, and inspected the elephants, to see if among them were any big-tusked bulls. There were no bulls, however; the little herd consisted of five cows and four calves, which were marching across a patch of burnt ground ahead of us, accompanied by about fifty white cow-herons. We stood where we were until they had passed; we did not wish to get too close, lest they might charge us and force us to shoot in self-defense. They walked in unhurried confidence, and yet were watchful, continually cocking their ears and raising and curling their trunks. One dropped behind and looked fixedly in our direction, probably having heard us talking; then with head aloft and tail stiffly erect it hastened after the others, presenting an absurd likeness to a baboon. The four calves played friskily about, especially a very comical little pink fellow which accompanied the leading cow. Meanwhile a few of the white herons rode on their backs, but most of the flock stalked sedately alongside through the burnt grass, catching the grasshoppers which were disturbed by the great feet. When, however, the herd reached the tall grass all the herons flew up and perched on the backs and heads of their friends; even the pink calf carried one. Half a mile inside the edge of the tall grass the elephants stopped for the day beside a clump of bushes; and there they stood, the white birds clustered on their dark bodies. At the time we could distinctly hear the doctor's shotgun, as he collected birds near camp; the reports did not disturb the elephants, and when we walked on we left them standing unconcernedly in the grass.

A couple of hours later, as we followed an elephant path, we came to where it was crossed by the spoor of two rhino. Our gun-bearers took up the trail, over the burnt ground, while Kermit and I followed immediately behind them. The trail wound about, and was not always easy to disentangle, but after a mile or two we saw the beasts. They were standing among the bushes and patches of rank, unburned grass; it was just ten o'clock, and they were evidently preparing to lie down for the day. As they stood they kept twitching their big ears; both rhino and elephant are perpetually annoyed, as are most game, by biting flies, large and small. We got up very close, Kermit with his camera and I with heavy rifle. Too little is known of these northern square-mouthed rhino for us to be sure that they are not lingering slowly toward extinction; and, lest this should be the case, we were not willing to kill any merely for trophies; while, on the other hand, we deemed it really important to get good groups for the National Museum in Washington and the American Museum in New York, and a head for the National Collection of Heads and Horns which was started by Mr. Hornaday, the director of the Bronz Zoological Park. Moreover, Kermit and Loring desired to get some photos of the animals while they were alive.

Things did not go well this time, however. The rhinos saw us before either Kermit or Loring could get a good picture. As they wheeled I fired hastily into the chest of one, but not quite in the middle, and away they dashed—for they do not seem as truculent as the common rhino. We followed them. After an hour the trails separated; Cuninghame went on one, but failed to overtake the animal, and we did not see him until we reached camp late that afternoon.

Meanwhile our own gun-bearers followed the bloody spoor of the rhino I had hit, Kermit and I close behind, and Loring with us. The rhino had gone straight off at a gallop, and the trail offered little difficulty, so we walked fast. A couple of hours passed. The sun was now high and the heat intense as we walked over the burned ground. The scattered trees bore such scanty foliage as to cast hardly any shade. The rhino galloped strongly and without faltering; but there was a good deal of blood on the trail. At last, after we had gone seven or eight miles, Kiboko the skinner, who was acting as my gun-bearer, pointed toward a small thorn-tree; and beside it I saw the rhino standing with drooping head. It had been fatally hit, and if undisturbed would probably never have moved from where it was standing; and we finished it off forthwith. It was a cow, and before dying it ran round and round in a circle, in the manner of the common rhino.

Loring stayed to superintend the skinning and bringing in of the head and feet, and slabs of hide. Meanwhile Kermit and I, with our gun-bearers, went off with a "shenzi," a wild native who had just come in with the news that he knew where another rhino was lying, a few miles away. While bound thither we passed numbers of oribi, and went close to a herd of water-buck which stared at us with stupid tameness; a single hartbeest was with them. When we reached the spot there was the rhino, sure enough, under a little tree, sleeping on his belly, his legs doubled up, and his head flat on the ground. Unfortunately the grass was long, so that it was almost impossible to photograph him. However, Kermit tried to get his picture from an ant-hill fifty yards distant, and then, Kermit with his camera and I with my rifle, we walked up to within about twenty yards. At this point we halted, and on the instant the rhino jumped to his feet with surprising agility and trotted a few yards out from under the tree. It was a huge bull, with a fair horn; much the biggest bull we had yet seen; and with head up and action high, the sun glinting on his slate hide and bringing out his enormous bulk, he was indeed a fine sight. I waited a moment for Kermit to snap him. Unfortunately the waving grass spoiled the picture. Then I fired right and left into his body, behind the shoulders, and down he went. In color he seemed of exactly the same shade as the common rhino, but he was taller and heavier, being six feet high. He carried a stout horn, a little over two feet long; the girth at the base was very great.

Leaving the gun-bearers (with all our water) to skin the mighty beast, Kermit and I started for camp; and as we were rather late Kermit struck out at a great pace in front, while I followed on the little ambling mule. On our way in we passed the elephants, still standing where we had left them in the morning, with the white cow-herons flying and walking around and over them. Heller and Cuninghame at once went out to camp by the skin and take care of it, and to bring back the skeleton. We had been out about eleven hours without food; we were very dirty from the ashes on the burnt ground; we had triumphed; and we were thoroughly happy as we took our baths and ate our hearty dinner.

It was amusing to look at our three naturalists and compare them with the conventional pictures of men of science and learning—especially men of science and learning in the wilderness—drawn by the novelists a century ago. Nowadays the field naturalist—who is usually at all points superior to the mere closet naturalist—follows a profession as full of hazard and interest as that of the explorer or of the big-game hunter in the remote wilderness. He penetrates to all the out-of-the-way nooks and corners of the earth; he is schooled to the performance of very hard work, to the endurance of fatigue and hardship, to encountering all kinds of risks, and to grappling with every conceivable emergency. In consequence he is exceedingly competent, resourceful and self-reliant, and the man of all others to trust in a tight place.

Around this camp there were no ravens or crows; but multitudes of kites, almost as tame as sparrows, circled among the tents, uttering their wailing cries, and lit on the little trees near by or waddled about on the ground near the cook fires. Numerous vultures, many marabou storks, and a single fish-eagle, came to the carcasses set for them outside the camp by Loring; and he took pictures of them. The handsome fish-eagle looked altogether out of place among the foul carrion-feeding throng; on the ground the vultures made way for him respectfully enough, but they resented his presence, and now and then two or three would unite to mob him while on the wing.

We wished for another cow rhino, so as to have a bull and a cow both for the National Museum at Washington and for the American Museum in New York; and Kermit was to shoot this. Accordingly he and I started off early one morning with Grogan—a man of about twenty-five, a good hunter and a capital fellow, with whom by this time we were great friends. It was much like our other hunts. We tramped through high grass across a big, swampy plain or broad valley between low rises of ground, until, on the opposite side, we struck a by-this-time familiar landmark, two tall royal palms, the only ones for some miles around. Here we turned into a broad elephant and rhinoceros path, worn deep and smooth by the generations of huge feet that had tramped it; for it led from the dry inland to a favorite drinking-place on the Nile. Along this we walked until Kassitura made out the trail of two rhino crossing it at right angles. They were evidently feeding and seeking a noonday resting-place; in this country the square-mouthed rhinoceros live on the grassy flats, sparsely covered with small thorn-trees, and only go into the high reeds on their way to drink. With Kassitura and Kongoni in the lead we followed the fresh trail for a mile or so, until we saw our quarry. The stupid beasts had smelt us, but were trotting to and fro in a state of indecision and excitement, tails twisting and ears cocked, uncertain what to do. At first we thought they were a bull and a small cow; but they proved to be a big cow with good horns, and a calf which was nearly full grown. The wind and sun were both exactly wrong, so Kermit could not take any photos; and accordingly he shot the cow behind the shoulder. Away both animals went, Kermit tearing along behind, while Grogan and I followed. After a sharp run of a mile and a half Kermit overtook them, and brought down the cow. The younger one then trotted threateningly toward him. He let it get within ten yards, trying to scare it; as it kept coming on, and could of course easily kill him, he then fired into its face, to one side, so as to avoid inflicting a serious injury, and, turning, off it went at a gallop. When I came up the cow had raised itself on its fore legs, and he was taking its picture. It had been wallowing, and its whole body was covered with dry caked mud. It was exactly the color of the common rhino, but a little larger than any cow of the latter that we had killed. We at once sent for Heller—who had been working without intermission since we struck the Lado, and liked it—and waited by the body until he appeared, in mid-afternoon.

Here in the Lado we were in a wild, uninhabited country, and for meat we depended entirely on our rifles; nor was there any difficulty in obtaining all we needed. We only shot for meat, or for museum specimens—all the museum specimens being used for food, too—and as the naturalists were as busy as they well could be, we found that, except when we were after rhinoceros, it was not necessary to hunt for more than half a day or thereabouts. On one of these hunts, on which he shot a couple of buck, Kermit also killed a monitor lizard, and a crocodile ten feet long; it was a female, and contained fifty-two eggs which, when scrambled, we ate and found good.

The morning after Kermit killed his cow rhino he and Grogan went off for the day to see if they could not get some live rhino photos. Cuninghame started to join Heller at the temporary camp which we had made beside the dead rhino, in order to help him with the skin and skeletons. Mearns and Loring were busy with birds, small beasts, and photographs. So, as we were out of fresh meat, I walked away from camp to get some, followed by my gun-bearers, the little mule with its well-meaning and utterly ignorant shenzi sais, and a dozen porters.

We first went along the river brink to look for crocodiles. In most places the bank was high and steep. Wherever it was broken there was a drinking-place, with leading down to it trails deeply rutted in the soil by the herds of giant game that had travelled them for untold years. At this point the Nile was miles wide, and was divided into curving channels which here and there spread into lake-like expanses of still water. Along the edges of the river and between the winding channels and lagoons grew vast water-fields of papyrus, their sheets and bands of dark green breaking the burnished silver of the sunlit waters. Beyond the farther bank rose steep, sharply peaked hills. The tri-colored fish-eagles, striking to the eye because of their snow-white heads and breasts, screamed continually, a wild eerie sound. Cormorants and snake-birds were perched on trees overhanging the water, and flew away, or plunged like stones into the stream, as I approached; herons of many kinds rose from the marshy edges of the bays and inlets; wattled and spur-winged plovers circled overhead; and I saw a party of hippopotami in a shallow on the other side of the nearest channel, their lazy bulks raised above water as they basked asleep in the sun. The semidiurnal slate-and-yellow bats flitted from one scantily leaved tree to another, as I disturbed them. At the foot of a steep bluff, several yards from the water, a crocodile lay. I broke its neck with a soft-nosed bullet from the little Springfield; for the plated skin of a crocodile offers no resistance to a modern rifle. We dragged the ugly man-eater up the bank, and sent one of the porters back to camp to bring out enough men to carry the brute in bodily. It was a female, containing thirty eggs. We did not find any crocodile's nest; but near camp, in digging a hole for the disposal of refuse, we came on a clutch of a dozen eggs of the monitor lizard. They were in sandy loam, two feet and a half beneath the surface, without the vestige of a burrow leading to them. When exposed to the sun, unlike the crocodile's eggs, they soon burst. Evidently the young are hatched in the cool earth and dig their way out.

We continued our walk and soon came on some kob. At two hundred yards I got a fine buck, though he went a quarter of a mile. Then, at a hundred and fifty yards, I dropped a straw-colored Nile hartbeest. Sending in the kob and hartbeest used up all our porters but two, and I mounted the little mule and turned toward camp, having been out three hours. Soon Gouvimali pointed out a big bustard, marching away through the grass a hundred yards off. I dismounted, shot him through the base of the neck, and remounted. Then Kongoni pointed out, some distance ahead, a bushbuck ram, of the harnessed kind found in this part of the Nile Valley. Hastily dismounting, and stealing rapidly from ant-heap to ant-heap, until I was not much over a hundred yards from him, I gave him a fatal shot; but the bullet was placed a little too far back, and he could still go a considerable distance. So far I had been shooting well; now, pride had a fall. Immediately after the shot a difficulty arose in the rear between the mule and the shenzi sais; they parted company, and the mule joined the shooting-party in front, at a gallop. The bushbuck, which had halted with its head down, started off and I trotted after it, while the mule pursued an uncertain course between us; and I don't know which it annoyed most. I emptied my magazine twice, and partly a third time, before I finally killed the buck and scared the mule so that it started for camp. The bushbuck in this part of the Nile Valley did not live in dense forest, like those of East Africa, but among the scattered bushes and acacias. Those that I shot in the Lado had in their stomachs leaves, twig tips, and pods; one that Kermit shot, a fine buck, had been eating grass also. On the Uasin Gishu, in addition to leaves and a little grass, they had been feeding on the wild olives.

Our porters were not as a rule by any means the equals of those we had in East Africa, and we had some trouble because, as we did not know their names and faces, those who wished to shirk would go off in the bushes while their more willing comrades would be told off for the needed work. So Cuninghame determined to make each readily identifiable; and one day I found him sitting, in Rhadamanthus mood, at his table before his tent, while all the porters filed by, each in turn being decorated with a tag, conspicuously numbered, which was hung around his neck—the tags, by the way, being Smithsonian label cards, contributed by Doctor Mearns.

At last Kermit succeeded in getting some good white rhino pictures. He was out with his gun-bearers and Grogan. They had hunted steadily for nearly two days without seeing a rhino; then Kermit made out a big cow with a calf lying under a large tree, on a bare plain of short grass. Accompanied by Grogan, and by a gun-bearer carrying his rifle, while he himself carried his "naturalist's graphlex" camera, he got up to within fifty or sixty yards of the dull-witted beasts, and spent an hour cautiously manœuvring and taking photos. He got several photos of the cow and calf lying under the tree. Then something, probably the click of the camera, rendered them uneasy and they stood up. Soon the calf lay down again, while the cow continued standing on the other side of the tree, her head held down, the muzzle almost touching the ground, according to the custom of this species. After taking one or two more pictures Kermit edged in, so as to get better ones. Gradually the cow grew alarmed. She raised her head, as these animals always do when interested or excited, twisted her tail into a tight knot, and walked out from under the tree, followed by the calf; she and the calf stood stern to stern for a few seconds, and Kermit took another photo. By this time the cow had become both puzzled and irritated. Even with her dim eyes she could make out the men and the camera, and once or twice she threatened a charge, but thought better of it. Then she began to move off; but suddenly wheeled and charged, this time bent on mischief. She came on at a slashing trot, gradually increasing her pace, the huge, square lips shaking from side to side. Hoping that she would turn, Kermit shouted loudly and waited before firing until she was only ten yards off. Then, with the Winchester, he put a bullet in between her neck and shoulder, a mortal wound. She halted and half wheeled, and Grogan gave her right and left, Kermit putting in a couple of additional bullets as she went off. A couple of hundred yards away she fell, rose again, staggered, fell again, and died. The calf, which was old enough to shift for itself, refused to leave the body, although Kermit and Grogan pelted it with sticks and clods. Finally a shot through the flesh of the buttocks sent it off in frantic haste. Kermit had only killed the cow because it was absolutely necessary in order to avoid an accident, and he was sorry for the necessity; but I was not, for it was a very fine specimen, with the front horn thirty-one inches long; being longer than any other we had gotten. The second horn was compressed laterally, exactly as with many black rhinos (although it is sometimes stated that this does not occur in the case of the white rhino). We preserved the head-skin and skull for the National Museum.

The flesh of this rhino, especially the hump, proved excellent. It is a singular thing that scientific writers seem almost to have overlooked, and never lay any stress upon, the existence of this neck hump. It is on the neck, forward of the long dorsal vertebra, and is very conspicuous in the living animal; and I am inclined to think that some inches of the exceptional height measurements attributed to South African white rhinos may be due to measuring to the top of this hump. I am also puzzled by what seems to be the great inferiority in horn development of these square-mouthed rhinos of the Lado to the square-mouthed or white rhinos of South Africa (and, by the way, I may mention that on the whole these Lado rhinos certainly looked lighter colored, when we came across them standing in the open, than did their prehensile-lipped East African brethren). We saw between thirty and forty square-mouthed rhinos in the Lado, and Kermit's cow had much the longest horn of any of them; and while they averaged much better horns than the black rhinos we had seen in East Africa, between one and two hundred in number, there were any number of exceptions on both sides. There are recorded measurements of white rhino horns from South Africa double as long as our longest from the Lado. Now this is, scientifically, a fact of some importance, but it is of no consequence whatever when com-

pared with the question as to what, if any, the difference
is between the average horns; and this last fact is very difficult to ascertain, largely because of the foolish obsession for
"record" heads which seems to completely absorb so many
hunters who write.   What we need at the moment is more
information about the average South American heads.   There
are to be found among most kinds of horn-bearing animals
individuals with horns of wholly exceptional size, just as
among all nations there are individuals of wholly exceptional
height.   But a comparison of these wholly exceptional horns,
although it has a certain value, is, scientifically, much like
a comparison of the giants of different nations.   A good
head is of course better than a poor one; and a special effort
to secure an exceptional head is sportsmanlike and proper.
But to let the desire for "record" heads, to the exclusion of
all else, become a craze, is absurd.   The making of such a
collection is in itself not only proper but meritorious; all I
object to is the loss of all sense of proportion in connection
therewith.   It is just as with philately, or heraldry, or collecting the signatures of famous men.   The study of stamps,
or of coats of arms, or the collecting of autographs, is an
entirely legitimate amusement, and may be more than a mere
amusement; it is only when the student or collector allows
himself to utterly misestimate the importance of his pursuit
that it becomes ridiculous.

Cuninghame, Grogan, Heller, Kermit, and I now went off
on a week's safari inland, traveling as light as possible.   The
first day's march brought us to the kraal of a local chief
named Sururu.   There were a few banana-trees and patches
of scrawny cultivation, round the little cluster of huts, ringed
with a thorn fence, through which led a low door; and the
natives owned goats and chickens.   Sururu himself wore a
white sheet of cotton as a toga, and he owned a red fez and
a pair of baggy blue breeches, which last he generally carried over his shoulder.   His people were very scantily clad
indeed, and a few of them, both men and women, wore ab-

solutely nothing except a string of blue beads around the waist or neck.   Their ears had not been pierced and stretched like so many East African savages, but their lower lips were pierced for wooden ornaments and quills.   They brought us eggs and chickens, which we paid for with American cloth; this cloth, and some umbrellas, constituting our stock of trade goods, or gift goods, for the Nile.

The following day Sururu himself led us to our next camp, only a couple of hours away.   It was a dry country of harsh grass, everywhere covered by a sparse growth of euphorbias and stunted thorns, which were never in sufficient numbers to make a forest, each little, well-nigh leafless tree, standing a dozen rods or so distant from its nearest fellow.   Most of the grass had been burnt, and fires were still raging.   Our camp was by a beautiful pond, covered with white and lilac water-lilies.   We pitched our two tents on a bluff, under some large acacias that cast real shade.   It was between two and three degrees north of the equator.   The moon, the hot January moon of the mid-tropics, was at the full, and the nights were very lovely; the little sheet of water glimmered in the moon-rays, and round about the dry landscape shone with a strange, spectral light.

Near the pond, just before camping, I shot a couple of young water-buck bulls for food, and while we were pitching the tents a small herd of elephants—cows, young bulls, and calves, seemingly disturbed by a grass fire which was burning a little way off, came up within four hundred yards of us.   At first we mistook one large cow for a bull, and running quickly from bush to bush, diagonally to its course, I got within sixty yards, and watched it pass at a quick shuffling walk, lifting and curling its trunk.   The blindness of both elephant and rhino has never been sufficiently emphasized in books. Near camp was the bloody, broken skeleton of a young wart-hog boar, killed by a lion the previous night.   There were a number of lions in the neighborhood, and they roared at intervals all night long.   Next morning, after Grogan and

I had started from camp, when the sun had been up an hour, we heard one roar loudly less than a mile away. Running toward the place we tried to find the lion; but near by a small river ran through beds of reeds, and the fires left many patches of tall, yellow, half-burned grass, so that it had ample cover, and our search was fruitless.

Near the pond were green parrots and brilliant wood-hoopoos, rollers, and sunbirds; and buck of the ordinary kinds drank at it. A duiker which I shot for the table had been feeding on grass tips and on the stems and leaves of a small, low-growing plant.

After giving up the quest for the lion Grogan and I, with our gun-bearers, spent the day walking over the great dry flats of burnt grass-land and sparse, withered forests. The heat grew intense as the sun rose higher and higher. Hour after hour we plodded on across vast level stretches, or up or down inclines so slight as hardly to be noticeable. The black dust of the burn rose in puffs beneath our feet; and now and then we saw dust-devils, violent little whirlwinds, which darted right and left, raising to a height of many feet gray funnels of ashes and withered leaves. In places the coarse grass had half resisted the flames, and rose above our heads. Here and there bleached skulls of elephant and rhino, long dead, showed white against the charred surface of the soil. Everywhere, crossing and recrossing one another, were game trails, some slightly marked, others broad and hard, and beaten deep into the soil by the feet of the giant creatures that had trodden them for ages. The elephants had been the chief road-makers; but the rhinoceros had travelled their trails, and also buffalo and buck.

There were elephant about, but only cows and calves, and an occasional bull with very small tusks. Of rhinoceros, all square-mouthed, we saw nine, none carrying horns which made them worth shooting. The first one I saw was in long grass. My attention was attracted by a row of white objects moving at some speed through the top of the grass. It took a second look before I made out that they were cow-herons perched on the back of a rhino. This proved to be a bull, which joined a cow and a calf. None had decent horns, and we plodded on. Soon we came to the trail of two others, and after a couple of miles' tracking Kongoni pointed to two gray bulks lying down under a tree. I walked cautiously to within thirty yards. They heard something, and up rose the two pig-like blinking creatures, who gradually became aware of my presence, and retreated a few steps at a time, dull curiosity continually overcoming an uneasiness which never grew into fear. Tossing their stumpy-horned heads, and twisting their tails into tight knots, they ambled briskly from side to side, and were ten minutes in getting to a dis-tance of a hundred yards. Then our shenzi guide mentioned that there were other rhinos close by, and we walked off to inspect them. In three hundred yards we came on them, a cow and a well-grown calf. Sixty yards from them was an ant-hill with little trees on it. From this we looked at them until some sound or other must have made them uneasy, for up they got. The young one seemed to have rather keener suspicions, although no more sense, than its mother, and after a while grew so restless that it persuaded the cow to go off with it. But the still air gave no hint of our where-abouts, and they walked straight toward us. I did not wish to have to shoot one, and so when they were within thirty yards we raised a shout and away they cantered, heads tossing and tails twisting.

Three hours later we saw another cow and calf. By this time it was half past three in the afternoon, and the two animals had risen from their noonday rest and were grazing busily, the great clumsy heads sweeping the ground. Watch-ing them forty yards off it was some time before the cow raised her head high enough for me to see that her horns were not good. Then they became suspicious, and the cow stood motionless for several minutes, her head held low. We moved quietly back, and at last they either dimly saw us, or heard us, and stood looking toward us, their big ears cocked forward. At this moment we stumbled on a rhino skull, bleached, but in such good preservation that we knew Heller would like it; and we loaded it on the porters that had followed us. All the time we were thus engaged the two rhinos, only a hundred yards off, were intently gazing in our direction, with foolish and bewildered solemnity; and there we left them, survivors from a long-vanished world, standing alone in the parched desolation of the wilderness.

On another day Kermit saw ten rhino, none with more than ordinary horns. Five of them were in one party, and were much agitated by the approach of the men; they ran to and fro, their tails twisted into the usual pig-like curl, and from sheer nervous stupidity bade fair at one time to force the hunters to fire in self-defense. Finally, however, they all ran off. In the case of a couple of others a curious incident happened. When alarmed they failed to make out where the danger lay, and after running away a short distance they returned to a bush near by to look about. One remained standing, but the other deliberately sat down upon its haunches like a dog, staring ahead, Kermit meanwhile being busy with his camera. Two or three times I saw rhino, when roused from sleep, thus sit up on their haunches and look around before rising on all four legs; but this was the only time that any of us saw a rhino which was already standing assume such a position. No other kind of heavy game has this habit; and indeed, so far as I know, only one other hoofed animal, the white goat of the northern Rocky Mountains. In the case of the white goat, however, the attitude is far more often assumed, and in more extreme form; it is one of the characteristic traits of the queer goat-antelope, so many of whose ways and looks are peculiar to itself alone.

From the lily-pond camp we went back to our camp outside Sururu's village. This was a very pleasant camp, because while there, although the heat was intense in the daytime, the nights were cool and there were no mosquitoes.

During our stay in the Lado it was generally necessary to wear head-nets and gloves in the evenings and to go to bed at once after dinner, and then to lie under the mosquito-bar with practically nothing on through the long hot night, sleeping or contentedly listening to the humming of the baffled myriads outside the net. At the Sururu camp, however, we could sit at a table in front of the tents, after supper—or dinner, whichever one chose to call it—and read by lamplight in the still, cool, pleasant air; or walk up and down the hard, smooth elephant path which led by the tents, looking at the large red moon just risen, as it hung low over the horizon, or later, when, white and clear, it rode high in the heavens and flooded the land with its radiance.

There was a swamp close by, and we went through this the first afternoon in search of buffalo. We found plenty of sign; but the close-growing reeds were ten feet high, and even along the winding buffalo trails by which alone they could be penetrated it was impossible to see a dozen paces ahead. Inside the reeds it was nearly impossible to get to the buffalo, or at least to be sure to kill only a bull, which was all I wanted; and at this time when the moon was just past the full, these particular buffalo only came out into the open to feed at night, or very early in the morning and late in the evening. But Sururu said that there were other buffalo which lived away from the reeds, among the thorn-trees on the grassy flats and low hills; and he volunteered to bring me information about them on the morrow. Sure enough, shortly before eleven next morning, he turned up with the news that he had found a solitary bull only about five miles away. Grogan and I at once started back with him, accompanied by our gun-bearers. The country was just such as that in which we had hitherto found our rhinos; and there was fresh sign of rhino as well as buffalo. The thorny, scantily leaved trees were perhaps a little closer together than in most places, and there were a good many half-burned patches of tall grass. We passed a couple of ponds which must have been permanent, as water-lilies were growing in them; at one a buffalo had been drinking. It was half past twelve when we reached the place where Sururu had seen the bull. We then advanced with the utmost caution, as the wind was shifty, and although the cover was thin, it yet rendered it difficult to see a hundred yards in advance. At last we made out the bull, on his feet and feeding, although it was high noon. He was stern toward us, and while we were stealing toward him a puff of wind gave him our scent. At once he whipped around, gazed at us for a moment with outstretched head, and galloped off. I could not get a shot through the bushes, and after him we ran, Kongoni leading, with me at his heels. It was hot work running, for at this time the thermometer registered one hundred and two degrees in the shade. Fortunately the bull had little fear of man, and being curious, and rather truculent, he halted two or three times to look around. Finally, after we had run a mile and a half, he halted once too often, and I got a shot at him at eighty yards. The heavy bullet went home; I fired twice again as rapidly as possible, and the bull never moved from where he had stood. He was an old bull, as big as an East African buffalo bull; but his worn horns were smaller and rather different. This had rendered Kongoni uncertain whether he might not be a cow; and when we came up to the body he exclaimed with delight that it was a "duck"—Kongoni's invariable method of pronouncing "buck," the term he used to describe anything male, from a lion or an elephant to a bustard or a crocodile; "cow" being his expression for the female of these and all other creatures. As Gouvimali came running up to shake hands, his face wreathed in smiles, he exclamed "G-o-o-d-e morning"; a phrase which he had picked up under the impression that it was a species of congratulation.

As always when I have killed buffalo I was struck by the massive bulk of the great bull as he lay in death, and by the evident and tremendous muscular power of his big-boned frame. He looked what he was, a formidable beast. Thirty porters had to be sent out to bring to camp the head, hide, and meat. We found, by the way, that his meat made excellent soup, his kidneys a good stew, while his tongue was delicious.

Next morning Kermit and I with the bulk of the safari walked back to our main camp, on the Nile, leaving Cuninghame and Heller where they were for a day, to take care of the buffalo-skin. Each of us struck off across the country by himself, with his gun-bearers. After walking five or six miles I saw a big rhino three-quarters of a mile off. At this point the country was flat, the acacias very thinly scattered, and the grass completely burnt off, the green young blades sprouting; and there was no difficulty in making out, at the distance we did, the vast gray bulk of the rhino as it stood inertly under a tree. Drawing nearer we saw that it had a good horn, although not as good as Kermit's best; and approaching quietly to within forty yards I shot the beast.

At the main camp we found that Mearns had made a fine collection of birds in our absence; while Loring had taken a variety of excellent photos, of marabou, vultures, and kites feeding, and, above all, of a monitor lizard plundering the nest of a crocodile. The monitors were quite plentiful near camp. They are amphibious, carnivorous lizards of large size; they frequent the banks of the river, running well on the land, and sometimes even climbing trees, but taking to the water when alarmed. They feed on mice and rats, other lizards, eggs, and fish; the stomachs of those we caught generally contained fish, for they are expert swimmers. One morning Loring surprised a monitor which had just uncovered some crocodile eggs on a small sandy beach. The eggs, about thirty in number, were buried in rather shallow fashion, so that the monitor readily uncovered them. The monitor had one of the eggs transversely in its mouth, and, head erect, was marching off with it. As soon as it saw

Loring it dropped the egg and scuttled into the reeds; in a few minutes it returned, took another egg, and walked off into the bushes, where it broke the shell, swallowed the yolk, and at once returned to the nest for another egg. Loring took me out to see the feat repeated, replenishing the rifled nest with eggs taken from a crocodile the doctor had shot; and I was delighted to watch, from our hiding place, the big lizard as he cautiously approached, seized an egg, and then retired to cover with his booty. Kermit came on a monitor plundering a crocodile's nest at the top of a steep bank, while, funnily enough, a large crocodile lay asleep at the foot of the bank only a few yards distant. As soon as it saw Kermit the monitor dropped the egg it was carrying, ran up a slanting tree which overhung the river, and dropped into the water like a snake-bird.

There was always something interesting to do or to see at this camp. One afternoon I spent in the boat. The papyrus along the channel rose like a forest, thirty feet high, the close-growing stems knit together by vines. As we drifted down, the green wall was continually broken by openings, through which side streams from the great river rushed, swirling and winding, down narrow lanes and under low archways, into the dim mysterious heart of the vast reed beds, where dwelt bird and reptile and water beast. In a shallow bay we came on two hippo cows with their calves, and a dozen crocodiles. I shot one of the latter—as I always do, when I get a chance—and it turned over and over, lashing with its tail as it sank. A half-grown hippo came up close by the boat and leaped nearly clear of the water; and in another place I saw a mother hippo swimming, with the young one resting half on its back.

Another day Kermit came on some black-and-white Colobus monkeys. Those we had shot east of the Rift Valley had long mantles, and more white than black in their coloring; west of the Rift Valley they had less white and less of the very long hair; and here on the Nile the change had gone still further in the same direction. On the west coast this kind of monkey is said to be entirely black. But we were not prepared for the complete change in habits. In East Africa the Colobus monkeys kept to the dense cool mountain forests, dwelt in the tops of the big trees, and rarely descended to the ground. Here on the Nile they lived in exactly such country as that affected by the smaller greenish-yellow monkeys, which we found along the Guaso Nyero, for instance; country into which the East African Colobus never by any chance wandered. Moreover, instead of living in the tall timber and never going on the ground except for a few yards as in East Africa, here on the Nile they sought to escape danger by flight over the ground in the scrub. Kermit found some in a grove of fairly big acacias, but they instantly dropped to the earth and galloped off among the dry, scattered bushes and small thorn-trees. Kermit also shot a twelve-foot crocodile in which he found the remains of a big heron.

One morning we saw from camp a herd of elephants in a piece of unburned swamp. It was a mile and a half away in a straight line, although we had to walk three miles to get there. There were between forty and fifty of them, a few big cows with calves, the rest half-grown and three-quarters-grown animals. Over a hundred white herons accompanied them. From an ant-hill to leeward we watched them standing by a mud-hole in the swamp; evidently they now and then got a whiff from our camp, for they were continually lifting and curling their trunks. To see if by any chance there was a bull among them we moved them out of the swamp by shouting; the wind blew hard, and as they moved away evidently smelled the camp strongly, for all their trunks went into the air; and off they went at a rapid pace, half of the herons riding on them, while the others hovered over and alongside, like a white cloud. Two days later the same herd again made its appearance.

Spur-winged plover were nesting near camp, and evidently

distrusted the carrion-feeders, for they attacked and drove off every kite or vulture that crossed what they considered the prohibited zone. They also harassed the marabous, but with more circumspection; for the big storks were short-tempered, and rather daunted the spur-wings by the way they opened their enormous beaks at them. The fish-eagles fed exclusively on fish, as far as we could tell, and there were piles of fish bones and heads under their favorite perches. Once I saw one plunge into the water, but it failed to catch anything. Another time, suddenly, and seemingly in mere mischief, one attacked a purple heron which was standing on a mud bank. The eagle swooped down from a tree and knocked over the heron; and when the astonished heron struggled to its feet and attempted to fly off, the eagle made another swoop and this time knocked it into the water. The heron then edged into the papyrus, and the eagle paid it no further attention.

In this camp we had to watch the white ants, which strove to devour everything. They are nocturnal, and work in the daytime only under the tunnels of earth which they build over the surface of the box, or whatever else it is, that they are devouring; they eat out everything, leaving this outside shell of earth. We also saw a long column of the dreaded driver-ants. These are carnivorous; I have seen both red and black species; they kill every living thing in their path, and I have known them at night drive all the men in a camp out into the jungle to fight the mosquitoes unprotected until daylight. On another occasion, where a steamboat was moored close to a bank, an ant column entered the boat after nightfall, and kept complete possession of it for forty-eight hours. Fire, and boiling water, offer the only effectual means of resistance. The bees are at times as formidable; when their nests are disturbed they will attack every one in sight, driving all the crew of a boat overboard or scattering a safari, and not infrequently killing men and beasts of burden that are unable to reach some place of safety.

The last afternoon, when the flotilla had called to take us farther on our journey, we shot about a dozen buck, to give the porters and sailors a feast, which they had amply earned. All the meat did not get into camp until after dark—one of the sailors, unfortunately, falling out of a tree and breaking his neck on the way in—and it was picturesque to see the rows of big antelope—hartbeest, kob, water-buck—stretched in front of the flaring fires, and the dark faces of the waiting negroes, each deputed by some particular group of gun-bearers, porters, or sailors to bring back its share.

Next morning we embarked, and steamed and drifted down the Nile; ourselves, our men, our belongings, and the spoils of the chase all huddled together under the torrid sun. Two or three times we grounded on sandbars; but no damage was done, and in twenty-six hours we reached Nimule. We were no longer in healthy East Africa. Kermit and I had been in robust health throughout the time we were in Uganda and the Lado; but all the other white men of the party had suffered more or less from dysentery, fever, and sun prostration while in the Lado; some of the gun-bearers had been down with fever, one of them dying while we were in Uganda; and four of the porters who had marched from Koba to Nimule had died of dysentery—they were burying one when we arrived.

At Nimule we were as usual greeted with hospitable heartiness by the English officials, as well as by two or three elephant-hunters. One of the latter, three days before, had been charged by an unwounded bull elephant. He fired both barrels into it as it came on, but it charged home, knocked him down, killed his gun-bearer, and made its escape into the forest. In the forlorn little graveyard at the station were the graves of two white men who had been killed by elephants. One of them, named Stoney, had been caught by a wounded bull, which stamped the life out of him and then literally dismembered him, tearing his arms from his body. In the African wilderness, when a man dies, his companion usually brings in something to show that he is dead, or some remnant of whatever it is that has destroyed him; the sailors whose companion was killed by falling out of the tree near our Lado camp, for instance, brought in the dead branch which had broken under his weight; and Stoney's gun-bearer marched back to Nimule carrying an arm of his dead master, and deposited his gruesome burden in the office of the district commissioner.

CHAPTER XV

DOWN THE NILE: THE GIANT ELAND

WE spent two or three days in Nimule, getting everything ready for the march north to Gondokoro.

By this time Kermit and I had grown really attached to our personal followers, whose devotion to us and whose zeal for our success and welfare and comfort had many times been made rather touchingly manifest; even their shortcomings were merely those of big, naughty children, and though they occasionally needed discipline, this was rare, whereas the amusement they gave us was unending. When we reached Nimule we were greeted with enthusiasm by Magi, Kermit's Kikuyu sais, who had been in charge of the mules which we did not take into the Lado. Magi was now acting as sais for me as well as for Kermit; and he came to Kermit to discuss the new dual relationship. "Now I am the sais of the Bwana Makuba, as well as of you, the Bwana Merodadi" (the Dandy Master, as for some inscrutable reason all the men now called Kermit); "well, then, you'll both have to take care of me," concluded the rusé Magi.

Whenever we reached one of these little stations where there was an Indian trading-store, we would see that those of our followers who had been specially devoted to us—and this always included all our immediate attendants—had a chance to obtain the few little comforts and luxuries, tea, sugar, or tobacco, for instance, which meant so much to them. Usually Kermit would take them to the store himself, for they were less wily than the Indian trader, and, moreover, in the excitement of shopping occasionally purchased something for which they really had no use. Kermit would march his tail of followers into the store, give them time to look around, and then make the first purchase for the man who had the least coming to him; this to avoid heart-burnings, as the man was invariably too much interested in what he had received to scrutinize closely what the others were getting. The purchase might be an article of clothing or a knife, but usually took the form of tobacco, sugar, and tea; in tobacco the man was offered his choice between quality and quantity; that is, either a moderate quantity of good cigarettes or a large amount of trade tobacco. Funny little Juma Yohari, for instance, one of Kermit's gun-bearers, usually went in for quality, whereas his colleague Kassitura preferred quantity. Juma was a Zanzibari, a wiry merry little grig of a man, loyal, hard-working, fearless; Kassitura a huge Basoga negro, of guileless honesty and good faith, incapable of neglecting his duty. Juma was rather the wit of the gun-bearers' mess, and Kassitura the musician, having a little native harp on which for hours at a time he would strum queer little melancholy tunes to which he hummed an accompaniment in undertone.

All the natives we met and the men in our employ were fond of singing, sometimes simply improvised chants, sometimes sentences of three or four words repeated over and over again. The Uganda porters who were with us after we left Kampalla did not sing nearly as freely as our East African safari, although they depended much on the man who beat the drum, at the head of the marching column. The East African porters did every kind of work to an accompaniment of chanting. When, for instance, after camp was pitched, a detail of men was sent out for wood—the "wood safari"—the men as they came back to camp with their loads never did anything so commonplace as each merely to deposit his burden at the proper spot. The first comers waited in the middle of the camp until all had assembled, and then marched in order to where the fire was to be made, all singing vigorously and stepping in time together. The leader,

or chantey-man, would call out "Kooni" (wood); and all the
others would hum in unison "Kooni telli" (plenty of wood).
"Kooni," again came the shout of the chantey-man; and the
answer would be "Kooni." "Kooni," from the chantey-man;
and this time all the rest would simply utter a long-drawn
"Hum-m-m." "Kooni," again; and the answer would be
"Kooni telli," with strong emphasis on the "telli." Then, if
they saw me, the chantey-man might vary by shouting that
the wood was for the Bwana Makuba; and so it would continue until the loads were thrown down.

Often a man would improvise a song regarding any small
incident which had just happened to him, or a thought which
had occurred to him. Drifting down the Nile to Nimule,
Kermit and the three naturalists and sixty porters were
packed in sardine fashion on one of the sailboats. At nightfall one of the sailors, the helmsman, a Swahili from Mombasa, began to plan how he would write a letter to his people
in Mombasa and give it to another sailor, a friend of his,
who intended shortly to return thither. He crooned to himself as he crouched by the tiller, steering the boat, and gradually, as the moon shone on the swift, quiet water of the
river, his crooning turned into a regular song. His voice was
beautiful, and there was a wild meaningless refrain to each
verse; the verses reciting how he intended to write this
letter to those whom he had not seen for two years; how a
friend would take it to them, so that the letter would be in
Mombasa; but he, the man who wrote it, would for two years
more be in the far-off wilderness.

On February 17 the long line of our laden safari left Nimule on its ten days' march to Gondokoro. We went through
a barren and thirsty land. Our first camp was by a shallow,
running river, with a shaded pool in which we bathed. After
that we never came on running water, merely on dry watercourses with pools here and there, some of the pools being
crowded with fish. Tall half-burnt grass, and scattered, well-
nigh leafless thorn-scrub covered the monotonous landscape,

although we could generally find some fairly leafy tree near which to pitch the tents. The heat was great; more than once the thermometer at noon rose to one hundred and twelve degrees in the shade—not real shade, however, but in a stifling tent, or beneath a tree the foliage of which let through at least a third of the sun-rays. The fiery heat of the ground so burnt and crippled the feet of the porters that we had to start each day's march very early.

At quarter of three in the morning the whistle blew; we dressed and breakfasted while the tents were taken down and the loads adjusted. Then off we strode, through the hot starlit night, our backs to the Southern Cross and our faces toward the Great Bear; for we were marching northward and homeward. The drum throbbed and muttered as we walked, on and on, along the dim trail. At last the stars began to pale, the gray east changed to opal and amber and amethyst, the red splendor of the sunrise flooded the world, and to the heat of the night succeeded the more merciless heat of the day. Higher and higher rose the sun. The sweat streamed down our faces, and the bodies of the black men glistened like oiled iron. We might halt early in the forenoon, or we might have to march until noon, according to the distance from water-hole to water-hole.

Occasionally in the afternoons, and once when we halted for a day to rest the porters, Kermit and I would kill buck for the table—hartbeest, reedbuck, and oribi. I also killed a big red ground-monkey, with baboon-like habits; we had first seen the species on the Uasin Gishu, and had tried in vain to get it, for it was wary, never sought safety in trees, and showed both speed and endurance in running. Kermit killed a bull and a cow roan antelope. These so-called horse-antelope are fine beasts, light roan in color, with high withers, rather short curved horns, huge ears, and bold face mark-ings. Usually we found them shy, but occasionally very tame. They are the most truculent and dangerous of all antelope; this bull, when seemingly on the point of death, rose like a flash when Kermit approached and charged him full tilt; Kermit had to fire from the hip, luckily breaking the animal's neck.

On the same day Loring had an interesting experience with one of the small cormorants so common in this region. Previously, while visiting the rapids of the Nile below Nimule, I had been struck by the comparative unwariness of these birds, one of them repeatedly landing on a rock a few yards away from me, and thence slipping unconcernedly into the swift water—and, by the way, it was entirely at home in the boiling rapids. But the conduct of Loring's bird was wholly exceptional. He was taking a swim in a pool when the bird lit beside him. It paid no more heed to the naked white man than it would have paid to a hippo, and although it would not allow itself to be actually touched, it merely moved a few feet out of his way when he approached it. Moreover it seemed to be on the lookout for enemies in the air, not in the water. It was continually glancing upward, and when a big hawk appeared, followed its movements with close attention. It stayed in and about the pool for many minutes before flying off. I suppose that certain eagles and hawks prey on cormorants; but I should also be inclined to think that crocodiles at least occasionally prey on them.

The very most attractive birds we met in middle Africa and along the Nile were the brave, cheery little wagtails. They wear trim black-and-white suits, when on the ground they walk instead of hopping, they have a merry, pleasing song, and they are as confiding and fearless as they are pretty. The natives never molest them, for they figure to advantage in the folk-lore of the various tribes. They came round us at every halting-place, entering the rest-houses in Uganda and sometimes even our tents, coming up within a few feet of us as we lay under trees, and boarding our boats on the Nile; and they would stroll about camp quite unconcernedly, in pairs, the male stopping every now and then to sing. Except the whiskey-jacks and Hudsonian chickadees of the North woods I never saw such tame little birds.

At Gondokoro we met the boat which the Sirdar, Major-General Sir Reginald Wingate, had sent to take us down the Nile to Khartoum; for he and all the Soudan officials— including especially Colonel Asser, Colonel Owen, Slatin Pasha, and Butler Bey—treated us with a courtesy for which I cannot too strongly express my appreciation. In the boat we were to have met an old friend and fellow countryman, Leigh Hunt; to our great regret he could not meet us, but he insisted on treating us as his guests, and on our way down the Nile we felt as if we were on the most comfortable kind of yachting trip; and everything was done for us by Captain Middleton, the Scotch engineer in charge.

Nor was our debt only to British officials and to American friends. At Gondokoro I was met by M. Ranquet, the Belgian commandant of the Lado district, and both he and M. Massart, the chief de poste at Redjaf, were kindness itself, and aided us in every way.

From Gondokoro Kermit and I crossed to Redjaf, for an eight days' trip after the largest and handsomest and one of the least known of African antelopes, the giant eland. We went alone, because all the other white men of the party were down with dysentery or fever. We had with us sixty Uganda porters and a dozen mules sent us by the Sirdar, together with a couple of our little riding mules, which we used now and then for a couple of hours on safari, or in getting to the actual hunting-ground. As always when only one or two of us went, or when the safari was short, we travelled light, with no dining tent and nothing unnecessary in the way of baggage; the only impedimenta which we could not minimize were those connected with the preservation of the skins of the big animals, which, of course, were throughout our whole trip what necessitated the use of the bulk of the porters and other means of transportation employed.

From the neat little station of Redjaf, lying at the foot

of the bold pyramidal hill of the same name, we marched
two days west, stopping short of the River Koda, where we
knew the game drank.   Now and then we came on flower-
bearing bushes, of marvellously sweet scent, like gardenias.
It was the height of the dry season; the country was covered
with coarse grass and a scrub growth of nearly leafless thorn-
trees, usually growing rather wide apart, occasionally close
enough together to look almost like a forest.   There were a
few palms, euphorbias, and very rarely scattered clumps of
withered bamboo, and also bright-green trees with rather thick
leaves and bean pods, on which we afterward found that the
eland fed.

The streams we crossed were dry torrent beds, sandy or
rocky; in two or three of them were pools of stagnant water,
while better water could be obtained by digging in the sand
alongside.   A couple of hours after reaching each camp everything was in order, and Ali had made a fire of some slivers
of wood and boiled our tea; and our two meals, breakfast and
dinner, were taken at a table in the open, under a tree.

We had with us seven black soldiers of the Belgian native
troops, under a corporal; they came from every quarter of
the Congo, but several of them could speak Swahili, the lingua
franca of Middle Africa, and so Kermit could talk freely with
them.   These black soldiers behaved excellently, and the attitude, both toward them and toward us, of the natives in
the various villages we came across was totally incompatible
with any theory that these natives had suffered from any mal-
treatment; they behaved just like the natives in British territory.   There had to be the usual parleys with the chiefs
of the villages to obtain food for the soldiers (we carried
the posho for our own men), and ample payment was given
for what was brought in; and in the only two cases where
the natives thought themselves aggrieved by the soldiers,
they at once brought the matter before us.   One soldier had
taken a big gourd of water when very thirsty; another, a
knife from a man who was misbehaving himself.   On care-

ful inquiry, and delivering judgment in the spirit of Solomon, we decided that both soldiers had been justified by the provocation received; but as we were dealing with the misdeeds of mere big children, we gave the gourd back to its owner with a reprimand for having refused the water, and permitting the owner of the knife, whose offense had been more serious, to ransom his property by bringing in a chicken to the soldier who had it.

The natives lived in the usual pointed beehive huts in unfenced villages, with shambas lying about them; and they kept goats, chickens, and a few cattle. Our permanent camp was near such a village. It was interesting to pass through it at sunrise or sunset, when starting on or returning from a hunt. The hard, bare earth was swept clean. The doors in the low mud walls of the huts were but a couple of feet high and had to be entered on all fours; black pickaninnies scuttled into them in wild alarm as we passed. Skinny, haggard old men and women, almost naked, sat by the fires smoking long pipes; the younger men and women laughed and jested as they moved among the houses. One day, in the course of a long and fruitless hunt, we stopped to rest near such a village at about two in the afternoon, having been walking hard since dawn. We—I and my gun-bearer, a black askari, a couple of porters, and a native guide—sat down under a big tree a hundred yards from the village. Soon the chief and several of his people came out to see us. The chief proudly wore a dirty jersey and a pair of drawers; a follower carried his spear and the little wooden stool of dignity on which he sat. There were a couple of warriors with him, one a man in a bark apron with an old breech-loading rifle, the other a stark-naked savage—not a rag on him—with a bow and arrows; a very powerfully built man with a ferocious and sinister face. Two women bore on their heads, as gifts for us, one a large earthenware jar of water, the other a basket of ground-nuts. They were tall and well shaped. One as her sole clothing wore a beaded cord around her waist and a breech-clout consisting of half a dozen long, thickly leaved, fresh sprays of a kind of vine; the other, instead of this vine breech-clout, had hanging from her girdle in front a cluster of long-stemmed green leaves, and behind a bundle of long strings, carried like a horse's tail.

The weather was very hot, and the country, far and wide, was a waste of barren desolation. The flats of endless thorn-scrub were broken by occasional low and rugged hills, and in the empty water-courses the pools were many miles apart. Yet there was a good deal of game. We saw buffalo, giraffe and elephant; and on our way back to camp in the evenings we now and then killed a roan, hartbeest, or oribi. But the game we sought was the giant eland, and we never fired when there was the slightest chance of disturbing our quarry. They usually went in herds, but there were solitary bulls. We found that they drank at some pool in the Koda before dawn and then travelled many miles back into the parched interior, feeding as they went; and, after lying up for some hours about midday, again moved slowly off, feeding. They did not graze, but fed on the green leaves, and the bean pods of the tree of which I have already spoken and of another tree. One of their marked habits—shared in some degree by their forest cousin, the bongo—was breaking the higher branches with their horns, to get at the leaves; they thus broke branches two or three inches in diameter and seven or eight feet from the ground, the crash of the branches being a sound for which we continually listened as we followed the tracks of a herd. They were far more wary than roan or hartbeest or any of the other buck, and the country was such that it was difficult to see more than a couple of hundred yards ahead.

It took me three hard days' work before I got my eland. Each day I left camp before sunrise and on the first two I came back after dark, while it always happened that at noon we were on a trail and could not stop. We would walk until we found tracks made that morning, and then the gun-bearers and the native guide would slowly follow them, hour after hour, under the burning sun. On the first day we saw nothing; on the next we got a moment's glimpse of an eland, trotting at the usual slashing gait; I had no chance to fire. By mid-afternoon on each day it was evident that further following of the trail we were on was useless, and we plodded campward, tired and thirsty. Gradually the merciless glare softened; then the sun sank crimson behind a chain of fantastically carved mountains in the distance; and the hues of the afterglow were drowned in the silver light of the moon, which was nearing the full.

On the third day we found the spoor of a single bull by eight o'clock. Hour after hour went by while the gunbearers, even more eager than weary, puzzled out the trail. At half past twelve we knew we were close on the beast, and immediately afterward caught a glimpse of it. Taking advantage of every patch of cover I crawled toward it on all fours, my rifle too hot for me to touch the barrel, while the blistering heat of the baked ground hurt my hands. At a little over a hundred yards I knelt and aimed at the noble beast; I could now plainly see his huge bulk and great, massive horns, as he stood under a tree. The pointed bullet from the little Springfield hit a trifle too far back and up, but made such a rip that he never got ten yards from where he was standing; and great was my pride as I stood over him, and examined his horns, twisted almost like a koodoo's, and admired his size, his finely modelled head and legs, and the beauty of his coat.

Meanwhile, Kermit had killed two eland, a cow on the first day, and on the second a bull even better than, although not quite so old, as mine. Kermit could see game and follow tracks almost as well as his gun-bearers, and in a long chase could outrun them. On each day he struck the track of a herd of eland, and after a while left his gun-bearers and porters, and ran along the trail accompanied only by a native guide. The cow was killed at two hundred yards with a

shot from his Winchester. The bull yielded more excitement. He was in a herd of about forty which Kermit had
followed for over five hours, toward the last accompanied
only by the wild native; at one point the eland had come upon
a small party of elephant, and trotted off at right angles to
their former course—Kermit following them after he had
satisfied himself that the elephants were cows and half-grown
animals. When he finally overtook the eland during the torrid heat of the early afternoon, they were all lying down, in a
place where the trees grew rather more thickly than usual.

Stalking as close as he dared he selected a big animal which
he hoped was a bull, and fired three shots into it; however, it
ran, and he then saw that it was a cow. As the rest of the
herd jumped up he saw the form of the master-bull looming
above the others. They crossed his front at a slashing trot,
the cows clustered round the great bull; but just as they came
to a little opening, they opened somewhat, giving him a clear
shot. Down went the bull on his head, rose, received another
bullet, and came to a standstill. This was the last bullet from
the magazine; and now the mechanism of the rifle refused to
work or to throw the empty shell out of the chamber. The
faithful Winchester, which Kermit had used steadily for ten
months, on foot and on horseback, which had suffered every
kind of hard treatment and had killed every kind of game,
without once failing, had at last given way under the strain.
While Kermit was working desperately at the mechanism, the
bull, which was standing looking at him within fifty yards,
gradually recovered, moved off step by step, and broke into
a slow trot. After it went Kermit as hard as he could go,
still fussing with the rifle, which he finally opened, and refilled
with five cartridges. Kermit could just about keep the eland
in sight, running as hard as he was able; after a mile or two
it lay down, but rose as he came near, and went off again,
while he was so blown that though, with four shots, he hit it
twice he failed to kill it. He now had but one bullet left, after
which he knew that the rifle would jam again; and it was

accordingly necessary to kill outright with the next shot. He was just able to keep close to the bull for a half-mile, then it halted; and he killed it. Leaving the shenzi by the carcass, he went off to see about the wounded cow, but after an hour was forced to give up the chase and return, so as to be sure to save the bull's skin. The gun-bearers and another shenzi had by this time reached the dead eland; they had only Kermit's canteen of water among them. One of the shenzis was at once sent to camp to bring back twenty porters, with rope, and plenty of water; and, with parched mouths, Kermit and the gun-bearers began to take off the thick hide of the dead bull. Four hours later the porters appeared with the ropes and the water; the thirsty men drank gallons; the porters were loaded with the hide, head, and meat; and they marched back to camp by moonlight.

It was no easy job in that climate, to care for and save the three big skins; but we did it. On the trip we had taken, besides our gun-bearers and tent-boys, Magi, the sais, and two of our East African skinners, Kiboko and Merefu; they formed in the safari a kind of chief petty officers' mess, so to speak. They were all devoted to their duties, and they worked equally hard whether hunting or caring for the skins; the day Kermit killed his bull he and the gun-bearers and skinners, with Magi as a volunteer, worked until midnight at the hide. But they had any amount of meat, and we shared our sugar and tea with them. On the last evening there was nothing to do, and they sat in the brilliant moonlight in front of their tents, while Kassitura played his odd little harp. Kermit and I strolled over to listen; and at once Kassitura began to improvise a chant in my honor, reciting how the Bwana Makuba had come, how he was far from his own country, how he had just killed a giant eland, and so on and so on. Meanwhile, over many little fires strips of meat were drying on scaffolds of bent branches, and askaris and porters were gathered in groups, chatting and singing; while the mighty tree near which our tents were pitched cast a black shadow on the silver plain. Then the shenzis who had helped us came to receive their reward, and their hearts were gladdened with red cloth and salt, and for those whose services had been greatest there were special treasures in the shape of three green-and-white umbrellas. It was a pleasant ending to a successful hunt.

On our return to Gondokoro we found Cuninghame all right, although he had been obliged single-handed to do the work of getting our porters safely started on their return march to Kampalla, as well as getting all the skins and skeletons properly packed for shipment. Heller had also recovered, and had gone on a short trip during which he trapped a leopard and a serval at the same carcass, the leopard killing the serval. Doctor Mearns and Loring were both seriously sick; so was the district commissioner, kind Mr. Haddon. One day a German missionary dined with us; the next he was dead of black-water fever. An English sportsman whom we had met at Nimule had been brought in so sick that he was at death's door; Doctor Mearns took care of him, badly off though he himself was. We had brought with us a case of champagne for just such emergencies; this was the first time that we made use of it.

On the last day of February we started down the Nile, slipping easily along on the rapid current, which wound and twisted through stretches of reeds and marsh-grass and papyrus. We halted at the attractive station of Lado for a good-by breakfast with our kind Belgian friends, and that evening we dined at Mongalla with Colonel Owen, the chief of the southernmost section of the Soudan. I was greatly interested in the Egyptian and Soudanese soldiers, and their service medals. Many of these medals showed that their owners had been in a dozen campaigns; some of the native officers and men (and also the Reis or native captain of our boat, by the way) had served in the battles which broke forever the Mahdi's cruel power; two or three had been with Gordon. They were a fine-looking set, and their obvious self-respect was a good thing to see. That same afternoon I witnessed a native dance, and was struck by the lack of men of middle age; all the tribes who were touched by the blight of the Mahdist tyranny, with its accompaniments of unspeakable horror, suffered such slaughter of the then young men that the loss has left its mark to this day. The English when they destroyed Mahdism rendered a great service to humanity; and their rule in the Soudan has been astoundingly successful and beneficial from every standpoint.*

We steamed onward down the Nile; sometimes tying up to the bank at nightfall, sometimes steaming steadily through the night. We reached the Sud, the vast papyrus marsh once so formidable a barrier to all who would journey along the river; and sunrise and sunset were beautiful over the endless, melancholy stretches of water-reeds. In the Sud the only tree seen was the water-loving ambatch, light as cork. Occasionally we saw hippos and crocodiles and a few water-birds; and now and then passed native villages, the tall, lean men and women stark naked, and their bodies daubed with mud, grease, and ashes to keep off the mosquitoes.

On March 4 we were steaming slowly along the reedy, water-soaked shores of Lake No, keeping a sharp lookout for the white-eared kob and especially for the handsome saddle-marked lechwi kob—which has been cursed with the foolishly inappropriate name of "Mrs. Gray's water-buck."

Early in the morning we saw a herd of these saddle-marked lechwi in the long marsh-grass and pushed the steamer's nose as near to the shore as possible. Then Cuninghame, keen-eyed Kongoni, and I started for what proved to be a five hours' tramp. The walking was hard; sometimes we were on dry land, but more often in water up to our ankles or knees, and occasionally floundering and wallowing up to our hips through stretches of reeds, water-lilies, green water, and foul

* The despotism of Mahdist rule was so revolting, so vilely cruel and hideous, that the worst despotism by men of European blood in recent times seems a model of humanity by comparison; and yet there were nominal "antimilitarists" and self-styled "apostles of peace" who did their feeble best to prevent the destruction of this infamy.

black slime. Yet there were ant-hills in the marsh. Once or twice we caught a glimpse of the game in small patches of open ground covered with short grass; but almost always they kept to the high grass and reeds. There were with the herd two very old bucks, with a white saddle-shaped patch on the withers, the white extending up the back of the neck to the head; a mark of their being in full maturity, or past it, for on some of the males, at least, this coloration only begins to appear when they seem already to have attained their growth of horn and body, their teeth showing them to be five or six years old, while they are obviously in the prime of vigor and breeding capacity. Unfortunately, in the long grass it was impossible to single out these old bucks. Marking as well as we could the general direction of the herd we would steal toward it until we thought we were in the neighborhood, and then cautiously climb an ant-hill to look about. Nothing would be in sight. We would scan the ground in every direction; still nothing. Suddenly a dozen heads would pop up, just above the grass, two or three hundred yards off, and after a steady gaze would disappear; and some minutes later would again appear a quarter of a mile farther on. Usually they skulked off at a trot or canter, necks stretched level with the back; for they were great skulkers, and trusted chiefly to escaping observation and stealing away from danger unperceived. But occasionally they would break into a gallop, making lofty bounds, clear above the tops of the grass; and then they might go a long way before stopping. I never saw them leap on the ant-hills to look about, as is the custom of the common or Uganda kob. They were rather noisy; we heard them grunting continually, both when they were grazing and when they saw us.

At last, from an ant-hill, I saw dim outlines of two or three animals moving past, a little over a hundred yards ahead. There was nothing to shoot at; but a moment afterward I saw a pair of horns through the grass tops, in such a position that it was evident the owner was looking at me. I guessed that he had been moving in the direction in which the others had gone, and I guessed at the position of the shoulder, and fired. The horns disappeared. Then I caught a glimpse, first of a doe, next of a buck, in full flight, each occasionally appearing for an instant in a great bound over the grass tops. I had no idea whether or not I had hit my buck; so Cuninghame stayed on the ant-heap to guide us, while Kongoni and I plunged into the long grass, as high as our heads. Sure enough, there was the buck, a youngish one, about four years old; my bullet had gone true. While we were looking at him we suddenly caught a momentary glimpse of two more of the herd rushing off to our right, and we heard another grunting and sneaking away, invisible, thirty yards or so to our left.

Half an hour afterward I shot another buck, at over a hundred and fifty yards, after much the same kind of experience. At this one I fired four times, hitting him with three bullets; three of the shots were taken when I could only see his horns and had to guess at the position of the body. This was a very big buck, with horns over twenty-nine inches long, but the saddle mark was yellow, with many whitish hairs, showing that he was about to assume the white saddle of advanced maturity. His stomach was full of the fine swamp grass.

These handsome antelopes come next to the situtunga as lovers of water and dwellers in the marshes. They are far more properly to be called "water-buck" than are the present proprietors of that name, which, like the ordinary kob, though liking to be near streams, spend most of their time on dry plains and hillsides. This saddle-marked antelope of the swamps has the hoofs very long and the whole foot flexible and spreading, so as to help it in passing over wet ground and soft mud; the pasterns behind are largely bare of hair. It seems to be much like the lechwi, a less handsome, but equally water-loving, antelope of southern Africa, which is put in the same genus with the water-buck and kob.

That afternoon Doctor Mearns killed with his Winchester

30–40, on the wing, one of the most interesting birds we obtained on our whole trip, the whale-billed stork. It was an old male and its gizzard was full of the remains of small fish. The whalebill is a large wader, blackish gray in color, slightly crested, with big feet and a huge, swollen bill; a queer-looking bird, with no near kinsfolk, and so interesting that nothing would have persuaded me to try to kill more than the four actually needed for the *public* (not private) museum to which our collections were going. It is of solitary habits and is found only in certain vast, lonely marshes of tropical Africa, where it is conspicuous by its extraordinary bill, dark coloration, and sluggishness of conduct, hunting sedately in the muddy shallows, or standing motionless for hours, surrounded by reed beds or by long reaches of quaking and treacherous ooze.

Next morning while at breakfast on the breezy deck we spied another herd of the saddle-marked lechwi, in the marsh alongside; and Kermit landed and killed one, after deep wading, up to his chin in some places, and much hard work in the rank grass. This buck was interesting when compared with the two I had shot. He was apparently a little older than either, but not aged; on the contrary, in his prime, and fat. He had the white saddle-like mark on the withers, and the white back of the neck, well developed. Yet he was smaller than either of mine, and the horns much smaller; indeed they were seven inches shorter than my longest ones. It looks as if, in some animals at least, the full size of body and horns were reached before the white saddle markings are acquired. The horns of these saddle-mark lechwis are, relatively to the body, far longer and finer than in other species of the genus; just as is the case with the big East African gazelle when compared with other gazelles.

That afternoon, near the mouth of the Rohr, which runs into the Bahr el Ghazal, I landed and shot a good buck, of the Vaughn's kob; which is perhaps merely a subspecies of the white-eared kob. It is a handsome animal, handsomer than its close kinsman, the common or Uganda kob; although much less so than its associate, the saddle-marked lechwi. Its hoofs are like those of the ordinary kobs and water-bucks, not in the least like those of the saddleback; so that although the does are colored alike, there is no chance of mistaking any lechwi doe for any true kob doe. We found these kobs in much drier ground than the saddlebacks, and therefore they were easier to get at. The one I shot was an old ram, accompanied by several ewes. We saw them from the boat, but they ran. Cuninghame and I, with Kongoni and Gouvimali, hunted for them in vain for a couple of hours. Then we met a savage, a very tall, lean Nuer. He was clad in fawn-skin, and carried two spears, one with a bright, sharp, broad-bladed head, the other narrow-headed with villainous barbs. His hair, much longer than that of a west coast negro, was tied back. As we came toward him he stood on one leg, with the other foot resting against it, and, raising his hand, with fingers extended, he motioned to us with what in civilized regions would be regarded as a gesture bidding us halt. But he meant it as a friendly greeting, and solemnly shook hands with all four of us, including the gun-bearers. By signs we made him understand that we were after game; so was he; and he led us to the little herd of kob. Kongoni, as usual, saw them before any one else. From an ant-hill I could make out the buck's horns and his white ears, which he was continually flapping at the biting flies that worried him; when he lowered his head I could see nothing. Finally, he looked fixedly at us; he was a hundred and fifty yards off and I had to shoot standing on the peak of the ant-heap, and aim through the grass, guessing where his hidden body might be; and I missed him. At the shot the does went off to the left, but he ran to the right, once or twice leaping high; and when he halted, at less than two hundred yards, although I could still only see his horns, I knew where his body was; and this time I killed him. We gave most of the meat to the Nuer. He was an utterly wild savage, and when Cuninghame suddenly lit a match he was so frightened that it was all we could do to keep him from bolting.

Kermit went on to try for a doe, but had bad luck, twice killing a spike-buck by mistake, and did not get back to the boat until long after dark.

The following day we were in the mouth of the Bahr el Ghazal. It ran sluggishly through immense marshes, which stretched back from the river for miles on either hand, broken here and there by flats of slightly higher land with thorn-trees. The whale-billed storks were fairly common, and were very conspicuous as they stood on the quaking surface of the marsh, supported by their long-toed feet. After several fruitless stalks and much following through the thick marsh-grass, sometimes up to our necks in water, I killed one with the Springfield at a distance of one hundred and thirty yards, and Kermit, after missing one standing, cut it down as it rose with his Winchester 30–40. These whalebills had in their gizzards not only small fish but quite a number of the green blades of the marsh-grass. The Arabs call them the "Father of the Shoe," and Europeans call them shoebills as well as whalebills. The Bahr el Ghazal was alive with water-fowl, saddlebill storks, sacred and purple ibis, many kinds of herons, cormorants, plover, and pretty tree-ducks which twittered instead of quacking. There were sweet-scented lotus water-lilies in the ponds. A party of waterbuck cows and calves let the steamer pass within fifty yards without running.

We went back to Lake No, where we met another steamer, with aboard it M. Solvé, a Belgian sportsman, a very successful hunter, whom we had already met at Lado; with him were his wife, his sister, and his brother-in-law, both of the last being as ardent in the chase, especially of dangerous game, as he was. His party had killed two whalebills, one for the British Museum and one for the Congo Museum. They were a male and female who were near their nest, which contained two downy young; these were on M. Solvé's boat, where we saw them. The nest was right on the marsh water; the birds had bent the long blades of marsh-grass into an interlacing foundation, and on this had piled grass which they had cut with their beaks. These beaks can give a formidable bite, by the way, as one of our sailors found to his cost when he rashly tried to pick up a wounded bird.

I was anxious to get a ewe of the saddleback lechwi for the museum, and landed in the late afternoon, on seeing a herd. The swamp was so deep that it took an hour's very hard and fatiguing wading, forcing ourselves through the rank grass up to our shoulders in water before we got near them. The herd numbered about forty individuals; their broad trail showed where they had come through the swamp, and even through a papyrus bed; but we found them grazing on merely moist ground, where there were ant-hills in the long grass. As I crept up they saw me and greeted me with a chorus of croaking grunts; they are a very noisy buck. I shot a ewe, and away rushed the herd through the long grass, making a noise which could have been heard nearly a mile off, and splashing and bounding through the shallow lagoons; they halted, and again began grunting; and then off they rushed once more. The doe's stomach was filled with tender marsh-grass. Meanwhile, Kermit killed, on drier ground, a youngish male of the white-eared kob.

Next morning we were up at the Bahr el Zeraf. At ten we sighted from the boat several herds of white-eared kob, and Kermit and I went in different directions after them, getting four. The old rams were very handsome animals with coats of a deep rich brown that was almost black, and sharply contrasted black-and-white markings on their faces; but it was interesting to see that many of the younger rams, not yet in the fully adult pelage, had horns as long as those of their elders. The young rams and ewes were a light reddish yellow, being in color much like the ewes of the saddleback lechwi; and there was the usual disproportion in size between the sexes. With each flock of ewes and young rams there was ordinarily one old black ram; and some of the old rams went by themselves. The ground was so open that all my shots had to be taken at long range. In habits they differed from the saddleback lechwis, for they were found on dry land, often where the grass was quite short, and went freely among the thorn-trees; they cared for the neighborhood of water merely as ordinary water-buck or kob care for it.

Here we met another boat, with aboard it Sir William Garstin, one of the men who have made Egypt and the Soudan what they are to-day, and who have thereby rendered an incalculable service not only to England but to civilization.

We had now finished our hunting, save that once or twice we landed to shoot a buck or some birds for the table. It was amusing to see how sharply the birds discriminated between the birds of prey which they feared and those which they regarded as harmless. We saw a flock of guinea-fowl strolling unconcernedly about at the foot of a tree in which a fish-eagle was perched; and one evening Doctor Mearns saw some guinea-fowl go to roost in a bush in which two kites had already settled themselves for the night, the kites and the guineas perching amiably side by side.

We stopped at the mouth of the Sobat to visit the American mission, and were most warmly and hospitably received by the missionaries, and were genuinely impressed by the faithful work they were doing, under such great difficulties and with such cheerfulness and courage. The medical mission was especially interesting. It formed an important part of the mission work; and not only were the natives round about treated, but those from far away also came in numbers. At the time of our visit there were about thirty patients, taking courses of treatment, who had come from distances varying from twenty-five miles to a hundred and fifty.

We steamed steadily down the Nile. Where the great river bent to the east we would sit in the shade on the forward deck during the late afternoon and look down the long glistening water street in front of us, with its fringe of reed bed and marshy grass-land and papyrus swamp, and the slightly higher dry land on which grew acacias and scattered palms. Along the river-banks and inland were villages of Shilluks and other tribes, mostly cattle-owners; some showing slight traces of improvement, others utter savages, tall, naked men, bearing bows and arrows.

Our Egyptian and Nubian crew recalled to my mind the crew of the dahabiyeh on which as a boy I had gone up the Egyptian Nile thirty-seven years before; especially when some piece of work was being done by the crew as they chanted in grunting chorus "Ya allah, ul allah." As we went down the Nile we kept seeing more and more of the birds which I remembered, one species after another appearing; familiar cow-herons, crocodile plover, noisy spurwing plover, black-and-white kingfishers, hoopoos, green bee-eaters, black-and-white chats, desert larks, and trumpeter bullfinches.

At night we sat on deck and watched the stars and the dark, lonely river. The swimming crocodiles and plunging hippos made whirls and wakes of feeble light that glimmered for a moment against the black water. The unseen birds of the marsh and the night called to one another in strange voices. Often there were grass fires, burning, leaping lines of red, the lurid glare in the sky above them making even more sombre the surrounding gloom.

As we steamed northward down the long stretch of the Nile which ends at Khartoum, the wind blew in our faces, day after day, hard and steadily. Narrow reed beds bordered the shore; there were grass flats and groves of acacias and palms, and farther down reaches of sandy desert. The health of our companions who had been suffering from fever and dysentery gradually improved; but the case of champagne, which we had first opened at Gondokoro, was of real service, for two members of the party were at times so sick that their situation was critical.

We reached Khartoum on the afternoon of March 14, 1910, and Kermit and I parted from our comrades of the trip with real regret; during the year we spent together there had not been a jar, and my respect and liking for them had grown steadily. Moreover, it was a sad parting from our faithful black followers, whom we knew we should never see again. It had been an interesting and a happy year; though I was very glad to be once more with those who were dear to me, and to turn my face toward my own home and my own people.

Kermit's and my health throughout the trip had been excellent. He had been laid up for three days all told, and I for five. Kermit's three days were due, two to tick fever on the Kapiti Plains, one probably to the sun. Mine were all due to fever; but I think my fever had nothing to do with Africa at all, and was simply a recurrence of the fever I caught in the Santiago campaign, and which ever since has come on at long and irregular intervals for a day or two at a time. The couple of attacks I had in Africa were very slight; by no means as severe as one I had while bear-hunting early one spring in the Rocky Mountains. One of these attacks came on under rather funny circumstances. It was at Lake Naivasha on the day I killed the hippo which charged the boat. We were in the steam-launch and I began to feel badly, and knew I was in for a bout of fever. Just then we spied the hippo and went after it in the rowboat. I was anxious to hold back the attack until I got the hippo, as when shaking with a chill it is of course very difficult to take aim. I just succeeded, the excitement keeping me steady; and as soon as the hippo was dead I curled up in the boat and had my chill in peace and comfort.

There are differences of opinion as to whether any spirituous liquors should be drunk in the tropics. Personally I think that the less one has to do with them the better. Not liking whiskey, I took a bottle of brandy for emergencies. Very early in the trip I decided that even when feverish or exhausted by a hard day's tramp, hot tea did me more good than brandy, and I handed the bottle over to Cuninghame. At Khartoum he produced it and asked what he should do with it, and I told him to put it in the steamer's stores; he did so, after finding out the amount that had been drunk, and informed me that I had taken just six ounces in eleven months.

LIST OF GAME SHOT WITH THE RIFLE DURING THE TRIP

	BY T. R.	BY K. R.
Lion	9	8
Leopard	—	3
Cheetah	—	7
Hyena	5	4
Elephant	8	3
Square-mouthed rhinoceros	5	4
Hook-lipped rhinoceros	8	3
Hippopotamus	7	1
Wart-hog	8	4
Common zebra	15	4
Big or Grevy's zebra	5	5
Giraffe	7	2
Buffalo	6	4
Giant eland	1	2
Common eland	5	2
Bongo	—	2
Kudu	—	2
Situtunga	—	1
Bushbuck		
East African	2	4
Uganda harnessed	1	2
Nile harnessed	3	3
Sable	—	3
Roan	4	5
Oryx	10	3
Wildebeest	5	2
Neumann's hartbeest	—	3
Coke's hartbeest	10	3
Big hartbeest		
Jackson's	14	7
Uganda	1	3
Nilotic	8	4
Topi	12	4
Common water-buck	5	3
Singsing water-buck	6	6
Common kob	10	6
Vaughn's kob	1	2

	BY T. R.		BY K. R.	
White-eared kob	3		2	
Saddle-backed lechwi (Mrs. Gray's)	3		1	
Bohor reedbuck	10		4	
Chanler's buck	3		4	
Impala	7		5	
Big gazelle				
Grant's	5		3	
Roberts's	4		6	
Notata	8		1	
Thomson's gazelle	11		9	
Gerenuk	3		2	
Klipspringer	1		3	
Oribi	18		8	
Duiker	3		2	
Steinbuck	4		2	
Dikdik	1		1	
Baboon	—		3	
Red ground-monkey	1		1	
Green monkey	—		1	
Black-and-white monkey	5		4	
Serval	—		1	
Jackal	—		1	
Aardwolf	—		1	
Ratel	—		1	
Porcupine	—		2	
Ostrich	2		—	
Great bustard	4	(1 on wing)	3	(1 on wing)
Lesser bustard	1		1	
Kavirondo crane	2	(on wing)	—	
Flamingo	—		4	
Whale-headed stork	1		1	(on wing)
Marabou	1		1	
Saddle-billed stork	1	(on wing)	—	
Ibis stork	2	(1 on wing)	—	
Pelican	1		—	
Guinea-fowl	5		5	
Francolin	1		2	
Fish-eagle	—		1	
Vulture	—		2	
Crocodile	1		3	
Monitor	—		1	
Python	3		1	
	296		216	

Grand total 512

In addition we killed, with the Fox shotgun, Egyptian geese, yellow-billed mallards, francolins, spur-fowl, and sand-grouse for the pot, and certain other birds for specimens.

Kermit and I kept about a dozen trophies for ourselves; otherwise we shot nothing that was not used either as a museum specimen or for meat—usually for both purposes. We were in hunting-grounds practically as good as any that have ever existed; but we did not kill a tenth, nor a hundredth, part of what we might have killed had we been willing. The mere size of the bag indicates little as to a man's prowess as a hunter, and almost nothing as to the interest or value of his achievement.

APPENDIXES

APPENDIX A

I WISH to thank Sir Edward Grey and Lord Crewe for the numerous courtesies extended to me by the British officials throughout the British possessions in Africa; and M. Renkin for the equal courtesy shown me by the Belgian officials in the Lado.

The scientific part of the expedition could not have been undertaken save for the generous assistance of Mr. Andrew Carnegie, Mr. Oscar Straus, Mr. Leigh Hunt, and certain others, to all of whom lovers of natural history are therefore deeply indebted.

I owe more than I can express to the thoughtful and unwearied consideration of Mr. F. C. Selous and Mr. E. N. Buxton, through whom my excellent outfit was obtained.

Mr. R. J. Cuninghame, assisted in East Africa by Mr Leslie J. Tarlton, managed the expedition in the field; and no two better men for our purposes could have been found anywhere. I doubt if Mr. Cuninghame's equal in handling such an expedition as ours exists; I know no one else who combines as he does the qualities which make a first-class explorer, guide, hunter, field naturalist and safari manager. Messrs. Newland and Tarlton, of Nairobi, did the actual work of providing and arranging for our whole journey in the most satisfactory manner.

APPENDIX B

THE following is a partial list of the small mammals obtained on the trip, except certain bats, shrews, and rodents which it is not possible to identify in the field; even some of these identifications are not final.

LIST OF SMALL MAMMALS

UNGULATA—HOOFED MAMMALS

Procavia mackinderi................Alpine Hyrax
Procavia brucei maculata.............Athi Rock-hyrax
Procavia (Dendrohyrax) bettoni.....Kikuyu Tree-hyrax
Procavia (Dendrohyrax) crawshayi..Alpine Tree-hyrax

GLIRES—RODENTS

Heliosciurus keniæ...................Kenia Forest Squirrel
Paraxerus bæhmi emini..............Uganda Striped Squirrel
Paraxerus jacksoni..................Jackson Forest Squirrel
Paraxerus jacksoni capitis..........Nairobi Forest Squirrel
Euxerus microdon fulvior..........Kenia Ground-squirrel
Graphiurus raptor...................Kenia Dormouse
Graphiurus parvus...................Pigmy Dormouse
Lophiomys testudo...................Nandi Maned Rat
Tatera mombasæ.....................Mombasa Gerbille
Tatera pothæ.. ....Highland Gerbille
Tatera fallax.......................Uganda Gerbille
Tatera varia........................Sotik Gerbille
Tatera emini................... ..Nile Gerbille
Tatera nigrita......................Dusky Gerbille
Dipodillus harwoodi.................Pigmy Gerbille
Otomys irroratus orestes............Alpine Velt Rat
Otomys irroratus tropicalis..........Masai Velt Rat
Dendromus nigrifrons...............Black-fronted Tree-mouse
Dendromus insignis...... ....Greater Tree-mouse
Dendromus whytei pallescens........Athi Tree-mouse
Steatomys athi......................East African Fat Mouse
Lophuromys ansorgei...............Uganda Harsh-furred Mouse

Lophuromys aquilus................	Masai Harsh-furred Mouse
Mus (Leggada) bellus..............	East African Pigmy Mouse
Mus (Leggada) gratus.............	Uganda Pigmy Mouse
Mus (Leggada) sorellus...........	Elgon Pigmy Mouse
Mus (Leggada) triton murillus......	Sooty Pigmy Mouse
Mus (Leggada) triton naivashæ.....	Naivasha Pigmy Mouse
Epimys hindei....................	Masai Bush-rat
Epimys endorobæ.................	Small-footed Forest Mouse
Epimys jacksoni............... ...	Uganda Forest Mouse
Epimys peromyscus................	Large-footed Forest Mouse
Epimys hildebranti................	Taita Multimammate Mouse
Epimys ugandæ...................	Uganda Multimam'te Mouse
Epimys panya....................	Masai Multimammate Mouse
Epimys nieventris ulæ.............	Athi Rock-mouse
Zelotomys hildegardæ.............	Broad-headed Bush-mouse
Thamnomys surdaster polionops......	Athi Tree-rat
Thamnomys loringi................	Masked Tree-rat
Œnomys hypoxanthus bacchante......	Rusty-nosed Rat
Dasymus helukus..................	East African Swamp Rat
Acomys wilsoni...................	East African Spiny Mouse
Arvicanthis abyssinicus nairobæ.....	Athi Grass Rat
Arvicanthis abyssinicus rubescens....	Uganda Grass Rat
Arvicanthis pulchellus massaicus.....	Spotted Grass Rat
Arvicanthis barbarus albolineatus.....	Striped Grass Rat
Arvicanthis pumilio diminutus.......	Pigmy Grass Rat
Arvicanthis dorsalis maculosus.......	Single-striped Grass Rat
Pelomys roosevelti................	Iridescent Creek Rat
Saccostomus umbriventer...........	Sotik Pouched Rat
Saccostomus mearnsi..............	Swahili Pouched Rat
Tachyoryctes annectens............	Rift Valley Mole-rat
Tachyoryctes splendens ibeanus......	Nairobi Mole-rat
Tachyoryctes rex.................	Alpine Mole-rat
Myoscalops kapiti................	Masai Blesmole
Pedetes surdaster.................	East African Springhaas
Hystrix galeata..................	East African Porcupine
Lepus victoriæ...................	East African Hare

FERÆ—CARNIVORA

Hyæna striata schillingsi...........	Masai Striped Hyena
Hyæna crocuta germinans..........	East African Spotted Hyena
Proteles cristatus septentrionalis.....	Somali Aardwolf
Genetta bettoni..................	East African Genet
Crossarchus fasciatus macrurus......	Uganda Banded Mongoose
Mungos sanguienus ibeæ...........	Kikuyu Lesser Mongoose
Mungos albicaudus ibeanus.........	Masai White-tailed Mongoose
Canis mesomelas.................	Black-backed Jackal
Canis variegatus.................	Silver-backed Jackal

Lycaon pictus lupinus..............East African Hunting-dog
Otocyon virgatus...................Masai Great-eared Fox
Mellivora ratel.....................Cape Honey Badger

INSECTIVORA—INSECTIVORES

Nasilio brachyrhynchus delamerei....Athi Lesser Elephant-shrew
Elephantulus pulcher................East African Elephant-shrew
Erinaceus albiventris................White-bellied Hedgehog
Crocidura flavescens myansæ........Giant Shrew
Crocidura alchemillæ................Alpine Shrew
Crocidura fumosa...................Dusky Shrew
Crocidura argentata fisheri..........Velt Shrew
Crocidura bicolor elgonius...........Elgon Pigmy Shrew
Crocidura allex.....................Rift Valley Pigmy Shrew
Surdisorex noræ....................Short-tailed Shrew

CHIROPTERA—BATS

Scotophilus nigrita colias............Kikuyu Green Bat
Pipistrellus kuhlii fuscatus..........Naivasha Pigmy Bat
Nyctinomus hindei..................Free-tailed Bat
Lavia frons........................East African Great-eared Bat
Lavia frons affinis..................Nile Great-eared Bat
Petalia thebaica....................Nile Wrinkle-nosed Bat
Rhinolophus hildebranti eloqueus.....Elgon Horseshoe Bat
Hipposiderus caffer centralis.........Uganda Leaf-nosed Bat

PRIMATES—MONKEYS

Galago (Ototemur) lasiotis..........Mombasa Lemur
Papio ibeanus.....................East African Baboon
Cercocebus albigena johnstoni.......Uganda Mangabey
Erythrocebus formosus..............Uganda Patas Monkey
Cercopithecus ascanius schmidti......Uganda White-nosed Monkey
Cercopithecus pygerythrus johnstoni.Masai Green Monkey
Cercopithecus kolbi.................Kikuyu Forest Green Monkey
Cercopithecus kolbi hindei...........Kenia Forest Green Monkey
Colobus abyssinicus caudatus........White-tailed Colobus Monkey
Colobus abyssinicus matschiei.......Uganda Colobus Monkey
Colobus palliatus cottoni............Nile Colobus Monkey

LIST OF LARGE MAMMALS

UNGULATA—HOOFED MAMMALS

Diceros simus cottoni..............Nile Square-nosed Rhinoceros
Diceros bicornis...................Black Rhinoceros
Equus burchelli granti..............Northern Burchell Zebra

Equus grevyi......................Grevy Zebra
Hippopotamus amphibius............Nile Hippopotamus
*Potamochærus chæropotamus dæmonis.*East African Bush Pig
Hylochærus meinertzhageni..........East African Forest Hog
*Phacochærus æthiopicus massaicus...*East African Wart-hog
Bos caffer radcliffei.................East African Buffalo
Bos æquinoctialis...................Abyssinian Buffalo
Taurotragus oryx livingstonii.......East African Eland
Taurotragus gigas..................Giant Eland
Boocercus isaaci....................East African Bongo
Strepsiceros strepsiceros............Greater Koodoo
Tragelaphus scriptus heywoodi.......Aberdare Bushbuck
Tragelaphus scriptus dama..........Kavirondo Bushbuck
Tragelaphus scriptus bor............Nile Bushbuck
Limnotragus spekii..................Uganda Situtunga
Ozanna roosevelti..................Roosevelt Sable Antelope
Ozanna equinus langheldi..........East African Roan Antelope
Ozanna equinus bakeri..............Nile Roan Antelope
Oryx beisa annectens...............East African Beisa
Gazella granti......................Grant Gazelle
Gazella granti robertsi..............Nyanza Grant Gazelle
Gazella granti notata................Boran Grant Gazelle
Gazella thomsoni...................Thomson Gazelle
Lithocranius walleri.................Gerenuk Gazelle
Æpyceros melampus suara..........Impala
Redunca fulvorufula chanleri.......East African Rock Reedbuck
Redunca redunca wardi.............Highland Bohor Reedbuck
Redunca redunca donaldsoni.........Uganda Bohor Reedbuck
Kobus kob thomasi..................Kavirondo Kob
Kobus vaughani....................Rufous White-eared Kob
Kobus leucotis......................White-eared Kob
Kobus defassa ugandæ..............Uganda Defassa Water-buck
Kobus defassa harnieri..............White Nile Defassa Water-buck
Kobus ellipsiprymnus................East African Water-buck
Kobus maria.......................White-withered Water-buck
Cephalophus abyssinicus hindei.......Masailand Duikerbok
Cephalophus abyssinicus nyansæ.....Kavirondo Duikerbok
Cephalophus ignifer.................Rufous Forest Duikerbok
Nototragus neumanni................East African Steinbok
Ourebia montana...................Abyssinian Oribi
Ourebia cottoni....................Guas Ngishu Oribi
Rhynchotragus kirki hindei..........Masai Dikdik
Oreotragus schillingsi...............East African Klipspringer
Connochætes albojubatus............White-bearded Wildebeest
Damaliscus corrigum jimela.........East African Topi
Bubalis jacksoni....................Jackson Hartbeest
Bubalis jacksoni insignis............Uganda Hartbeest

Bubalis cokei.......................Kongoni Hartbeest
Bubalis neumanni...................Neumann Hartbeest
Bubalis lelwel niediecki.............White Nile Hartbeest
Giraffa reticulata..................Somali Giraffe
Giraffa camelopardalis tippelskirchi...Masailand Giraffe
Giraffa camelopardalis rothschildi....Five-horned Giraffe
Elephas africanus peeli..............British E. African Elephant

FERÆ—CARNIVORA

Felis leo massaica..................East African Lion
Felis pardus suahelica..............East African Leopard
Felis capensis hindei...............East African Serval-cat
Cynælurus jubatus guttatus..........African Cheetah

The following is a partial list of those species obtained by Heller concerning which he (and occasionally I) could make observations as to their life histories. In the comparisons with or allusions to our American species there is, I need hardly say, no implication of kinship; the differences are generally fundamental, and I speak of the American animals only for the purpose of securing a familiar standard of comparison. The central African fauna is of course much more nearly allied to that of Europe than to that of North America, and were I familiar with small European mammals, I should use them, rather than the American, for purposes of illustration.

Heliosciurus keniæ (Kenia Forest Squirrel). Mount Kenia, B. E. A. Heller shot one in a tree in the heavy forest by our first elephant camp. In size and actions like our gray squirrel. Shy.

Paraxerus jacksoni. Shot at same camp; common at Nairobi and Kijabe, B. E. A. A little smaller than our red squirrel; much less noisy and less vivacious in action. Tamer than the larger squirrel, but much shyer than our red squirrel or chickaree. Kept among the bushes and lower limbs of the trees. Local in distribution; found in pairs or small families.

Graphiurus parvus (Pigmy Dormouse). Everywhere in B. E. A. in the forest; arboreal, often descending to the ground at night, for they are strictly nocturnal. Found in the woods fringing the rivers in the Sotik and on the Athi Plains, but most common in the juniper forests of the higher levels. Spend the daytime in crevices and hollows in the big trees. Build round, ball-like nests of bark fibre and woolly or cottony vegetable fibre. One of them placed in a hollow, four inches across, in a stump, the entrance being five feet above the ground. Caught in traps baited with walnuts or peanuts.

Tatera pothæ Heller (n. s.) (Athi Gerbille). Common on the Athi Plains, in open ground at the foot of the hills. Live in short grass, not bush. Nocturnal. Live in burrows, each burrow often possessing several entrances, and sometimes several burrows, all inhabited by same animal, not communicating.

Tatera varia Heller (n. s.) (Sotik Gerbille). A large form, seemingly new. Lives in the open plains, among the grass; not among bushes, nor at foot of hills. Lives in burrows, one animal apparently having several, each burrow with a little mound at the entrance. Nocturnal. In aspect and habits bears much resemblance to our totally different kangaroo-rats.

Dipodillus harwoodi (Naivasha Pigmy Gerbille). Common around Naivasha, also in Sotik. A small form, quarter the size of the above; about as big as a house-mouse. Same habits as above, but apparently only one burrow to each animal; much more plentiful. The burrows in the Sotik were in hard ground and went straight down. Round Naivasha the ground was soft and dry, and most of the burrows entered it diagonally.

Otomys irroratus tropicalis (Velt Rat). Generally throughout B. E. A. but always in moist places, never on dry plains. Abundant on top of Aberdares, and ten thousand feet up on slopes of Kenia. Always in open grass. Make very definite trails which they cut with their teeth through the grass. Feed on the grass which they cut into lengths just as our meadow-mice—mirotus—do. Largely diurnal, but also run about at night. The gravid females examined had in each of them two embryos only. Live in burrows, in which they place nests of fine grass six inches in diameter.

Dendromus nigrifrons (Black-fronted Tree-mouse). On Athi Plains and on the Sotik. Size of our harvest-mouse. Do not go into forest, but dwell in bush country and thin timber along streams. Nocturnal; not abundant. Live in covered nests in bushes; nests made of long wiry grass, not lined, and very small, less than three inches in diameter. They are globular, and entered by a hole in one side, as with our marsh-wrens. Only one mouse to a nest, as far as we saw; Heller caught two in their nests. The nests were in thorn-bushes only about a foot and a half from the ground; once or twice these mice were found in what were apparently abandoned weaver-birds' nests. If frightened, one would drop out of its nest to the ground and run off; but if Heller waited quietly for ten minutes the mouse would come back, climb up the twigs of the bush, and re-enter the nest. It never stayed away long, seeming to need the nest for protection.

Dendromus insignis. Although belonging to the genus of tree-mice this large dendromys lives on the ground, seemingly builds no nest, and is most often found in the runways of the *Otomys.*

Lophuromys aquilus (Harsh-furred Mouse). Common in Rift Valley, on the top of the Aberdares, and in the Kenia forest. Go up to timber-line, but are not found in the deep forest, save above the edges of the stream. Very fond of brush. Do not go out on the grassy plains. Usually, but not strictly, nocturnal; and in the cold, foggy uplands, as on the Aberdares, become diurnal.

(*Leggada*) *Mus gratus* (Pigmy Harvest-mouse). As small as our smallest harvest-mouse. A grass mouse, usually entirely away from bushes and trees. Usually taken in the runways of the larger species. Occasionally come into tents. Nocturnal. Found generally throughout East Africa, but nowhere as abundant as many other species.

Epimys hindei (Masai Bush-rat). Trapped on the Kapiti and Athi Plains. About the size of the Southern wood-rat of California; almost the size of the wood-rat of the Eastern States. Is a ground-loving species, fond of bushes; in habits like the Mus panya; but less widely distributed, and entering houses less freely.

Epimys peromyscus Heller (n. s.) (African White-footed Mouse). Externally strikingly like our white-footed mouse. Found in thick forest, along the edges of the Rift Valley and on Mount Kenia. Near our elephant camp Heller failed to trap any white-footed mice in the open glades, even when the glades were of small size, but caught them easily if the traps were set only a few yards within the dense forest. Evidently very abundant in the forest, but not venturing at all into the open. Strictly nocturnal. Dwell under logs and in decayed places around stumps, and the trunks of big trees.

Epimys panya (East African House-mouse). Common in B. E. A., coming into the houses, and acting like a house-mouse, but twice the size. Frequently came into our camps, entering the tents. Very common on the edges of the forest and in brush country and long grass, and among the shambas; not in the deep forests, except along streams, and not in the bare open plains. Nocturnal. Found in the runways of *Otomys* and *Arvicanthis.* Does not seem to be a grass-feeding species, like *Otomys;* eats grain, beans, etc.

Epimys nieventris ulæ (Athi Rock-mouse). On the Athi Plains, in the Sotik, around Naivasha, and in the Rift Valley. Body only slightly larger than that of a house-mouse, but tail at least a third longer than the head and body together. Yellowish brown above and whitish beneath. Never found except among rocks; we always found it where there were cliffs or on stony koppies.

Lives in crevices in the rocks and along the ledges of the cliffs. Nocturnal. Caught in traps with nuts.

Zelotomys hildegardæ (Broad-headed Bush-mouse). Looks like a small-eared, broad-headed house-mouse. Rather common on Athi Plains, in same localities with Uganda mouse, but rare, and seldom enters houses.

Thamnomys surdaster polionops (Long-tailed Tree-mouse). Arboreal; more like a mouse than a rat. On the Athi Plains, in the Sotik and Rift Valley. Not found in heavy forest, but in the open acacia woods and in bushy country. Apparently lives much of the time on the ground, and builds no nests in the trees, but runs up and down them and among their branches freely. Nocturnal.

Thamnomys loringi Heller (n. s.) (Masked Tree-rat). In the Rift Valley; common around Naivasha. Has a black ring around each eye, the color spreading over the nose like a mask. Arboreal and nocturnal. Much the habits of our neotoma, but do not build large nests. Build nests about six inches in diameter, made of sticks, placed in the branches of the thorn-trees; also in burrows near the bottom of the trunks; runways lead from the trees containing the nests to the burrows. Trapped on the ground and in traps set in notches of the trees.

Oenomys hypoxanthus bacchante (Rusty-nosed Rat). Found in same country as above, and with similar habits, but somewhat less arboreal. A handsome species.

Dasymus helukus Heller (n. s.) (Swamp Rat). In appearance much like the Alexandrian or roof rat, but with longer hair and shorter, much less conspicuous ears. Found all over the Athi Plains where there was brush, especially along stream-beds. Nocturnal.

Arvicanthis abyssinicus nairobæ (Athi Grass Rat). The commonest mouse in B. E. A. on the plains. Outnumbers any other species. Found everywhere in grass and brush, but not in deep forest. Often lives in shallow burrows round the bases of thorn-trees, from which its well-marked runways radiate into the grass. Strictly diurnal. Often seen running about in bright sunlight. Never found in traps at night. A striped mouse that has lost its stripes, vestiges of which are occasionally found in the young.

Arvicanthis pulchellus massaicus (Nairobi Striped Mouse). Diurnal. Common on the Athi Plains and on the Sotik and in Rift Valley. Around Neri we often saw them running about through the shambas. Live in brush and cultivated fields. In pattern of coloration much like our thirteen-striped gopher.

Arvicanthis pumilio diminutus (Naivasha Striped Rat). Common in Rift Valley, and on the Aberdares and around Kenia. Sometimes occurs in company with Nairobi mouse, but less widely distributed; much more abundant where found, and ascends to much higher altitudes.

Pelomys rooselvelti Heller (n. s.). About the size of our cotton-rat, and with much the same build. Coarse, bristly hair; the dorsal coloration is golden yellow overlaid by long hairs with an olive iridescence; the under parts are silky white. It is a meadow-mouse found at high altitudes, seven to nine thousand feet high; usually lives close to streams in heavy grass, through which it makes runways. Not common.

Saccostomus umbriventer (Sotik Pouched Rat). Heller trapped several on the Sotik at the base of the southernmost range of mountains we reached. Found in the longish grass along a dry creek-bed. Trapped in their rather indistinct runways. The pockets or pouches are internal; not external as in our pocket-mice.

Tachyoryctes splendens ibeanus (Nairobi Mole-rat). A mole-rat of B. E. A. with general habits of above, but avoiding rocky places, and not generally found many miles out on the plains away from the forest. Rarely found in the bamboos—in spite of its name.

Myoscalops kapiti Heller (n. s.) (Kapiti Blesmole). On the Kapiti and Athi Plains and in the Sotik. Smaller than German East African form and no white occipital spot. A cinnamon wash on its silvery fur. Burrows like our pocket-gophers, and has same squat look and general habits. Lives in rocky ground, where bamboo-rat does not penetrate. It does not run just below the surface of the soil, as the pocket-gopher does in winter. The blesmole's burrows are about a foot below the surface. Eats roots.

Pedetes surdaster (Springhaas). (See body of book.) One young at birth. A colony of four to eight open burrows, all inhabited by a single animal.

Hystrix galeata. (See body of book.) Heller found in stomach the remains of a root or tuber and seeds like those of the night-shade.

Lepus victoriæ. Generally distributed on plains; much the habits and look of a small jack-rabbit. Does not burrow.

Elephantulus pulcher (Elephant-shrew). Fairly common throughout B. E. A. in bush and on hills, not in deep forests or on bare plains. Often out at dusk, but generally nocturnal. A gravid female contained a single embryo. One in a trap had its mouth full of partly masticated brown ants. A gentle thing, without the fierceness of the true shrews. Trapped in the runways of arvicanthis.

Erinaceus albiventris (Hedgehog). Fairly common in the Sotik. In certain places under trees Heller found accumulations of their spiny skins, as if some bird of prey had been feeding on them.

Crocidura fisheri. The common shrew of the Athi Plains and the Sotik in the Rift Valley. Largely diurnal. Males quite yellowish, females smoky brown. Generally trapped in runways of arvicanthis. Pregnant females contained three to five embryos, usually four. Not found in heavy forest or swamp.

Crocidura fumosa (Dusky Shrew). A darker form found in the rush swamps and sedgy places of the same region. Number of young usually three. Diurnal. Occasional in forests.

Crocidura alchemillæ Heller (n. s.). Aberdare shrew; a diurnal form, occurring above timber-line on the Aberdare; perhaps identical with the foregoing.*

Crocidura allex. A pigmy shrew, taken at Naivasha.

Crocidura nyansæ. Very big for a shrew. Chiefly in the high country, near watercourses; found round the edge of the forest, at Kenia and Kijabe. A fierce, carnivorous creature, preying on small rodents as well as insects; habitually ate mice, rats, or shrews which it found in the traps, and would then come back and itself be readily trapped.

Surdisorex noræ. A shrew in shape not unlike our mole-shrew. On the high, cold, wet Aberdare plateau. Diurnal.

Scotophilus nigrita colias. Common at Nairobi; flying among the tree-tops in the evenings. Greenish back, with metallic glint; belly sulphur. Has the same flight as our big brown bat— vespertilio fuscus.

Pipistrellus kuhlii fuscatus. Common at Naivasha and Nairobi. Very closely kin to our Myotis, or little brown bat, with same habits. Fly high in the air after dusk and are easily shot. We never found its day roosts.

Nyctinomus hindei (Free-tailed Bat). At Naivasha. Very swift flight, almost like a swallow's, fairly high in the air. Live in colonies; one such in a house at Naivasha. On the Athi Plains they were found in daytime hanging up behind the loose bark of the big yellow-trunked acacias.

Lavia frons (Great-eared Bat). Bluish body and yellowish wings; very long ears. Almost diurnal, flies well by day; hangs from

---

* *Crocidura alchemillæ,* new species (Heller). Type from the summit of the Aberdare Range; altitude, 10,500 feet; British East Africa; adult male, number 163,087, U. S. Nat. Mus.; collected by Edmund Heller, October 17, 1909; original number, 1177.

Allied to *fumosa* of Mount Kenia, but coloration much darker, everywhere clove brown, the underparts but slightly lighter in shade; feet somewhat lighter sepia brown but much darker than in *fumosa;* hair at base slaty black. Hair long and heavy, on back 6 to 7 mm. long; considerably longer than in *fumosa.* Musk-glands on sides of body clothed with short brownish hairs, the glands producing an oily odor very similar to that of a petrel. Skull somewhat smaller than *fumosa* with relatively smaller teeth.

Measurements: Head and body, 90; tail, 55; hind foot, 15.3. Skull: Condyloincisive length, 21; mastoid breadth, 9.7; upper tooth row (alveoli), 8.3.

This species is an inhabitant of the dense beds of *Alchemilla* which clothe the alpine moorland of the Aberdare Range.

the thorn-tree branches, in the sunlight, and flies as soon as it sees a man approaching. One young, which remains attached to the mother until it is more than half her size.

Petalia thebaica (Large-eared Nycterine Bat). Caves in the Rift Valley; also in the Sotik, spending the day in the tops of the limestone wells or caverns which contained water. Both sexes occurred together in company with a bat of another genus—Rhinolophus. Fly very close to the ground, only two or three feet above it, and usually among trees and brush and not in the open, so that it is almost impossible to shoot them.

Rhinolophus. Found at the Limestone Springs in the Sotik, and in great numbers in a cave at Naivasha, no other bat being found in the cave. Same general habits as the nycteris. Specimens flew among our tents in the evening.

Papio ibeanus. The baboon is common all over the plains, in troops. It digs up lily bulbs, and industriously turns over stones for grubs and insects. Very curious, intelligent, and bestial.

Cercopithecus kolbi. Found in company with the Colobus in heavy forest along the Kikuyu escarpment. The subspecies *Hindei* is found in Kenia.

Cercopithecus pygerythrus johnstoni (Green Monkey). In the yellow thorns of the Sotik and Rift Valley, and along the northern Guaso Nyero. Leaves and acacia pods in their stomachs. Live in troops of from ten to twenty individuals. Exceedingly active and agile. Often sit motionless on the very tops of the trees, when they cannot be seen from below. Run well on the ground.

Colobus caudatus (Black-and-white Monkey). Heavy mountain forests, Kijabe and Kenia, and on the Aberdares. Only foliage in the stomachs of those shot. Goes in small troops, each seemingly containing both males and females; not as agile as the other monkeys, and less wary. The natives prize their skins.

On the Guas Ngishu the small mammals were in general identical with those of the Aberdares and Mount Kenia.

In Uganda Heller shot an old male, Cercopithecus ascanius schmidti, a red-backed, red-tailed, white-nosed monkey; it was alone in a small grove of trees surrounded by elephant-grass. In the same grove he shot a squirrel, Paraxerus, very different from the Kenia species. In Uganda there were fewer species of small mammals than in East Africa, in spite of the abundance of vegetation and water.

In the Lado we found rats, mice, and shrews abundant, but the number of species limited, and for the most part representing wide-spread types. Some of the bats were different from any yet obtained; the same may be true of the shrews. The small carnivora, and hyenas also, were very scarce.

North of Nimule Kermit shot another *Funisciurus,* while it was climbing a bamboo.

At Gondokoro there were many bats in the houses chiefly *Nyctinomus,* the swift-flying, high-flying, free-tailed bats, with a few leaf-nosed bats, and yellow bats.

I wish field naturalists would observe the relation of zebras and wild dogs. Our observations were too limited to be decisive; but it seemed to us that zebras did not share the fear by the other game for the dogs. I saw a zebra, in a herd, run toward some wild dogs, with its mouth open and ears back; and they got out of the way, although seemingly not much frightened. Loring saw a solitary zebra seemingly unmoved by the close neighborhood of some wild dogs.

Once, on the Nile, while Loring and I were watching a monitor stealing crocodiles' eggs, we noticed a hippo in midstream. It was about ten in the morning. The hippo appeared regularly, at two or three minute intervals, always in the same place, breathed, and immediately sank. This continued for an hour. We could not make out what he was doing. It seemed unlikely that he could be feeding; and the current was too swift to allow him to rest; all other hippos at that time were for the most part lying in the shallows or were back among the papyrus beds.

APPENDIX C

The following notes were made by Loring in East Africa:

Alpine Hyrax (*Procavia mackinderi*). On Mount Kenia at altitudes between 12,000 and 15,000 feet we found these animals common wherever protective rocks occurred. Under the shelving rocks were great heaps of their droppings, and in the places where for centuries they had sunned themselves the stone was stained and worn smooth. At all times of the day, but more frequently after the sun had risen, they could be seen singly, in pairs, and in families, perched on the peaks. At our highest camp (14,700 feet), where on the 22d of September more than half an inch of ice formed in buckets of water outside the tent, they were often heard. They emit a variety of chatters, whistles, and catlike squalls that cannot be described in print, and we found them very noisy. Whenever they saw any one approaching they always sounded some note of alarm, and frequently continued to harangue the intruder until he had approached so close that they took fright and disappeared in the rocks or until he had passed. All along the base of cliffs and leading from one mass of rocks to another they made well-worn trails through the grass. At this time of the year many young ones about one-third grown were seen and taken.

Kenia Tree-hyrax (*Procavia crawshayi*). From the time that we reached the edge of the forest belt (altitude 7,000), on Mount Kenia, we heard these tree-dassies every night, and at all camps to an altitude of 10,700 feet they were common. I once heard one on a bright afternoon about four o'clock, and on a second occasion another about two hours before sundown. Although I searched diligently on the ground for runways, and for suitable places to set traps, no such place was found. In a large yew-tree that had split and divided fifteen feet from the ground, I found a bed or bulky platform of dried leaves and moss of nature's manufacture. On the top of this some animal had placed a few dried green leaves. In this bed I set a steel trap and carefully covered it, and on the second night (October 14) captured a dassie containing a fœtus almost mature. We were informed by our "boys" that these animals inhabited hollow stumps and logs as well as the foliage of the live trees, but we found no signs that proved it, although, judging from the din at night, dassies were abundant everywhere in the forests.

At evening, about an hour after darkness had fully settled, a dassie would call and in a few seconds dassies were answering from all around, and the din continued for half an hour or an hour. The note began with a series of deep frog-like croaks that gradually gave way to a series of shrill tremulous screams, at times resembling the squealing of a pig and again the cries of a child. It was a far-reaching sound and always came from the large forest-trees. Often the cries were directly over our heads and at a time when the porters were singing and dancing about a bright camp-fire. Although we tried many times to shine their eyes with a powerful light, we never succeeded, nor were we able to hear any rustling of the branches or scraping on the tree trunks as one might expect an animal of such size to make. The porters were offered a rupee apiece for dassies, but none was brought in.

Rock-hyrax (*Procavia brucei maculata*). These animals inhabited the rocks and cliffs on Ulukenia Hills in fair numbers. None lived in burrows of their own make, but took advantage of the natural crevices for cover. I heard their shrill calls at night, usually when the moon was out. Several were shot and two trapped in traps set in narrow passages through which the animals travelled.

Klipspringer (*Oreotragus oreotragus*). Several pairs of these little antelopes were seen on Ulukenia Hills, but never were more than two found at a time. They lived on the rocky hillsides and were quite tame, allowing one to approach within twenty-five yards before taking fright and dashing into the rocks, invariably their shelter when alarmed. When thoroughly frightened they made a loud sneezing sound. Two were collected; one of which was a female with horns. A young Boer who had lived in that neighborhood three years told me that all the females of proper age had horns.

Pigmy Gerbille (*Dipodillus harwoodi*). These little sand-mice resemble very closely some of our American pocket-mice (*Perognathus*). Heller took several on the Njoro O Solali and found them common, and I caught one specimen on the South Guaso Nyero River. On the sandy desert flats on the southwest side of Lake Naivasha they were abundant. The holes running obliquely into the ground were sometimes blocked with sand from the inside. On the opposite side of the lake there was less sand, and here the gerbilles were found only in spots. In sand alone their burrows resembled those described, but where the ground was hard they entered almost perpendicular, and were never blocked with sand. Often seed pods and tiny cockle burrs were strewn about the entrances.

Pigmy Mouse (*Mus [Leggada] gratus*). Various forms of this tiny little mouse were taken all along the route we travelled. They were caught in traps set at random in the brushy thickets in the lowland, as well as in the open grassy spots on the rocky hillsides where they frequented the runways made by various species of *Mus*. A few were collected on Mount Kenia.

Athi Rock-mouse (*Epimys nieventris ulæ*). This mouse proved to be a new species. It was common in and about the rocks on Ulukenia Hills, which is the only place where we found them. Those taken were caught in traps baited with peanut butter, dried apple, and rolled oats and set among the rocks.

Forest Mouse (*Epimys peromyscus*). At our camp at 8,500 feet altitude we first met with this mouse, and although a good line of traps well baited was set about stumps, tree trunks, and logs for three nights, but one mouse was captured, that being taken under a large log. Several others were trapped in the thick brush bordering the bamboo. At 10,000 feet several were caught in the bamboo, and at 10,700 feet a good series was collected on a well-thicketed and timbered rocky ridge.

Masked Tree-rat (*Thamnomys loringi*). None were taken until we reached the southwest end of Lake Naivasha. Here and also at Naivasha Station a number were collected in traps baited with rolled oats and dried apple and set at the base of large trees and in brushy thickets in groves. In some of these trees and in the bushes, nests of sticks, grass, and leaves were found. While setting traps one afternoon I saw what might have been one of these rats dart from a deserted bird's nest, and run down a limb to the ground. The following morning I caught a masked tree-rat in a trap set beneath the nest.

Four-striped Grass Rat (*Arvicanthus pumilio diminutus*). At Naivasha we first came across this species, where it was found on the east side of the lake only, although the spotted rat was common on both the east and the west side. At Naivasha these two animals inhabited slightly different regions. In the brushy and grassy thickets bordering the lake spotted rats were abundant, but a few four-striped rats were captured. As soon as the traps were transferred to thorn-tree groves where there was plenty of underbushes, and not so much grass and weeds, the spotted rats were found in great numbers, but no four-striped rats. All the way from Fort Hall to Mount Kenia and as high as 10,700 feet, where Doctor Mearns secured one specimen, this species was common. We also caught them along the route between Kampalla and Butiaba.

Giant Rat (*Thrynomys gregorianus*). Along the skirtings of the rivers in the thick weeds, grass, and bushes at Fort Hall signs of these animals were common. There were no well-defined paths. Footprints the size and shape of those made by our muskrats (*Fiber*) were found in the mud at the water's edge, and here and there were clusters of grass and weed stems cut in lengths averaging six inches. In sections where the vegetation had been burned were innumerable holes where some animal had dug about the base of grass tufts. Their signs did not extend farther than fifty feet from water. While passing through a thicket close to the water, I started a large rodent which darted through the grass and plunged into the water.

Mole-rat (*Tachyoryctes splendens ibeanus*). Mounds of earth that these rats had thrown from the mouth of their burrows at the time that the tunnels were made were found as far west as Oljoro O'Nyon River, but none at N'garri Narok River. At our camp on the South Guaso Nyero River a pale mole-colored mole-rat took this animal's place. Some fifteen miles west of Lake Naivasha mole-rats became common, and on the sandy flats within five miles of the lake they were so abundant that our horses broke into their runways nearly every step. Their underground tunnels and the mounds of earth that were thrown out were similar to those made by the pocket-gophers of western United States. Many were snared by the porters and brought to camp alive. They would crawl about slowly, not attempting to run away, but looking for a hole to enter. After the lapse of a few seconds they would begin to dig. In any slight depression they began work, and when small roots or a tussock of grass intervened, they used their teeth until the obstruction was removed, and then with the nails of their front feet only, continued digging. As the hole deepened they threw the dirt out between their hind legs and with them still farther beyond. After the earth had accumulated so that it drifted back they faced about and using their chest as a scoop, pushed it entirely out of the way. They were most active in the evening, at night, and in early morning. Several were found dead near their holes, having evidently been killed by owls or small carnivorous mammals.

Alpine Mole-rat (*Tachyoryctes rex*). Mole-rat mounds were common about the West Kenia Forest Station, but none were seen between 7,500 and 8,500 feet, and from this altitude they ranged to 11,000 feet. They inhabited all of the open grassy plots in the bamboo belt and in the open timber. The "boys" snared many in nooses ingeniously placed in the runs that were opened and closed after the trap was set. While digging into the burrows, several times I found bulky nests of dried grass in side pockets just off the main runway. Most of them were empty, but one was filled with the animal's droppings.

Kapiti Blesmole (*Myoscalops kapiti*). This mole-rat, which proved to be new to science, was first encountered at Potha on Kapiti Plains and it was again met with at Ulukenia Hills. I was shown several skins that were taken about fifteen miles east of Nairobi. They were the most difficult of all mole-rats to catch because they lived in the very sandy soil and almost invariably covered the trap with sand without themselves getting into it. I found a number of their skulls in the pellets of barn and other species of owls.

Springhaas (*Pedetes surdaster*). Very common at Naivasha Station where their burrows were numerous on a sandy flat practically in the town, and many were taken within a hundred yards of the station. They are nocturnal, although one instance came under my observation where a springhaas was seen on a dark day to run from one burrow to another. By hunting them on dark nights, with the aid of an acetylene light we were able to secure a good series of skins. When the light was flashed on them, their eyes shone like balls of fire the size of a penny, and it was not uncommon to see from two to five and six within the radius of the light at one time. They were usually flashed at a distance of about a hundred yards, and as the light drew near they would watch it, frequently bobbing up and down. Often they hopped away to right or to left, but very seldom did their fright carry them into their burrows unless a shot was fired; in fact even then we sometimes followed up one of their companions and secured it. Some allowed us to approach within ten feet before moving, and then off they would go in great bounds, but I was never able in the dim light to see whether or not their tails aided them in jumping. I once shot a fox from a cluster of eyes that I am positive were those of springhaas; this together with the fact that the stomachs of all of the foxes killed contained termites and insects leads me to believe that these two animals are more or less congenial. Doctor Mearns saw a springhaas sitting with its tail curled around to one side of its body, similar to the position often assumed by a house cat.

Several small colonies of springhaas were discovered on sandy flats near Ulukenia Hills. Two females taken from the same burrow showed great variation in size, one having a tail several inches longer and ears larger than the other. Although I never discovered a burrow that was completely blocked with sand, in the morning one could find quantities of fresh sand that had been thrown out of the entrance during the night.

Great-eared Fox (*Otocyon virgartus*). This new species of fox we discovered at Naivasha and found it very common there. All of the seven specimens secured were taken by "jacking" at night, although while travelling over the Uganda Railroad we frequently saw them singly or in pairs in broad daylight. The white people knew nothing of a fox in this country and had always called them "jackals." They seemed to live in pairs and groups of three to six. On dark nights it was usually easy to shine their eyes and approach within shooting range. We would shine a fox, then suddenly the glare of its eyes would disappear and we would walk about casting the light in all directions until we again saw the two balls of fire glaring some fifty or a hundred yards away. Often the foxes would slink about for some time before we got within gunshot range. Frequently we saw two and sometimes three and four standing so close together that it was surprising that the spread of the shot did not kill more than one. One evening Doctor Mearns and I started out about nine o'clock and returned about midnight. Most of the hunting was done on an elevated brushy plateau within short distance of a native village where the occupants were singing, dancing, and playing their crude stringed instruments. We ran into a bunch of five of these foxes and got four of them, none of which was the young of the year. After shooting one, we would search about in the dark until the light picked up another pair of eyes, and in this way we kept circling about close to the village. One fox was killed within two hundred yards of the railroad-station, and at dusk one evening I saw a fox emerge from a burrow close to a group of natives and scamper across the flat. The stomachs of several were examined and found to contain about a quart of termites and other insects.

Giant Shrew (*Crocidura nyansæ*). Giant shrews were common at Lake Naivasha, where most of them were caught in the thick reeds and rank grass bordering the lake. One was taken at Nyeri and another on Mount Kenia at an altitude of 10,700 feet. They seemed to be as much diurnal as nocturnal and were captured in traps baited with rolled oats, dried apple, and raw meat. They inhabited the dense parts of the thickets where the foliage had to be parted and a clearing made for the traps. These localities were the home of a large rat, and many of the rats captured were decapitated or partly eaten by animals that probably were giant shrews. A shrew captured alive was very ferocious and would seize upon anything that came within its reach. When fully excited and lifted into the air by its tail, it would emit a loud shrill chirping note.

Short-tailed Shrew (*Surdisorex noræ*). Collected between altitudes of 10,000 and 12,100 feet on Mount Kenia. With the exception of those collected at 10,000 feet, where they were trapped in open grassy and brushy parks in the bamboo, most of them were taken in runways of *Otomys*, and all of those taken at 12,100 were caught in such runways in tall marsh-grass.

Elephant-shrew (*Elephantulus pulcher*). Both diurnal and nocturnal. While riding over the country I frequently saw them darting through the runways from one thicket to another. Nearly every clump of bushes and patch of rank vegetation in the Sotik and Naivasha districts was traversed with well-worn trails used by different species of *Mus* and shrews. The elephant-shrews were most common on the dry flats where clumps of fibre plants grew, and their trails usually led into some thorny thicket and finally entered the ground.

Yellow-winged Tree-bat (*Lavia frons*). These large semi-diurnal bats lived in the thorn-tree groves and thick bush along the Athi, South Guaso Nyero, and Nile Rivers, where we found them more or less common, and at the latter place abundant. At the first two named places they were almost always found in pairs hanging from the thorn-trees by their feet, their wings folded before their faces. When disturbed they fly a short distance and alight, but when we returned to the spot a few minutes later they would often be found in the same tree from which they had been started. On the Nile at Rhino Camp, and in suitable places all along the trail between Kampalla and Butiaba, it was not unusual to find three and four in a single thorn-tree. On dark days, and once in the bright sunlight, I saw these bats flying about and feeding. At evening they always appeared an hour or so before the sun went down. Their method of feeding was quite similar to that of our fly-catching birds. They would dart from the branches of a thorn-tree, catch an insect, then return and hang head downward in the tree while they ate the morsel. One was captured with a young one clinging to it head downward, its feet clasped about its mother's neck.

APPENDIX D

DOCTOR MEARNS, accompanied by Loring, spent from the middle of September to after the middle of October, 1909, in a biological survey of Mount Kenia. I take the following account from his notes. In them he treats the mountain proper as beginning at an altitude of 7,500 feet.

Mount Kenia is the only snow-capped mountain lying exactly on the equator. Its altitude is about 17,200 feet. The mountain is supposed to support 15 glaciers; those that Mearns and Loring examined resembled vast snow-banks rather than clear ice-glaciers. The permanent snow-line begins at the edge of the glacial lakes at 15,000 feet; on October 18 there was a heavy snow-storm as low down as 11,000 feet. For some distance below the snow-line the slopes were of broken rock, bare earth, and gravel, with a scanty and insignificant vegetable growth in the crannies between the rocks. These grasses and alpine plants, including giant groundsels and lobelias, cover the soil. At 13,000 feet timber-line is reached.

The Kenia forest belt, separating this treeless alpine region from the surrounding open plains, is from 6 to 9 miles wide. The forest zone is only imperfectly divided into successive belts of trees of the same species; for the species vary on different sides of the mountain. Even the bamboo zone is interrupted. On the west side the zones may be divided into:

(1) A cedar zone from 7,000 or 7,500 to 8,500 feet. The cedars are mixed with many hardwood-trees.

(2) A belt composed mainly of bamboo and yellow-wood (African yew) from 8,500 to 10,700 feet. Here the true timber zone ends.

(3) A zone of giant heath, mixed with giant groundsels and shrubs, extending to 13,000 feet. The heaths may be 30 feet high and can be used as fuel. In this zone are many boggy meadows.

Loring and Mearns occupied five collecting camps in the forest zone and one above it, at 13,700 feet. One day Mearns followed the snow-line for a mile without seeing any traces of large animals, although leopards and smaller cats sometimes wander to this height. The grove-toothed rat, otomys, was numerous in the grass bordering the glacial lakes at a height of 15,000 feet; so were the big mountain hyrax; and Mearns shot one of these animals at 15,500 feet, by a snowbank; it was the highest point at which any mammal was collected. Various kinds of rats and shrews were numerous about the 13,700-foot camp. Above 12,000 feet only three small birds were seen: a long-tailed sunbird, a stone-chat, and a fantail warbler.

On the entire Mount Kenia trip 1,112 birds, of 210 species, were collected; 1,320 mammals and 771 reptiles and batrachians were collected, but the species represented were much fewer. Mearns also made an excellent collection of plants and a good collection of invertebrates. Fresh-water crabs were numerous in the streams up to 10,000 feet, frogs went as high as 10,700, a chameleon was taken at 11,000, and a lizard at 12,100.

Loring ascended the mountain to the base of the pinnacle, at about 16,500 feet. He started from the highest camp, where the water froze each night. The ascent was easy and he carried his camera; but the glare of the snow gave him snow-blindness.